THE JFK ASSASSINATION

CHOKEHOLDS

That Prove There Was a Conspiracy

By James DiEugenio, Paul Bleau, Matt Crumpton, Andrew Iler, and Mark Adamczyk

Cover design by

Larouche

Branding and
Communications

larouchemc.com

CONTENTS

Introduction   1

1   The Official Record Impeaches the Warren Commission   27

2   Oswald's Intelligence Connections: He was No Lone Nut   93

3   Oswald Was Impersonated   128

4   Oswald Could Not Have Been on the

        Sixth Floor When the Shots Were Fired   164

5   Jack Ruby Was On a Mission   181

6   Prior Plots, The Fair Play for Cuba

        Committee, and Useful Idiots   197

7   The Evidentiary Mess of the Twentieth Century   238

8   The Single Bullet Fabrication   256

9   Proof of a Front Shots Overwhelming   275

10 Sixty Years of Obstruction of Justice   328

    Conclusion   416

    Index   423

THE AUTHORS

James DiEugenio

James DiEugenio has an MA in history from California State University Northridge. He is a retired teacher who has written or co-edited four books on the assassinations of the sixties: *Destiny Betrayed, The Assassinations, The JFK Assassination: The Evidence Today* and *JFK Revisited*. The last volume is the companion piece to Oliver Stone's two recent documentaries on the Kennedy assassination, *JFK Revisited: Through the Looking Glass,* and *JFK: Destiny Betrayed.* Jim wrote the screenplays for both of those films. He has lectured widely and made many appearances on many broadcast programs about the subject. He is the editor and publisher of the online journal KennedysandKing.com which features articles, news stories and critiques of works about the four major assassinations of the sixties: JFK, Malcolm X, MLK and RFK.

Paul Bleau

Paul holds an MBA from McGill University, Montreal, Canada. With over 25 years' experience as a strategic planner on national accounts, Paul eventually took ownership of, and presided Bleau Marketing Communications. He cofounded Harmonia in 2006 which has grown to become a leading commemorative services provider in the Quebec Market. Paul has also sat on many boards. He now is in his eighteenth year as a teacher in the P. W. Sims Business Program at Champlain St., Lawrence College. Presently a CAPA member, he has a long track record of research and writing about the JFK assassination which includes appearing in Oliver Stone's documentary JFK Revisited: Through the Looking Glass, writing numerous articles for KennedysandKing.com, and speaking regularly as a guest on BlackOp Radio and on other podcasts.

Matt Crumpton

Matt Crumpton is an entrepreneur, attorney (franchising, small business, and entertainment), and podcaster. Matt previously acquired, developed, and sold the D.P. Dough franchise restaurant brand. In addition to his law practice, Matt now owns and operates a campground in central Ohio and serves on the board of directors for Music Loves Ohio, the non-profit youth music charity that he founded.

In 2022, Matt launched the podcast Solving JFK, which analyzes each issue in the JFK Assassination from the perspective of both Warren Report defenders and critics. In its first season, the podcast reached the top 15 in the United States (as well as the top 35 in the UK and Australia) on Spotify and the top 25 in the United States on Apple Podcasts. Matt also appears as a commentator on JFK: What the Doctors Saw on Paramount Plus.

Andrew Iler

Andrew A. Iler B.A. LL. B. is an Ontario-based lawyer, practicing in the areas of corporate, commercial and administrative law, having served on or chaired provincial and federal government tribunals, and having appeared as counsel at the Federal Court, Ontario Court of Appeal, Ontario Superior Court and numerous federal and provincial tribunals. Over the last several years, Andrew has developed a comprehensive base of knowledge in and around the John F. Kennedy Assassination Records Collection Act 1992 and legal aspects of the official investigations into the assassination of President Kennedy.

Mark Adamczyk

Mark E. Adamczyk is an attorney from Naples, Florida, practicing in the areas of real estate and community association law. Mark is admitted to practice in Florida and Georgia. Since 2003, Mark has provided legal guidance to hundreds of corporations and community associations throughout the State of Florida. Mark attended Tulane University in New Orleans from 1996 to 2000, where he competed in Division 1 men's golf. While at Tulane, Mark also had the opportunity to research the JFK assassination and the New Orleans connections. Throughout his legal career, Mark continued his research into the assassination and developed a balanced view of what happened in Dallas, and why. In 2017, Mark started focusing on the JFK Assassination Records Collections Act of 1992. Mark has become an expert on that law, and has dedicated a significant amount of time to ensuring that agencies and the President provide complete disclosure and transparency with respect to the government's assassination records.

INTRODUCTION

IN APRIL 2016 CTKA, now KennedysandKing, ran an article by Paul Bleau that revealed how history books portray the JFK assassination as a crime perpetrated by Lee Harvey Oswald alone and how authors' sources are restricted to the Warren Commission and a few books that mostly support the *Lone Nut* scenario. The study he had conducted was updated in 2022 with very little change. Information and conclusions coming from other major investigations and pro-conspiracy authors are almost completely ignored.

Historians also tend to find that independent researchers lack credibility. One of the consequences of this is that captive audiences of young students have been unfairly exposed to a biased, unsound and incomplete account of the Kennedy assassination in most history textbooks.

So far, textbook writers seem oblivious to what they can easily learn from the official investigations and the opinions and statements from the actual investigators, lawyers, and staff members who were involved in seven investigations that were mostly (all but one) government initiated and managed. The Warren Commission was the first one, the one most historians count on almost entirely for their writings, and as we will see, it is the most obsolete and least reliable.

For this reason, historians are disrespecting the American Historical Association statement of conduct about honoring the historical record when they assert that Oswald alone assassinated the president based on the conclusions of the Warren Commission.

Compounding this problem is the breach of the law through the refusals of the U.S. Government (including presidents Trump and Biden) to declassify documents pertaining to the JFK assassination, as prescribed by the JFK Records Collection Act of 1992.

1

Studies show that since the JFK assassination, there has been a steady drop in the confidence American citizens have in their leaders as well as the media. The political murders of the sixties, Vietnam, Watergate, Iran-Contra, weapons of mass destruction in Iran accompanied with the lies fed to distrusting citizens has contributed to the world's most powerful nation polarized in a climate of mistrust that has cast a depressing cloud over ordinary people's lives, and has brought many of them to see their institutions as the enemy within.

In November 2022, during the CAPA Conference in Dallas, there was a casual discussion that would lead five researchers to join forces with the goal of putting together the most compelling bodies of evidence that would convince a jury that what happened on November 22, 1963, was the result of a conspiracy to eliminate the duly elected sitting president.

It went something like this:

MATT: What do you guys think of the backyard photo of Oswald?
MARK: Fake
PAUL: Odds are it's a fake, there seems to be crop lines along the chin
MATT: Same facial expression on all photos
PAUL: Marina did not even know how to operate the camera that they said she took the picture with
MATT: Really?
MARK: It was made to sell his guilt to the public.
PAUL: The alleged rifle, the alleged pistol and magazines that paint him as communist all on his person ... talk about over selling it.
MATT: What about the shadows that don't seem to align?
PAUL: I don't know about that, shadows are tricky... Anyway, for me this does not really matter as I really only focus on chokeholds. Madeleine Brown, Prayer man, Badge man... Too many of these are debatable. There are too many other solid arguments that are impossible to deny if explained properly.
MARK: That's an interesting concept: Chokeholds!

.... Sometime later, Jim joins the fray.

MARK: As an attorney, I am intrigued by this discussion about chokeholds.
PAUL: Malcolm Blunt used this term, when he described how the CIA handled Oswald's file.
JIM: That is a chokehold.
MATT: We need to define what we mean by a "chokehold."
PAUL: It refers to a body of evidence that allows you to draw an indisputable conclusion: JFK's assassination was part of a conspiracy. There are about ten such chokeholds.
JIM: In JFK Revisited we dealt with solid proof and stayed away from disputable stuff.
MARK: I agree, and that's what swayed audiences.
PAUL: Key to the notion of proof is the concept of consilience. That is that even if one element cannot prove a fact on its own, the concordance of evidence from unrelated sources converges on a conclusion. Example: It is difficult to not conclude a front shot when you see the Zapruder Film but a few might. The same goes with witness testimony, the exit wound in the back of Kennedy's head, acoustical evidence, spatter analysis and so on and so forth... However, it is difficult to not imagine a jury concluding anything else but there being a conspiracy with such a preponderance of proof when seen in its totality.
MATT: So, would you say that proof of a front shot is a chokehold?
JIM: Definitely!
PAUL: People get so bogged down on sideshows like Judy Baker that naysayers have a field day with. But whenever you bring up Oswald and 544 Camp Street, they turn themselves into knots.
MARK: What are the other Chokeholds?
JIM: CE399
PAUL: Jim, would you agree that there can be no denial that Oswald was impersonated in Mexico City?
JIM: Yes, there are simply too many people who heard a tape

recording of Oswald when they were questioning him after the assassination who said the voices were not those of the same person.
MARK: What about Jack Ruby?

This discussion led two teachers and two attorneys who would later be joined by Andrew, a third lawyer, to form a team that would deliver the all-defining body of work that would prove *that the public is being consistently misled about the JFK assassination, that there was a conspiracy to remove the president and that there has been a cover-up that has been going for sixty years.*

On the positive side, during the last couple of years, the tide has turned in the mainstream media when it comes to reporting on the assassination. The delays in declassification by Trump and Biden have been panned and are seen with suspicion by a number of leading networks. The landmark Oliver Stone documentary JFK Revisited received very positive reviews in the foreign press and specialized media in the U.S. after its 2021 premiere. More recently, ex-Secret Service agent Paul Landis broke his silence about information that, if true, would be a further nail in the coffin of the lone nut theory. So far mainstream media has not been dismissive of what he has to say.

While the authors are well beyond the point of determining if there was a conspiracy and have been more focused on putting the pieces together in what is still an unsolved murder, the sixtieth anniversary of JFK assassination represents an opportunity to share with a larger audience why those who have seriously looked into the case have concluded that there was a sinister plot.

Readers will find in The Chokeholds a number of characteristics that we hope will render it unique and meaningful:

First, the expertise mix of the writers ensures an optimal blend of research proficiency and legal soundness in the construction of the argumentative. Jim DiEugenio is one of the leading researchers in the field. His knowledge, archive of articles and network of collaborators is unparalleled. This was all put to good use and made available to the whole team. Jim contributed two chapters to the book. He ensured quality

4

control, provided expert contacts and kept the whole team clued in on the facts new and old. Paul, who had already performed intensive research in many of the topics that were discussed at CAPA led the way in the writing of six of the chapters. Our lawyers, Matt and Andrew ensured that our writings would be impactful in terms of legal standards and convincing to a jury if ever there were to be a trial. Matt also contributed two chapters while Andrew developed what is meant by a legal standard of proof and also wrote about how the JFK Records Collection Act of 1992 has been breached by Presidents Trump and Biden in Chapter 10. Except for perhaps a few liberal expressions of bewilderment, the style of writing tends to be factual and void of hyperbole thanks to the lawyer influence. There is some repetition as some of the evidence is related to more than one chokehold.

Second, the concepts of chokeholds and consilience were top of mind throughout our work. We settled on ten different arguments which independently prove that 1. there was a conspiracy in the murder of JFK, and 2. that the chokehold issues provide more than a reasonable doubt that would have made it impossible to convict Lee Harvey Oswald in a criminal trial. In some cases, just one piece of evidence within one of the chokeholds is so compelling that on its own, the case against Oswald being a lone nut would collapse. In other areas, one may find that a particular piece of evidence does not constitute a chokehold, but when combined with all the other evidence, the cumulative effect becomes overwhelmingly compelling, and the concept of consilience would lead a jury to only one conclusion. Logically, the only way a critic could convince a jury that Oswald was a lone nut would be to negate every single chokehold which would imply negating many smoking gun facts. When one considers that there are ten chokeholds and each rests on multiple highly incriminating pieces of evidence, it would require a formidable effort to take down every one of the chokeholds. Another challenge critics will have will be to somehow prop up the Warren Commission findings which will be proven beyond any doubt to be completely unreliable ... as confirmed by subsequent investigations. The authors are confident that the highest ceiling we set out to attain will be met: Most readers of this book will be equipped with ten solid, indisputable bodies of evidence that put to rest forever the already impeached lone gunman narrative. The lowest floor imaginable for the remaining unconvinced would be a loss of confidence in what history books claim to be the official story. Both reactions would imply that the JFK murder is still unsolved.

Third, our team was determined to shed the conspiracy quack label painted on researchers in our field by the likes of Vincent Bugliosi, John McAdams and others, who knew how to capitalize on some of the weaker bodies of work and by applying a well-honed stratagem used to counter assassination research which we will discuss later. Chapter 1 will convince readers that the authors of this book are actually corroborated by a vast majority of the investigation insiders as well as by many of the conclusions we can read in the reports of the governmental inquiries. It is clear that Warren Commission backers are on the wrong side of the actual historical records. Critics will be pitted not only against the authors, but also numerous commissioners, lawyers, investigators and expert witnesses who agree with the authors. The other element that was paramount for the authors was to use primary documents, recorded statements, reliable exhibits as our sources which readers will find in the footnotes or through hyperlinks. In total there are over 700 references that back up the statements made by the authors. In cases where we refer to our own previous writings or those of other respected researchers, readers will find that these secondary sources link to reliable primary sources. In the few cases where material proof was not available, corroboration and credibility were taken into consideration.

Fourth, other guidelines we followed were to be up to date and thorough. Historians are frozen in the year 1964 when the Warren Commission completed its investigations and Gerald Posner named his book, *Case Closed,* before the Government even began declassifying the JFK files as per the 1992 act. Our facts come from sources that precede the assassination and are sprinkled throughout six decades all the way back to 1963. It will be in this book that most readers will discover tactics that were used to smear alternate patsies; what the Russians had to say about Oswald's shooting skills; a hand-written report about a spectrographic analysis of JFK neckband and tie; how Arlen Specter was compelled to come up with the Single Bullet theory and how he got the Warren Commission to buy in; how a Secret Service agent disposed of JFK's brain—or at least a portion of it and a lot more ... all relevant, all factual and all completely ignored by historians, journalists and other usual architects of denial.

Finally, fifth, our work was also enriched by input given to us by highly regarded researchers who looked over some of the chapters and provided insights. For this we would like to thank Gerry Simone, David Josephs, Peter McGrath, David Boylan, Jeff Meek, Brian Edwards, Larry Hancock, Matt Douthit, and Gary Murr for their valuable help and friendship.

One of the daunting challenges faced by the authors was how to make the cases palatable for a wide audience. JFK researchers are familiar with the Zapruder Film, the Bethesda Autopsy, the Single Bullet Theory, the Tippit murder ... and persons of interest such as Dulles, D. A. Phillips, David Ferrie but many have not been exposed to the finer details of the case including historians and journalists. We hope to have assisted the readers by beginning every chapter with an executive summary, including easily accessible citations, and producing a brief timeline of the investigations that took place over sixty years from which is where we found many of our sources. Readers are encouraged to follow links to access more background information that is complementary to what they will find in this book.

THE INVESTIGATIONS TIMELINE[1]

The President's Commission on the Assassination of President Kennedy (aka The Warren Commission)

Established on November 29, 1963, it was set up by President Lyndon Johnson to investigate the November 22, 1963, assassination of Presi-

---

[1] https://www.kennedysandking.com/content/jfk-and-the-unforgivable-how-the-historians-version-of-the-jfk-assassination-dishonors-the-historical-record-part-1

dent Kennedy. The Commission presented an 888 page report and twenty-six volumes of evidence on September 24, 1964. Its major conclusions were that Lee Harvey Oswald acted alone in killing JFK and that nightclub owner Jack Ruby also acted alone in killing Oswald two days later.

The Commission had *"not found evidence"* linking either Oswald or Ruby to a conspiracy.

The Jim Garrison Investigation

Starting in 1966, New Orleans DA Jim Garrison investigated the assassination. This led to the 1969 trial of Clay Shaw, a well-known local businessman, who was accused of being part of a conspiracy. While the jury found Shaw not guilty, according to Mark Lane—who had advised Garrison—most jurors felt there had nevertheless been a conspiracy

The United States President's Commission on CIA Activities within the United States (The Rockefeller Commission)

After a 1974 New York Times report on illegal acts committed by the CIA, Gerald Ford set up the Rockefeller Commission headed by his Vice-President Nelson Rockefeller in 1975. It publicized the CIA MK/Ultra mind control experiments and revealed its illegal mail opening and U.S. protester surveillance programs (MH/Chaos). It also held a very narrow investigation into the Kennedy assassination focusing on the Zapruder film, some of the medical evidence and whether Frank Sturgis and E. Howard Hunt, who had just gained notoriety because of their roles in the Watergate scandal, were involved in the assassination. In a short eighteen-page chapter about the assassination, it concluded that the CIA had not been involved and that only three shots were fired from behind the motorcade. The Executive Director of this commission was David Belin, who served on the Warren Commission.

United States Senate Select Committee to Study Governmental Operations with Respect to Intelligence Activities (The Church Committee)

This U.S. Senate Committee was chaired by Senator Frank Church and issued 14 reports in 1975 and 1976 after interviewing hundreds of witnesses and studying thousands of files from the FBI, CIA and other agencies.

It delved into U.S. assassination plots against foreign leaders, which were a key component of CIA regime control or change operations. Their targets included Congo's Lumumba, Castro of Cuba, the Diem brothers of Vietnam, General Schneider of Chile, President Trujillo of the Dominican Republic. Ex CIA leader Allen Dulles' pact with the mafia to assassinate Castro was also part of their findings.

Volume 4 of the report sheds light on HT/LINGUAL, the illegal mail intercept programs involving both the CIA and the FBI.

The Committee also reported on the extent the CIA partnered with media and academia, in an effort to control the media, later called Operation Mockingbird.

Led by Senators Gary Hart and Richard Schweiker, the Church Committee also conducted a focused investigation (Book 5) of the Kennedy assassination, concentrating on how the FBI and CIA supported the Warren Commission. Its report was very critical of these agencies: " ... *developed evidence which impeaches the process by which the intelligence agencies arrived at their own conclusions about the assassination, and by which they provided information to the Warren Commission. This evidence indicates that the investigation of the assassination was deficient.*"

United States House of Representatives Select Committee on Assassinations (HSCA)

Established in 1976 to investigate the assassinations of Martin Luther King and John F. Kennedy, the HSCA issued its final report in 1979. It found that there was a "probable conspiracy" in the JFK case.

Liberty Lobby vs. E. Howard Hunt

Contrary to the other investigations which were governmental, this instance was a civil trial which pitted CIA operative and Watergate burglary planner E. Howard Hunt against Mark Lane. Lane came in because *Spotlight* was a publication which ran a piece in 1985 reporting that the CIA had a memo confirming its intention to out Hunt as having been involved in the JFK assassination, acting as something like a rogue agent. Hunt sued and won for slander but lost on appeal after Liberty Lobby hired Lane to represent them.

Spotlight wrote the following about its victory: "Scattered news reports did mention Hunt had lost a libel case against The SPOTLIGHT. However, no media reported what the jury forewoman had told the press: 'Mr. Lane was asking us to do something very difficult. He was asking us to believe John Kennedy had been killed by our own government. Yet when we examined the evidence closely, we were compelled to conclude that the CIA had indeed killed President Kennedy.'" While it is true that some jurors may have simply determined that Liberty Lobby failed to meet the elements of defamation, it is striking that the jury foreperson believed that the CIA's complicity in the murder of President Kennedy was established.

ARRB Assassination Records Review Board

This Board was created in 1994 after the movie *JFK* put pressure on Congress to pass the 1992 JFK Assassination Records Collection Act. During a four-year period, it declassified tens of thousands of documents. <u>Its mandate</u> was different from the other investigations: The major purpose of the Review Board was to reexamine for release the records that the agencies still regarded as too sensitive to open to the public. In addition, Congress established the Review Board to help restore government credibility. To achieve these lofty goals, Congress designed an entity that was unprecedented.

All files were to be declassified by 2017 except for very specific and unique cases. As of the year 2023, thousands of files still remain inaccessible to the public.

Foreign Government Research Into the Assassination[2]

Russia has extensive files on Lee Harvey Oswald because of his sojourn there, and also came up with their own conclusions about the assassination which they kept for the most part private. Cuba through its espionage network in the U.S. and the capture of Cuban exiles of interest developed their own intelligence about the case. The French also used spies in the U.S. during the de Gaulle era, and they too collected pertinent intelligence about the murder. We will discuss these in a later chapter. All three foreign governments concluded there was a right-wing conspiracy.

Despite attempts to cover up, obfuscate, hide and destroy material evidence that has gone on for decades, it was impossible to cover all the tracks and silence the many brave ones who did speak out … sometimes at a great cost. The writers of this book understand this. But they too live by a code: what we do in life echoes in eternity … may these reverberations be the truth. The truth is that JFK's murder was a conspiracy. This is not just an opinion… It is a matter of record.

---

[2] https://www.kennedysandking.com/john-f-kennedy-articles/the-cia-and-mafia-s-cuban-american-mechanism-and-the-jfk-assassination

Standard of Proof

Definition: *the level of certainty and the degree of evidence necessary to establish proof in a criminal or civil proceeding*

A Brief History of Standards of Proof

In law, the "standard of proof" (also known as the "burden of persuasion") is a specified level of certainty that a judge, jury or other decision-maker requires in order to determine the outcome of a proceeding. The standard is based on the level of evidence needed to establish guilt in a criminal proceeding, liability in a civil proceeding, or a finding or conclusion in administrative matters.

Everyone who has served on a criminal or civil jury has definitely been exposed to detailed explanations about the applicable standard of proof, whether it be the *preponderance of evidence, balance of probabilities*, or the most well-known standard, *beyond a reasonable doubt*. Each of these terms (and several others) have incredibly important implications to fact-finding proceedings, ranging from high-profile criminal murder trials, to serious civil trials involving fraud, personal injury, product liability, and every other conceivable kind of claim. In a whole other realm of legal proceedings, typically categorized under the heading of "administrative law," tribunals, boards, commissions, agencies, and other decision-making bodies tasked with reviewing facts and evidence pursuant to statutes and regulations must make findings based on some specified standard of proof, typically mandated by the relevant authorizing statute or regulation.

Beyond a Reasonable Doubt

The history of the most well-known standard of proof, *beyond a reasonable doubt*, has an interesting backstory according to author James Q. Whitman, who explains the premise of his 2008 book, *The Origins of Reasonable Doubt: Theological Roots of the Criminal Trial* [Yale University Press],

In the criminal trial of past centuries, there was more at stake than the fate of the accused. The fate of those who sat in judgment was at stake as well. In part this was because jurors had to fear vengeance on the part of the relatives of the convicted man. But it was also for religious reasons. Convicting an innocent defendant was regarded, in the older Christian tradition, as a potential mortal sin. The reasonable doubt rule developed in response to this disquieting possibility. It was originally a theological doctrine, intended to reassure jurors that they could convict the defendant without risking their own salvation.[3]

For both the religious and the unreligious among us, one would like to think that triers of fact (juries) need to be seriously concerned for their own states of mind, soul and conscience in determining the guilt of another human being, especially with the potential consequences being life imprisonment or the death penalty. To wrongfully convict someone is the ultimate failure of our justice system. In this light, the expression "to be damned sure about something" seems only natural.

The criminal standard of proof — "beyond a reasonable doubt" is such a fundamentally important concept of natural justice, the Supreme Court *In re Winship*, 397 U.S. 358, 364 (1970) stated,

> The reasonable-doubt standard plays a vital role in the American scheme of criminal procedure. It is a prime instrument for reducing the risk of convictions resting on factual error. The standard provides concrete substance for the presumption of innocence-that bedrock "axiomatic and elementary" principle whose "enforcement lies at the foundation of the administration of our criminal law." Coffin v. United States, supra, 156 U.S., at 453. As the dissenters in the New York Court of Appeals observed, and we agree, "A person accused of a crime ... would be at a severe disadvantage, a disadvantage amounting to a lack of fundamental fairness, if he

---

[3] https://historynewsnetwork.org/article/47018#:~:text=In%20the%20criminal%20trial%20of,was%20also%20for%20religious%20reasons

could be adjudged guilty and imprisoned for years on the strength of the same evidence as would suffice in a civil case." 24 N.Y.2d, at 205, 299 N.Y.S.2d, at 422, 247 N.E.2d, at 259.

The requirement of proof beyond a reasonable doubt has this vital role in our criminal procedure for cogent reasons. The accused during a criminal prosecution has at stake interest of immense importance, both because of the possibility that he may lose his liberty upon conviction and because of the certainty that he would be stigmatized by the conviction. Accordingly, a society [397 U.S. 358, 364] that values the good name and freedom of every individual should not condemn a man for commission of a crime when there is reasonable doubt about his guilt.

It was, in part, for these reasons, that the Supreme Court in *Winship* held that the *due process* clauses of the Fifth and Fourteenth Amendments "protects the accused against conviction except upon proof beyond a reasonable doubt of every fact necessary to constitute the crime with which he is charged."

Equally important to the Supreme Court *In re Winship* was the notion that the beyond a reasonable doubt standard was critical to the American public having faith and confidence in its criminal justice system, as Justice Brennan, writing for the Court explained,

moreover, use of the reasonable-doubt standard is indispensable to command the respect and confidence of the community in applications of the criminal law. It is critical that the moral force of the criminal law not be diluted by a standard of proof that leaves people in doubt whether innocent men are being condemned. It is also important in our free society that every individual going about his ordinary affairs have confidence that his government cannot adjudge him guilty of a criminal offense without convincing a proper factfinder of his guilt with utmost certainty.

Readers should keep these principles from *Winship* in mind as they consider how the two main investigations of the Kennedy assassination, the Warren Commission and the House Select Committee on Assassinations ("HSCA"), both failed to hold themselves accountable to any standard of proof, yet purported to make findings and come to conclusions that have ended up creating deep skepticism and doubt on the part of a very large majority of the American public. The shortcomings and failures of the Warren Commission and the HSCA have also created serious uncertainty and mistrust in respect to many of the country's most important institutions.

In criminal trials, both prosecutors and defense attorneys usually spend a considerable amount of time in their opening and closing submissions explaining to juries how the beyond a reasonable doubt standard of proof is a critical component of their weighing the evidence. At the commencement of a criminal trial, judges also take time to explain the beyond a reasonable doubt standard of proof and how the jury is to always have it on their mind when evidence is being considered throughout the course of a trial. Once both the state and the defense have rested their respective cases, the presiding judge must instruct, or charge the jury before it starts its deliberations. A critical part of every jury instruction in a criminal trial is the judge's instructions on the applicable standard of proof and how it is the state's burden to prove its case beyond a reasonable doubt. If a judge incorrectly instructs a jury in regard to the standard of proof, either side may seek a mistrial.

Civil Standards of Proof

In non-criminal cases, there are less demanding civil standards of proof, that require a far reduced level of certainty in order for a trier of fact to render a decision. Part of the reasoning for this reduced standard is that the consequences of a negative finding will not result in imprisonment, a loss of freedom or the death penalty. In civil matters, the plaintiff and defendant are typically placed on even footing and there is no "presumption of innocence" granted by right to the defendant. While the initial burden of persuasion is on the plaintiff/claimant to prove their case, and the level of evidence required is only that to tip the scales slightly to one side or the other.

The most common standard of proof in civil law proceedings is the "preponderance of evidence" standard. In the most basic of terms, the preponderance of evidence standard is often explained as being the "more likely than not" standard of proof. A claimant need only prove its burden of persuasion to tip the scale just over the 50% level.... 50.1% will typically suffice.

There is a third standard of proof, called the "clear and convincing evidence" standard that exists on the spectrum somewhere between the preponderance of evidence and beyond a reasonable doubt standard. The clear and convincing standard of proof requires a higher level of evidence to support a finding than does the preponderance of evidence standard but is not as high a standard as that demanded by beyond a reasonable doubt.

The clear and convincing evidence standard is typically found in processes where the consequences of the issues being reviewed are significantly high, such quasi-criminal matters involving civil fraud or "where particularly important individual interests or rights are at stake, such as the termination of parental rights, involuntary commitment, and deportation." [*T.B. et al., as Coconservators, etc., Petitioners and Respondents, v. O.B., Objector and Appellant*. Cali Supreme Court July 27, 2020]

In its discussion regarding the clear and convincing standard of proof, the California Supreme Court in *T.B. et al., as Coconservators, etc., Petitioners and Respondents, v. O.B., Objector and Appellant* stated,

> The standard of proof that applies to a particular determination serves "to instruct the fact finder concerning the degree of confidence our society deems necessary in the correctness of factual conclusions for a particular type of adjudication, to allocate the risk of error between the litigants, and to indicate the relative importance attached to the ultimate decision."

Section 6 of the *John F. Kennedy Assassinations Records Collection Act 1992* provides that,

> disclosure of assassination records or particular information in assassination records to the public may be postponed subject to the limitations of this Act if there is ***clear and convincing evidence*** that.... [Emphasis added.]

This section of the JFK Records Act specifically mandates that the clear and convincing standard of proof applies to all decisions regarding the postponement of the disclosure of assassination records by the ARRB and the President. By requiring that clear and convincing evidence of a demonstrable identifiable threat or harm that fits one of the five very limited criteria under section 6 of the Act, Congress made it clear that the mandated release of all of the assassination records was an extremely serious and profound issue for the country, that is demanding a higher standard of proof than a simple balance of probabilities/preponderance of evidence standard.

Every kind of legal or quasi-legal proceeding from a low-level university or college non-academic discipline committee or a local landlord tenant or small claims court matter, right up to appeals at the Supreme Court of the United States is subject to having a decision-maker apply a standard of proof to its decision-making process. Standards of proof are a critical and necessary element of a legitimate, fair and defensible legal process. The result of not applying a standard of proof to a legal proceeding is the inevitability of an arbitrary and illegitimate process that will not be able to withstand even the mildest level of public scrutiny.

And this brings us to the two official government investigations of the assassination of President John F. Kennedy...... The Warren Commission (1963–1964) and the House Select Committee on Assassinations (1976–1978).

Background of the JFK Assassination Investigative Processes

On November 29, 1963, seven days after the assassination of President Kennedy in Dallas, in an attempt to head off a local judicial investigation in Dallas and congressional investigations in Washington, D.C., President Lyndon Johnson issued Executive Order 11,130—Appointing a Commission to Report Upon the Assassination of President John F. Kennedy. The stories behind President Johnson's strong-arm tactics in appointing Chief Justice Earl Warren and Senator Richard B. Russell to the Commission are well known to historians. Other appointees like John McCloy, Allen Dulles and Gerald Ford took *less pressure* to ensure their appointments to the President's Commission.

Executive Order 11,130 sets out the Commission's terms of reference in very broad strokes, stating that,

> The purposes of the Commission are to examine the evidence developed by the Federal Bureau of Investigation and any additional evidence that may hereafter come to light or be uncovered by Federal or State authorities; to make such further investigation as the Commission finds desirable; to evaluate all the facts and circumstances surrounding such assassination, including the subsequent violent death of the man charged with the assassination, and to report to me its findings and conclusions.
>
> The Commission is empowered to prescribe its own procedures and to employ such assistants as it deems necessary.

Executive Order 11,130 tasks the Commission with examining and evaluating the evidence and circumstances around the assassination of President Kennedy and reporting the Commission's findings and conclusions. The Commission was also authorized to establish its own procedures. President Johnson's Executive Order did not, however, mandate or specify any particular *standard of proof* on which his Commission was to base its findings and conclusions.

One would think that since the President omitted to establish a standard of proof for his Commission in his Executive Order that the Commission itself would consider this extremely important starting point for its investigation, especially given the gravity of its task, the seriousness with which its findings would be scrutinized by the American public and by the global community, not to mention the fact that the Commission was chaired by the Chief Justice of the United States and all six of the other members of the Commission were powerful attorneys.

How did the Warren Commission handle the issue of standards of proof and other fundamental requirements to a fair and impartial fact-finding process? It is best to let the words of the Commission speak for itself. Under the heading titled, "**The Commission's Functions**," the Commission Report states,

The Commission's most difficult assignments have been to uncover all the facts concerning the assassination of President Kennedy and to determine if it was in any way directed or encouraged by unknown persons at home or abroad. In this process, its objective has been to identify the person or persons responsible for both the assassination of President Kennedy and the killing of Oswald through an examination of the evidence. The task has demanded unceasing appraisal of the evidence by the individual members of the Commission in their effort to discover the whole truth. The procedures followed by the Commission in developing and assessing evidence necessarily differed from those of a court conducting a criminal trial of a defendant present before it, since under our system there is no provision for a posthumous trial. If Oswald had lived, he could have had a trial by American standards of justice where he would have been able to exercise his full rights under the law. A judge and jury would have presumed him innocent until proven guilty beyond a reasonable doubt. He might have furnished information which could have affected the course of his trial. He could have participated in and guided his defense. There could have been an examination to determine whether he was sane under prevailing legal standards. All witnesses, including possibly the defendant, could have been subjected to searching examination under the adversary system of American trials.

The Commission has functioned neither as a court presiding over an adversary proceeding nor as a prosecutor determined to prove a case, but as a fact-finding agency committed to the ascertainment of the truth. In the course of the investigation of the facts and rumors surrounding these matters, it was necessary to explore hearsay and other sources of information not admissible in a court proceeding obtained from persons who saw or heard and others in a position to observe what occurred. In fairness to the alleged assassin and his family, the Commission on February 25, 1964, requested Walter E. Craig, president of the American Bar Association, to participate in the investigation and to advise the Commission whether in his opinion the proceedings conformed to the basic principles of American justice. Mr. Craig accepted this assignment and participated fully and without limitation. He attended Commission hearings in person or through his appointed assistants. All working papers, reports, and other data in Commission files were made available, and Mr. Craig and his associates were given the opportunity to cross-examine witnesses, to recall any witness heard prior to his appointment, and to suggest witnesses whose testimony they would like to have the Commission hear. This procedure was agreeable to counsel for Oswald's widow.

The above excerpt, taken directly from the opening pages of the *Report of the President's Commission on the Assassination of President Kennedy*, is the full extent of the Commission's explanation of their procedures and standards of conducting the government's investigation into the assassination of President John F. Kennedy, and in respect to the basis and parameters of determining their findings and conclusions.

The Commission Report states that had Oswald lived, he would have been afforded the presumption of innocence and a public trial whereby his guilt would have been required to have been proven beyond a reasonable doubt, but since Oswald was dead, there is no reason to even discuss the issue of standards of proof. Further, the Commission acknowledged that they would allow hearsay testimony and other kinds of evidence into the process that would have otherwise not been permitted if Oswald had survived to contest the allegations against him at trial. The Commission Report also admitted that because there would be no defense, Oswald would not have the chance to defend himself through bringing his own evidence before a jury or having his own legal counsel cross-exam the witnesses. In addition, the Commission decided that almost all of its hearings would be held in secret, with the public excluded from all but a few hearings. Any one of these procedural decisions on its own would have rendered a judicial proceeding unlawful and any conclusions completely illegitimate. Coupled together, all of these deficiencies are fatal to the concept of a fair process. The Commission's failure to at least impose a standard of proof to which they would hold themselves accountable in weighing the testimony and evidence imposed such an arbitrary and baseless process, it is no surprise that the Commission's findings and conclusions were quickly deemed unacceptable to the American public from almost the time that the Commission Report came off the presses.

The HSCA Standard of Proof

For eleven years the American public struggled to accept the conclusions foisted upon it by the Warren Commission and a feckless media. Much of the evidence gathered by the Warren Commission was kept from the public and unlawfully classified by the Commission, which had no authority granted to it to impose any level of classification. One of the pieces of evidence that had been withheld and suppressed from the public was the short film of the assassination taken by Dallas resident, Abraham Zapruder. On March 6, 1975, photography technician, Robert Groden, appeared on the ABC late-night program, Good Night America, hosted by Geraldo Rivera, bringing with him and publicly broadcasting for the very first time a bootleg copy of the Zapruder film. The public reaction to the Zapruder film was electrifying, as it demonstrably showed in horrifyingly graphic clarity a far different series of events than the public had been told by the Warren Commission and the media.

As a result of the public broadcast of the Zapruder film and the massive demand by the American people, the House Select Committee on Assassinations was formed by way of House Resolution 1540 on September 17, 1976. The terms of reference for this select committee were to conduct a full and complete investigation of the circumstances surrounding the deaths of President John F. Kennedy and Dr. Martin Luther King Jr.

In the HSCA Report's Introduction and History of the Committee, effort is made to advise the public of the limitations of a congressional committee and the differences between a judicial process and the Committee's process. Like the Warren Commission, the HSCA made it clear that the proceedings would differ from those found in the judicial branch of government, in that hearsay testimony would be permitted, there would be no right to cross-examine or challenge admissibility, and no impartial judge would preside over the hearings. The Committee Report also specifically stated that as a result of being a congressional hearing, it would not be required, "in its finding of facts for the purpose of legislation, to establish facts beyond a reasonable doubt. A committee may base its legislation on facts it finds as probable, or even likely."

Interestingly, the HSCA Report noted that, "It can be forcefully argued that when evidence of conduct that may be termed criminal is introduced before a congressional committee, but in the end falls short of a clear and convincing or similar high standard of persuasion, the responsible course would be to refrain from making the evidence public to protect the reputation of the person involved."

On January 2, 1979, The Final Report of the Select Committee on Assassinations—U.S. House of Representatives (HSCA) was publicly released. The Final Report included numerous findings and conclusions, some agreeing with the Warren Commission's findings and conclusions, others substantially differing. Among the differing conclusions, the HSCA Final Report found a "high probability that two gunmen fired at President John F. Kennedy." And "on the basis of the evidence available to it, that

President John F. Kennedy was probably assassinated as a result of a conspiracy."

Other specific findings of the HSCA repeated the phrase, "The committee believes, on the basis of the evidence available to it..." This phrase suggests that the available evidence supports a finding, however, there is no gradation of whether such evidence met a high or a low standard of proof in order to tie some level of certainty or reliability to each finding or conclusion.

Once again, without holding itself accountable to any standard of proof, the HSCA's findings and conclusions, not to mention the process through which it conducted its proceedings was met with skepticism and more questions from the public. Like the Warren Commission Report, the HSCA Final Report ultimately fell far short in terms of providing the American people with definitive answers to the continuing questions about the true facts and circumstances surrounding the assassination.

The Assassinations Record Review Board Standard of Proof

In 1991, Oliver Stone released his feature film JFK. In addition to winning two Academy Awards, the film sparked renewed interest in the Kennedy assassination and a reinvigorated demand for public transparency in the millions of records that remained classified and held secret from public view under the guise of "national security." In the closing sequence of the film JFK, Oliver Stone brought to light the continuing secrecy around the classified assassination records. The public was once again outraged that almost thirty years after the assassination of President Kennedy, its government was still holding millions of pages of documents and materials about the assassination secret on baseless grounds of national security. The movie sparked congressional hearings which led to the creation of the Assassination Records Review Board ("ARRB").

The statute that Congress quickly and unanimously passed in 1992 included a provision (section 6), that mandated that records could only warrant continuing postponement of public disclosure if there was *clear and convincing evidence* of current demonstrable harm to a very limited

23

class of criteria that justified the postponement of the public disclosure of each specific assassination record.

This was the first time in the course of any government process dealing with the assassination that a bona fide standard of proof had been mandated. The John F. Kennedy Assassination Records Collection Act 1992, also imposed a burden on the government agencies seeking to withhold assassination records to prove to the high standard of clear and convincing evidence that postponement was justified. The imposition of the clear and convincing evidence standard and the burden on the agencies was a marked departure from the Warren Commission and HSCA processes. What resulted was the release of a massive trove of assassination-related documentation that has punched massive holes in the Warren Commission's findings and conclusion over the thirty years since the passage of the JFK Records Act. The ARRB's mandate to apply the high clear and convincing evidence standard of proof set the table for a more rigorous and accountable process of review of the determining evidence, that was simply not present in either the Warren Commission or the HSCA proceedings.

The JFK Assassination Chokeholds Standards of Proof

When reading this book, we ask readers to apply the high level of the standard of proof of clear and convincing evidence in reviewing the evidence pertaining to conspiracy and obstruction of justice and the beyond a reasonable doubt standard of proof with respect to the evidence regarding Lee Harvey Oswald's guilt as the "lone nut assassin". The information and evidence put forward with respect to the ten topic areas of assassination that the authors have presented as "chokeholds" issues, or irrefutable proof when viewed through these standards of proof should provide solid ground on which any reasonable person will determine that the findings and conclusions of the Warren Commission cannot be deemed to be a true and accurate record of the history of the assassination and that there was a conspiracy in the murder of JFK. It is our hope that when weighed against the clear and convincing standard of proof that readers will determine to a very high level of certainty that the Warren Commission's findings should be repudiated and deemed not to be the official and true history of the assassination.

What will such a finding achieve now that 60 years have passed since the 35th President of the United States, John F. Kennedy was publicly executed on the streets of Dallas, Texas? It is the hope of the authors of this book, that the government of the United States will align its "official history" with the views and conclusions reached by an enormous bipartisan majority of Americans, that the Warren Commission Report was a fabrication and is not an accurate account of the assassination and that the true nature of the Kennedy assassination (most particularly a reliable and complete forensic report on the President's actual cause of death) still has not been told to the American public.

CHAPTER 1

THE OFFICIAL RECORD IMPEACHES THE WARREN COMMISSION

BY PAUL BLEAU

STATEMENT

U.S. INVESTIGATIONS into the assassination, statements made by investigation insiders and foreign government conclusions about the assassination prove that there is a strong consensus by the independent investigative authorities that there was a conspiracy in the murder of President John F. Kennedy.

INTRODUCTION

This chapter focuses on what is revealed by the official investigations and the opinions and statements from actual investigators, lawyers, experts and staff members who were involved in seven investigations. We will also present what some foreign governments concluded after their own probes into the case.

EXECUTIVE SUMMARY

While the Warren Commission concluded that Lee Harvey Oswald was the lone assassin of JFK and that they could find no evidence of a larger conspiracy, some of the writings in its final report and conflicting evidence or findings in the volumes of its hearings and exhibits as well as affirmations made by a number of its commissioners and other participants in this investigation impeached both the process followed by the WC and the report itself.

Later investigations that lasted longer, were more fact-based and relied on a higher quality of information concluded that the Warren Commission's investigation into a conspiracy was inadequate.

The House Select Committee on Assassinations (HSCA) concluded: "That since the Warren Commission and FBI's investigation into a possibility of a conspiracy was seriously flawed, their failure to develop evidence of a conspiracy could not be given independent weight."

More importantly the HSCA, based on photographic, witness, acoustic, documentary evidence concluded that there was a probable conspiracy. While some have made attempts to discredit this conclusion by casting doubt on the acoustic evidence, they failed to sway the main architects of these findings who have spoken publicly, written on the subject and in some cases signed a petition expressing without a doubt their beliefs that there was a dark plot involving a number of people.

In their combined form, the writings of six government inquiries, one civil trial, statements of over ninety persons closely connected to these inquiries, results from three foreign investigations prove that the most informed specialists with arm's length access to evidence and witnesses, who were involved in the investigations for their expertise and independence refute the Warren Commission findings and believe that something more sinister than three *lone-nut* murders occurred between November 22 and November 24, 1963.

THE OFFICIAL RECORDS AND KEY STATEMENTS

The President's Commission on the Assassination of President Kennedy (aka The Warren Commission)

Established on November 29, 1963, it was set up by President Lyndon Johnson to investigate the November 22, 1963, assassination of President Kennedy. The Commission presented an 888-*page report* and twenty-six volumes of evidence on September 24, 1964. Its major conclusions were that Lee Harvey Oswald acted alone in killing JFK and that nightclub owner Jack Ruby also acted alone in killing Oswald two days later.

The Commission had *"not found evidence"* linking either Oswald or Ruby to a conspiracy.[1]

The first powerful hint of dissent among the members of the Commission can be seen in the following bewildering statement in the report which points to a rift concerning the Single Bullet Theory and Governor John Connally's testimony: *"Although it is not necessary to any essential findings of the Commission to determine just which shot hit Governor Connally, there is very persuasive evidence from the experts to indicate that the same bullet which pierced the President's throat also caused Governor Connally's wounds. However, Governor Connally's testimony and certain other factors have given rise to some difference of opinion as to this probability but there is no question in the mind of any member of the Commission that all the shots which caused the President's and the Governor's wounds were fired from the sixth floor of the Texas School Book Depository."[2]*

What is not being said directly here is that certain members of the Commission, as well as *John Connally*[3] and his wife, did not believe that a single bullet caused all seven wounds in JFK and Connally that it is credited for, which is in fact necessary to the essential conclusion

---

[1] Warren Report, p. 21. One must remember that on November 25, 1963, within just 24 hours of the murder of Lee Harvey Oswald, Nicholas Katzenbach, who then served as Deputy Attorney General wrote a memo to Bill Moyers, Special Assistant to President Johnson, stating that it was important that the public be made to believe that Oswald acted alone and that all speculation of conspiracy should be "cut-off". This was all decided before the Warren Commission was formed and before the evidence had even been gathered. See Katzenbach Memo: https://www.maryferrell.org/show-Doc.html?docId=62268#relPageId=29

[2] Warren Report, p. 19.

[3] https://www.youtube.com/watch?v=4svgOqQmS3o

The FBI Summary Report—Wounds to Connally and JFK Caused by Three Separate Bullets[4]

This preliminary scientific finding, which obliterates the Single Bullet Theory (ergo a lone gunman), can be found on page 8 of the FBI summary report prepared in December 1963. As a matter of fact, the FBI at this point did not even attempt to connect the Kennedy back wound to his throat-wound. The report indicates that medical evidence describes the back entry injury as one caused by a missile entering on a 45 to 60% downward slope beneath the right shoulder blade. It was only in March 1964 that the unproven trajectory would be made. And finally, the Single Bullet Theory (SBT) came about in June 1964, when the injuries to bystander James Tague had to be accounted for.[5] This theory came from Arlen Specter, Junior Counsel on the WC, whom we will see in Chapter 8 was cornered into this fabulation and not necessarily guided by science, physics or any actual evidence. According to this controversial theory "Specter solved the multiple injury problem by arguing that one bullet had caused all the seven non-fatal wounds to both JFK and Connally... Specter's theory remains the keystone on which the edifice of Oswald's sole guilt rests. For if one bullet did not cause all of Kennedy's and Connally's wounds that were below the neck, the only explanation of their injuries is that they were caused by two gunmen and some kind of conspiracy."[6]

Roger Craig—Dallas Deputy Sheriff

Roger Craig[7] was very well regarded up until the assassination. He was on duty and in Dealey Plaza at the time of the murder. In a number of interviews he explains what he witnessed on November 22, 1963: He was in the Book Depository when the alleged murder weapon was found

---

[4] Commission Document 1—FBI Summary Report p. 8 and Commission Document 1— FBI Summary Report (maryferrell.org)
[5] The JFK Assassination Single-Bullet Theory Explained (22november1963.org.uk)
[6] https://spartacus-educational.com/JFKspecter.htm
[7] https://spartacus-educational.com/JFKcraigR.htm

which he confirmed to be a Mauser and not the Mannlicher-Carcano that the Warren Commission claimed Oswald owned.[8] Furthermore, Craig said he had seen Oswald entering a station wagon a few minutes after the murder, which would contradict the Warren Commission's chronology of Oswald's movements and implicated a getaway driver—the following is part of his Warren Commission testimony:

David Belin: *All right. Then, what did Captain Fritz say and what did you say and what did the suspect (Oswald) say?*

Roger Craig: *Captain Fritz then asked… "What about this station wagon?" And the suspect interrupted him and said, "That station wagon belongs to Mrs. Paine"… I believe that is what he said. "Don't try to tie her into this. She had nothing to do with it."*

Craig's description of the Rambler driver goes a long way in vindicating his account: *He said that the man driving the vehicle was not a Negro but that he was dark-skinned—possibly Latin. His skin, he said, appeared to be very smooth. The driver had a powerful face, neck and shoulders. Craig repeatedly used the words "powerful" and "muscular" to describe his neck and shoulders.*

The description of this escort comes up repeatedly in other sightings of Oswald with a stocky homunculus.

Jim Leavelle—DPD Detective

In 1988, he told author Gary Fannin that "Oswald would never have been found guilty of killing Tippit or JFK at the time of his death."[9]

Jesse Curry—Dallas Chief of Police

Curry, who was in the motorcade just in front of the President and interviewed Oswald after the assassination is on the record for saying: "*There*

---

[8] https://www.kennedysandking.com/john-f-kennedy-articles/the-mauser-the-carcano-and-the-lt-day-rifle
[9] The Innocence of Oswald, Fannin p.175

is a possibility that one (a shot) came from in front of us… By the direction of the blood and the brains of the president from one of the shots, it just seems it would have to be fired from the front… I can't say that I could swear that there was one man and one man alone, I think that there is the possibility that there could be another man…". He also stated they were never able to place Oswald on the sixth floor with the rifle in his hands.[10]

James Sibert and Francis O'Neill—FBI Agents

Sibert and O'Neill witnessed the autopsy in Bethesda and wrote a report about it which disproves the Single Bullet theory and explains why Junior Counsel Arlen Specter, who interviewed them, prevented them from talking to the Warren Commission and also kept their report hidden.[11]

The eventually declassified report, Sibert's deposition to the ARRB and his interview with William Matson Law for his 2005 book *In the Eye of History: Disclosures in the JFK Assassination Medical Evidence* do not help Specter's case whatsoever:

Law: *I've talked to Mr. O'Neill quite a bit about this and asked him about his belief in the single-bullet theory, and he said, "Absolutely not, it did not happen!"*
Sibert: *Well, you can put me in the same category! Have you read Arlen Specter's latest book, Passion for Truth? …*
Sibert: *I told them before they asked me to come up for the [ARRB] deposition, I said: "Well, before I come up, I want to tell you one thing: I don't buy the single-bullet theory." And they said, "We don't expect you to."*
Law: *Yes, when I talked to Mr. O'Neill, he was adamant that it did not happen…*
… Law: *Were you surprised you weren't called before the Warren Commission?*

---

[10] Spartacus Educational—and The Killing of President Kennedy 1978
[11] http://22november1963.org.uk/sibert-and-oneill-report#sibert-oneill-report

Sibert: *I was at the time, but now I can understand why.*

Law: *Why do you think you weren't called?*

Sibert: *Why? In other words, with that single-bullet theory, if they went in there and asked us to pinpoint where the bullet entered the back and the measurements and all that stuff, how are you going to work it? See, the way they got the single-bullet theory, was by moving that back wound up to the base of the neck.*

... Law: *I was going to ask you to tell me your thoughts on Mr. Specter and the single-bullet theory.*

Sibert: *Well I—that single-bullet theory—when they had me come up to the ARRB deposition there at College Park, I said, "Well before I come up there, I want you to know one thing. I'm not an advocate of the single-bullet theory." I said, "I don't believe it because I stood there two feet from where that bullet wound was in the back, the one that they eventually moved up to the base of the neck. I was there when Boswell made his face sheet and located that wound exactly as we described it in the FD 302." And I said, "Furthermore, when they examined the clothing after it got into the Bureau, those bullet holes in the shirt and the coat were down 5 inches there. So there is no way that bullet could have gone that low then rise up and come out the front of the neck, zigzag and hit Connally and then end up pristine on a stretcher over there in Dallas."*

Law: *You don't believe in the single-bullet theory. Period.*

Sibert: *There is no way I will swallow that. They can't put enough sugar on it for me to bite it. That bullet was too low in the back.*

Law also interviewed O'Neill:

Law: *Were you surprised you were not called before the Warren Commission?*

O'Neill: *Yes. Because we had pertinent information and the information that was given to the Warren Commission as a result of our interview with Mr. Specter was not a hundred percent accurate...*

As Law concluded, O'Neill and Sibert are adamant that the single-bullet theory is wrong. *"That's Arlen Specter's theory,"* O'Neill told me. It's quite evident from my conversations with them that they have no respect for the one-time assistant counsel to the Warren Commission, now Senator from Pennsylvania. When I questioned Jim Sibert about the single-bullet theory and Arlen Specter, he went as far as to say, *"What a liar. I feel he got his orders from above—how far above I don't know."*[12]

Law enforcement, Doctors and Medical Personnel in Dallas, at Parkland Memorial Hospital and Bethesda who Made Descriptions of Wounds Indicating a Front Shot

Parkland—doctors: Robert McClelland, Charles Crenshaw, Paul Peters, William Zedlitz, Ronald Jones, Richard Dulany, Charles Carrico, Ken Salyer, Kemp Clark, James Duke, Malcolm Perry, Charles Baxter, Don Curtis, Marion Jenkins, Robert Grossman, Adolph Giesecke, Fouad Bashour, William Midgett, Jackie Hunt, David Stewart; Nurses: Diana Bowron, Audrey Bell, Doris Nelson, Phyliss Hall, Pat Hutton, Margaret Hinchliffe; Other Parkland personnel and onlookers—Justice of the Peace Theron Ward, Ambulance driver Aubrey Rike, Darrell Tomlinson

Bethesda Personnel: Dennis David, Jerrol Custer, Floyd Riebe, Paul O'Connor, James Curtis, Dr. James Humes, Dr. Thornton Boswell, Saundra Spencer, Godfrey McHugh, Joe O'Donnell, Dr. John Ebersole, John Stringer, Dr. Robert Karnel, James Metzler, Chester Boyers, Joseph Hagan, Tom Robinson, John Van Hoesen, Robert Knudsen ;

Law enforcement: James Courson D. P. D. Police Officer, Milton Wright, Texas, Highway Patrolman, Vincent Drain FBI Special Agent, Samuel Kinney Secret Service Agent, Joe Cody DPD Police Officer, Clint Hill Secret Service, Bill Greer Secret Service, Roy Kellerman Secret Service, James Sibert and Frank O'Neill FBI.[13]

As we can see one of the biggest lies told by the HSCA was the statement that people present at the Bethesda autopsy contradicted the

---

[12] https://spartacus-educational.com/JFKsibertW.htm and In the Eye of History: Disclosures in the JFK Assassination Medical Evidence (William Matson Law)
[13] *JFK Absolute Proof*, Robert Groden, pages 149 to 156

back of the head exit wound Parkland doctors witnessed, or as Gary Aguilar put it:

They said that all the witnesses at the autopsy, they all agreed to those autopsy photographs (showing no damage to the back of JFK's head). But they suppressed the witness statements them-selves. When the ARRB came along, and out come those witness statements, out come the diagrams. And lo and behold, it turns out that the witnesses at the autopsy all agreed with the doctors at Dal-las: That the defect involved the rear of the head. They basically lied about what was there...[14]

Doctor James Humes—the chief of anatomic pathology at the Be-thesda Naval Hospital... Performed JFK autopsy

In his 1964 testimony during the Warren Commission, Humes had this to say about CE399, the pristine Magic Bullet: *"I think that is extremely unlikely..."* Aware that the Parkland doctors had spoken of fragments of bullet remaining in Connally's thigh, Humes said, *"... I can't conceive of where they came from with this missile."*

---

[14] JFK Revisited, page 283, also see Chapter 9 in this book

Admiral Doctor George Burkley—President Kennedy's personal physician (present in the motorcade, at Parkland Hospital and Bethesda)

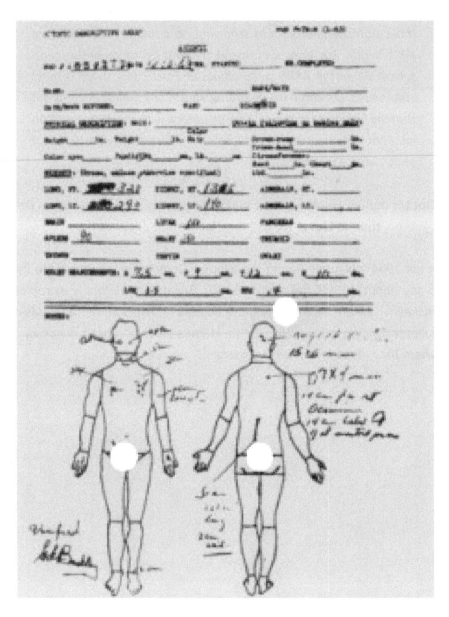

NAMED N (Rev. 6-58) BACK

25 NAME

John Fitzgerald Kennedy

30 SUMMARY OF FACTS RELATING TO DEATH:

President John Fitzgerald Kennedy, while riding in the motorcade in Dallas, Texas, on November 22, 1963, and at approximately 12:30 p.m., was struck in the head by an assassin's bullet and a second wound occurred in the posterior back at about the level of the third thoracic vertebra. The wound was shattering in type causing a fragmentation of the skull and evulsion of three particles of the skull at time of the impact, with resulting maceration of the right hemisphere of the brain. The President was rushed to Parkland Memorial Hospital, and was immediately under the care of a team of physicians at the hospital under the direction of a neurosurgeon, Kemp Clark. I arrived at the hospital approximately five minutes after the President and immediately went to the emergency room. It was evident that the wound was of such severity that it was bound to be fatal. Breathing was noted at the time of arrival at the hospital by several members of the Secret Service. Emergency measures were employed immediately including intravenous fluid and blood. The President was pronounced dead at 1:00 p.m. by Dr. Clark and was verified by me.

31. DISPOSITION OF REMAINS

To the White House, Washington, D.C.

32.

DATE SIGNED November 23, 1963   SIGNATURE   George Gregory Burkley   RADM   (MC)
Physician to the President   (Rank)

33.

APPROVED: COURT OF INQUIRY OR BOARD OF INVESTIGATION _____ BE HELD.
(will or will not)

DATE SIGNED _____   SIGNATURE _____   USN
(Commanding Officer)   (Rank)

COPY

000091

Images: *the autopsy facing sheet and flip side*

These corroborate Sibert and O'Neill's testimonies and contradict Gerald Ford's (and the Warren Commission's) description of the location of the Single Bullet entry point (back of the neck) ... thus disqualifying the Single Bullet theory that it alone caused seven wounds to Governor Connally and the President.

Once asked the question: *"Do you agree with the Warren Report on the number of bullets that entered the President's body?"* Burkley answered: *"I would not care to be quoted on that."*[15]

In 1976, Burkley's lawyer William Illig contacted Richard Sprague of the HSCA, saying that his client had information that *"others besides Oswald must have participated."*[16]

James Young-White House Physician, White House Corpsman Chief Petty Officers Mills and Martinell

Young was a White House physician who ordered Chiefs Mills and Martinell, his assistants, to go to the White House and retrieve what they knew were skull fragments at that time… He was the first one at the autopsy to see these materials recovered from the limousine… He described a bullet (among the materials) brass-colored with a bent tip and five millimeters in diameter… *They said it was in the back seat…* (This would imply a fourth shot, therefore multiple shooters.)[17]

Young was ignored by Gerald Ford, Arlen Specter and some at the ARRB, and was shunned because he mistakenly referred to the limousine as the Queen Mary instead of the SX 100X presidential limousine. Mills remembered the event but refused to elaborate when questioned by a reporter.[18]

Alex Rosen—Former FBI Assistant Director

Alex Rosen told the Committee (*Church Committee testimony*) that the FBI was not actively investigating a conspiracy, but *was "in the position*

---

[15] George Burkley interview with the JFK Library (page 18 of transcript)
[16] Letter from Illig to Sprague, March 18, 1977
[17] Mary Ferrell — The Missing Physician
[18] JFK Revisited, Through the Looking Glass, pp. 434–437) James Young letter to Gerald Ford, December 27, 2000, https://aarclibrary.org/white-house-physician-autopsy-eyewitness-questions-president-ford-about-missing-bullet/

of standing on the corner with our pockets open, waiting for someone to drop information into it…"[19]

Charles Shaffer—Staff member—Former Justice Department Investigator

In a 2014 Washington Post interview, Charles Shaffer admitted that he *now* thinks that JFK was assassinated as a result of a mob-related conspiracy involving Santo Trafficante and Carlos Marcello. He also claimed that Warren's biggest blunder was not allowing Ruby to testify in Washington where he may have exposed a conspiracy.[20]

Alfredda Scobey—Staff member—Law Assistant to Court of Appeals Georgia

Scobey wrote down notes taking the position of what a defense lawyer for Oswald could have argued with respect to the evidence presented by the Warren Commission. Her observations underscore many problems the prosecution would have faced including: The denial of Oswald's right to legal counsel; the inadmissibility of his wife's testimony; the poor quality of Helen Markham as witness to the Tippit assassination; the number of witnesses that refused to identify Oswald as Tippit's assassin; the lack of pertinence of the Walker incident; the evidence obtained from the Paines without a proper warrant; the chain of possession of the rifle, etc.[21]

Burt Griffin and Leon Hubert—Assistant Counsels

Burt Griffin and Leon Hubert were charged with investigating Jack Ruby and while they had not concluded that Ruby was involved in a cons-

---

[19] *Mary Ferrell Foundation: TESTIMONY OF ALEX ROSEN, 30 APR 1976*
https://www.maryferrell.org/showDoc.html?docId=1433#relPageId=1&search=testimony_of%20alex%20rosen
[20] Washington Post-September 19, 2014
[21] Weisberg Collection: http://jfk.hood.edu/Collection/Weisberg%20Subject%20Index%20Files/S%20Disk/Scobey%20Alfredda/Item%2001.pdf

piracy, they were clearly not satisfied with the investigation and information transferred to them by the FBI or CIA. This is made clear by memos written by them and answers Judge Griffin gave in his HSCA testimony.

In the documentary *The Killing of President Kennedy*, Griffin is even blunter: *"I feel betrayed … the CIA lied to us…"* He goes on to state that the CIA concealed their efforts to kill Castro and their links with the mafia, which would have been very important for the investigation. Griffin also is on the record as saying: *"In any area where Oswald's relation to the FBI… We could not trust Hoover."*[22]

J. Lee Rankin—Chief Counsel to the Warren Commission

In 1978, before an executive session appearance, the top legal expert of the Warren Commission, J. Lee Rankin, was interviewed by Michael Ewing, a staff member for the HSCA. A report on the phone conversation was declassified in the mid-1990s which clearly underscores his dissatisfaction with the FBI and the CIA in their investigations and their cooperation, and the doubts he had about the Warren Commission conclusions.

The following are some of the key statements he made:

First, he stated that he believed that *"hindsight makes it clear that both Hoover and the CIA were covering up a variety of items"*;

He said that he finds the FBI performance *"quite disturbing in hindsight. We would have found their conduct nearly unbelievable if we had known about it at the time."* He commented that the destruction of the Hosty (FBI) note (a message from Oswald just days before the assassination) was *"a crime—a crime committed by the FBI, and one which directly related to the assassin's most important actions and motivations during the final days"*;

---

[22] HSCA Volume XI: The Warren Commission—Attachment F: Executive session testimony of Judge Burt W. Griffin and Howard P. Willens. SUBCOMMITTEE HEARING THURSDAY, NOVEMBER 17, 1977 —The Killing of the President and https://www.kennedysandking.com/john-f-kennedy-articles/gunrunner-ruby-and-the-cia

... that the decision to use the FBI for investigative work might have changed. He agreed, saying, *"We couldn't have used the people involved in any further way, that's clear. The FBI would have to have been regarded as a suspect in that instance and that in turn would have affected everything."*;

... and that the CIA/Mafia plots would have had a *"very direct bearing on the areas of conspiracy which we tried to pursue."* He also asked, *"Are you looking into the plots on the basis of whether they were covered up by the CIA because some of the very people involved in them could have been involved in the President's assassination?"[23]*

Senator Richard Russell—Warren Commissioner

Senator Russell in a stunning phone conversation with LBJ on September 18, 1964, voiced his disagreement with the Single Bullet theory very directly:

"They were trying to prove that the same bullet that hit Kennedy first was the one that hit Connally, went through him and through his hand, his bone, into his leg and everything else. ... The commission believes that the same bullet that hit Kennedy hit Connally. Well, I don't believe it."... "And so I couldn't sign it. And I said that Governor Connally testified directly to the contrary, and I'm not going to approve of that. So I finally made them say there was a difference in the commission, in that part of them believed that that wasn't so. And of course, if a fellow was accurate enough to hit Kennedy right in the neck on one shot and knock his head off in the next one ... and he's leaning up against his wife's head ... and not even wound her ... why, he didn't miss completely with that third shot. But according to their theory, he not only missed the whole automobile, but he missed the street! Well, a man that's a good enough shot to put two bullets right into Kennedy, he didn't miss that whole automobile."

---

[23] *May-June 1997 issue (Vol. 4, No. 4) of Probe*

Senator John Cooper—Warren Commissioner

Senator John Cooper is also on the record for having written about the Single Bullet theory: *"It seems to me that Governor Connally's statement negates such a conclusion."* He later confirmed his stance in an interview for the BBC documentary.[24]

Congressman Hale Boggs—Warren Commissioner

Boggs was neither convinced that Oswald was the assassin, nor that Ruby acted alone. According to legal advisor Bernard Fensterwald:

> *"Almost from the beginning, Congressman Boggs had been suspicious over the FBI and CIA's reluctance to provide hard information when the Commission's probe turned to certain areas, such as allegations that Oswald may have been an undercover operative of some sort. When the Commission sought to disprove the growing suspicion that Oswald had once worked for the FBI, Boggs was outraged that the only proof of denial that the FBI offered was a brief statement of disclaimer by J. Edgar Hoover. It was Hale Boggs who drew an admission from Allen Dulles that the CIA's record of employing someone like Oswald might be so heavily coded that the verification of his service would be almost impossible for outside investigators to establish."*

> According to one of his friends: *"Hale felt very, very torn during his work (on the Commission) ... he wished he had never been on it and wished he'd never signed it (the Warren Report)."* Another former aide argued that *"Hale always returned to one thing: Hoover lied his eyes out to the Commission—on Oswald, on Ruby, on their friends, the bullets, the gun, you name it."*[25]

---

[24] *The Killing of President Kennedy*
[25] https://spartacus-educational.com/JFKboggs.htm

Congressman Gerald Ford—Warren Commissioner

In public Gerald Ford was a staunch defender of the Warren Commission's findings and conclusions, describing the report as a Gibraltar of factual literature. However, in private he seems to have held a very different discourse. Valérie Giscard d'Estaing, ex-president of France, claimed the following in an interview he gave to RTL:

> *"Gerald Ford (president of the United States from 1974 to 1977, editor's note) was a member of the Warren Commission,"* he resumes. *"Once I was making a car trip with him, he was then President as I was myself. I said to him: 'Let me ask you an indiscreet question: you were on the Warren Commission, what conclusions did you arrive at?' He told me: 'It's not a satisfactory one. We arrived at an initial conclusion: it was not the work of one person, it was something set up. We were sure that it was set up. But we were not able to discover by whom.'"[26]*

In 1997 the Assassination Records Review Board (ARRB) released a document that revealed that Ford had altered the first draft of the Warren Report to read: *"A bullet had entered the base of the back of his neck slightly to the right of the spine."* Something he admitted to before his death.[27]

John Moss Whitten—Chief of CIA Covert Operations in Mexico and Central America

Whitten was assigned by Richard Helms to be the CIA liaison to the Warren Commission. Though he initially posited that Oswald acted alone, he learned of hidden evidence by the CIA and argued for more examination. Helms eventually replaced him with James Jesus Angleton.

---

[26] http://www.rtl.fr/actu/international/kennedy-le-reve-a-ete-assassine-avec-l-homme-dit-giscard-7767111282 and https://jfkfacts.org/president-ford-spoke-jfk-plot-says-former-french-president/#google_vignette
[27] JFK Absolute Proof, Groden, page 265

Whitten was also later to discover that CIA officer George Joannides had in 1963 been the case officer for the Student Revolutionary Directorate, the Cuban exile group Lee Harvey Oswald had multiple interactions within New Orleans. This was unknown to the HSCA when he became an obfuscating liaison for that investigation.

Whitten testified to the HSCA that his team of thirty agents was provided with no details about *"Oswald's political activity in the United States, especially the 'pro-Castro activity' and autobiographical sketches … found among his effects."* … that had he known about Oswald's activities in New Orleans and contacts with the DRE Cubans, he would have focused his investigation on the *"possible involvement of the Miami station."*

Whitten also knew nothing about William Harvey (a madman according to him) and the CIA's executive action programs.[28]

William C. Sullivan-Assistant Director of the FBI's Intelligence Division

By the time of the assassination, Sullivan was third in the FBI hierarchy after Hoover and Tolson. He was the leading FBI representative during the in-house investigation and coordinated with the CIA's James Angleton. He wrote a book, *The Bureau: My Thirty Years in Hoover's FBI* (1979), highly critical of Hoover and LBJ.

Here are just a few of his explosive revelations which contradicted his own reports to the Warren Commission:

> *"-Hoover was delighted when Gerald Ford was named to the Warren Commission. The director wrote in one of his internal memos that the bureau could expect Ford to 'look after FBI interests,' and he did, keeping us fully advised of what was going on behind closed doors. He was our man, our informant, on the Warren Commission.*
> *—… after we zeroed in on Oswald, there were huge gaps in the*

---

[28] *Whitten Deposition to HSCA, ARRB*

case, gaps we never did close. For example, we never found out what went on between Oswald and the Cubans in Mexico.

—On the other hand, it seemed extremely likely to me that Jack Ruby, a local nightclub owner who knew a lot of low characters, who was a police buff, and who had a working relationship with the local police, could easily have been a police informer. That certainly could explain Ruby's presence at the jail where he shot Oswald.

—Oswald didn't have a record of being an outstanding marksman and yet he hit the president with two shots while his car was moving slowly down the road. His third shot hit Governor Connally. I went to the book depository from which Oswald fired at the president and I looked out the window where he was positioned. I've been around guns all my life and I'm a reasonably good shot, but I must say that that would be quite a task for me. It was, tragically, damn good shooting."

J. Edgar Hoover—Director of the FBI

Less than 24 hours after the assassination of President Kennedy, FBI Director J. Edgar Hoover reported to the new President Johnson on the state of the investigation. Noting that the evidence against [Oswald] is *"not very, very strong."* But when LBJ then asked: *"Have you established any more about the visit to the Soviet Embassy in Mexico in September,"* an event of no little interest to the inner circles of government, Hoover replied, *"No, that's one angle that's very confusing for this reason. We have up here the tape and the photograph of the man who was at the Soviet Embassy, using Oswald's name. The picture and the tape do not correspond to this man's voice, nor to his appearance. In other words, it appears that there is a second person who was at the Soviet Embassy down there."[29]*

---

[29] Transcripts of Hoover-LBJ phone calls Nov. 24, 1963, https://www.history-matters.com/archive/jfk/lbjlib/phone_calls/Nov_1963/html/LBJ-Nov-1963_0030a.htm

LBJ—President

In a 1969 interview with Walter Cronkite, Lyndon Johnson said that he had not completely discounted the possibility of international connections to the murder.

He is also on the record for stating the following: *"I never believed that Oswald acted alone ...."* He added that the government *"had been operating a damned Murder Inc. in the Caribbean."*[30]

The Jim Garrison Investigation

Starting in 1966, New Orleans DA Jim Garrison investigated the assassination. This led to the 1969 trial of Clay Shaw, a well-known local businessman, who was accused of being part of a conspiracy. While the jury found Shaw not guilty, according to Mark Lane—Garrison advisor—most jurors felt there had nevertheless been a conspiracy.

This investigation shed light on many, up to then under-reported, issues:

Pierre Finck (Pathologist at JFK Autopsy) Shaw Trial Testimony Excerpts:

Mr. Oser:

How many other military personnel were present at the autopsy in the autopsy room?

Col. Finck:

The autopsy room was quite crowded. It is a small autopsy room, and when you are called in circumstances like that to look at the wound of the President of the United States who is dead, you don't look around too much to ask people for their names and take notes on who they are and how many there are. I did not do so. The room was crowded with military and civilian personnel and federal agents, Secret Service agents, FBI agents, for part of the autopsy,

---

[30] https://www.theatlantic.com/magazine/archive/2013/08/lbj-oswald-wasnt-alone/309486/

46

but I cannot give you a precise breakdown as regards the attendance of the people in that autopsy room at Bethesda Naval Hospital.

Mr. Oser:

Colonel, did you feel that you had to take orders from the Army General that was there directing the autopsy?

Col. Finck:

No, because there were others, there were Admirals.

Mr. Oser:

There were Admirals?

Col. Finck:

Oh, yes, there were Admirals, and when you are a Lieutenant Colonel in the Army you just follow orders, and at the end of the autopsy we were specifically told—as I recall it, it was by Admiral Kenney, the Surgeon General of the Navy—this is subject to verification— we were told not to discuss the case.

Mr. Oser:

You were told not to discuss the case?

Col. Finck:—to discuss the case without coordination with the Attorney General.

... Mr. Oser : Did you have an occasion to dissect the track of that particular bullet in the victim as it lay on the autopsy table?

Col. Finck:

I did not dissect the track in the neck...

... Mr. Oser :

Your Honor, I would ask Your Honor to direct the witness to answer my question. I will ask you the question one more time: Why did you not dissect the track of the bullet wound that you have described today and you saw at the time of the autopsy at the time you examined the body? Why? I ask you to answer that question.

Col. Finck:

As I recall I was told not to, but I don't remember by whom.[31]

---

[31] State of Louisiana vs. Clay L. Shaw, Criminal District Court, Parish of Orleans, State of Louisiana, 198–059 1426 [30] section C, transcript, pp.51f and Ibid., pp. 114–118

Aloysius A. Habighorst—New Orleans Police Officer

Many witnesses have confirmed that Clem and Clay Bertrand were Clay Shaw aliases. He used this name in an airport lounge[32] and in a probable moment of absent-mindedness gave it away to Officer Aloysius A. Habighorst after he was arrested. (See line 10 to the left in the Alias box.)

---

[32] Garrison Files—Materials Clay Shaw 2, p. 20

Even though Judge Haggerty ruled the following piece inadmissible… There is no reasonable explanation for the name Bertrand being in this field. This would have gone a long way in proving Shaw's connections to Oswald.

OFFICE OF THE DISTRICT ATTORNEY

STATE OF LOUISIANA
PARISH OF ORLEANS

January 23, 1969

STATEMENT OF: ALOYSIUS J. HABIGHORST
New Orleans Police Department

RESIDING AT: 3426 Pittari Place
New Orleans, La.

RE: FINGERPRINTING AND FACTS CONTAINED ON
FINGERPRINTING CARD, (BEARING NO. 125-389
NEW ORLEANS POLICE DEPARTMENT)

STATEMENT

On March 1, 1967, at approximately 8:55 P.M. I had an occasion to print and process a white male who identified himself as CLAY LEVERGNE SHAW who was booked under police item number C-466-67 of the New Orleans Police Department.

MR. SHAW was given three fingerprint cards and asked to sign his name in a designated spot on the card. After having been fingerprinted by Patn. James Millet who is a New Orleans Police Officer and was assigned in the B of I of the Central Lockup along with myself on the above date. In order to fill these cards I asked MR. SHAW related questions as to his date of birth, middle name, occupation, birth date and place, scars or marks or tattoos of identification on his body, and also asked him "what other names other than CLAY L. SHAW do you use" and in reply MR. SHAW gave me the name of CLAY BERTRAND.

I would not consider MR. SHAW's attitude as being facetious in fact he was most cooperative during the entire time.

The above statement is true and correct and I have made same of my on free will.

ALOYSIUS J. HABIGHORST

(Habighorst affidavit)

49

Francis Fruge—Garrison Case Investigator—Louisiana State Police Lieutenant

Francis Fruge's entry into the case actually began a few days before the assassination when he first encountered and questioned Rose Cheramie, a heroin-addicted call girl and drug courier, who predicted the assassination, and talked about her links with Jack Ruby while she was hospitalized from November 20 to 22, 1963. He met her again right after the murder. Fruge later became an important investigator for Jim Garrison. His account of this extremely incriminating story was summarized[33] in a thoroughly documented July 1999 *Probe Magazine* article:

> *As Fruge so memorably recalled to Jonathan Blackmer of the HSCA, Cheramie summed up her itinerary in Dallas in the following manner:* "She said she was going to, number one, pick up some money, pick up her baby, and to kill Kennedy."[34]
>
> At the hospital, Cheramie again predicted the assassination. Again, before it happened on November 22nd, to more than one nurse. *The nurses, in turn, told others of Cheramie's prognostication.*[35] Further, according to a psychiatrist there, Dr. Victor Weiss, Rose " ... *told him that she knew both Ruby and Oswald and had seen them sitting together on occasions at Ruby's club."* Fruge later confirmed the fact that she had worked as a stripper for Ruby.[36]
>
> Fruge had discounted Cheramie's earlier comments to him as drug-induced delusions. Or, as he said to Blackmer, *"When she came out with the Kennedy business, I just said, wait a minute, wait a minute, something is wrong here somewhere."*[37]
>
> The word spread throughout the hospital that she had predicted Kennedy's murder. Dr. Wayne Owen, who had been interning from LSU at the time, later told the *Madison Capital Times* that

---

[33] Ibid., 3/13/67
[34] p. 9 of Fruge's 4/18/78 HSCA deposition
[35] Memo of Frank Meloche to Louis Ivon (Garrison lawyer), 5/22/67
[36] *Louisiana State Police report of 4/4/67*
[37] *Fruge, HSCA deposition, p. 9*

he and other interns were told of the plot in advance of the assassination. Amazingly, Cheramie even predicted the role of her former boss Jack Ruby because Owen was quoted as saying that one of the interns was told " ... *that one of the men involved in the plot was a man named Jack Rubinstein.*" (2/11/68) Owen said that they shrugged it off at the time. But when they learned that Rubinstein was Ruby they grew quite concerned. *"We were all assured that something would be done about it by the FBI or someone. Yet we never heard anything." (Ibid)* In fact, Cheramie's association with Ruby was also revealed to Dr. Weiss. In an interview with him after the assassination, Rose revealed that she had worked as a drug courier for Jack Ruby.[38]

In the same memo, there is further elaboration on this important point:

"I believe she also mentioned that she worked in the nightclub for Ruby and that she was forced to go to Florida with another man whom she did not name to pick up a shipment of dope to take back to Dallas, that she didn't want to do this thing but she had a young child and that they would hurt her child if she didn't." These comments are, of course, very revealing about Ruby's role in both an intricate drug smuggling scheme and, at the least, his probable acquaintance with men who either had knowledge of, or were actually involved in, the assassination.

Although Fruge had discounted the Cheramie story on November 20th, the events of the 22nd made him a believer. Right after JFK's murder, Fruge " ... *called that hospital up in Jackson and told them by no way in the world to turn her loose until I could get my hands on her."[39]* So, on November 25th, Fruge journeyed up to Jackson State Hospital again to talk to Cheramie. This time he conducted a much more in-depth interview. Fruge found out that Cheramie had been traveling with the two men from Miami. He also found that the men seemed to be a part of the conspiracy...

---

[38] *Memo of Frank Meloche to Jim Garrison, 2/23/67*
[39] *Fruge's HSCA deposition, p. 12*

After the assassination, they were supposed to stop by a home in Dallas to pick up around eight thousand dollars plus Rose's baby. From there Cheramie was supposed to check into the Rice Hotel in Houston under an assumed name. Houston is in close proximity to Galveston, the town from which the drugs were coming in. From Houston, once the transaction was completed, the trio headed for Mexico.

Cheramie proved to be reliable: Fruge decided to have the drug deal aspect of her story checked out by the state troopers and U. S. Customs. The officers confirmed the name of the seaman on board the correct ship coming into Galveston. The customs people checked the Rice Hotel and the reservations had been made for her under an assumed name. The contact who had the money and her baby was checked, and his name showed that he was an underworld, suspected narcotics dealer. Fruge checked Cheramie's baggage and found that one box had baby clothes and shoes inside.

Aftermath of the Garrison Case and General Comments

Perhaps no other person who believed there was a conspiracy was more vilified than Jim Garrison. He has been called a charlatan, a publicity seeker and crazy, among other things. With time, however, many of his claims have been vindicated.

While some described his case as a farce, it is often overlooked that Garrison had presented his evidence beforehand to a three-judge panel who concluded that he was justified to bring it to court, and that the subsequent HSCA investigation concluded the following about Garrison and his office:

"As noted, the committee believed the Clinton witnesses to be telling the truth as they knew it. It was, therefore, inclined to believe that Oswald was in Clinton, La., in late August, early September 1963, and that he was in the company of David Ferrie, if not Clay Shaw. The committee was puzzled by Oswald's apparent associa-

tion with Ferrie, a person whose anti-Castro sentiments were so distant from those of Oswald, the Fair Play for Cuba Committee campaigner. But the relationship with Ferrie may have been significant for more than its anti-Castro aspect, in light of Ferrie's connection with G. Wray Gill and Carlos Marcello[40] ... and also...

The committee also found that there was at least a possibility that Oswald and Guy Banister were acquainted. —and also: *Further, the committee's investigation of Oswald and Ruby showed a variety of relationships that may have matured into an assassination conspiracy. Neither Oswald nor Ruby turned out to be "loners," as they had been painted in the 1964 investigation.[41]*

Other information from later investigations reveals that Garrison's efforts were sabotaged by adversaries who infiltrated his volunteer team and weakened his efforts; well-orchestrated propaganda attacking both his case and reputation; refusals to his subpoenas for out-of-state witnesses and the harassment, turning of witnesses, and untimely deaths of some of his key witnesses, including the suspicious death of star-witness David Ferrie and the murder of Eladio Del Valle.

Over time evidence that began to emerge showed that Clay Shaw, despite his denials, was in fact a CIA asset and part of an organization of interest to the CIA called Permindex. The latest documents, even before this last release by NARA, revealed that Shaw was a highly valued and compensated CIA contract agent, a fact that the Agency had done all it could to conceal from the public.[42] It now turns out that the internal deception by the CIA about Shaw seems to have gone even further. One of the ARRB releases from when it was active, from 1994 to 1998, revealed that the Agency had destroyed something called Shaw's "Y" files. It now appears that the destruction of Shaw's files extended even further, into his 201 file. (See this ARRB memo)[43]

---

[40] HSCA Final Report, p. 145
[41] HSCA Final Report, p. 180
[42] *Joan Mellen, Our Man in Haiti,* pp. 54–55
[43] MEMORANDUM November 14, 1996, To: Jeremy Gunn, Michelle Combs, Irene Marr, Robert J. Skwirot cc: From: Manuel E. Legaspi Subject: CIA and related files

The United States President's Commission on CIA Activities within the United States (The Rockefeller Commission)

After a 1974 New York Times report on illegal acts committed by the CIA, Gerald Ford set up the Rockefeller Commission headed by his Vice-President Nelson Rockefeller in 1975. It publicized the CIA MK/Ultra mind control experiments and revealed its illegal mail opening and U.S. protester surveillance programs (MH/Chaos). It also held a very narrow investigation into the Kennedy assassination focusing on the Zapruder film, some of the medical evidence and whether Frank Sturgis and E. Howard Hunt, who had just gained notoriety because of their roles in the Watergate scandal, were involved in the assassination. In a short eighteen-page chapter about the assassination, it concluded that the CIA had not been involved and that only three shots were fired from behind the motorcade.

Many distrusted this Commission because of the involvement of key Warren Commission members such as Ford and David Belin. The final report was on orders of Gerald Ford heavily edited by none other than Dick Cheney. It was largely superseded by the Church, Pike and HSCA committees that succeeded it.

United States Senate Select Committee to Study Governmental Operations with Respect to Intelligence Activities (The Church Committee)

This U.S. Senate Committee was chaired by Senator Frank Church and issued 14 reports in 1975 and 1976 after interviewing hundreds of witnesses and studying thousands pages of of files from the FBI, CIA and other agencies.

It delved into U.S. assassination plots against foreign leaders, which were a key component of CIA regime control or change operations. Ex-CIA leader Allen Dulles' pact with the Mafia to assassinate Castro was also part of their findings. This information, which could have impacted

---

pertaining to New Orleans, Hunter Leake, Clay Shaw, QKENCHANT, and ZRCLIFF the Warren Commission investigation, was kept secret by Dulles from the other commissioners.

Volume 4 of the report sheds light on HT/LINGUAL, the illegal mail intercept programs involving both the CIA and the FBI. The Committee also reported on the extent the CIA partnered with media and academia, in an effort to control the media, later called Operation Mockingbird:

"The CIA currently maintains a network of several hundred foreign individuals around the world who provide intelligence for the CIA and at times attempt to influence opinion through the use of covert propaganda. These individuals provide the CIA with direct access to a large number of newspapers and periodicals, scores of press services and news agencies, radio and television stations, commercial book publishers, and other foreign media outlets."

Led by Senators Gary Hart and Richard Schweiker, the Church Committee also conducted a focused investigation (Book 5) of the Kennedy assassination, concentrating on how the FBI and CIA supported the Warren Commission. Its report was very critical of these agencies: *"In the days following the assassination of President Kennedy, nothing was more important to this country than to determine the facts of his death; no one single event has shaken the country more. Yet the evidence the Committee has developed suggests that, for different reasons, both the CIA and the FBI failed in, or avoided carrying out, certain of their responsibilities in this matter...*

... developed evidence which impeaches the process by which the intelligence agencies arrived at their own conclusions about the assassination, and by which they provided information to the Warren Commission. This evidence indicates that the investigation of the assassination was deficient."

Paul Wallach—Church Committee Counsel
(Wendel Roache Interviews)

INS investigator Wendel Roache, when called by Church Committee investigators, replied that he had been expecting a call for twelve years.
What he said about Oswald is so damning that it likely contributed to
Richard Schweiker's suspicions that Oswald was a double agent spying
on both anti and pro-Castro groups:

> *"Included in this surveillance was the group of "nuts" headed by Da-*
> *vid Ferrie. Roache knew the details on Ferrie i.e., dismissal from*
> *Eastern Airlines, homosexual with perverse tendencies ("nuttier*
> *than a fruitcake"), etc. He stated that Ferrie's office—on a side*
> *street between St. Charles and Camp—(we'll have a street map for*
> *him) was under surveillance (although he never surveilled it, an-*
> *other inspector drove him past it and identified it); that Lee Harvey*
> *Oswald—who was identified by INS as an American when he first*
> *appeared on the New Orleans street scene (he does not recall the*
> *circumstances surrounding the identification)—was seen going into*
> *the offices of Ferrie's group, and "Oswald was known to be one of*
> *the men in the group."[44]*

Senator Gary Hart—Church Committee Member
(Democrat Senator)

An interview Hart gave to the *Denver Post* after his stint on the committee clearly showed that he did not buy the Warren Commission depiction
of Oswald, nor did he find that the FBI and the CIA were transparent with
what they knew:

> *"Who Oswald really was—who did he know? What affiliation did*
> *he have in the Cuban network? Was his public identification with*

---

[44] *MEMORANDUMS To: Files* From: *Paul Wallach Date: December 3, 1975, Re: Telephone conversations with Wendall Roache; See pages 35 and 40:* https://docu-
ments.theblackvault.com/documents/jfk/NARA-Oct2017/2018/157-10014-10120.pdf

the left-wing a cover for a connection with the anti-Castro right-wing?"

Hart believed that Oswald was a double agent which was one of the reasons why the FBI and CIA had made *"a conscious decision to withhold evidence from the Warren Commission."*

During the fiftieth anniversary of the Kennedy assassination, Hart was interviewed by the Huffington Post.[45]

One can only deduce that his views about the inadequacy of the Warren Commission investigation and mainstream media's efforts into getting to the bottom of things had hardened based on the following statements when talking about the suspicious and timely deaths of two key Mafiosi persons of interest while his committee was investigating them:

"It's amazing to me that American journalism never followed up on that story very much, because if you found out who killed those two guys, you might have some really interesting information on your hands."

"I went down to Miami when [Johnny] Roselli was killed and talked to this Dade County sheriff from the Miami Police Department, and they showed me pictures of him being fished out of the water in the barrel and how he'd been killed—nightmarish stuff. And [Momo Salvatore] Giancana was killed in his own basement with six bullet holes in his throat with a Chicago police car and an FBI car outside his house."

"I was always amazed in that particular instance of the CIA-Mafia connection and the Cuban connection 12 years—coming up 12 years—after Kennedy was killed that somebody didn't go after that story... New York Times, Washington Post, anybody. And they didn't. They reported the deaths and that was it, and the strange quirky coincidence, you know, but nothing more."

"You don't have to be a genius to believe that they knew

45 https://www.huffpost.com/entry/jfk-assassination-gary-hart_n_4302598

something about the coincidence of events—Cuba, Mafia, CIA and Kennedy—that somebody didn't want that out in the public 12 years later."

During a day-long symposium[46] in May 2015 featuring former Church Committee members and staff, held by the Brennan Center for Justice at NYU School of Law at the Constance Milstein and Family Global Academic Center of the New York University in Washington, D.C., Hart on a panel with former Church Committee colleague Senator Mondale, added this powerful affirmation:

"... THE THREE MAFIA FIGURES INVOLVED IN THE CASTRO PLOT WITH THE CIA. WE HEARD FROM ONE OF THEM TWICE. THE 2nd TIME—THE 1st TIME HE CAME AND WENT WITH NO PUBLIC NO-TICE AT ALL. HIGHLY SECRET. THE QUESTIONS OBVIOUSLY WERE WHO ORDERED CASTRO KILLED, WHAT ROLE DID YOU PLAY SO FORTH. I FELT AT THE TIME THAT HE WAS GENERALLY FORTHCOM-ING HE STILL KNEW A LOT HE WASN'T TELLING US. HE WENT HOME TO MIAMI AND DISAPPEARED AND ENDED UP DEAD. HE WAS IN HIS 70s. AND MAFIA TIMES IN THOSE DAYS THAT WAS RETIRE-MENT. FOR THE REST OF US NOW IT'S MIDDLE-AGED. THE 2nd FIG-URE WAS PROBABLY THE TOP MAFIA FIGURE IN AMERICA. PRE-PARED TO SUBPOENA HIM WITH THE HOUSE COMMITTEE. HE WAS KILLED IN HIS BASEMENT. KILLED IN HIS BASEMENT WITH SIX BUL-LET HOLES IN HIS THROAT. NEITHER OF THESE CRIMES HAVE BEEN SOLVED. NOW, BY AND LARGE THE MEDIA INCLUDED WITH THESE WERE DISMISSED AS MAFIA STUFF. THERE IS NO DOUBT IN MY MIND THEY WERE KILLED IN CONNECTION WITH OUR COMMITTEE. THE QUESTION IS WHY? WHO DID IT AND WHY?"

---

[46] https://www.c-span.org/video/?326284-1/intelligence-oversight-part-1

Sen. Richard Schweiker—Church Committee Member
(Republican Senator)

Schweiker's comments are even more explosive.

In 1975 he made the following statement to the *Village Voice*: <u>"We do know Oswald had intelligence connections. Everywhere you look with him, there are fingerprints of intelligence."</u>

In 1976 he told CBS News that the CIA and FBI lied to the Warren Commission and that the case could be solved if they followed hot new leads. He also claimed that the White House was part of the cover-up.[47]

In a BBC documentary *the Killing of President Kennedy (min. 6:36)*, he made the following blistering statements about the Warren Commission investigation:

"The Warren Commission has in fact collapsed like a house of cards and I believe it was set up at the time to feed pablum to the American people for reasons not yet known, and one of the biggest cover-ups in the history of our country occurred at that time."...

"The most important thing was that the intelligence agencies did all the wrong things if they were really looking for a conspiracy or to find out who killed John Kennedy."...

"The key is why did they let him (Oswald) bring a Russian-born wife out contrary to present Russian policy, he had to get special dispensation from the highest levels to bring his Russian-born wife out, that in itself says somebody was giving Oswald highest priority either because we had trained and sent him there and they went along and pretended they did not know to fake us out, or they had in fact inculcated him and sent him back and were trying to fake us out, but he had gotten a green light no other American had gotten."

In the documentary he goes on to say that the highest levels of government were behind him and his committee being misled and were continuing the cover-up and also that Oswald was clearly involved with pro-

---

[47] Rome News Tribune, May 14, 1976

Castro and anti-Castro groups, which smacks of an intelligence role as a double agent, and that these relationships were not investigated.

In an **interview Bob Tanenbaum** (first Deputy Counsel for the HSCA) gave to *Probe Magazine*, here is how he describes an exchange he had with Schweiker where the senator directly accuses the CIA[48]:

Q: One of the more interesting subjects you've mentioned in some of your talks is this meeting you had with Senator Schweiker which, I'm assuming, you give a lot of weight to, because of the evidence and because of who it was coming from.

A: *Well, it was shocking! I went up there with Cliff Fenton and Schweiker told me in his opinion the CIA was responsible for the assassination. That's a heck of a statement to come from a United States Senator and one who had even been Ronald Reagan's running mate in 1976, even though they didn't make it.*

Q: Was it just you in the room when he told you that?

A: *Yeah, it was just the two of us. I was stunned! He had asked Cliff to leave and he had his own staff people leave. I had that material he had given us which contained all that information about Veciana and the Alpha 66 group and this Bishop character.*

Q: When I interviewed Schweiker, one of the last questions I asked him was if he had been on the oversight committee, for which he had not been nominated, which avenue would he have pursued. And he said, "I would have gone after Maurice Bishop."

A: *Well, as I said, I was stunned. Even after investigating this case, I'm not going to say that the CIA did it. He was saying it definitively. What the evidence suggested when we were in Washington was there were certain rogue elements who were involved with Bishop and others, the "plumber" types in the Nixon White House, who were involved with Oswald, who were substantially involved with anti-Castro Cubans who, the evidence suggests, were involved in the assassination. I keep saying that the evidence suggested it because we weren't there long enough to make the case. So, there*

---

[48] Probe July-August 1996, Vol. 3, No. 5

was a short-circuiting that occurred. But that's the area we were moving inexorably toward. And then I spoke with Gaeton Fonzi and Gaeton would corroborate this to the extent that he worked with Schweiker, he knew what Schweiker's feelings were and he knew all about that file on Veciana. And that's when we asked Gaeton to come on board, because he had worked on the Church senate over-sight committee and he had a lot of connections that would be very helpful. And he's a very honest guy.

U.S. House of Representatives Select Committee on Assassinations (<u>HSCA</u>)[49]

Established in 1976 to investigate the assassinations of Martin Luther King and John F. Kennedy, the HSCA issued its final report in 1979. It found that there was a "probable conspiracy" in the JFK case.

The following is a summary of their conclusions:

Findings of the Select Committee on Assassinations in the Assassination of President John F. Kennedy in Dallas, Tex., November 22, 1963, that rebuke or contradict the WC investigation

1. Scientific acoustical evidence establishes a high probability that two gunmen fired at President John F. Kennedy. Other scientific evidence does not preclude the possibility of two gunmen firing at the President. Scientific evidence negates some specific conspiracy allegations.

2. The committee believes, on the basis of the evidence available to it, that President John F. Kennedy was probably assassinated as a result of a conspiracy. The committee is unable to identify the other gunman or the extent of the conspiracy.

3. The committee believes, on the basis of the evidence available

---

[49] https://www.archives.gov/research/jfk/select-committee-report/part-1c.html

to it, that anti-Castro Cuban groups, as groups, were not involved in the assassination of President Kennedy, but that the available evidence does not preclude the possibility that individual members may have been involved.

4. The committee believes, on the basis of the evidence available to it, that the national syndicate of organized crime, as a group, was not involved in the assassination of President Kennedy, but that the available evidence does not preclude the possibility that individual members may have been involved.

5. Agencies and departments of the U.S. Government performed with varying degrees of competency in the fulfillment of their duties. President John F. Kennedy did not receive adequate protection. A thorough and reliable investigation into the responsibility of Lee Harvey Oswald for the assassination of President John F. Kennedy was conducted. The investigation into the possibility of conspiracy in the assassination was inadequate. The conclusions of the investigations were arrived at in good faith, but presented in a fashion that was too definitive.

6. The Secret Service was deficient in the performance of its duties.

7. The Secret Service possessed information that was not properly analyzed, investigated or used by the Secret Service in connection with the President's trip to Dallas; in addition, Secret Service agents in the motorcade were inadequately prepared to protect the President from a sniper.

8. The responsibility of the Secret Service to investigate the assassination was terminated when the Federal Bureau of Investigation assumed primary investigative responsibility.

9. The Department of Justice failed to exercise initiative in super-

vising and directing the investigation by the Federal Bureau of Investigation of the assassination.

10. The Federal Bureau of Investigation performed with varying degrees of competency in the fulfillment of its duties.

11. The Federal Bureau of Investigation failed to investigate adequately the possibility of a conspiracy to assassinate the President.

12. The Federal Bureau of Investigation was deficient in its sharing of information with other agencies and departments.

13. The Central Intelligence Agency was deficient in its collection and sharing of information both prior to and subsequent to the assassination.

14. The Warren Commission performed with varying degrees of competency in the fulfillment of its duties.

15. The Warren Commission failed to investigate adequately the possibility of a conspiracy to assassinate the President. This deficiency was attributable in part to the failure of the Commission to receive all the relevant information that was in the possession of other agencies and departments of the Government.

16. The Warren Commission presented the conclusions in its report in a fashion that was too definitive.

The committee had other troubling conclusions: Neither Lee Harvey Oswald nor Jack Ruby were the loners depicted by the Warren Commission, and were involved in relationships that could have matured into a conspiracy; Lee Harvey Oswald was connected to David Ferrie and Guy Banister if not Clay Shaw—three conspirators according to Jim Garrison;

Jack Ruby was in fact connected to the Mafia (an issue sidestepped by the Warren Commission); Marina Oswald's incriminating statements against her husband were found to be lacking in credibility; they were inclined to believe Sylvia Odio, who asserted that she was visited before the assassination by two Cuban exiles and a Leon Oswald in an attempt to portray Oswald as unbalanced and hostile to JFK. Her testimony was rejected by the Warren Commission even though she had related the event before the assassination; *The Lopez Report*[50], (Corroborated by statements made by J. Edgar Hoover) established that someone was impersonating Oswald seven weeks before the assassination in Mexico City in an attempt to get a visa to travel to Cuba and that the CIA had tampered with the electronic evidence.

While the HSCA asked the Justice Department to reinvestigate the case—it chose to only look at the acoustical evidence, which it rejected based on science, but that itself is also contested.

For those who have used this final point to argue that the Warren Commission got it right and discard all the other incriminating findings—It will prove useful to read what the key members of the Committee had to say.

Robert Groden-HSCA, Staff Photographic Consultant, and Dr. Mark Weiss and Ernest Ashkenasy Acoustic Experts

Perhaps no one masters the photographic evidence of the JFK assassination better than Robert Groden. He first worked under Moses Weitzman in 1968 on a contract for Life Magazine to blow up the 8 mm Zapruder film to 35 mm. Groden kept a copy of it. He testified for several days before Executive Director David Belin of the Rockefeller Commission and senior counsel Robert Olsen. It was his showing of the Zapruder Film on national television that helped lead to the reinvestigation of the case by the HSCA, where he ended up contributing as a photo-optic technician/analyst.

---

[50] https://www.history-matters.com/archive/contents/hsca/contents_hsca_lopezrpt_2003.htm

Robert Groden played a key role in demonstrating how the damage alleged to have been caused by the Magic Bullet was simply impossible based on geometric, timing and photographic evidence; the synchronization of acoustic evidence with Zapruder film images and further proof of a front shot which was stymied by Robert Blakey's disagreement. According to Groden, every congressional committee member who heard the evidence presented by Groden and his colleagues, including worldwide acoustic expert Dr. Mark Weiss and Ernest Ashkenasy, were unanimous in their belief that a shot from the front had struck JFK's head… Only Blakey refused to admit this. But he did concede that there was a fourth shot.

Groden also contends that Blakey refused to extend acoustic testing in order to pinpoint the provenance of other shots (there were at least five and probably more). Groden also performed an analysis of bullet damage to Connally's clothing which also negates the single-bullet theory.[51]

Betsy Wolf—HSCA Staffer

Betsy Wolf was tasked with mapping out CIA files on Oswald. Her handwritten notes were kept classified for decades. Thanks to her persistence, we are now able to confirm that Oswald's opening of a 201 file was unusually late despite the fact that Oswald and his mother were spied upon through HT/LINGUAL (mail-intercept program); that his file was located secretly in the Office of Security (purpose of investigating employees of CIA under suspicion) instead of them going to the SR division (for people residing in Russia); and how Henry instead of Harvey was given as his name in the file. This is evidence that Oswald was a false defector, perhaps being used in a mole hunt.[52]

---

[51] JFK Absolute Proof, Groden, pp. 127 and 146
[52] *HSCA, record 180-10142-10332, file 24-05-02*

Gaeton Fonzi—Church Committee and HSCA Investigator

Gaeton Fonzi was interviewed a number of times after the investigations. The information he brought forward in his 1993 book, *The Last Investigation* was considered credible and explosive. Fonzi described an exchange he had with Arlen Specter (the Warren Commission's principal proponent of the Single Bullet theory) where he described him as being unnerved when discussing the Commission's evidence. He also revealed how Cuban exile group Alpha 66 leader Antonio Veciana exposed his CIA handler Maurice Bishop (a cover name for top-ranking CIA officer David Atlee Phillips) whom he claimed to have witnessed meeting with Oswald. He discussed how close contacts of CIA officer David Sanchez Morales heard him admit a conspiracy in the assassination. He described how the HSCA was stonewalled by the CIA. He also complained about second Commission head Robert Blakey's submissive relationship with the CIA. In a speech in 1998 while receiving the Mary Ferrell JFK Lancer Pioneer Award, he had this to say about the Warren Commission: *Is there any doubt that the Warren Commission deliberately set out not to tell the American people the truth?*

In a 1999 interview he gave to Michael Corbin, Fonzi contradicted Robert Blakey by stating that the HSCA investigation also lacked thoroughness. He also wonders out loud whether the *" … the Government itself or a power elite within the government was a controlling element here."*

He opined that the failed Bay of Pigs, the Missile Crisis followed by the cessation of secret anti-Castro operations were probably a guiding motivation for operatives linked to the JM/WAVE CIA station in Miami to remove the President and which end up dovetailing with Oswald's movements in 1963.

He claimed that Oswald was an agent of the intelligence establishment who was coded as a leftist. He was not a lone nut. He believes that he was also a patsy who did not fire a shot and that Dealey Plaza became a shooting gallery on November 22, 1963.

He also describes how David Phillips was not only seen with Oswald by Antonio Veciana, which admittedly is an uncorroborated allegation, but how a lot of the cover-up and misinformation campaigns about Oswald were linked to him, which is a fact. Note: Veciana survived a gunshot to the head after he revealed what he witnessed.[53]

He concludes the interview by stating: *"There is no doubt that it was a coup d'état!*

Dan Hardway and Edwin Lopez—HSCA "Staffers" (authors of appendix 13 of the HSCA Report, "Oswald, the CIA and Mexico City," aka the *Lopez Report—released in 1996*). History Matters provides an excellent introduction about this report:

> *The so-called Lopez Report, written by HSCA staffers Dan Hardway and Edwin Lopez, was released in a redacted form in 1996. It is a good starting place for grappling with some of the many mysteries of the Mexico City affair. Newly released files have provided new information not present in this report. The LBJ taped phone conversations for instance, include startling corroboration for the claim that audio intercepts of an Oswald impersonator were listened to by FBI agents in Dallas while Oswald was in custody. Declassified testimony of David Phillips, the Tarasoff couple who translated the tapes for the CIA, and others illuminate some areas and deepen the mystery in others.*

In 2014, for an ARRC conference, both Hardway and Lopez talked about their experience on the HSCA and the report. A lot of focus was put on how they had been making progress in the HSCA investigation until the CIA placed George Joannides as their resource person in charge of supervising the CIA's interaction with the HSCA. Despite claims that Joannides was impartial, it was confirmed that he was directly involved with the Cuban exile organization called the DRE in 1963. Oswald had direct interaction with the DRE in events that became very public and were used to paint him as a communist. Hardway concludes his speech with:

---

[53] https://www.youtube.com/watch?v=zy4MWRKM89E

"The CIA had something to hide; Joannides knew what they had to hide. The CIA knew he knew and knew we did not know who or what he was hiding; Joannides hid what he had to hide."

Edwin Lopez confirmed the stonewalling and gave examples on how they were being spied on. He referred to the continued holding back of documents as a mess we all needed to work on together.

They also confirmed that they felt that there were either fake phone calls done by an Oswald imposter while he was allegedly in Mexico, or at least faked transcripts.

In an interview Hardway gave to Black Op Radio, he recommended *The Devil's Chessboard* by David Talbot, a book which exposes incriminating information about Alan Dulles and William Harvey, who can be seen now as persons of high interest in the case.

In 2015, for a civil action where plaintiff Jefferson Morley, was suing the CIA for access to information, Dan Hardway signed a sworn deposition that underscores CIA obfuscation techniques as well as some of his findings during the investigation. The following are some of his statements:

Beginning in May of 1978, the CIA assigned George Joannides to handle liaison with Edwin Lopez and me. In the summer of 1978, Mr. Joannides began to change the way file access was handled. We no longer received prompt responses to our requests for files and what we did receive no longer seemed to provide the same complete files that we had been seeing. The obstruction of our efforts by Mr. Joannides escalated over the summer, finally resulting in a refusal to provide unexpurgated access to files in violation of the Memorandum of Understanding previously agreed to by the HSCA and the CIA;

During the course of the spring and summer of 1978, I had been looking into several areas of research which were actively impeded under Mr. Joannides's direction. These included back channel communications methods used by the CIA's Mexico City Station, William

Harvey's Office of Security files and his continuing relationship with certain Mafia figures, the use of an impulse camera to photograph the Cuban Consulate in Mexico City, missing production from one of the photographic installations that covered the Soviet Embassy in Mexico City as well as the impulse camera at the Cuban Consulate, and David Atlee Phillips's possible involvement in stories about LHO that appeared after the assassination of John F. Kennedy.

Before our unexpurgated access was cut off by Joannides, I had been able to document links between David Phillips and most of the sources of the disinformation that came out immediately after the assassination about Oswald and his pro-Castro proclivities. I confronted Phillips with those in an interview at our offices on August 24, 1978. Phillips was extremely agitated by that line of questioning, but was forced to admit that many of the sources were not only former assets that he had managed, in the late '50s and early 1960s, but were also assets whom he was personally managing in the fall of 1963. Mr. Phillips was asked, but could not explain, why the information that came from anti-Castro Cuban groups and individuals pointing to Cuban connections, all seemed to come from assets that he handled personally, but acknowledged that that was the case.

We have, since 1978, learned that George Joannides was running the propaganda shop at the CIA's Miami JMWAVE Station in 1963. It is extremely unlikely that Mr. Joannides could have occupied that position and not have known, and worked with, David Atlee Phillips. In addition, in 1963, we now know, George Joannides was the case officer handling the DRE. In 1977 the CIA specifically denied that DRE had a case officer assigned when asked that question by the HSCA.

Gary Cornwell—Assistant Chief Counsel HSCA

In 1999, Cornwell had his book *Real Answers* published which was very critical of the FBI and WC investigations: *"The case should have been solved in 1963 and 1964, and because the government decided not to look for the real answers when it had the chance, the opportunity was probably lost forever."*

"We confirmed that much of what the Warren Commission said was wrong"[54]

He also made this candid remark: *" ... the one thing that can be said about the Kennedy case with absolute certainty is that the statement Case Closed is as much a lie today as it was thirty-five years ago."*

Robert Tanenbaum—Chief Counsel HSCA (under Sprague)

In a Probe Magazine interview in 1993, Tanenbaum explained why he and Richard Sprague resigned from the Commission:

> *"In my opinion, Congress never wanted to go forward with these investigations at all. That's just based upon my having spoken with a lot of the membership of the House as I was asked to do by the Committee, in order to get funding. That's something I never thought would be an issue before I went down there. They sort of politicized into it with some very distinguished members of Congress who were retiring in 1976, requesting that the Kennedy portion be investigated because they had seen Groden's presentation of the Zapruder film and were very persuaded by it."*[55]

He also reveals troubling information about David Atlee Phillips:

> BT: *... The most significant one was when [David Atlee] Phillips came up before the Committee and then had to be recalled because it was*

---

[54] Real Answers, Cornwell, p. 45
[55] Probe Magazine, Vol. 3, No 5.

clear that he hadn't told the truth. That had to do with the phony commentary he made about Oswald going to Mexico City on or about October 1, 1963.

JD: Would you describe that whole sequence, because I feel that is one of the real highlights of your book?

BT: *As I said, I had never followed the sequence of these events and I wasn't aware of any of this before I went to Washington. If you had told me all this before I went, I would have said, "This is madness. Talk to me about reality!" So, Phillips was saying that an individual went to Mexico City on or about October 1st and the CIA was claiming this was Lee Harvey Oswald, just as the Warren Commission claimed. However, the following occurred: "Oswald" goes to the Russian Embassy and identifies himself as Lee Henry Oswald. He wants to fake everybody out by changing his middle name. There were tapes of what he said because the CIA was bugging the Embassy the same as they were doing to the U.S. Embassy, according to Phillips. And the CIA was photographing people going in and out of the Embassy, the same as they were doing to the U.S. (We found out, from our own sources that the CIA had a contract employee named Lee Henry Oswald, in their files). Phillips's testimony was that there was no photograph of "Oswald" because the camera equipment had broken down that day and there was no audio tape of "Oswald's" voice because they recycled their tapes every six or seven days. The problem with his story was, we had obtained a document, it was from the desk of J. Edgar Hoover, it was dated November 23, 1963, the very next day after the assassination. This document was a memo to all FBI supervisorial staff stating, in substance, that FBI agents who have questioned Oswald for the past 17 hours approximately, have listened to the tape made on October 1st, by an individual identifying himself as Lee Henry Oswald inside the Russian Embassy, calling on the phone to someone inside the Cuban Embassy and the agents can state unequivocally that the voice on the tape is not the voice of Lee Harvey Oswald, who is in custody.*

Tanenbaum also vindicated Garrison, incriminated Clay Shaw and shared thoughts about leads that were not followed up on:

JD: You've said that you've actually seen a CIA document that says they were monitoring and harassing Jim Garrison's witnesses.

BT: *Right. We had that information. I was shocked to read that because I remember discounting everything Garrison had said. I had a negative point of view about Garrison based upon all the reportage that had gone on. And then I read all this material that had come out of Helm's office, that in fact what Garrison had said was true. They were harassing his witnesses, they were intimidating his witnesses. The documents exist. Where they are now, God only knows. It's a sad commentary on the lack of oversight on the executive intelligence agencies.*

JD: I read something about you to the effect that during the brief period you ran the Committee, after Sprague left, one of the areas that really interested you was New Orleans and its connection to JMWAVE and Miami. Also, Delsa told me, as far as he was concerned, that was one of the most productive areas they were working.

BT: *That's correct. The meeting in Clinton and the Clay Shaw connection and the fact that the government was lying about Clay Shaw and the aliases and so on. That the fact that the government and the executive intelligence agencies, not Garrison, were lying about that, was definitely an area to probe to find out what the justification for that was. Why were they involved in all this, if in fact, nothing had occurred? If it was meaningless, why get involved in creating a perjurious situation for a prosecutor in New Orleans? What was he really on to?*

JD: What's interesting about the day that Sprague resigns, is that's the day de Mohrenschildt is found dead.

BT: *Right. The night before the Committee vote, we had sent an investigator to serve him a subpoena. The night of the day he received the subpoena from the Committee is when he was found dead.*

In 2003, Tanenbaum spoke at the Wecht Conference and what he had to say would certainly give students of American History new insights in the assassination that would not have pleased Earl Warren or Gerald Ford and some of their disciples.

Here are but a few of the points he made:

What I am saying is that from the evidence we produced, there were substantial questions about the assassination...

... from a prosecutorial point of view, from what our investigation revealed, there was, in my judgment, no case to convict Lee Harvey Oswald of murdering the President...

The assassination was approximately 12:30; at 12:48 a description of a suspect was sent out: "white male, approximately thirty, slender build, height: five-foot-ten inches, weight 165 pounds." Where did that description come from? And the answer the WC gives is that this fellow Brennan was ... looking up at the Depository window. And he allegedly sees this person—the shooter—Oswald the Warren Commission maintains, and was able to give a description, a miraculous feat ... because if he stood up in the window you would only see a partial of his body [his knees] because the first few feet was opaque [the window was close to the floor]. Whoever the shooter was that was in that window—in that Sniper's Nest, he was crouched down looking out that window which was raised about 12 inches. At best, if anybody saw anybody in that window, they would have seen a partial of their face, at best.

Richard Sprague—Chief Counsel (Pre-Blakey)

Historians can be illuminated by what this top-level insider of impeccable credentials thought about the assassination and the ensuing cover-up from the many interviews he gave.

In the BBC Documentary, *the Killing of President Kennedy*, Sprague related the following about Oswald:

His trip to Russia raised a number of questions that we wanted to get into. For example, when any American went to Russia and re-nounced his American citizenship and subsequently changed his mind and wanted to come back to this country, upon returning to this country there was a thorough debriefing by the CIA, with one exception as far as we could ascertain—Oswald...

The photographs allegedly of Oswald going into the Cuban em-bassy as we all know in fact are not photographs of Oswald. Sec-ondly, it turns out that those photographs, even if they were of the wrong person, you would expect they would be of a person entering the Cuban embassy but it turns out they are photographs of some-one entering the Russian embassy and the question raised how could they so mix up even what building they are talking about. In addition when we inquire where are the photographs you took of the people entering the Cuban embassy the day in question, we are told the cameras were not working that day. I want to talk to the camera people. I want to find out if that's true and that's where we got stopped.

The CIA said they had reused the tape prior to the assassination of President Kennedy, yet the FBI has a document stating that some of their agents listened to the tape after the assassination of Presi-dent Kennedy and that the voice on there was not Oswald's. In ad-dition the CIA presented a transcript of that conversation; we had interviewed the typist who typed it up who said that the transcript presented was not in fact what was typed up by whoever it was who spoke in that conversation. These are areas that I wanted to get into.

Sprague so wanted to lead a thorough investigation that he was pressured out.

How did it happen? According to Gaeton Fonzi in *The Last Investi-gation:*

The key factors that drove Richard Sprague to resign as Chief Counsel of the Assassinations Committee appeared, at the time, to be apparent and on the surface. His proposed use of certain investigative equipment, his demand for an expensive, unrestricted investigation, his refusal to play politics with Chairman Gonzalez—all were apparent grounds for the vociferous criticism which, in the long run, was debilitating to the Committee's efforts to get on with its job. However, after his resignation and a brief respite from the turmoil of Washington, Sprague was able to view his experience in a broader perspective... "If he had it to do over again, he would begin his investigation of the Kennedy assassination by probing "Oswald's ties to the Central Intelligence Agency." Recently, I asked Sprague why he had come to that conclusion. "Well," he said, "when I first thought about it I decided that the House leadership really hadn't intended for there to be an investigation. The Committee was set up to appease the Black Caucus in an election year. I still believe that was a factor. But when I looked back at what happened, it suddenly became very clear that the problems began only after I ran up against the CIA. That's when my troubles really started.

Robert Blakey—Chief Counsel and staff director 1977-79

While Sprague's replacement, Robert Blakey, frustrated some investigators for being too trusting of the CIA, he too did not buy the Warren Commission's final conclusions.

While at first Blakey felt that the HSCA had investigated the CIA enough to absolve them of any role in the assassination, in 2003 in an addendum to an interview with PBS, his opinion evolved. Because he found out that the CIA misled him and the HSCA by bringing George Joannides out of retirement as the CIA liaison with the Committee and hiding the role he had with an anti-Castro group called the DRE which played an important role by its interaction with Oswald:

*I am no longer confident that the Central Intelligence Agency coop-
erated with the Committee. My reasons follow:*

*The Committee focused, among other things, on (1) Oswald, (2)
in New Orleans, (3) in the months before he went to Dallas, and, in
particular, (4) his attempt to infiltrate an anti-Castro group, the Di-
rectorio Revolucionario Estudiantil or DRE.*

*These were crucial issues in the Warren Commission's investi-
gation; they were crucial issues in the committee's investigation.
The Agency knew it full well in 1964; the Agency knew it full well in
1976-79. Outrageously, the Agency did not tell the Warren Commission or our committee that it had financial and other connections
with the DRE, a group that Oswald had direct dealings with!*

*What contemporaneous reporting is or was in the Agency's DRE
files? We will never know, for the Agency now says that no reporting is in the existing files. Are we to believe that its files were silent
in 1964 or during our investigation?*

*I don't believe it for a minute. Money was involved; it had to be
documented. Period. End of story. The files and the Agency agents
connected to the DRE should have been made available to the Commission and the Committee. That the information in the files and
the agents who could have supplemented it were not made available to the Commission and the Committee amounts to willful obstruction of justice.*

*Obviously, too, it did not identify the agent who was its contact
with the DRE at the crucial time that Oswald was in contact with it:
George Joannides.*

*During the relevant period, the Committee's chief contact with
the Agency on a day-to-day basis was Scott Breckinridge. (I put
aside our point of contact with the office of chief counsel, Lyle Miller.) We sent researchers to the Agency to request and read documents. The relationship between our young researchers, law students who came with me from Cornell, was anything but "happy."
Nevertheless, we were getting and reviewing documents. Breckinridge, however, suggested that he create a new point of contact*

person who might "facilitate" the process of obtaining and review-
ing materials. He introduced me to Joannides, who, he said, he had
arranged to bring out of retirement to help us. He told me that he
had experience in finding documents; he thought he would be of
help to us.

I was not told of Joannides' background with the DRE, a focal
point of the investigation. Had I known who he was, he would have
been a witness who would have been interrogated under oath by
the staff or by the committee. He would never have been accepta-
ble as a point of contact with us to retrieve documents. In fact, I
have now learned, as I note above, that Joannides was the point of
contact between the Agency and DRE during the period Oswald was
in contact with DRE.

That the Agency would put a "material witness" in as a "filter"
between the committee and its quests for documents was a flat-out
breach of the understanding the committee had with the Agency
that it would cooperate with the investigation.

The Committee's researchers immediately complained to me
that Joannides was, in fact, not facilitating, but obstructing our ob-
taining of documents. I contacted Breckinridge and Joannides. Their
side of the story wrote off the complaints to the young age and at-
titude of the people.

They were certainly right about one question: The Committee's
researchers did not trust the Agency. Indeed, that is precisely why
they were in their positions. We wanted to test the Agency's integ-
rity. I wrote off the complaints. I was wrong; the researchers were
right. I now believe the process lacked integrity precisely because of
Joannides.

For these reasons, I no longer believe that we were able to con-
duct an appropriate investigation of the Agency and its relationship
to Oswald. Anything that the Agency told us that incriminated, in
some fashion, the Agency may well be reliable as far as it goes, but
the truth could well be that it materially understates the matter.

What the Agency did not give us, none but those involved in the

Agency can know for sure. I do not believe any denial offered by the Agency on any point. The law has long followed the rule that if a person lies to you on one point, you may reject all of his testimony.

I now no longer believe anything the Agency told the Committee any further than I can obtain substantial corroboration for it from outside the Agency for its veracity. We now know that the Agency withheld from the Warren Commission the CIA-Mafia plots to kill Castro. Had the commission known of the plots, it would have followed a different path in its investigation. The Agency unilaterally deprived the commission of a chance to obtain the full truth, which will now never be known.

Significantly, the Warren Commission's conclusion that the agencies of the government cooperated with it is, in retrospect, not the truth.

We also now know that the Agency set up a process that could only have been designed to frustrate the ability of the committee in 1976-79 to obtain any information that might adversely affect the Agency.

Many have told me that the culture of the Agency is one of prevarication and dissimulation and that you cannot trust it or its people. Period. End of story.

I am now in that camp.[56]

During his appearance for the AARC Conference in 2014, Blakey's views seem to have crystallized by stating that at first, he felt the CIA had cooperated but that he had come to change his mind.

During this presentation and on a 2015 *Black Op Radio* program he confirmed his belief in the single-bullet theory, but also that a shot came from the grassy knoll due to witness testimony from several people whom the Warren Commission made every effort to undermine. This includes Secret Service agents, S. M. Holland, and presidential assistant

---

[56] Anyone interested in pursuing this story further should consult the reporting by Jefferson Morley of the *Washington Post*. See, e.g., Jefferson Morley, "Revelation 1963," *Miami New Times* (April 2001).

Dave Powers. He said this caused him to lose confidence in the Warren Commission report. He said that *"it's not an investigation… It's a justification to assert that Oswald acted alone… They used the testimony of Lenny Patrick—a mob shooter—to exculpate Ruby from mob connections…"* He concluded that the committees, including the ARRB, were had.

Comments About the Liberty Lobby—Hunt Trial

Few historians and journalists ever bring up a civil trial that concluded, in the appeal phase, that E Howard Hunt, for all practical purposes was wrong when he claimed that Liberty Lobby defamed him by linking him to the JFK assassination.

As mentioned in the introduction, *while many Warren Commission defenders have tried to discredit Mark Lane through the years, an open-minded historian should consider the jury members who were asked to play an important role in ensuring that justice was served. They took in and evaluated all the evidence. And have added themselves to the already overwhelming number of insiders who do not buy what is written in most history books, i.e., the Warren Commission version of events.*

Steven Jaffe—Assistant to Mark Lane, Investigator for Jim Garrison

Steven Jaffe is perhaps the most important living witness to some of the key investigations of the JFK assassination. He was an investigator/photo analyst for Jim Garrison who played a key role in exposing Oswald's backyard photos as fakes, analyzing all the views witnesses in Dealey Plaza had, casing out possible shooting positions and obtaining a quality copy of the Zapruder Film from French Intelligence. This last mandate allowed Jaffe to obtain insights from Intelligence.

Steven was also a close friend and collaborator of Mark Lane's.

On April 4, 2018, co-author Paul Bleau had a conversation with Jaffe. He related that he had three sources who confirmed that Bobby Kennedy did in fact consult French Intelligence and that they did report that there was a conspiracy, and he mentioned that one of these sources was Senator Daniel Patrick "Pat" Moynihan.

ARRB Assassination Records Review Board

This Board was created in 1994 after Oliver' Stone's film, *JFK,* put pressure on Congress to pass the 1992 JFK Assassination Records Collection Act. During a four-year period, it declassified millions of documents. Its mandate was different from the other investigations: The major purpose of the Review Board was to reexamine for release the records that the agencies still regarded as too sensitive to open to the public. In addition, Congress established the Review Board to help restore government credibility. To achieve these lofty goals, Congress designed an entity that was unprecedented.

It was *not* set up to re-investigate the case, nor to solve what happened on November 22, 1963. It nevertheless provided valuable information to assassination researchers that historians seem oblivious to. It achieved the following:

—Reviewed and voted on over 27,000 previously redacted assassination records.

—Obtained agencies' consent to release an additional 33,000+ assassination records.

—Ensured that the famous Zapruder Film of the assassination belonged to the American people and arranged for the first known authenticity study of the Zapruder Film.

—Opened previously redacted CIA records from the Directorate of Operations.

—Released 99% of the "Hardway/Lopez Report" documenting the CIA's records on Lee Harvey Oswald's trip to Mexico City before the assassination.

—Conducted its own inquiry into the medical record of President Kennedy's autopsy and his treatment at Parkland Hospital by deposing 10 Bethesda autopsy participants, five Parkland Hospital treating physicians, and conducting numerous unsworn interviews of Parkland and Bethesda personnel.

—Secured records relating to District Attorney Jim Garrison's prosecution of Clay Shaw for conspiracy to assassinate President Kennedy, including Shaw's diaries, records from Shaw's defense attorneys, investigative records from the District Attorney's office, and grand jury records.

—Made available to the public all FBI and CIA documents from previous official investigations, like the HSCA.

—Sponsored ballistics and forensic testing of Warren Commission Exhibit 567, the bullet "nose fragment" from the front seat of the Presidential limousine (the HSCA Firearms Panel first recommended the testing in 1978, but the testing was not conducted until the Review Board existed).

—Permanently preserved *all* the extant autopsy photographs of President Kennedy in digitized form, and conducted sophisticated digital enhancement of selected, representative images.

Thomas Samoluk—Deputy Director and Press Officer of the ARRB

For the documentary *Destiny Betrayed*, Samoluk was interviewed by Oliver Stone. He described a lot of obfuscation to their research. He proves that New Orleans D.A. Harry Connick tried to destroy the Garrison Files and claimed that it was the Garrison team who pilfered them. A former employee of his who was supposed to bring these files to the incinerator on Connick's orders had kept them and made them available to the ARRB. He also revealed that the Secret Service destroyed files about JFK's 1963 travels and how the FBI and CIA attempted stonewalling when the ARRB tried to access some of their files. He also said that the continued hiding of files beyond October 26, 2017, was in breach of the law.[57]

---

[57] *JFK Revisited, Through the Looking Glass (book version),* pp. 383 to 389

John Tunheim—Chairman of the ARRB

Tunheim was also interviewed extensively by Oliver Stone. The revelations from this high-ranking insider are also very significant:

"Angleton took control of the CIA's investigation into the assassination and compiled a large series of records. Those records, when we tried to find them, some existed in various parts of the agency. Most were no longer maintained as part of a collection. I think it is pretty clear Angleton destroyed records before he was dismissed from the CIA." He also confirmed CIA attempts to resist transfers of files and how George H. W. Bush tried to oppose the bill before it became law, and then moved very slowly to cooperate once he was elected. Finally, he stated that the CIA misled the ARRB, as they had the HSCA, about the HSCA-CIA liaison to that investigation: George Joannides, by hiding his involvement with the CIA Miami Station at the time of the assassination.[58]

Jeremy Gunn—Executive Counsel

On November 10, 2013, he made the following remarks for NPR:

"There were many things that were disturbing." "I can recite a litany of other unresolved questions surrounding the Kennedy assassination—ones the Warren Commission failed to answer. For example, in New Orleans in 1963, Oswald came in contact with the FBI. When he was arrested after a scuffle at a demonstration, he asked to meet with the FBI. Why would Oswald ask to see someone from the FBI?" Gunn asks. *"But an FBI agent went and interviewed Oswald, came back and wrote a memo on it, put it in the file."* "For me, it's quite simple," Gunn says. *"I don't know what happened."*

"There is substantial evidence that points toward Oswald and incriminates Oswald," he says, *"and the only person we can name where there is evidence is Oswald. But there's also rather important exculpatory evidence for Oswald, suggesting he didn't do it, and*

---

[58] *Ibid, p. 341*

that he was framed, 'unstable, and that's that the explanation for what happened. Since the facts aren't clear, though, that document can look like a whitewash.'

For the Warren Commission, transparency had its own difficulties. *'There are serious problems with the forensics evidence, with the ballistics evidence, with the autopsy evidence,'* Gunn says. *'And, in my opinion, if they had said that openly, it would have not put the issue to rest.'*

'If the president had been killed as part of a conspiracy, that needed to be known.'

'The institution that had the opportunity to best get to the bottom of this, as much as it was possible, was the Warren Commission, and they didn't do it,' he says. *'Now it's too late to do what should have been done originally.'*

When Gunn pored over the material, what stuck out most for him was the medical evidence. For instance, what he learned in his 1996 deposition of James Joseph Humes. Humes, who died three years later, was one of the doctors who performed the autopsy on Kennedy's body.[59]

For one thing, Humes told Gunn that the autopsy was not performed strictly by the book; some procedures were left out, such as removing and weighing all the organs. Then, Humes made an eye-opening revelation.

'Dr. Humes admitted that the supposedly original handwritten version of the autopsy that is in the National Archives is in fact not the original version,' Gunn says. He says Humes had never said that publicly before, even to the Warren Commission. When Gunn showed Saundra Spencer, the Navy Warrant Officer who processed the autopsy film, the official photos from the National Archives during her deposition in 1997, she said they were not the pictures she

---

[59] BEFORE THE ASSASSINATION RECORDS REVIEW BOARD PRESIDENT JOHN F. KENNEDY College Park, Maryland, Tuesday, February 13, 1996, The deposition of DR. JAMES JOSEPH HUMES

remembered processing. What's more, the official pictures weren't anything like the ones she remembered. *'The prints that we printed did not have the massive head damages that is visible here,' she told Gunn.* "... The face, the eyes were closed and the face, the mouth was closed, and it was more of a rest position than these show... "So, they wanted to write the document in a way that would reassure the American public that it was a single gunman acting alone, somebody who's a little bit unstable, and that that's the explanation for what happened."[60]

Doug Horne—Senior Analyst

Doug Horne reviewed the military records, including the military autopsy for the ARRB. What he found was revealed during interviews as well as the book he wrote, *Inside the ARRB*, published in 2009.

Numerous persons the ARRB deposed or interviewed (FBI agents Sibert and O'Neill, mortician Tom Robinson, and others) have essentially disowned the autopsy photographs showing the back of JFK's head intact. O'Neill said the photos of the back of the head looked *"doctored"* (by which he meant that he thought the wound had been repaired—put back together—not that the photo looked altered), and Sibert said the back of the head looked "reconstructed." Tom Robinson of Gawler's Funeral Home said there was a large hole in the back of the head where it looks intact in the photos. Pathologist J. Thornton Boswell said that there was a lot of bone missing in the right rear of the head behind where the scalp looks intact, but did not explain how the scalp could be intact if the bone in the right rear of the skull was missing! (See the ARRB deposition transcripts of Frank O'Neill, James Sibert, and J. Thornton Boswell, as well as the unsworn report of the ARRB interview with Tom Robinson.)

---

[60] *https://jfkfacts.org/counsel-for-the-jfk-review-board-found-many-things-that-were-disturbing/*

But perhaps Horne's most stunning conclusion was that the photographs of "the President's brain" in the autopsy collection are really photographs of someone else's brain ... a major deception in this case. These images, which appear to show damage consistent with a shot from above and behind, were disowned under oath to the ARRB by John Stringer, the photographer who took the official brain photos at JFK's supplementary autopsy. He disowned the images because of the angles at which they were shot, and because they were taken on the wrong film—film he did not use. (FBI agent O'Neill also disowned the brain photos in the autopsy collection, saying that there was too much tissue present, and that at autopsy a large part of the President's brain was missing.) These photos have been used for years by supporters of the Warren Commission's conclusions to support their shooting scenario, and to discount those who claim there were shots from the front or right front.

Horne also explained that, contrary to other depositions done of the autopsists during other investigations, the ARRB questioned Dr. Humes and Dr. Boswell separately. This yielded a stunning result: "While Humes contended under oath that there was no bone missing in the back of JFK's skull, Boswell said there was bone missing in the rear skull and actually made a sketch on a three-dimensional skull model (now at the archives) showing missing bone skull from the top of the head, part of the right side, and the entire right rear of the cranium."[61]

Horne also revealed the following: Oswald's last quarter of earnings in the United States before he defected to the Soviet Union should have been paid by the Marine Corps. And they weren't... That has serious implications to me because of the speculation that he was a fake defector.[62] (Writer Paul Hoch has tried to question this but researcher Miles

---

[61] JFK Revisited, p. 301
[62] Ibid., p. 308

Massicotte effectively countered Hoch at the Education Forum, by refer-ring to Commission Exhibit No, 3099.)

Cuba, France and Russia Conclusions

As noted earlier, these three countries collected intelligence in the U.S. and were able to form independent opinions. Neither France nor Russia sought to pour gasoline on a fire to undermine U.S. institutions. Castro, on the other hand, suspected that the U.S. would use the assassination to blame Cuba and have an excuse to invade. He said so immediately after the assassination. Their intelligence forces in both Cuba and the U.S. painted a dark picture of machinations that were contrary to the Warren Commission account. The following is taken from this author's article: *The CIA and Mafia's "Cuban American Mechanism" and the JFK Assassination at KennedysandKing, April 2018*:[63]

The French Say Non

Neither Jackie Kennedy nor Bobby Kennedy believed the Warren Com-mission, nor did they trust U.S. intelligence to find the underlying cause of what really happened. According to the late William Turner and Jim Garrison investigator Steve Jaffe, they received information from French intelligence, which had monitored Cuban exiles and right-wing targets in the U.S. (perhaps because they felt some of the attempts on de Gaulle's life stemmed from the U.S.). They reported that the president had been killed by a large right-wing domestic conspiracy.

Nyet Nyet Soviet

As for the Russian reaction to the JFK assassination, the most recent ARRB releases leave no doubt about where they stood on the matter. In 2017, a CIA note describing Nikita Khrushchev's feelings about the

---

[63] https://www.kennedysandking.com/john-f-kennedy-articles/the-cia-and-mafia-s-cuban-american-mechanism-and-the-jfk-assassination

assassination was declassified. It revealed a May 1964 conversation between the Soviet leader and reporter Drew Pearson, where the head of state said he did not believe American security was so "inept" that Kennedy was killed without a conspiracy. Khrushchev believed the Dallas Police Department to be an "accessory" to the assassination. The CIA source "got the impression that Chairman Khrushchev had some dark thoughts about the American Right Wing being behind this conspiracy." When Pearson said that Oswald and Ruby both were, "mad" and "acted on his own... Khrushchev said flatly that he did not believe this."

The research community also gained access to a J. Edgar Hoover memo sent to Marvin Watson, Special Assistant to the President on December 2, 1966, which described what Russian intelligence believed about the murder:

JFK Assassination System Identification Form		Date:	8/27/201

Agency Information	
AGENCY: KISS/SCOW	Released under the John
RECORD NUMBER: 178-10003-19131	F. Kennedy Assassination Records
RECORD SERIES: CHURCH COM.	Collection Act of 1992 (44 USC 2107 Note).
IENCY FILE NUMBER: 7602957 (3)	Case#:NW 54653 Date: 10-23-2017

Document Information

ORIGINATOR: FBI
FROM: HOOVER, J. EDGAR
TO: WATSON, MARVIN

TITLE: REACTION OF SOVIET AND COMMUNIST PARTY OFFICIALS TO JFK ASSASSINATION

DATE: 12/01/1963
PAGES: 7

```
        According to our source, officials of the Communist
Party of the Soviet Union believed there was some well-
organized conspiracy on the part of the "ultraright" in the
United States to effect a "coup." They seemed convinced that
the assassination was not the deed of one man, but that it
arose out of a carefully planned campaign in which several
people played a part. They felt that those elements interested
in utilizing the assassination and playing on anticommunist
sentiments in the United States would then utilize this act
to stop negotiations with the Soviet Union, attack Cuba and
thereafter spread the war. As a result of these feelings,
the Soviet Union immediately went into a state of national
alert.
```

The Memo also adds this explosive point made after two years of Russian intelligence efforts that had been intended for internal use only:

> On September 16, 1965, this same source reported that the KGB Residency in New York City received instructions approximately September 16, 1965, from KGB headquarters in Moscow to develop all possible information concerning President Lyndon B. Johnson's character, background, personal friends, family, and from which quarters he derives his support in his position as President of the United States. Our source added that in the instructions from Moscow, it was indicated that "now" the KGB was in possession of data purporting to indicate President Johnson was responsible for the assassination of the late President John F. Kennedy.

We can safely guess that this only hardened Khrushchev's opinions.

Lee Harvey Oswald and the Subterfuge According to Fabian Escalante (Cuba)

Fabian Escalante joined the *Department of State Security* in 1959. Escalante was head of a counterintelligence unit and also part of a team investigating a CIA operation called *Sentinels of Liberty*, an attempt to recruit Cubans willing to work against Castro. At the request of the U.S., he presented the HSCA with a report on Cuban findings about the JFK assassination that was never published by the committee because of some of the information it contained. He is recognized as a leading authority on the CIA in Cuba and Latin America.

Like most Americans, the Cubans found Oswald's murder by a nightclub owner in the basement of the Dallas Police headquarters simply too convenient. Oswald's immediate portrayal as communist and pro-Castro made them strongly suspect that this was all a ruse to attack Cuba.

Within days of the assassination, Castro stated the following: "... It just so happened that in such an unthinkable thing as the assassination a guilty party should immediately appear; what a coincidence, he (Oswald) had gone to Russia, and what a coincidence, he was associated with FPCC! That is what they began to say... It just so happens that these incidents are taking place precisely at a time when Kennedy was under heavy attack by those who felt his Cuba policy was weak..."

When Escalante analyzed all they could find on Oswald (post-assassination cryptonym: GPFLOOR), he was led to the following hypothesis:

1. Oswald was an agent of the U.S. intelligence service, infiltrated into the Soviet Union to fulfill a mission.
2. On his return, he continued to work for U.S. security services.
3. Oswald moved to New Orleans in April 1963 and formed links with Cuban organizations and exiles.
4. In New Orleans, Oswald received instructions to convert himself into a sympathizer with the Cuban Revolution.
5. Between July and September 1963, Oswald created evidence that he was part of a Cuba-related conspiracy.
6. In the fall of 1963, Oswald met with a CIA officer and an agent of Cuban origin in Dallas, Texas, to plan a covert operation related to Cuba.
7. In September 1963, Oswald met with the Dallas Alpha 66 group and tried to compromise Cuban exile Silvia Odio.
8. Oswald attempted to travel to Cuba from Mexico.
9. Oswald was to receive compromising correspondence from Havana linking him to the Cuban intelligence service.
10. The mass media, directed by the CIA and Mafia's "Cuban American Mechanism," was primed to unleash a far-reaching campaign to demonstrate to the U.S. public that Cuba and Fidel Castro were responsible for the assassination.

Through his investigation, Escalante found evidence of the parallel nature of plans of aggression against Cuba and the assassination of Kennedy. The Cubans simply found that there were too many anti-Castro Cuban exiles in Oswald's realm, suggesting a role in a sheep-dipping operation. They show that his history as a provocateur in his pre-Russia infiltration days was similar to his actions in New Orleans, and that James Wilcott, a former CIA officer in Japan, testified to the HSCA that "… Oswald was recruited from the military division with the evident objective of turning him into a double agent against the Soviet Union…" Escalante also received material on Oswald in 1977 from their KGB representative in Cuba, Major General Piotr Voronin. Then, in 1989, while in the Soviet Union, he met up with Pavel Iatskov, colonel of the first Directorate of the KGB, who had been in Mexico City during Oswald's visit.

Iatskov stated the following: "At the end of the 1970s, when the investigation into the Kennedy assassination was reopened, I was in Moscow, and at one point ... one of the high-ranking officers from my directorate ... commented that Oswald had been a U.S. intelligence agent and that his defection to the Soviet Union was intended as an active step to disrupt the growing climate of détente..." They speculated that Oswald was there to lend a blow to Eisenhower's peace endeavors by giving away U2 military secrets, which dovetailed into the downing of Gary Powers a few short weeks before a crucial Eisenhower/Khrushchev *summit.*

While the authors recognize the limitations that should be put on foreign opinions, because of potential bias—bias that should be weighed against the bias of Warren Commission backers—it is important to let the reader consider this added information.

Paul Landis—Secret Service Agent

To know more about the explosive revelations of Secret Service Agent Paul Landis who had bird's eye view of the presidential limousine after the assassination see chapter 8.[64]

General Conclusions

According to a study conducted in 2013,[65] most historians who wrote school books that cover the JFK assassination were not aware of the ARRB and the wealth of new evidence made available starting a year

---

[64] The revelation of Paul Landis regarding finding CE 399 and placing it on Kennedy's stretcher was breaking news at the time of the publishing of this book.

[65] https://www.kennedysandking.com/john-f-kennedy-articles/the-jfk-assassination-according-to-the-history-textbooks-part-1

after Gerald Posner wrote *Case Closed*. As a matter of fact, not one cited any of the official investigations as a source other than the Warren Commission. Which, of course, is the oldest, most contested, highly rushed, poorly investigated, biased governmental source possible.

The overwhelming consensus that there were serious flaws with the Warren Commission conclusions and that there was a likely conspiracy does not come from independent authors who are trying to sell books. It comes from written reports of subsequent investigations and the statements of a very significant cross-section of over 90 insiders that participated in the investigations including the Warren Commission: Senators (some Republican, some Democrat), legal counsel, staff members, attorneys, researchers, medical personnel, autopsy physicians, historians, archivists, investigators, jury members, FBI, DPD and Louisiana State law enforcement agents. These include some of the highest-ranking members of the Warren Commission, Church and HSCA committees and the ARRB. There is an impressive number of dissenting participants from the Warren Commission itself—still the go-to investigation for lone-nut proponents—who have voiced their opinions in reputable magazines, newspapers, documentaries and books, all easily accessible on the web. We are not talking about zany, fringe, book peddling conspiracy theorists here. These are persons that witnessed the autopsy, questioned persons of interest under oath while looking them in the eye, poured over reports and secret documents, worked in teams to analyze the evidence, attended executive sessions, etc.—people who the U.S. government entrusted to investigate the crime of the century and who curious historians may learn from.

While they may not all know what in fact happened, they all agree on certain key points: The Warren Commission conclusions are not reliable; the investigations into the assassination were deficient (especially the Warren Commission's); and they are far from certain that Oswald and Ruby acted alone. Many of them believe that: that there was demonstrable obstruction of justice by numerous agencies and individuals; government agencies hid the truth; the Single Bullet Theory is a fabrication; that there has been a long-lasting cover-up; that Oswald and Ruby were involved in very suspicious relationships, and the list goes on and on. The three foreign governments (Cuba, Russia and France) that had reason to have their eyes and ears open in the U.S. also concluded that there was a conspiracy. All diametrically opposed to what historians, for money, are telling adolescents as part of a captive audience! Which is that Oswald did it and the Warren Commission got it right. End of story.

The American Historical Association statement of conduct stipulates that historians are to honor the historical record. To do so they first need to know what it is! If the next edition of their history books continues to support the cover-up, their behavior should be considered nothing less than unforgivable.

The next time someone decides to cite expert endorsements for their positions on the case, see how they compare with the highly credible experts and reports cited in this section. There can be no comparison. One would have to be quite paranoid to believe that the ninety investigation insiders were somehow part of a misinformation conspiracy.

CHAPTER 2

OSWALD'S INTELLIGENCE CONNECTIONS: HE WAS NO LONE NUT

BY PAUL BLEAU

STATEMENT

THE WARREN COMMISSION portrayed Lee Oswald as a lone nut, Marxist, and drifter who was not on anyone's radar. The New York Times coverage of the Warren Commission's Report release included the following statement:

> "The Warren Commission also rejected, after complete access to the files of the FBI and the Central Intelligence Agency, the claim that Oswald may have been some kind of American undercover agent."

This section will prove that he was in fact a low level, disposable intelligence pawn who was used in a stratagem to blame opponents for the assassination of JFK which was quickly overridden after the assassination and evolved into his lone-nut persona becoming part of the final scenario the deciders went with.

EXECUTIVE SUMMARY

As seen in section one, several investigation insiders including some of the top guns for the Church Committee and the HSCA made strong statements about Oswald's intelligence connections.

Oswald's sojourn in Russia as well as his launch of an FPCC chapter in New Orleans were clearly intelligence missions. CIA officer Peter Bagley's analysis of Oswald's defection was that he had to be a witting false defector.[1] Otto Otepka who worked at the State Department was railroaded out of his job because of his inquiries about Oswald and false defectors. Officer William Kent, who oversaw the DRE Cuban Exile group, referred to Oswald as a "useful idiot."[2] Ex-CIA staffer, Jane Roman, confirmed to John Newman and Jefferson Morley that CIA documents proved that there was a level of high interest in Oswald.

The simultaneous splitting of Oswald's file at CIA, so no one had all the information on him, plus his removal from the FBI Watch List shortly before the assassination, is what allowed him to be on the motorcade route in Dallas.

Oswald's intelligence files were handled in a way that was contrary to how normal defectors' files are administered. After being arrested for a minor street fight, Oswald while in jail, met with an FBI agent for hours. This and his relationships in New Orleans confirm his provocateur/informant mandate.

Oswald possessed six wallets, a Minox spy camera, a top of a small cardboard box with "Cox's Fort Worth" printed on top (speculated that this was to be used to make contact with a handler at the Texas Theater) and a notebook with suspicious entries including the word microdot.

When Oswald died shortly after his 24th birthday, he had experienced upwards of 65 plausible touch points with over thirty of them being definite intelligence assets/employees. This would have been impossible for any high-school dropout drifter. His relations with David Ferrie, Guy Banister and Clay Shaw and his use of the 544 Camp Street address for his Fair Play for Cuba Committee office in New Orleans baffled the HSCA. The INS confirmed that Oswald was seen entering the building with Ferrie and his right-wing nuts.

---

[1] https://www.kennedysandking.com/john-f-kennedy-reviews/the-devil-is-in-the-details-by-malcolm-blunt-with-alan-dale from The Devil is in the Details, Malcolm Blunt (exchange with Peter Bagley)

[2] Dan Hardway, "An Operational Sketch," 2014

Oswald himself made a Freudian slip during an interview in the summer of 1963 when he admitted being under U.S. government protection while in Russia. Oswald was seen in the company of at least one Cuban/Latin escort by over 45 witnesses. His last attempted phone calls after his arrest for the assassinations of JFK and Officer Tippit were likely directed to intelligence contacts in North Carolina. All of this proves that Oswald was an intelligence connected fall guy.

EVIDENCE

At a very early age, Oswald was fascinated by espionage. His favorite show was the spy series *I Led Three Lives* and he enjoyed James Bond novels. As a Marine he received security clearance and worked as a radar operator in Atsugi, Japan on a U2 spy plane base. He learned Russian while in the Marines in a way which New Orleans district attorney Jim Garrison, himself an ex-marine, concluded he could only have been through special training for an intelligence assignment.

While a marine in California, Oswald applied to a very obscure Swiss college called Albert Schweitzer that appears to be intelligence-linked.[3]

Oswald was discharged from the Marines compassionately after his mother sustained a minor injury. After spending very little time with her, he booked travel arrangements in New Orleans's International Trade Mart (managed by Garrison trial defendant Clay Shaw), transited mysteriously from England to Finland and eventually—after staying in a luxurious five-star Helsinki hotel—entered Russia through a favorite spy-friendly crossing point at the height of a false defector program, threatened theatrically to give away secrets to the Russians in the U.S. embassy, and returned over two years later to the U.S. with his Russian wife, who had ties to Russian intelligence. There is no plausible explanation for how Oswald managed to fund his travels to the USSR through

---

[3] https://www.archives.gov/files/research/jfk/releases/2022/104-10418-10344.pdf and http://coverthistory.blogspot.com/2005/07/oswald-and-albert-schweitzer-college.html

Finland. He did not have the money to afford luxury accommodations and intercontinental travel.[4]

A few writers have researched this strange travel and have noted that it was likely a mole-hunt maneuver, stimulated by the loss of the U.S.'s own mole, Pyotr Popov. According to John Newman, it was orchestrated by the CIA using Oswald and his U2 knowledge as a lure to flush out the mole.[5]

How Real Defectors Are Investigated vs. Oswald

The following is taken verbatim from this author's article Oswald's Intelligence Connections:[6]

In part 2 of his excellent essay "Tokyo Legend? Oswald and Japan,"[7] Kevin Coogan compared the investigation into two genuine defectors who embraced the Soviet Union almost one year after Oswald defected with the one conducted for Oswald. On September 6, 1960, two former National Security Agency (NSA) employees named Bernon Mitchell and William Martin held a press conference in Moscow. The mathematician/cryptographers formally announced their defection. As it so happened, the two men had earlier worked at the U.S. military base at Atsugi, Japan.

Contrary to what happened with Oswald, in this case the level of alarm and degree of scrutiny were off the charts: The Mitchell-Martin defection was a tremendous shock to the NSA, which launched an internal investigation that involved speaking to some 450 witnesses. The FBI, the CIA, and military intelligence all worked the case. The inquiry included a microscopic look at both men's earlier experiences in Japan.

Mark Lane found that intelligence investigation into Oswald's defect-

---

[4] https://www.kennedysandking.com/john-f-kennedy-articles/oswald-s-intelligence-connections-how-richard-schweiker-clashes-with-fake-history and *(Destiny Betrayed, Jim DiEugenio Chapter 7)*

[5] Uncovering Popov's Mole, John Newman, Introduction

[6] *https://www.kennedysandking.com/john-f-kennedy-articles/oswald-s-intelligence-connections-how-richard-schweiker-clashes-with-fake-history*

[7] Tokyo legend? Lee Harvey Oswald and Japan, Kevin Coogan

ion was very shallow and *pro forma*. Schweiker added this telling insight: "The most important thing was that the intelligence agencies did all the wrong things if they were really looking for a conspiracy or to find out who killed John Kennedy."

James Botelho, former roommate of Oswald who would later become a California judge, in an interview with assassination researcher Mark Lane stated the following.

"Oswald, it was said, was the only Marine ever to defect from his country to another country, a Communist country, during peacetime... When the Marine Corps and American intelligence decided not to probe the reasons for the 'defection,' I knew then what I know now: Oswald was on an assignment in Russia for American intelligence."

When Oswald's commanding officer, John Donovan was questioned by the Warren Commission, he noted that they did everything they could to avoid exchanges about Oswald and the U2 program.[8]

In his book, *The Other Oswald,* Gary Hill chronicled the following: Defector Robert Webster (also, like Oswald, in 1962) upon his return to the U.S. testified intensely for two weeks before *the Senate Internal Security Subcommittee* ... a fate Oswald avoided. This, on its own, is noteworthy. Does anyone really believe that Oswald was not debriefed? Can anyone explain why Webster's debriefing was done openly and Oswald was given special treatment? But there is more... Webster could no longer work at *Rand*, because of the classified projects it was involved in, whereas Oswald was parked at Jaggars Chiles Stovall where he was involved in sensitive work involving military mapmaking of Cuba.

Betsy Wolf and Oswald's File

British researcher Malcolm Blunt is known for his painstakingly meticulous sleuthing. Perhaps no one spends as much time as he does unearthing documentary trails from the archives. What he found around the HSCA's Betsy Wolf provides solid proof of the CIA's special interest in Oswald from the get-go—He was not an ordinary defector. For this part

---

[8] John Newman interview with John Donovan, Oswald and the CIA, p. 45

I quote directly from the *2020 Creating the Oswald Legend—Part 4 Written by Vasilios Vazakas*[9]

> Betsy Wolf was one of the researchers for the House Select Committee on Assassinations. She interacted with attorneys Michael Goldsmith and Dan Hardway on matters related to the CIA. On page 514 of the HSCA report, she is listed as a researcher under the name Elizabeth Wolf, but she signed all of her work with the first name of Betsy. Researchers only have access to her handwritten notes as the HSCA did not have them typed up.
>
> Why was her work not transcribed? Why did it take so long to get it declassified? It appears to be because one of her major areas of inquiry was exploring the mystery surrounding the Oswald file at CIA. One of the key points she addressed was this: Why was there no opening of a 201 file on Oswald once it was known he had defected to the USSR in late October of 1959, which was the common practice for such subjects? When Oswald arrived in Moscow, he talked to former CIA employee Richard Snyder at the American Embassy. (Snyder's formal Agency employ was discovered by Wolf and is in her notes.) What made the late opening even more perplexing was the fact that the State Department knew that Oswald had threatened to give away top secrets to the Soviets. That threat was magnified because the former Marine Oswald had been a radar operator and his military service associated him with the ultra-strategic U2 spy plane.[10] The fact that the Agency did not open a 201 file—one of its most common files—upon learning this information greatly puzzled Wolf. Oswald's 201 file was not opened until thirteen months after his defection, in spite of the fact that the U2 was a CIA project...
>
> According to three witnesses that Wolf interviewed, CIA Officer William Larson, CI/SIG chief Birch O'Neil (sometimes spelled O'Neal), and CIA Director Dick Helms, that information should

---

[9] https://www.kennedysandking.com/content/author/322-vasiliosvazakas
[10] Newman, *Oswald and the CIA*, pp. 29–46

have caused the opening of a 201 file.[11] In other words, there were two reasons to open the 201 file on Oswald over a year prior to when it happened. Neither one triggered the opening. Further, when Wolf looked at the 201 file, it only contained copies and the two naval dispatches were gone. She later discovered that the Office of Security (OS) had the originals, and these were not dated as to when they arrived or who handled them...

As Malcolm Blunt explained, OS Chief Robert Gambino described incoming mail dissemination. This was in an HSCA interview that cannot be found anywhere except in Betsy Wolf's surviving notes. (Wolf interviewed Gambino on 7/26/78) Gambino revealed to her that it was CIA Mail Logistics, a component of the Office of Central Reference (OCR)—part of the Deputy Director of Intelligence (DDI)—that was responsible for disseminating all incoming documents. In the case of Oswald, his files bypassed the General Filing System and went straight into the Office of Security and its SRS component. (This is illustrated in the file routing graph below; note the detour at the second step from the top.) If someone wanted to get a file from Mail Logistics, they would have to request it ahead of time.

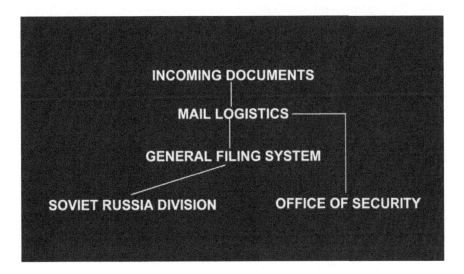

INCOMING DOCUMENTS

MAIL LOGISTICS

GENERAL FILING SYSTEM

SOVIET RUSSIA DIVISION   OFFICE OF SECURITY

---

[11] Wolf notes of 7/20/78 and 9/9/78

So, the SR Division would have to ask Mail Logistics for Oswald's incoming documents. But, in this case, Mail Logistics closed off the SR Division.

Jane Roman

Another key finding is revealed in Alan Dale's book about Malcolm Blunt, *The Devil Is in the Details,* and relates to what a CIA employee told John Newman and Jefferson Morley. The following is from a KennedysandKing review:[12] "With Jefferson Morley visiting, Malcolm and Alan review what they consider another landmark on the road to discovery about the JFK case. This was the Morley/Newman interview with Jane Roman.

In 1963, Jane Roman was a senior liaison officer for the CIA's Counterintelligence staff, which meant—among other things—that she handled communications with other federal offices. Morley saw her name on a routing slip concerning documents about Oswald *before* the assassination. He located her in the Washington area and he and Newman talked to her in the autumn of 1994. Morley had fished out a document that Roman had signed and sent to Mexico City saying that, as of 10/10/63, the latest information CIA had on Oswald was a State Department report from May of 1962.

Here was the problem: that Oswald cable was clearly false. Because—as was her position—she had read and signed off on, at the minimum, two FBI reports on Oswald from 1963. They arrived on her desk just a week prior to October 10th and one described Oswald being arrested in New Orleans. Her signature was on both Bureau reports. When presented with this puzzle as to why she had been part of a false declaration to Mexico City, Roman replied that her only rationale would be that the Office of Security staff had all the data about Oswald under their tight control. She also added that she was not in on any sabotage aspect as far as Cuba went. She then said that the person in control of the cable

---

[12] https://www.kennedysandking.com/john-f-kennedy-reviews/the-devil-is-in-the-details-by-malcolm-blunt-with-alan-dale and The Devil is in the Details page 29

to Mexico City would have been Tom Karamessines, who was the right-hand man to Richard Helms. Helms was the Director of Plans in 1963, in other words, he was in charge of covert operations.[13]

When Newman pressed her on what this all meant, Roman replied with something that was probably a milestone at the time. She said, 'To me it's indicative of a keen interest in Oswald held very closely on a need-to-know basis.' She then added that there must have been a reason to withhold that information from Mexico City.[14] For the first time, someone had an oral declaration from a CIA employee that the Agency had a keen interest, on a need-to-know basis, about Oswald. This was just weeks before the assassination. And Richard Helms' assistant was the principal officer on the cable. Later in the book, Malcolm will relate another conversation with a different CIA employee, and it will echo this one, except it will be about Oswald back in 1959—before his defection to Russia."[15]

Oswald's Return from Russia

Since the ARRB cleared the release of a large number of classified documents, a number of CIA files have shed light on the person assigned by the U.S. State Department to greet the Oswald family on June 12, 1962, when they stepped off the ocean liner *Maasdam* in Hoboken, New Jersey. Spas Raikin was a representative of the Traveler's Aid Society who helped them pass smoothly through immigration and customs.

---

[13] Jefferson Morley, "What Jane Roman Said," at History Matters.com

[14] *John Newman, Oswald and the CIA*, p. 405

[15] https://www.kennedysandking.com/john-f-kennedy-reviews/the-devil-is-in-the-details-by-malcolm-blunt-with-alan-dale

Spas Raikin

Here is how James Douglass describes what the Warren Report did not reveal about him: "Raikin was at the same time secretary-general of the American Friends of the Anti-Bolshevik Nations, an anti-communist organization with extensive intelligence connections—like the American government, an unlikely source of support for a traitor."[16]

The FPCC Front[17]

When Oswald moved to New Orleans to start a Fair Play for Cuba chapter, he was clearly following instructions. The author of this section performed an analysis of the FPCC and wrote a three-part article on the subject that merits reading in full. Let's review the highlights.

---

[16] RAIKIN'S SECURITY FILE As a result of the 1992 JFK Documents Act, Spas T. Raikin's CIA Office of Security File was declassified on November 20, 1957- and *JFK and the Unspeakable-James Douglass.*

[17] https://www.kennedysandking.com/john-f-kennedy-articles/exposing-the-fpcc-part-1 (also follow links to parts 2 and 3)

In 1993, author Van Gosse wrote *Where the Boys Are: Cuba, Cold War America and the Making of the New Left*. It gives one of the more complete accounts of this odd association. The FPCC was founded in the spring of 1960 by Robert Taber and Richard Gibson——CBS newsmen who covered Castro's ascent to power——as well as Alan Sagner, a New Jersey contractor. Its original mission was to correct distortions about the Cuba revolution. It was first supported by writers, philosophers, artists and intellectuals such as Norman Mailer, Truman Capote and Jean-Paul Sartre. It also touched a chord with university students. Some estimates place its African American membership at one third of its roster. In April 1960, Taber and Gibson ran a full-page ad in the *New York Times*.

When it became clear that the U.S. would not tolerate the revolution, it began dissipating. After a short-lived peace demonstration binge during the missile crisis in 1962, its spiral downward was accelerated and the FPCC died not long after one of its members allegedly killed JFK.

The FPCC was also characterized as "Castro's Network in the U.S.A." by the HUAC;

By the time Oswald opened his Crescent City chapter of the FPCC, it was under the intense intelligence scrutiny which had started in 1960, the year of the national launch. An FBI document[18] in response to NSAM 43 and 45 to the attorney general, dated April 24, 1961, outlines steps taken by then to counter pro-Castro organizations. It was already a full-court blitz.

In this writer's first prior plots article,[19] a rather important number of informants and potential patsies shared similar traits with Oswald. My research greatly benefited from and expanded upon author Van Gosse's excellent work (*Where the Boys are*) to estimate maximum FPCC membership to be between 5 and 7 thousand in 1961 and argued that such a low number made it impossible for persons of interest like Richard Case Nagell, Oswald, Policarpo Lopez, Vaughn Marlowe, Harry Dean, John

---

[18] *FBI report (CR-109-12 210-2990)*
[19] https://www.kennedysandking.com/john-f-kennedy-articles/the-three-failed-plots-to-kill-jfk-the-historians-guide-on-how-to-research-his-assassination

Glenn, Santiago Garriga—who were potential patsies to varying degrees—to all be coincidentally linked to the FPCC; especially for those in the Deep South where the FPCC had much less activity. Based on more recent data (likely fewer than 1500 national members in 1963), the odds are astronomically worse than what I first thought.

According to one of its national leaders, Barry Sheppard, the Socialist Workers Party (SWP) was very involved with the FPCC. From his memoirs we can see that by the time Oswald became active with the FPCC it was in a death spiral.

The following points concerning the July 1963 SWP convention cast even more suspicion around the timing and motives of the already bizarre late openings of FPCC chapters in the deep south by Santiago Garriga in Miami and Oswald in New Orleans and the continued involvement with the FPCC by other odd subjects.

"At the convention, a meeting of pro-Cuba activists discussed the situation in the Fair Play for Cuba Committee. Cubans living in the United States who supported the 26th of July Movement had helped us build the FPCC. Now most of them had returned to Cuba. In most areas, the FPCC had dwindled to supporters of the SWP and YSA [Socialist Workers Party and Young Socialist Alliance]. Since we did not want the FPCC to become a sectarian front group, the meeting decided to stop trying to build it. The FPCC then existed for a while as a paper organization, until the assassination of President John Kennedy dealt it a mortal blow."[20]

FBI reports confirm that FPCC National Chapter meetings plummeted from 25 meetings a year to 3 in its last year of existence.

According to Malcolm Blunt, Vincent T. Lee, who was the last head of the organization, stated that the number of members had dwindled to about 1500 by mid-1963, finances were very poor and that the other FPCC officers were no longer even answering to him. Even the Treasury Department noted that the FPCC was almost inactive. Furthermore, members in the Deep South tended to be disproportionately African American, and the FPCC was riddled with informants. In other words, the statistical probability of seeing a white person in the Deep South

---

[20] Sheppard, *The Party*, p. 103

genuinely involved with such a vegetative outfit was infinitely small ... seeing seven of the subjects profiled in the Prior Plots articles ... well, no comment.

When Oswald joined, the FPCC was infested with informants. The FBI and CIA were countering it through their respective COINTELPRO and AMSANTA programs, and New Orleans intelligence was fully prepared for the arrival of the FPCC. In fact, records show that William Stuckey, who eventually interviewed Oswald on WSDU, was on the prowl for the FPCC two years in advance.

The two most dangerous places to open chapters in the U.S. at the time were probably Miami and New Orleans. Dallas would not have been far behind. New Orleans perhaps stood out as the worst because of its dependence on North-South trade. Its proximity to Cuba caused many sleepless nights during the October 1962 missile crisis. FPCC director Vincent T. Lee had urged Oswald to avoid New Orleans.

When the HSCA published its completed Final Report in 1979, it showed two areas related to the FPCC that the Warren Commission failed to investigate adequately. One overlooked area was the identity of occupants at the address Oswald used for his FPCC literature distribution. The 544 Camp Street address appeared on materials that Oswald was handing out. This location was the New Orleans Newman Building. The Warren Report stated that, at an earlier date, the building was occupied by an anti-Castro group, but the name was not revealed in the final report.

Later it was found to be the Cuban Revolutionary Council. Another resident of the Newman Building was the private detective agency of Guy Banister. He also was not mentioned in the Warren Report. Banister was the retired FBI Special Agent in Charge of the Chicago FBI field office. After his FBI retirement in the mid-1950s, he moved to New Orleans and helped set up that city's police intelligence unit. Guy Banister, a staunch anti-communist, continued his anti-subversion work well after his official ties with the FBI were severed. The HSCA determined in their investigation that in 1961 Banister and Sergio Arcacha Smith of the CRC were working together in the anti-Castro cause.[21]

The 544 Camp Street address, which Oswald foolishly stamped on some of his handouts, was also surrounded by intelligence organizations, including the ONI, CIA, Secret Service and the FBI.

The HSCA did take a closer look at the Camp Street enigma. Here were some of the findings:

> During the course of that investigation, however, the Secret Service received information that an office in the Newman Building had been rented to the Cuban Revolutionary Council from October 1961 through February 1962.[22]
>
> The investigation of a possible connection between Oswald and the 544 Camp Street address was closed. The Warren Commission findings concurred with the Secret Service report that no additional evidence had been found to indicate Oswald ever maintained an office at the 544 Camp Street address.[23]
>
> The committee investigated the possibility of a connection between Oswald and 544 Camp Street and developed evidence pointing to a different result.[24]
>
> The overall investigation of the 544 Camp Street issue at the time of the assassination was not thorough. It is not surprising, then, that significant links were never discovered during the original investigation. Banister was involved in anti-Communist activities after his separation from the FBI and testified before various investigating bodies about the dangers of communism. Early in 1961, Banister helped draw up a charter for the Friends of Democratic Cuba, an organization set up as the fundraising arm of Sergio Arcacha Smith's Branch of the Cuban Revolutionary Council.[25]

---

[21] https://www.kennedysandking.com/john-f-kennedy-articles/exposing-the-fpcc-part-1#_edn20
[22] HSCA Report, p 467
[23] Ibid., p 466
[24] Ibid., p 469
[25] Ibid., p 482

The long-standing relationship of Ferrie and Banister is significant since Ferrie became a suspect soon after it occurred.[26]

Witnesses interviewed by the committee indicate Banister was aware of Oswald and his Fair Play for Cuba Committee before the assassination. Banister's brother, Ross Banister, who is employed by the Louisiana State Police, told the committee that his brother had mentioned seeing Oswald hand out Fair Play for Cuba literature on one occasion.[27]

Ivan F. "Bill" Nitschke, a friend and business associate and former FBI agent, corroborates that Banister was cognizant of Oswald's leaflet distributing.[28]

Delphine Roberts, Banister's long-time friend and secretary, stated to the committee that Banister had become extremely angry with James Arthus and Sam Newman over Oswald's use of the 544 Camp Street address on his handbills.[29]

The committee questioned Sam Newman regarding Roberts' allegation. Newman could not recall ever seeing Oswald or renting space to him... Newman theorized that if Oswald was using the 544 Camp Street address and had any link to the building, it would have been through a connection to the Cubans.[30]

Roberts claimed Banister had an extensive file on Communists and fellow travelers, including one on Lee Harvey Oswald, which was kept out of the original files because Banister "never got around to assigning a number to it."

Significant to the argument that Oswald and Ferrie were associated in 1963 is evidence of prior association in 1955 when Ferrie was captain of a Civil Air Patrol squadron and Oswald a young cadet. This pupil-teacher relationship could have greatly facilitated

---

[26] Ibid., p 489
[27] Ibid., p 491
[28] Ibid., p 492
[29] Ibid., p 494
[30] Ibid., p 495

their reacquaintance and Ferrie's noted ability to influence others could have been used with Oswald.[31]

D. Ferrie's experience with the underground activities of the Cuban exile movement and as a private investigator for Carlos Marcello and Guy Banister might have made him a good candidate to participate in a conspiracy plot. He may not have known what was to be the outcome of his actions, but once the assassination had been successfully completed and his own name cleared, Ferrie would have had no reason to reveal his knowledge of the plot.[32]

On page 145 of its final report, the HSCA states that "it was inclined to believe that Oswald was in Clinton, August—early September 1963, and that he was in the company of David Ferrie, if not Clay Shaw. The Committee was puzzled by Oswald's apparent association with David Ferrie, a person whose anti-Castro sentiments were so distant from those of Oswald, the Fair Play for Cuba Committee campaigner."

Research conducted after this very accusatory report has only reinforced its conclusion. We now know for certain that Clay Shaw was a well-paid CIA asset, something that he vehemently denied during the Garrison inquiry. He was also using the alias Clay Bertrand and that he was seen in the company of Oswald in Clinton.

Oswald's First Letter to the FPCC

For this important clue, we need to go back to 1964 and quote directly from Harold Feldman, <u>OSWALD and the FBI</u>.[33]After presenting arguments that Oswald was an FBI informant, Harold astutely makes the following points:

"If the FBI did not employ Oswald or work with him, then who wrote the letters he addressed to the Fair Play for Cuba Committee

---

[31] Ibid., p 514
[32] Ibid., p 515
[33] https://ratical.org/ratville/JFK/OswaldAndFBI.html

in New York? Oswald alone certainly didn't. Whoever wrote the letters to New York was coherent, commanded a good vocabulary, rarely misspelled a word, and punctuated decently. Oswald himself wrote English that a sixth grader would blush to acknowledge. Here is a letter he wrote to his mother from Russia on June 28, 1963. I preserve the original spelling and punctuation:

"Dear Mother.

Received your letter today in which you say you wish to pay me back the money you used last year, that, of course, is not necessary however you can send me somethings from there every now and than. If you decide to send a package please send the following: One can Rise shaving cream (one razor (Gillet) Pocket novels westerns and scienace fiction—Time or Newsweek magazine, Chewing Gum and chocolate bars. That's about all. Ha-ha

I very much miss sometime to read you should try and get me the pocket novel "1984" by Wells. I am working at the local Radio plant as a mettal worker. We live only five minutes from there so it is very conveinant.

Well thats about all for now. I repeat you do not have to send me checks or money!

Love XX

Lee

P.S. Marina sends a big Hello to you also"

Now compare this semiliterate effusion with the following addressed to the Fair Play for Cuba Committee about two years later. (A *New York Times* report on the letters to FPCC indicates that they were handwritten, so presumably no public stenographer improved their style.)

Dear Mr. Lee: I was glad to receive your advice concerning my try at starting a New Orleans F.P.C.C. chapter. I hope you won't be too disapproving at my innovations but I do think they are necessary for this area.

As per your advice I have taken a P.O. Box (N.O. 30,061).
Against your advice I have decided to take an office from the very
beginning. I u c [apparently meaning, as you see] from the circular
I had jumped the gun on the charter business but I don't think it's
too important. You may think the circular is too provocative, but I
want it to attract attention even if it's the attention of the lunatic
fringe. I had 2,000 of them run off.

The major change in tactics you can see from the small mem-
bership blanks, in that I will charge $1 a month dues for the new
Orleans chapter only and I intend to issue N.O. F.P.C.C. membership
cards also. This is without recourse to the $5 annual F.P.C.C. mem-
bership fee.

However, you will lose nothing in the long run because I will
forward $5 to the national F.P.C.C. for every New Orleans chapter
member who remains a dues paying member for 5 months in any
year...

And so on for several more well-integrated paragraphs. He now spells "receive" and "necessary" correctly. He has mastered the apostrophe. His ideas cohere. He tackles words like "innovations," "provocative," "recourse," "disapproving," "approaching," and "application" with success, something that would have been clearly beyond the powers of the voluntary exile in Minsk.

In the following you will see that the actual handwritten version indicates a few differences with the above-typed version (for example its vs. it's). In my view the analysis by Mr. Feldman remains valid and astute given what he had to work with. He is correct in saying that this letter is so much better in grammar, word selection and style than other Oswald correspondence.

V.T. Lee Exhibit #4

even if its the attention of the
lunatic fringe. I had heard of
them ...

The dues change no attention
you can see from the small membership I have, in that it will
charge $1.00 a month dues for the
new Orleans chapter, only, and I
intend to issue N.O. F.P.C.C. membership cards also.

This is without ... to
the $5.00 annual national F.P.C.C.
membership fee.

However, you will lose nothing
in the long run because I will
forward $5.00 to the national F.P.C.C.
for every new Orleans chapter
member who remains a dues paying
member for 5 months in any year.

To just that the people I am
approaching will not pay 5 dollars.

LEE (VINCENT T.) EXHIBIT No. 4—Continued

Until the authorship of the letters to the FPCC is settled, it is reasonable to suppose that Oswald did not compose them, at least not without help. Who, and where, is the invisible scribe? No associate of his New Orleans period has been found, or even hinted at. If Oswald was employed by the FBI to operate in "Castro groups," as the news report suggests, it is also reasonable to suppose that in the letters to FPCC his pen was guided by the FBI.

Even Hale Boggs of the Warren Commission had serious doubts about this letter. Boggs and Commission General Counsel Lee Rankin had early on discussed such an idea:

> "Rankin: They [the Fair Play for Cuba Committee] denied he was a member and also he wrote to them and tried to establish as one of the letters indicate, a new branch there in New Orleans, the Fair Play for Cuba.
>
> Boggs: That letter has caused me a lot of trouble. It is a much more literate and polished communication than any of his other writing."[34]

John Quigley and Warren DeBrueys

After the altercation with Carlos Bringuier of the DRE, while under arrest, Oswald made a bizarre request. He asked to see an FBI agent. The FBI sent agent John Quigley, who spent somewhere between 90 minutes and three hours with Oswald. It's safe to say that they were not discussing Bringuier simply being mean to the alleged communist. Quigley stated that Martello told him that Oswald wanted to pass on information about the FPCC to him. Joan Mellen's research finds that Oswald actually asked specifically for Warren DeBrueys. DeBrueys, who ran Cuban exile Frank Bartes as an informant, was in charge of monitoring the FPCC in New Orleans. This would further nail down the real reason Oswald started an FPCC chapter in a hostile place like New Orleans. William Walter, an employee at the New Orleans FBI office, claimed to have seen an FBI informant file on Oswald with DeBrueys' name on it.[35] This

---

[34] **Bernard Fensterwald, *Assassination of JFK: Coincidence or Conspiracy* (1974)**
[35] Destiny Betrayed, Jim DiEugenio pages 109, 158 and Farewell to Justice, Joan Mellen page 59.

is even more interesting given that Ruth and Michael Paine and Guy Banister each had files filled with names of communists.

Orestes Peña, Joseph Oster, David Smith, and Wendell Roache

Curiously, the evidence that Oswald collaborated with Customs is stronger than with almost any other agency. Cuban exile Orestes Peña testified that he saw Oswald chatting on a regular basis with FBI Cuban specialist Warren DeBrueys, David Smith at Customs, and Wendell Roache at INS. Peña told the Church Committee that Oswald was employed by Customs. Informant Joseph Oster went farther, saying that Oswald's handler was David Smith at Customs. Church Committee staff members knew that David Smith "was involved in CIA operations." Orestes Peña's handler Warren DeBrueys admitted he knew David Smith.

Roache, when called by Church Committee investigators, replied that he had been expecting a call for twelve years. As we have seen in Chapter 1, what he said about Oswald and his 544 Camp Street connections is so damning that it likely contributed to Richard Schweiker's suspicions that Oswald was a double agent spying on both anti and pro-Castro groups.[36]

Follow the Money

"Forensic accounting" is one of the things that the FBI and Warren Commission did not do thoroughly in trying to understand how such a destitute person like Oswald could run an FPCC chapter, raise a family, and save money for Marina (at least $1600 in today's money). He was so poor that the White Russians paid for his YMCA fees.

The FPCC added the following to this drifter's cost of living: FPCC membership fees, renting of a space, hiring leafleteers, paying a fine for disturbing the peace, the purchase of rubber-stamping equipment, personal displacements, printing of up to five different pieces of literature,

---

[36] https://documents.theblackvault.com/documents/jfk/NARA-Oct2017/2018/157-10014-10120.pdf pages 35, 36, 37, 40, 41, 51

correspondence with the FPCC, and use of a Post Office Box … with not one single member to help absorb the costs.

The following exchange between Oswald's lawyer and Wesley Liebeler of the Warren Commission suggests something more plausible than Oswald giving away time and money for a passé organization rather than focusing on his growing family—he was paid $25 a day. This was about double what Oswald's $1.50/hour job at the Texas Schoolbook Depository would later yield him.

Mr. LIEBELER. And did you talk about different subjects at different times? As I understand it, the first time he came there, he was primarily concerned about his discharge, is that correct?

Mr. ANDREWS. Well, I may have the subject matter of the visits reversed because with the company he kept and the conversation—he could talk fairly well—I figured that this was another one of what we call in my office free alley clients, so we didn't maintain the normalcy with the file that—might have scratched a few notes on a piece of pad, and 2 days later threw the whole thing away. Didn't pay too much attention to him. Only time I really paid attention to this boy, he was in the front of the Maison Blanche Building giving out these kooky Castro things.

Mr. LIEBELER. When was this, approximately?

Mr. ANDREWS. I don't remember. I was coming from the NBC building, and I walked past him. You know how you see somebody, recognize him. So I turned around, came back, and asked him what he was doing giving that junk out. He said it was a job. I reminded him of the $25 he owed the office. He said he would come over there, but he never did.

Mr. LIEBELER. Did he tell you that he was getting paid to hand out this literature?

Mr. ANDREWS. Yes.

Mr. LIEBELER. Did he tell you how much?

Mr. ANDREWS. No.

Mr. LIEBELER. Do you remember telling the FBI that he told you that he was being paid $25 a day for handing out these leaflets?

Mr. ANDREWS. I could have told them that. I know I reminded him of the $25. I may have it confused, the $25. What I do recall, he said it was a job. I guess I asked him how much he was making. They were little square chits a little bit smaller than the picture you have of him over there [indicating].

Mr. LIEBELER. He was handing out these leaflets?

Mr. ANDREWS. They were black-and-white pamphlets extolling the virtues of Castro, which around here doesn't do too good. They have a lot of guys, Mexicanos and Cubanos, that will tear your head off if they see you fooling with these things.

Oswald's Slip was Showing

Admitting his remuneration to Dean Andrews and stamping 544 Camp Street on his handouts were not Oswald's only mistakes that would ultimately blow his cover. Shortly after launching the FPCC Chapter in New Orleans, Lee sent out two honorary membership cards to Gus Hall and Benjamin Davis, two senior members of the American Communist Party.

Even though after his return from Russia he wrote the following in his diary:

> The Communist Party of the United States has betrayed itself! It has turned itself into the traditional lever of a foreign power to overthrow the government of the United States; not in the name of freedom or high ideals, but in servile conformity to the wishes of the Soviet Union and in anticipation of Soviet Russia's complete domination of the American continent.

In a letter dated August 1, 1963, postmarked August 4, Oswald wrote to Vincent T. Lee, head of the Fair Play for Cuba Committee in New York:

> In regards to my efforts to start a branch of the Fair Play for Cuba Committee in New Orleans... I rented an office as planned and was promptly closed 3 days later for some obsure [sic] reasons by the renters, they said something about remodeling, ect. [sic] I'm sure you understand after that I worked out of a post office box and by useing [sic] street demonstrations and some circular work have substained [sic] a great deal of interest but no new members. Through the efforts of some cuban-exial [sic] "gusanos" a street demonstration was attacked and we were oficialy [sic] cautioned by the police.

The problem with this letter was that the incident Oswald seems to be referring to occurred on August 9th, more than a week after he first wrote about it. Was Oswald describing a scenario for the upcoming theatrics on Canal Street over which he would be arrested and arraigned in court?

When Oswald was interviewed on WSDU, he was asked how he lived in Russia: "Did you have a government subsidy?" Oswald answered, "Well, I worked in Russia and, I was under the protection of the United States, Uh I was under the Uh that is to say, I was not under the protection of the United States Government. But, I was always considered a United States citizen."[37]

John Newman shows how Dallas FBI claims that they lost track of Oswald, while he was setting up the FPCC in New Orleans all the way up to August 5, lack credibility, especially given his multiple FBI scrutinized correspondences—all occurring before June 6—with the Post Office, the Communist Party, the Soviet Embassy in Washington, and the FPCC, where his New Orleans address was easy to find.[38]

Another astute observation by Newman is that before August 5th, Oswald's FPCC recruitment activities were done quietly, almost undercover. They were likely done that way in order to help Banister and the CRC with their background investigations. As of August 5, when he meets Bringuier up until September 25 when he meets Silvia Odio, Oswald repeatedly acts overtly with anti-Castro Cubans while, at the same time, seeking media attention for his FPCC activities.[39]

On September 16, 1963, the CIA informed the FBI that it was considering action to counter the activities of the Fair Play for Cuba Committee in foreign countries. In New Orleans, on September 17, 1963, Oswald applied for, and received, a Mexican travel visa.[40]

Another indicator of Oswald's informant role is what the FBI did not do: Infiltrate the New Orleans FPCC. The FBI did this with FPCC chapters throughout the country, often with multiple informants. And as we saw with Bill Stuckey, New Orleans was well prepared for an FPCC presence in their city. It would have been very easy to have informants answer Oswald's leafleting by signing up to spy on him—as they did in Tampa, New York, Detroit, Chicago, Los Angeles, Indiana, and elsewhere. But, for whatever reason, they chose not to.

There seems to be a logical deduction from all this. Oswald was informing on both pro- and anti-Castro operations in New Orleans. But he was also creating a portfolio like other FPCC participants in the past to

---

[37] https://www.youtube.com/watch?v=F_mg5-KCjRU&t=12s just passed minute 49
[38] Newman, Oswald and the CIA, Chapter 16
[39] Ibid., Chapter 17
[40] Dan Hardway, "Declaration," Case 1:03-cv-02545-RJL Document 156-1, Civil Action No. 03–02545 (RJL)

be able to eventually travel to Cuba by way of the Mexico City-Cubana Airlines route.

Carlos Quiroga

Oswald's landlady Jesse Garner saw Quiroga meet Oswald at his apartment. Quiroga claimed that he was trying to infiltrate the FPCC. This could have been done by filling out one of the flyers that Oswald was distributing. According to Jesse Garner in her Warren Commission testimony, Quiroga seems to have brought way more than one application: Note how both lawyer Wesley Liebeler and Jim Garrison (handwritten note in the margin) underscore the quantity of flyers Quiroga brought:

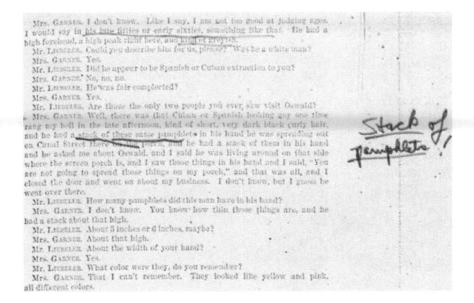

Another false claim made by Quiroga was that this had been the only time that he had met Oswald.

The following lie detector test results reveal that: Quiroga met Oswald a number of times. He also knew that Oswald's association with the FPCC was but a front and that Oswald was part of an anti-Castro operation. That he knew that David Ferrie knew Guy Banister and he had seen Oswald with at least one other Latino subject.

Scientific Lie Detection
Examinations

Polygraph, Inc.

Polygraph Examinations

ROY L. JACOB, SR.
Phone HU. 6-5120

P. O. Box 711
METAIRIE, LA.

Page (2)   Carlos Quiroga Cuban Male 30

After careful analysis of this subject's second polygram
it is the opinion of the examiner that he gave specific
reactions indicative of deception to the relevant questions
under examination:

QUESTION #2.

In the Summer of 1963 did you see Lee Oswald with any
Latin decent subject?   Answer No.

QUESTION #3.

Isn't it a fact that you know that the Fair Play for Cuba
activities were merely a cover?   Answer No.

QUESTION #5.

Was Oswald in reality part of af an anti-Castro operation?
Answer No.

QUESTION#12.

According to your own knowledge, did David Ferrie know
Sergio Arcacha?   Answer No.

TEST #3.

After careful analysis of this subject's third polygram it
is the opinion of the examiner that he gave specific reactions
indicative of deception to the relevant questions under examination:

QUESTION #3.

According to your own knowledge, did David Ferrie know
Guy Banister? Answer No.

QUESTION #6.

Verify Job Applicants – Fidelity – Integrity – Frauds – Inventory Shortages – Criminal – Personnel Screening – Portable Equipment Available

EXAMINERS TRAINED BY WORLD FAMOUS
KEELER POLYGRAPH INSTITUTE OF CHICAGO, ILLINOIS

Two witnesses—one who had also been polygraphed—contradicted Quiroga's statements.

David Lewis, a roommate of Banister employee Jack Martin, saw Quiroga with Oswald a number of times. While his testimony and character have been the subject of numerous attacks, there was no denying that his own polygraph results bolster the proof of deception brought forward by Quiroga's polygraph. We can also add Ricardo Davis as one other witness who accompanied Quiroga when he was with Oswald on an occasion.[41]

Oswald's choices in terms of timing, location, networking, recruitment activities, as well as the budget constraints he overcame, along with the lack of infiltration of his chapter, these all point to his being an informant on pro-Castro and anti-Castro goings-on in New Orleans.

The campaign to position Oswald as Castro-linked in and around the assassination was clearly coordinated and performed by intelligence assets. Two persons of extreme interest linked to the operatives and the strategies used were George Joannides and David Phillips. By 1963, the FPCC appears to have been no more than a tool for intelligence gathering, creating a portfolio to enter Cuba and lying in wait to be a perfect platform on which to hoist a patsy, and through him, implicate Castro.

Oswald's Last Call

On Saturday night, November 23rd, 1963, Oswald placed a call that even the head of the HSCA described as very troublesome. Doctor Grover B. Proctor, Jr. wrote a comprehensive article about that phone call.[42] It shows that Lee Oswald tried to make a phone call on Saturday night that the Secret Service did not allow to go through. Proctor then investigated why.

Surell Brady, a Senior Staff Counsel for the House Select Committee on Assassinations (HSCA), summarized phone operator Alveeta Treon's version of events this way:

Mrs. Treon stayed on the line. She said she was therefore able to hear everything Oswald said and she is sure he asked for the name John Hurt and gave the two numbers. She said that as she listened

---

[41] http://www.aarclibrary.org/publib/jfk/garr/grandjury/pdf/Quiroga.pdf, page 29
[42] http://groverproctor.us/jfk/jfk80.html

she wrote the information down on a regular telephone call slip. However, since Mrs. Swinney actually handled the call, Mrs. Treon signed her [Mrs. Swinney's] name to the slip she intended to keep as a souvenir. She said the notations on the slip of 'DA' and 'CA' stand for did not answer and canceled, because the call was never actually put through. Mrs. Treon said she never retrieved any paper from the wastebasket on which Mrs. Swinney supposedly entered the information.

Billie & John D. Hurt

Had Mrs. Treon not kept the call slip that she filled out as a souvenir, this story would be no more than the most minor of footnotes in the tragedy of the Kennedy Assassination. However, years later, when the identity became known of the man to whom Oswald was trying to place a call, its significance would rise to the "very troublesome" and "deeply disturbing" levels ascribed to it by HSCA Chief Counsel Blakey.

Grover goes on to write:

"What Mrs. Treon recorded for history on her LD slip is that Lee Oswald requested to call a 'John Hurt' in Raleigh, North Carolina. But what would become important is the fact that the John Hurt who had the first phone number on the slip was a former Special Agent in U.S. Army Counterintelligence. In short, Oswald attempted to place a call *from the Dallas jail* to a member of the American Intelligence community on Saturday evening, November 23, 1963, but was mysteriously prevented from completing the call."

Other Incriminating Statements

According to stenographer, Paulina Virginia Bates, Oswald hired to make records of notes he brought from Russia, he hinted that he was an agent.[43]

CIA officer George Joannides ran the DRE in New Orleans when Oswald got into a likely staged fight with DRE leader, Carlos Bringuier. Many years later, Joannides' reviewing officer William Kent answered a question about Oswald to his daughter.

Kent had been chief of JM/WAVE psychological warfare before Joannides took over that position in August 1963 and was quite familiar with the activities of the DRE. When interviewed by Gaeton Fonzi, Kent's daughter recalled asking her father about Lee Oswald. His only response was that Oswald had been a *"useful idiot."*[44] When asked who killed JFK, his response was *"It's better you don't know."*

Consider this by Senator Richard Schweiker: "We do know Oswald had intelligence connections. Everywhere you look with him, there are fingerprints of intelligence."[45]

Senator Richard Schweiker was a well-respected Republican politi-

---

[43] https://www.youtube.com/watch?v=HlnpOHfhLvQ
[44] https://www.maryferrell.org/pages/Tipping_Point_Part2.html
[45] *Senator Richard Schweiker, The Village Voice, 1975*

cian who served under President Reagan from 1981 to 1983 as Secretary of Health and Human Services. He served over 20 years as a Pennsylvania U.S. Representative (1961–1969) and U.S. Senator (1969–1981). In 1976, he had an unsuccessful run to become Vice President in Reagan's losing presidential campaign.

Most crucial for the purposes of these writings, from 1975 to 1976, Schweiker was a member of the United States Senate Select Committee to Study Governmental Operations with Respect to Intelligence Activities. Senator Frank Church appointed Schweiker and Colorado Senator Gary Hart to be a two-person subcommittee to look into the "performance or non-performance" of intelligence agencies during the initial investigation of the assassination.

Oswald's Intelligence Connections

Oswald had just turned 24 years-old when he was assassinated by Jack Ruby. He never finished high school and is portrayed as a lone nut drifter by Warren Commissioner backers. In 2017, in the article Oswald's Intelligence Connections[46] by Paul Bleau, it is clearly demonstrated that this is fake history.

The author chronicles touch points Oswald had with 64 plausible or definite intelligence assets (over 30 are definite): David Ferrie, The Paines, Carlos Bringuier, Guy Banister, George de Mohrenschildt, Kerry Thornley, Priscillia Johnson, Spas Raikin, Thomas Vicente, William Gaudet, Ed Butler are a but a few of a cast of characters that the alleged assassin had contact with. Since the article was written, more than a dozen other links have been identified. These encounters take place before Oswald even became a marine all the way to his death and they occur in California, Japan, Russia, New Jersey, Dallas, New Orleans, Mexico City and elsewhere.

Among some of the people who kept an eye on Oswald and Marina,

---

[46] https://www.kennedysandking.com/john-f-kennedy-articles/oswald-s-intelligence-connections-how-richard-schweiker-clashes-with-fake-history; The Killing of President Kennedy at 6:36, 20:42, 34:50, 46:25

George de Mohrenschildt and Ruth and Michael Paine had connections to Allen Dulles and Ruth Kloepfer had connections to both Ruth Paine and Clay Shaw.

In another article called <u>The Garrison Files and Oswald's Escort</u>,[47] over thirty testimonies are chronicled of witnesses who saw Oswald, or a double, accompanied by at least one Latino escort during the last ten months of his life. Another five sightings have since been identified, bringing this number to nearly forty. One of the Latinos frequently seen was described as short and very stocky.[48]

Warren Commission apologists have often painted witnesses like Richard Case Nagell, Sylvia Odio, Roger Craig, Perry Russo and others as unreliable, possibly demented, mixed up or brainwashed, all in a desperate attempt to dismiss their stories. Yet a number were given shortly after the assassination and they all describe the strikingly similar company held by Oswald. How could all the corroborating testimonies align that much?

Carlos Bringuier, Orest Pena and Arnesto Rodriguez all stated that the FBI was on the lookout for Oswald's Latin companions. There is testimony that he was in fact identified, but never talked about.

Given the corroborative value of these accounts, should we not be taking each and every one of these sightings very seriously? The implications are monumental. The myth of Oswald the lone nut should be torn down once and for all.

David Atlee Phillips[49]

Among all of Oswald's intelligence links, the most eye-popping has to be the one he shares with David Atlee Phillips. According to John Newman in Oswald & the CIA, the Agency began monitoring the FPCC in 1961. CIA officer E. Howard Hunt, affirmed that Phillips started the DRE.

---

[47] https://www.kennedysandking.com/john-f-kennedy-articles/oswalds-escort
[48] Ibid.
[49] https://www.kennedysandking.com/john-f-kennedy-articles/oswald-s-intelligence-connections-how-richard-schweiker-clashes-with-fake-history section: Where There's Smoke, There's Fire

Phillips also had links to Ed Butler of INCA (an anti-communist propaganda mill).

In August 1963, there was an infamous televised debate in New Orleans after Oswald and Bringuier were arrested for what the arresting officer felt was a staged fight because of Oswald's provocative FPCC leafleting. The debate helped paint Oswald as an unhinged Castro loving Marxist. The participants were Oswald, who was the sole member of his FPCC chapter in New Orleans, Carlos Bringuier who headed the New Orleans DRE, and Ed Butler.

This is not the only place where David Atlee Phillips's universe overlaps with Oswald's. There are nearly 20 common touch points between Oswald and Phillips involving Cuban exiles, propaganda tools, the FPCC, Mexico City, Oswald babysitters, etc. Case linkage shows that no fewer than six of the eight alternate patsies were also marked as pro-Castro with their bizarre FPCC links, the very organization Phillips was turning inside out in his plots to counter Castro sympathizers. Throw in his lies, quasi-confessions to the murder, and his being thrown under the bus by colleague E. H. Hunt, and we have a strong case to make about whom some of the leading plotters were and Oswald's role as a *useful idiot*.

Dan Hardway's 2016 Declaration

HSCA investigative attorneys Dan Hardway and Ed Lopez co-authored a section for the HSCA's Final Report on the CIA and Oswald in Mexico City which remained classified in full until 1996. The draft, after further declassification in 2003, was published by the Mary Ferrell Foundation Press as <u>Oswald, The CIA, And Mexico City: The Lopez-Hardway Report</u>, and shed light on missing/destroyed tapes and photos, Oswald impersonations, lying CIA officials and peculiar behavior by Oswald or a frame-up artist—all completely fluffed over by the Warren Commission.

As noted in Chapter 1, in 2016, Dan Hardway prepared <u>a written declaration</u> in support of a Jefferson Morley Freedom of Information civil action which should trouble mainstream historians who are holding on to the Warren Report's myths about what happened to President Kennedy.

Conclusion

Oswald was well known to the FBI and CIA. His relationships with intelligence agencies are still being suppressed and covered up. Oswald was not a lone-nut. His sojourn into Russia was a false defector mission, as was his opening of a FPCC front in New Orleans where he was maneuvered into his role as a patsy. Early strategies were developed to point the finger at Castro and Russia using Oswald as the patsy.

CHAPTER 3

OSWALD WAS IMPERSONATED

BY MATT CRUMPTON

STATEMENT

THERE ARE NUMEROUS documented accounts of Lee Harvey Oswald being impersonated, which begs the question: Who was impersonating Oswald and why?

INTRODUCTION

There are many instances of someone else saying that they saw Oswald when we know that Lee Harvey Oswald was elsewhere. The fact of these observations, combined with the details of what the impersonator was saying in each respective instance, demonstrate by clear and convincing evidence that Oswald was impersonated. The fact of impersonation reinforces the conclusion that Oswald alone did not kill President Kennedy. There is no plausible reason why a lone gunman would be impersonated so many times. The frequency of these instances clearly increased in the days, weeks and months before the assassination, and also on the day of the assassination, which clearly shows a designed plot to lay the blame on Oswald within hours of the assassination.

EXECUTIVE SUMMARY

Oswald was seen running out of the back of the Texas School Book Depository Building by Helen Forrest, James Pennington, and Roger Craig, when we know that the real Oswald was on a bus. Multiple witnesses saw a man who looked like Oswald and was an excellent shooter at Sports Drome rifle range in October and November of 1963 at times when Oswald was known to be with Marina and his children.

In November of 1963, Oswald is impersonated at a Fort Worth gun store, a car dealership, and the Red Bird Airfield. According to Laura Kittrell, she met with two different people who claimed to be Lee Harvey Oswald while working at the Texas Employment Commission. Oswald is also impersonated in writing, specifically with letters to the Soviet Embassy and the FPCC. On the Wednesday before the assassination when we know Oswald was at work, a hitchhiker who had curtain rods in a paper sack obtained a ride from Ralph Yates near Oswald's rooming house. On the way, the man asked Yates if he thought someone could kill the president with a rifle from a tall building. The hitchhiker said he worked at the Texas School Book Depository.

Oswald was even impersonated while he was in Russia. A man

named Lee Oswald attempted to buy vehicles on behalf of Friends of Democratic Cuba—a group that had opposing views from the Cuba group Oswald is publicly associated with, Fair Play for Cuba Committee. Even J. Edgar Hoover acknowledged that Oswald was being impersonated in a June 3, 1960, memo to the State Department. In total, there are at least seven reports of alleged Oswald sightings in the U.S. while Oswald was supposed to be in the USSR.

Finally, we know that Oswald was impersonated in Mexico City because the FBI did not recognize the man's appearance or voice to be Oswald, whom the FBI had met with in Dallas. The FBI concluded that Oswald had been impersonated in Mexico City.

Running Down the Grassy Knoll in Dealey Plaza
After the Assassination

Shortly after the assassination in Dealey Plaza, there are five people who claim to have seen a man resembling Oswald running down the hill and getting into a Rambler. This was at the same time, according to the Warren Commission, that Oswald was heading east on Elm Street boarding a bus.

When Marvin Robinson was driving through Dealey Plaza immediately after the assassination, he had to slam on the brakes in his Cadillac to avoid hitting the light-colored Rambler just ahead of him that had suddenly pulled over beside the curb on Elm Street. Robinson says the Rambler picked up a man running down the grass from the Depository who then got into the Rambler which was pulled over near the grassy knoll side of Elm Street.[1]

Robinson's story is supported by Roy Cooper, Robinson's employee who was in the car behind Robinson. Cooper says he saw the man coming down the incline wave at the Rambler and then jump in.[2] Neither

---

[1] *HSCA Report* at 97. https://archive.org/stream/investigationofa12unit/investigation-ofa12unit_djvu.txt

[2] *FBI Memorandum by Special Agent Earle Haley on Interview with Roy Cooper, November 23, 1963, Reproduced in Harvey and Lee by John Armstrong*

Robinson nor Cooper were able to identify the person they saw running to the Rambler.[3]

Helen Forrest and James Pennington, however, did get a good look at the man. Both Forrest and Pennington also say they saw a man running from the rear of the Depository building, down the incline into Dealey Plaza, and then get into a Rambler station wagon. They both said that the man they saw looked exactly like Lee Harvey Oswald.[4]

Sheriff Roger Craig is the fifth witness to corroborate that story. Sheriff Craig was standing in front of the Sheriff's Department when the motorcade passed. He heard gunshots and started running into Dealey Plaza, where he began looking for bullet marks.[5]

Here's what Roger Craig said he saw:

"As I was searching the South curb of Elm Street, I heard a shrill whistle. And I looked up. It just drew my attention. It was coming from across the street. And there was a light green Rambler station wagon driving real slow West on Elm Street and the driver was leaning to his right, looking up at a man running down the grass. So, I immediately tried to cross the street to take these two people into custody for questioning. Everybody else was coming to the scene. These were the only two people leaving. And this was suspicious in my mind. I wanted to talk to them, but the traffic was so heavy across the street that I couldn't get across to them. But I did get a good look at the man coming down the Grassy Knoll and he got in the station wagon, and he drove west on Elm Street."[6]

Craig described the driver of the station wagon as a "husky looking Latin, with dark wavy hair, wearing a tan windbreaker type jacket." Sheriff

---

[3] *HSCA Report* at 97

[4] *Helen Forrest interview by Michael L. Kurtz, May 17, 1974. Michael L. Kurtz, Crime of the Century: The Kennedy Assassination from a Historian's Perspective (Knoxville: University of Tennessee Press, 1993), p 132 For James Pennington, see Id. at 189*

[5] *Roger Craig, When They Kill a President, p. 9; James Douglass, JFK and the Unspeakable* at 275

[6] *JFK Assassination: The Roger Craig Story*—https://www.youtube.com/watch?v=-TLHx8dlGjE, at 4:20

Craig then went into the School Book Depository Building and up to the sixth floor to see what evidence he could find.[7] After securing and searching the depository building, Craig contacted the Dallas Police to let them know what he had seen regarding the suspicious man getting into the Rambler.

Craig said: "I called Captain Fritz at his office and gave him a description of the man I saw get into the Rambler. He told me, 'It sounds like the suspect we have in custody. Come on and take a look at him. So, I went directly to Captain Fritz's office … and a man was sitting at a chair behind a desk and there was another gentleman, I assumed he was one of Fritz's people because he had the white cowboy hat on which was the trademark of the Dallas Homicide Bureau. And Fritz turned to me and said, "Is this the man you saw?" I said yes. And it was.'[8]

Sheriff Roger Craig's positive identification of Oswald running down the hill getting into the Rambler makes Craig the fifth witness to see the same thing, with three of those witnesses identifying Oswald. He backs up what Helen Forest and James Pennington saw. Someone who looked just like Oswald was running out of the back of the Texas Schoolbook Depository Building and then got into a Nash Rambler waiting alongside the curb on Elm Street. His description of the Latino driver matches over twenty sightings of Oswald being accompanied by a short stocky escort.[9]

The Ralph Yates Incident

It is well known that Warren Report alleges that Oswald snuck his rifle in on the morning of the Assassination after receiving a ride from Buell Wesley Frazier. What is less known is the other story involving curtain rods being delivered to the Texas School Book Depository by Ralph Yates.

On Wednesday, November 20 at 10:30 a.m.-one day before Oswald

---

[7] *Craig at p. 9; Douglass at 275*
[8] *JFK Assassination: The Roger Craig Story*—https://www.youtube.com/watch?v=-TLHx8dlGjE, at 9:40
[9] https://www.kennedysandking.com/john-f-kennedy-articles/oswalds-escort

asked Frazier for a ride to pick up curtain rods from the Paine house—Ralph Yates picked up a hitchhiker near Beckley Avenue who he claimed was a 'dead ringer' for Lee Harvey Oswald. Yates said the man had a four-foot-long package covered in brown wrapping paper. And he told Yates that the long paper sack contained curtain rods.[10]

This hitchhiker asked Yates, 'If he thought a person could assassinate the President.' Yates said he supposed it was possible. The man then asked Yates, 'Could it be done from the top of a building or out a window high up?' Yates said it would be possible if someone had a good rifle with a scope and was a good shot.[11] The man then asked Yates if he knew the President's motorcade route. Yates said he did not, but that it was in the newspaper.

Yates then dropped off the man where he asked to be taken—the intersection of Elm and Houston Street, which happens to be where the Texas School Book Depository Building is located. After the hitchhiker exited the vehicle, Yates saw the man carrying the long brown paper sack across Elm Street.

When Yates returned to work that Wednesday afternoon, he told his co-worker, Dempsey Jones, about the hitchhiker and what the man had said about killing the president.[12] Once Yates heard about the assassination and saw Oswald on the news, he said the man he gave a ride to was 'identical with Oswald.'[13]

Yates immediately went to the FBI to tell them his story. But the FBI told Yates that he was mistaken. They interviewed Yates over 4 days on November 26, December 10, and then again on January 3rd and 4th, 1964.[14] We know that Yates" testimony must have been at least somewhat important to the case because FBI director J. Edgar Hoover *personally wrote* an urgent teletype regarding the Yates testimony and

---

[10] *Ralph Yates FBI Statement, December 10, 1963*—https://www.maryferrell.org/showDoc.html?docId=57741&relPageId=67

[11] Ibid. at https://www.maryferrell.org/showDoc.html?docId=57741#relPageId=68

[12] Ibid. at https://www.maryferrell.org/showDoc.html?docId=57741#relPageId=69

[13] James Douglass, *JFK and the Unspeakable*, p 351, *citing Statement by Ralph Leon Yates to FBI special agent Ben S. Harrison, November 26, 1963, Dallas, Texas, reproduced by John Armstrong on his CD-ROM for Harvey and Lee*, image 22

[14] Ibid. at 351

ordered Yates to be re-interviewed with the polygraph lie detector, which was administered on January 4th.[15]

After the January 4th interview, the FBI told Yates that he had passed the lie detector test because the test showed that Yates believed what he was saying was true. However, because the FBI said that they knew what Yates was saying could not be true, *Yates was declared to be mentally insane and needed to immediately check in to a mental institution.*

Yates, who was a twenty-eight-year-old husband with five children, was then admitted immediately to Woodlawn Hospital for the Mentally Ill as a psychiatric patient.[16] From that point on, Yates spent most of the remainder of his life in and out of mental health hospitals until he died at the age of 39.[17] He received over 40 shock treatments, but he never backed down or changed his story about picking up the hitchhiker who looked like Oswald and had foreknowledge of the curtain rods, the long paper sack, the shooting from high up with a rifle, and Oswald's place of employment.

When one reads the story of the FBI forcibly committing Yates, it is difficult to understand why the FBI would take such an extreme measure. Yates was providing information that was consistent with Oswald wanting to kill Kennedy from a location identical to the sixth floor of the Texas School Book Depository, where Yates dropped the hitchhiker, and potentially possessing a rifle to do it. How was this problematic to the Warren Report?

It's problematic because there is already an official story for how Oswald got the rifle into the building, which, incidentally, also involves curtain rods in a brown paper bag as the concealment method for sneaking the rifle in. The official story is that Buell Wesley Frazier gave Oswald a ride to work on Friday morning. The story of Yates dropping off a hitch-

---

[15] *To Special Agent in Charge, Dallas from Director, FBI (105–82555), January 2, 1964, JFK Record Number 180-10033-10242; See also* https://www.maryferrell.org/show-Doc.html?docId=57753#relPageId=3

[16] *January 17, 1964, FBI Report, C. Ray Hall*—https://www.maryferrell.org/show-Doc.html?docId=96528#relPageId=44&search=%22ralph_yates%22

[17] *Douglass* at 353-54 (citing Author's interview with Dorothy Walker, formerly Dorothy Yates, widow of Ralph Yates, October 6 and 16, 2006)

hiker on Wednesday morning is not the official story and is ignored in the Warren Report. Instead, the FBI had Yates committed to mental institutions until he perished. We know that Oswald was working his regular hours at the depository on Wednesday when Yates says he picked up the hitchhiker. So, Yates hitchhiker CANNOT be the real Lee Harvey Oswald![18]

This story sounds crazy. But the facts of Yates' 4 interviews with the FBI and his subsequent involuntary commitment to a mental health facility are not disputed. There are multiple FBI documents discussing the interviews with Yates. The FBI also checked Yates's whereabouts on Wednesday morning at 10:30 a.m., and, sure enough, Yates was out on a service call in the area of Beckley Avenue, which corroborates his story.[19]

Ralph Yates is where the analysis of the case really starts to diverge between conspiracy researchers and lone gunman researchers. For people who are suspicious of Oswald acting alone, the Yates story is a showstopper. The Feds committed this man to a mental institution without due process all because he told what was apparently an inconvenient truth.

And what was his truth that got him in trouble? —Telling the FBI that he picked up an Oswald lookalike who was apparently impersonating Oswald, given his foreknowledge of Oswald's place of work and curtain rods in a paper sack. Yates relayed his encounter with the hitchhiker to his co-worker Dempsey *before* the assassination on that Wednesday. How could Yates have possibly known to make that up?

Leading Warren Report defenders do not have a substantive counterpoint to the story of Ralph Yates.

Dobbs House

On Wednesday, November 20, 1963, the same day that Ralph Yates claims that he picked up a hitchhiker who looked just like Oswald on the

---

[18] Ibid. at 352
[19] https://www.maryferrell.org/showDoc.html?docId=57741&relPageId=67

highway near Oswald's Beckley Avenue rooming house, there was another sighting of someone who looked just like Oswald at the Dobbs House restaurant.

The Dobbs House sighting of Oswald included Oswald seeing Officer J. D. Tippit, who is said to have been murdered by Oswald shortly after the JFK assassination, and Tippit shooting him a glance. The FBI report says that former waitress Mary Dowling " ... last saw Oswald in the restaurant at 10 a.m. on Wednesday Nov. 20, at which time he was nasty and used curse words in connection with his order. JD Tippit was in the restaurant, as was his habit at the time each morning, shot a glance at Oswald. But there was no indication they knew each other."[20]

What is even more interesting is that the Dobbs House sighting of Oswald occurred at 10:00 a.m. Dobbs House was two blocks away from Oswald's rooming house on North Beckley. If Yates picked up this Oswald impersonator at 10:30 a.m. near the rooming house and there was someone else who looked like Oswald at 10:00 a.m. at Dobbs House, it appears possible that Yates may have been picking up the same man who was seen at Dobbs House. We know this man was not the actual Lee Harvey Oswald because Oswald was at work at the time.

Sports Drome

The fact that the Warren Commission went to great lengths to discredit the following witnesses further bolsters the fact that Oswald was impersonated and that the Warren Commission wanted to stay away from that at all costs. The Warren Report says, "Several witnesses believed that in the weeks preceding the assassination, they observed a man resembling Oswald practicing with a rifle in the fields and wooded areas surrounding Dallas, and at rifle ranges in that area... In most instances, the investigation has disclosed that there is no substantial basis for believing that the person reported by the various witnesses was Oswald."[21]

---

[20] CE 3001 — https://history-matters.com/archive/jfk/wc/wcvols/wh26/pdf/WH26_CE_3001.pdf
[21] Warren Report at 318

The Report continues, "The witnesses who claimed to have seen Oswald at the firing range had more than a passing notice of the person they observed. Malcolm H. Price, Jr., adjusted the scope on the individual's rifle on one occasion; Garland G. Slack had an altercation with the individual on another occasion because he was shooting at Slack's target; and Sterling C. Wood, who on a third date was present at the range with his father, Dr. Homer Wood, spoke with his father and very briefly with the man himself about the individual's rifle. All three of these persons, as well as Dr. Wood, expressed confidence that the man they saw was Oswald."[22]

So, according to the Warren Report, there were witnesses who say they saw Oswald at a shooting range, but the Commission did not believe them.

But what did the witnesses actually say? Let's start with the Woods.

Thirteen—year-old Sterling Wood was with his father Dr. Homer Wood at the Sports Drome shooting range when they saw a man who they claimed was Oswald.

On November 16, 1963, the Saturday before the assassination, Dr. Wood said his son was shooting next to a man with an unusual rifle that shot a "ball of fire."[23] Dr. Wood then told his son jokingly referencing the gun shooting the balls of fire used by the man next to him, "Watch out for the 105 Howitzer" and his son, Sterling, said, "Don't worry. It's only an Italian carbine."[24] Most of this man's shots were inside the target.

When Dr. Wood saw Oswald on TV after the assassination, he immediately told his wife that Oswald looked just like the man who was shooting next to their son at the range.[25] Dr. Wood decided to not mention it to his son to see if his son would first mention it. Thirty minutes later, Sterling said, "Daddy, is that the fellow that was sitting next to me out on the rifle range?"

Sterling Wood and his father Dr. Homer Wood both testified before

---

[22] Ibid.

[23] 10H 386, Dr. Homer Wood Testimony to Warren Commission

[24] Ibid.

[25] Ibid., 10H 387

the Warren Commission. During that testimony, Sterling added that he "asked the man if his rifle was a "6.5 Italian carbine with a four-power scope" and the man replied, "Yes."[26] Sterling also told the Commission that the man left the rifle range with another man in a newer model car. The boy identified a photo of Oswald and said that he was the same man he saw. Sterling was also shown a photo of the rifle and confirmed that it <u>was</u> the same rifle, but Sterling said the <u>sight</u> was different than the one he remembered seeing.[27]

So, a boy and his father testified that they saw Oswald shooting at a rifle range with a Carcano the weekend before the assassination of President Kennedy. One would think that this would be a compelling piece of evidence to use against Oswald, because it would establish that 1) he possessed a Carcano rifle, 2) he was an excellent shot with it, and 3) he practiced shooting at a rifle range only 6 days before the assassination. Even if the sight was different than what Sterling remembered, this should not have been reasonable grounds for the Warren Commission to give essentially zero weight to Woods's testimony. This bolsters the conclusion that the Commission wanted to stay away from any evidence, even if credible, that Oswald was impersonated shortly before the assassination.

In addition to the purported sighting by Woods, someone believed to have been Oswald at a shooting range was also seen by Malcolm Price and Garland Slack.[28] Price said that he saw the man on Saturday, September 28th at the Sports Drome shooting range. He drove a 1940 or 41 Ford and arrived alone, even though Oswald did not have a driver's license. The man asked Price to help him sight the weapon. Price actually fired the man's gun and helped him get his rifle sight zeroed in. He then gave the gun back to the man, who fired three shots, all of them in a tight pattern inside the bullseye.[29] Price says that he also saw the man again

---

[26] 10H 390–398, Sterling Wood Testimony to Warren Commission
[27] Ibid.
[28] Warren Report at 318
[29] Malcolm Price Testimony to Warren Commission, http://www.aarclibrary.org/pub-lib/jfk/wc/wcvols/wh10/pdf/WH10_Price.pdf

on October 12, October 13, and the Sunday before the assassination at Sports Drome.

Garland Slack says he saw Oswald at the Sports Drome on November 10 and November 17. He says that on November 17, Oswald was shooting at his rifle targets. Slack said that the type of gun he saw at the range had been cut off and was not the same one that he saw in the papers.[30]

Why does the Warren Report conclude that Oswald was not seen practicing with his rifle and that the Woods and others must have seen someone else? There are two primary reasons why the Commission rejected all testimony regarding Oswald at shooting ranges.

First, Oswald didn't have a car. So, he would have had to get a ride to a shooting range or take a bus. There's no evidence that he was on a bus with a rifle. But there is testimony from Sterling Wood that he departed in a car. If Oswald left in a car, then who was the person who drove him? If someone drove Oswald, that suggests that he was potentially working with others. Also, while at the Sports Drome, many witnesses stated that he was in the company of at least one Latino. That question did not need to be explored if the Commission determined that the man Sterling and Dr. Wood saw was not Oswald.

The second reason the Commission rejected the notion that Oswald was seen at shooting ranges has to do with timing. The days when Oswald was supposedly seen around Dallas at shooting ranges conflicts with the Warren Report's timeline for what Oswald was supposed to have been doing on those days. For example, there are some witnesses who say they saw Oswald at the shooting range when it is known that Oswald was in Irving with Ruth Paine, Marina, and his children. And one of the Oswald sightings occurred when Oswald was supposed to have been in Mexico City—according to the Warren Report. Clearly, the Warren Commission needed to stay away from these witnesses since it was so laser focused on Oswald visiting the Cuban and Soviet embassies in Mexico City.

---

[30] Garland Slack Testimony to Warren Commission, https://history-matters.com/archive/jfk/wc/wcvols/wh10/pdf/WH10_Slack.pdf

There is another critical detail from the Woods's Oswald sighting. The FBI collected 23 pounds of shells from the Sports Drome range to see if they could find any Carcano ammo. They did not find one single Carcano shell.[31]

The idea that Oswald ever had any practice at all with a rifle in Dallas comes from the Warren Commission testimony of Oswald's wife, Marina. In her first Commission interview in December 1963, Marina says that Oswald never left or returned to the home carrying a rifle. He never said that he was going to go shooting. He never went to shoot with the rifle to her knowledge.[32] She did admit that it was possible that Oswald went shooting without her knowledge when he was supposed to be in typing class.

At a Fort Worth Gun Store

On Friday, November 1, a man bought ammunition for his rifle at Morgan's Gun Shop in Fort Worth, Texas in a way that was memorable for those present. Witness Dewey Bradford told the FBI that the man was "rude and impertinent."[33] The man told Bradford that he had been in the Marine Corps. Bradford did not recall the caliber of ammo that the man bought. Later, when Bradford (and his wife and brother-in-law who were also with him) saw the photos of Oswald in Life magazine, all three of them agreed that the person they saw at Morgan's Gun Shop was Lee Harvey Oswald.[34]

Despite this FBI report, the Warren Report ignored the Morgan's Gun Shop incident. The Warren Report goes out of its way to address other instances of alleged Oswald sightings, but it never mentioned what Dewey Bradford saw at Morgan's Gun Shop.

---

[31] *CE 3049*

[32] *CE 1785 ; CE 1401, p. 286 ; E 1790; CE 1403*, p. 735, *Meagher* at 132

[33] FBI Report from San Antonio Office by John M. Kemmy, April 30, 1964; Warren Commission Exhibit Number 2129, WCH, Exhibits, vol. 24, p 704

[34] Ibid.

At a Car Dealership

On Saturday, November 9, 1963 (the day after the incident at Morgan's Gun Shop as discussed above), a young man entered the Lincoln-Mercury showroom near Dealey Plaza. He told car salesman Albert Guy Bogard that he was interested in buying a red Mercury Comet. He told Bogard that he didn't currently have any money, but "he said he had some money coming in within two or three weeks and would pay cash for the car." He said his name was Lee Oswald!

This man then test-drove the Comet on Stemmons Freeway at speeds of up to 75 to 85 miles per hour. After the test drive, Bogard's associate, Eugene Wilson, tried to convince the man to buy the car that day using credit. The man then said, "Maybe I'm going to have to go back to Russia to buy a car." Bogard asked the man for a phone number or address, and he refused to provide either. Bogard says he gave the man a card and wrote the name Lee Oswald down after the man refused to provide his phone or address.

Bogard says that after seeing pictures of Lee Harvey Oswald on television, he said he was positive that the Oswald who visited his dealership, went on a test drive, and said his name was Lee Oswald was the same man he saw on television in connection with the murder of President Kennedy.[35]

Bogard's claim about seeing this man who said he was Oswald and looked like Oswald is supported by assistant sales manager Frank Pizzo, and Eugene Wilson (who also interacted with the man). Another salesman Oran Brown recalled that he also wrote down the customer's name and that the name was Oswald. Brown's wife says he had a piece of paper that said Oswald on it before the assassination.[36]

The Warren Report specifically addressed Bogard's claim. It said that the man Bogard saw could not have been Lee Harvey Oswald because their descriptions didn't match, Oswald couldn't drive, and the

---

[35] Commission Exhibit 2969, pages 1–4, Statement by Albert Guy Bogard, December 11, 1963
[36] Warren Report at 321

stories of Pizzo, Wilson and Bogard did not match exactly regarding whether the man wanted to use credit to buy a car. The Warren Report also said that Oswald could not have visited the car dealership because the testimony of Marina Oswald and Ruth Paine make it clear that he was somewhere else that day.[37]

At the Red Bird Airfield

On the morning of Wednesday, November 20, 1963, three people arrived at Red Bird Airfield, south of Dallas. A heavy-set young man and young woman got out of the car and entered the office, leaving a second young man sitting in the right front passenger seat. The man and woman spoke to Wayne January, the owner of American Aviation Company, about renting a small airplane for the afternoon of Friday, November 22 so that they could go to the Yucatan Peninsula, which is near Cuba in Southeast Mexico.[38]

January suspected that the couple may have been trying to hijack the plane to Cuba, so he did not rent it to them.[39] As this couple left January's office, he took a good look at the man sitting in the front passenger seat of the car. A few days later, after President Kennedy was assassinated, January recognized the man who had stayed in the passenger seat on Wednesday morning as the same man accused of killing the president on TV—Lee Harvey Oswald.[40]

The FBI report that notes Wayne January's story says that January was unsure whether the individual was Oswald and that the incident happened in July of 1963—four months before the assassination—as opposed to two days before the assassination.[41] But author Matthew Smith interviewed January who said that the incident happened on the Wed-

---

[37] Ibid.
[38] James Douglass, JFK & the Unspeakable, p 243; Richard H. Popkin, The Second Oswald, p 92
[39] Popkin at 92
[40] Ibid.
[41] Wayne January, November 29, 1963, FBI Interview, reproduced in Matthew Smith, JFK: The Second Plot, pp. 272-73

nesday before the assassination and that he could identify Oswald "nine out of ten."

In Front of the Texas Employment Commission

Laura Kittrell worked for the Texas Employment Commission and interviewed Oswald on October 3, two weeks before he started working at the Texas School Book Depository. Then, on October 22, while Oswald was working at the School Book Depository, another person named Lee Oswald showed up for an interview.

According to a July 18, 1978, memo from HSCA investigator Gaeton Fonzi to HSCA Chief Robert Blakey, "Kittrell said that she later found that Oswald was already working at the Book Depository when he appeared for the last interview at the TEC. That is when she began to think how different Oswald looked the last time she saw him. She has concluded that the person she saw the last time wasn't really Oswald, but perhaps someone he sent in his place in order to maintain his unemployment claim."[42]

Kittrell said that the second time she saw Oswald (when we know the real Oswald was working in the School Book Depository), that "he looked the same. The same general outline and coloring and build, but there was something so different in his bearing. He was slouchy, he was kind of unkempt and very unmilitary looking. That was one thing about Mr. Oswald. He always looked very military, neat as a pin. And this fellow wasn't. And he had this peculiar way of laughing and talking so that people all over the room could hear him, and Mr. Oswald wasn't like that at all. She said that although she suspected the fellow might not have been Oswald at the time, she wasn't sure, and she didn't want to call him a liar and create a scene without being sure."[43]

According to an FBI report, the FBI tracked Oswald's return trip on a La Frontera bus from Mexico City to the border town of Nuevo Laredo

---

[42] July 18, 1978, Memorandum from HSCA investigator Gaeton Fonzi to Chief Counsel Robert Blakey
[43] Ibid.

on October 3, 1963. The report concluded that "it appears highly improbable that Oswald could have traveled [the 426 miles] from Laredo, Texas to Dallas, Texas in time to appear personally before the [Texas Employment Commission]."[44]

Exiting the Rear of the Texas Theater

We have another one of these potential double Oswald sightings at the Texas Theater. The mystery has to do with which exit Oswald was taken out of the theater by police after his arrest. There is also some confusion as to why some parts of the official record state that Oswald was discovered in the balcony—and not the main floor of the theater.

First, let's look at the exit scenarios. The official story, which I believe is correct, is that Oswald was taken out of the front door. There is a famous photo of Oswald struggling with police as he is taken out the front door—which resolves the issue alone.[45] Numerous statements from officers that day, including Sergeant Hill, also support the idea that Oswald exited the Texas Theater through the lobby and then the front door.[46]

But, if it isn't really disputed that Oswald went out the front door, then why are there two witnesses who say that they saw Oswald taken out the back door?

According to Butch Burroughs—the concessions guy who sold Oswald popcorn at 1:15—he saw a second arrest with the suspect taken out the back of the theater. In an interview with Jim Douglass, Burroughs said that the Dallas Police arrested "an Oswald lookalike" three or four minutes after they arrested Oswald and took him out the front.[47] Burroughs said he could see the second man just as well as he could see Oswald and that man, "Looked almost like Oswald, like he was his brother or something."

Bernard Haire—who owned Bernie's Hobby House, two doors down

---

[44] https://harveyandlee.net/Kittrell/Legat.htm

[45] https://time.com/3804560/an-end-to-conspiracy-rare-photo-of-lee-harvey-oswalds-arrest-suggests-why-hes-guilty/

[46] https://jfkwitnesses.omeka.net/items/show/265

[47] Douglass at 291

from the Texas Theater—also saw an arrest happen in the back of the Texas Theater. At first, Haire couldn't see what was happening because of the crowd. So, he went back through his store into the alley out back. The alley was full of police cars, but there were fewer spectators. There in that back alley, Haire witnessed what he thought for years was the arrest of Lee Harvey Oswald.[48] It wasn't until 1987 that Haire found out that Oswald had actually been taken out the front of the theater.

So, from the stories of Bernie Haire and Butch Burroughs, there is some evidence for the idea that another person who resembled Oswald was taken out the back door after being arrested. But is there any documentary evidence to support the idea of an Oswald lookalike? Sort of.

In the official homicide report for J. D. Tippit, it says, "Suspect was later arrested in the balcony of the Texas Theater."[49] Dallas police detective LD Stringfellow said in a letter to Captain W.P. Gannaway that is now in the Dallas City Archives that, "Oswald was arrested in the balcony of the Texas Theater."[50]

In The Parking Lot of El Chico Restaurant Just After Oswald Was Arrested

TF White was an employee of Mack Pate's Garage in Oak Cliff, near the Texas Theater. At 2 p.m. on the day of the assassination and Tippit murder, White saw a red 1961 Falcon drive into the parking lot of the El Chico restaurant across the street from his garage. The man appeared to be trying to hide.

White then walked across the street to investigate—thinking that this man could be the assassin who shot the president. White stopped ten to fifteen feet from the car. He could see the driver was wearing a white t-shirt. The driver then turned toward White and looked him in the eyes. White then retreated because he feared the man would shoot him. But he did write down the license plate: Texas PP 4537. White was watching

---

[48] Ibid., p 292
[49] Ibid.
[50] Ibid.

TV with his wife that night and recognized Lee Harvey Oswald on television as the person he had made eye contact with who was hiding in the Falcon across the street.[51] White was not aware of the fact that Oswald was already in police custody at the time he saw the man hiding in the Falcon.[52]

Normally, this would be one more Oswald sighting that could not be connected with anything else. However, the fact that White wrote down the license plate made it possible that the owner of that vehicle could be tracked down.

When Dallas newscaster, Wes Wise, was giving a talk to the Oak Cliff Exchange Club at the El Chico Restaurant on December 4, 1963, the talk was attended by White's boss, Mack Pate. Pate told Wise about White seeing the Oswald lookalike in the Falcon around 2 p.m. and provided him with the license plate number. When Wise gave the plate numbers to an FBI contact, the license plate was traced back to a 1957 Plymouth owned by Carl Amos Mather. An FBI Agent then drove to Mather's house and found the same license plate that White said was on a red Falcon on Mather's 1957 Plymouth.[53]

So, who was Carl Mather? According to the FBI, Mather did high security communications work for Collins Radio, a CIA contractor. For example, Carl Mather personally installed the special electronic equipment in Vice President Johnson's Air Force Two plane.[54] Mather refused to speak to the FBI. Instead, his wife spoke to the FBI. When she did, she shared the bizarre information that Mather was a close friend of slain Officer J. D. Tippit. In fact, they were so close that Tippit's wife called the house to tell them that he had been shot on the day it happened.[55]

Eventually, Carl Mather consented to an interview with the House Select Committee on Assassinations. However, his agreement to an interview was conditioned upon him being granted immunity. He told the

---

[51] Ibid., p 293

[52] The Warren Report says that Oswald was on the way to the police station in the police car at 1:51 pm. Warren Report at 179

[53] Douglass at 294–295

[54] Ibid.

[55] Ibid.

HSCA that he could not explain how his license plate could possibly have been on a Falcon with another driver who looked like Oswald.[56]

Letters to the Russian Embassy and the FPCC

There are several instances of Oswald writing letters to the Soviet Embassy in Washington, D.C. There is evidence that the last letter, sent on November 9, 1963, appears to be a forgery. On November 26, 1963, the Soviet Embassy sent a Top Secret/Highest Priority telegram to Moscow regarding this letter. The telegram claims that the letter was "clearly a provocation" and was likely a forgery since it was typed, unlike previous letters from "Oswald."[57]

Soviet ambassador Anatoly Dobrynin said in the telegram, "One gets the definite impression that the letter was concocted by those who, judging from everything, are involved in the President's assassination."[58]

As previously noted in this book by Paul Bleau, Oswald's first letter to the FPCC had very few errors. A number of researchers, including Warren Commissioner Hale Boggs were convinced that he was aided.

---

[56] Ibid., p 296

[57] A. Dobrynin, Cipher Telegram, Special no. 2005, November 26, 1963, Russian original and English translation, National Archives, College Park, Maryland.

[58] Ibid.

At the Atomic Energy Museum

On July 26, 1963 visitor log of the Atomic Energy Museum of Nashville we can find the name of Oswald with USSR written beside it.

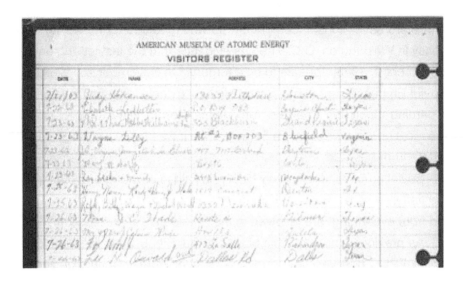

The person who signed the registry just before Oswald is certain Oswald was not there: "Mr. WOOD stated that he had observed LEE HARVEY OSWALD on several television broadcasts and had seen his picture in numerous newspapers and magazine articles and to the best of his remembrance, he never saw LEE HARVEY OSWALD at the American Museum of Atomic Energy on July 26, 1963."[59]

Buying a Beer in Dealey Plaza

On the morning of the assassination around 8:30 a.m., Fred Moore, who worked at the Jiffy Store at 310 South Industrial in Dallas, says that he sold two bottles of beer to Lee Oswald. According to a December 2, 1963, FBI Report, Moore said that he asked for identification for him to

---

[59] https://jfkcountercoup.blogspot.com/2010/10/lee-h-oswald-at-atomic-energy-museum.html?m=0 and CD1066 p. 612-613 – FBI Gemberling Report of 28 May, 1964 and Oswald-Russia/Cubahttp://www.maryferrell.org/mffweb/archive/viewer/showDoc.do?docId=11462&relPageId=624

buy the alcohol and the man provided an ID that said Lee Oswald or H. Lee Oswald. He recalled that the birthdate was 1939. He is sure of the name because he told his boss that "Lee Oswald was a good Jewish name."[60]

Moore said that this man then came back about thirty minutes later and bought candy. This strange combination of beer and candy in the morning is another reason Moore remembered the man. When shown a photo of Oswald, Moore said that the man he saw was thinner in the face than Oswald in the photo.

The FBI followed up with Moore's boss, George Worthington, to confirm what Moore said. Worthington confirmed that Moore had mentioned something about the man at the time and that Worthington was entering the back of the building as the man identified as Oswald was leaving the front. The time of the citing according to Worthington would have been around 9:30 a.m. (but this would be for the second trip for the candy only).

The distance from the Texas Schoolbook Depository Building to the Jiffy Store is about 15 minutes on foot. There is no record of Oswald leaving his work at the Depository on the morning of the assassination.

Seen By Silvia Odio When Oswald Was Supposed to Be In Mexico

Lee Harvey Oswald is known by many mainstream historians as a Marxist who actively defended Fidel Castro and handed out pamphlets supporting Fair Play for Cuba Committee. However, the testimony of Silvia Odio to the Warren Commission, as corroborated by her sister, Annie Odio portrays an Oswald who is ardently anti-Castro, to the point of working with anti-Castro Cubans to *kill* Castro.

Odio said that a man she later identified as Lee Harvey Oswald visited her apartment in Dallas in late September 1963. He was with two Latin men who said they were soliciting funds for JURE, the more peace-

---

[60] https://www.maryferrell.org/showDoc.html?do-cId=95645#relPageId=128&search=fred_moore%20jiffy%20oswald

ful anti-Castro group led by Manolo Ray, with whom Odio's father was a close friend.[61] Odio's mother and father were both political prisoners in Cuba at the time. She said the three men wanted her to introduce them to the Cuban underground because they assumed she would have connections because of her parents.[62] Odio's sister Annie also believes that the man who was at their apartment door was Oswald.[63]

Odio said that Leopoldo, the man who did all of the talking, introduced the American man as "Leon Oswald."[64] Leopoldo called Odio the next day and mentioned that "the American, Leon" was "kind of nuts" and "he told us we don't have any guts, you Cubans, because President Kennedy should have been assassinated after the Bay of Pigs, and some Cubans should have done that, because he was the one that was holding the freedom of Cuba actually."[65] He also told her that Leon was "an excellent shot" and had been in the Marines. Leopoldo then said, "it's so easy to do it," referring to assassinating the president.[66]

The Warren Report determined that Odio's story was not accurate, without providing a rationale. But, the apparent reason was that Odio's story conflicted with the timeline of the Warren Report for Oswald's whereabouts. The Warren Report stated that Oswald was in Mexico City at the time Odio claims he was visiting her, around September 26, 1963.

Odio's credibility would later be challenged by the fact that she blacked out when she found out about the assassination of the president and required hospitalization. This, combined with her regularly seeing a psychiatrist, Dr. Burton Einspruch, led people to believe that she was not a reliable witness. Dr. Einspruch told the FBI that Odio had "the kind of personality… where she would not lie, she could be — has a degree of suggestibility -- that she could believe something that did not really trans-

---

[61] Warren Commission Testimony of Sylvia Odio, Vol 11, p 370, http://www.aarcli-brary.org/publib/jfk/wc/wcvols/wh11/pdf/WH11_Odio.pdf
[62] Ibid., p 372
[63] Ibid., p 371
[64] Ibid.
[65] Ibid.
[66] Ibid.

pire."[67] However, Dr. Einspruch also told the FBI that Odio is a thoroughly credible person.

Additionally, an FBI report dated September 26 said that a man named Loran Hall claimed to be the person who was in Dallas at Odio's apartment and that he was with Lawrence Howard and Larry Seymour. However, the FBI interviewed both Howard and Seymour and both men denied having ever met Odio. Loren Hall later retracted his statement.[68]

The House Select Committee on Assassinations found Odio's testimony to be "essentially credible" and that "there is a strong probability that one of the men was or appeared to be Lee Harvey Oswald."[69] This means that either Oswald was being impersonated in Mexico as noted below, or Oswald was being impersonated in front of Silvia Odio and her sister.

Leonard Hutchison's Grocery Store

Leonard Hutchison, who owned a grocery store in Irving, Texas only eight blocks from Ruth Paine's House, said that he saw Oswald at the store four or five times.[70] Hutchison said the Oswald visits always occurred between Monday and Friday, not on the weekends when Oswald would normally visit Marina at Ruth Paine's home.

In late October 1963, Hutchison claimed to see Lee and Marina Oswald in the store between 6:45 and 7:30 on a Wednesday night, speaking a foreign language that he believed to be Russian, and accompanied by an elderly woman.[71] He recognized Lee and Marina from coverage on television.

We know that Oswald did not stay at the Paine home on any Wed-

---

[67] United States House of Representatives, House Select Committee on Assassinations, Sworn Testimony of Dr. Burton C. Einspruch, July 11, 1978 (JFK Document 010069) 1979, p. 35-36.

[68] HSCA Report, Volume 10, p 21 https://history-matters.com/archive/jfk/hsca/reportvols/vol10/pdf/HSCA_Vol10_AC_2_Odio.pdf

[69] Ibid., p 31

[70] Warren Commission Testimony of Leonard Hutchison, p 327, https://history-matters.com/archive/jfk/wc/wcvols/wh10/pdf/WH10_Hutchison.pdf

[71] Ibid., p 330

nesday evenings in late October. That means that this Oswald and Marina couple lookalike, speaking Russian, with an old lady matching the description of Oswald's mother, Marguerite, doesn't fit the record. It appears that Oswald, and his wife and mother, were being impersonated.

Hutchison also said that Oswald came in to the store alone and attempted to cash a check for $189 on Friday, November 8th. The amount of the check was higher than the store's limit of $25, so Hutchison told the man that he was unable to cash the check.[72] It is possible that Oswald could have been at Hutchison's store to cash that check because it was on a Friday afternoon. However, we have no evidence of anyone writing Oswald a personal check for $189, which is the 1963 equivalent of almost $1,896 today.

Changing a Postal Forwarding Order in New Orleans When Oswald Was In Dallas

On October 11, 1963, postal form 3546, Notice to Change Forwarding Order, was sent from New Orleans to Dallas. The purpose was to forward mail from a New Orleans PO Box to Ruth Paine's home address in Irving, Texas. However, as Warren Commission counsel Wesley Liebeler pointed out, we know that Oswald was in Dallas on October 11, not New Orleans.[73] Postal Inspector (and FBI Informant), Harry Holmes told Liebeler that Oswald probably mailed the form to someone in an envelope in New Orleans, and that person probably then mailed the form from New Orleans. But there is no evidence of that actually happening. It is merely speculation from Holmes. We have no evidence of anyone receiving mail for Oswald and then sending it from New Orleans. Who would have done that for him? It is more likely that someone else mailed the postal forwarding order.

---

[72] Ibid., p 338

[73] Warren Commission Testimony of Harry Holmes, p 529 - https://www.history-matters.com/archive/jfk/wc/wcvols/wh7/pdf/WH7_Holmes_2nd.pdf

Applying for a Job at the Southland Hotel One Week Before the Assassination

Exactly one week before the day of the assassination, Hubert Anderson Morrow, the manager of the Southland Hotel Garage, says Oswald asked him for a job in the morning.[74] Morrow recalled that the man asked him how high the parking lot building was and whether it would provide a good view of downtown Dallas. He also remembered that he had written down "Lee Harvey Osburn" and the man then corrected him and said "My name is Oswald." The man waited for 45 minutes to be interviewed by Morrow's boss, and then left at 7:50am. Morrow's story is supported by testimony from two other employees, Emmett Montgomery and Charlie Dabbs.[75]

While this person could theoretically be Oswald because there is no way to prove when Oswald left his rooming house that morning. We have no other evidence to support that Oswald was looking for another job at the time. Thus, the Southland Hotel garage story is a bit of an enigma.

In Washington D.C.

A key witness to seeing an unhinged Oswald near Washington's Willard Hotel was Bernard Thompson, the chauffeur for the Secretary of Agriculture Orville Freeman. He described an agitated Oswald or Oswald lookalike as acting bizarrely and unhinged on September 27, 1963, to a police officer. His behavior is reminiscent of the unstable, visibility seeking events involving Oswald or his double, that took place in New Orleans and Dallas during the months leading up to the assassination. After the homicide, this dossier was passed on to none other than Secret Service field officer Floyd Boring who interviewed Thompson on December 3 and who Secret Service expert, Vince Palamara, considers to be a leading

---

[74] Dallas Municipal Archives, Box 1, Folder 11, Item 10; Box 4, Folder 5, Item 50; DPD Interviews of Hubert Anderson Morrow, Emmett Montgomery, and Charlie Dabbs, 1/23/64 and 1/27/64
[75] Ibid.

suspect in the security failures in Dallas. Oswald is referred to in the report as Harvey Lee Oswald.[76]

While in Russia

From October 1959 through June of 1962, it is an established fact that Lee Harvey Oswald was in the Soviet Union.[77] Thus, it is very strange that there are numerous appearances of Lee Oswald in the United States at the same time.

On January 20, 1961, two men visited the Bolton Ford dealership in New Orleans. They spoke with assistant manager Oscar Deslatte about purchasing ten Ford Econoline Trucks. Deslatte then told his boss, Fred Sewell, about these two men who wanted to buy ten trucks and said that they represented the "Friends of Democratic Cuba." Sewell testified and provided the bid form from this interaction. The individuals associated with Friends of Democratic Cuba were Joseph Moore and Lee Oswald. The bid form itself only says "Oswald" and does not have a first name. However, Sewell testified in the Clay Shaw trial that the man did identify himself as "Lee Oswald."[78] Thus, we have yet another incident of Oswald being impersonated while he was in the Soviet Union.

What is perhaps more interesting about the Friends of Democratic Cuba is that, according to their Louisiana articles of incorporation, one of their incorporators was private investigator and former FBI man Guy Banister, who is known for renting offices adjacent to the 544-Camp Street address printed on flyers used by Oswald in New Orleans while Oswald was handing out flyers for Fair Play for Cuba.[79] Another incorporator was Gerard Tujague, who briefly employed Oswald in 1955 and 1956 at the Sanlin Building in New Orleans.[80]

---

[76] Who's Who in the Secret Service, Palamara p. 276 and 277 (United Secret Service Treasury Department report)

[77] Warren Report at 390

[78] https://harveyandlee.net/Misc/Bolton.html

[79] Articles of Incorporation, Friends of Democratic Cuba, January 9, 1961.- https://harveyandlee.net/Misc/Bolton.html

[80] CE 2228 - http://www.aarclibrary.org/publib/jfk/wc/wcvols/wh25/pdf/WH25_CE_2228.pdf

Perhaps it is a coincidence that two of the incorporators of this anti-Castro Cuban group had other ties to Oswald and also tried to rent trucks using Oswald's name when we know that he was in Russia. But, if it is, then how do we explain all the other Oswald sightings? They can't all be coincidences.

Indeed, the director of the FBI, J. Edgar Hoover himself, wrote a memo to the Office of Security at the State Department on June 3, 1960, acknowledging the possibility that someone was impersonating Oswald. Hoover said, "Since there is a possibility that an imposter is using Oswald's birth certificate, any current information the department of state may have concerning [Oswald] will be appreciated."[81]

On March 31, 1961, State Department official Edward Hickey wrote a memo to fellow official John White saying, "It has been stated that there is an imposter using Oswald's identification data."[82]

James Spencer, who worked at a car dealership in New Orleans, said that sometime between February and August of 1961, he met with Lee Oswald about purchasing a 1958 Chevrolet.[83] During the second meeting, he had coffee with this man claiming to be Oswald. Spencer said that the man made quite an impression on him because he "talked at length about Cuba and appeared to be very enthusiastic about Castro." Spencer recognized the man on television when he saw Lee Harvey Oswald and he recognized the name, but he could not place it initially. Spencer then found a business card that said "Lee Oswald, Magazine St." in Spencer's handwriting.[84]

Ray Carney was a news correspondent in Dallas during the Cuban Revolution, during which time he was contacted by an anti-Castro Cuban who attempted to recruit him as a pilot and wanted his assistance in getting publicity. Carney then obtained names of pilots who wanted to volunteer for the anti-Castro force and provided them to the Cuban general and to the FBI. Carney says that he was also contacted by Lee Harvey

---

[81] Memo from J. Edgar Hoover to Office of Security, Department of State, June 3, 1960, FBI File No. 105–82555

[82] Memo from Edward Hickey to John White, March 31, 1961, JFK No. 102–526

[83] FBI Report, December 14, 1963, S. A. Leonard Johnson

[84] Ibid.

Oswald in the latter part of 1960 or the early part of 1961. This person asked Carney for the names of the volunteers and expressed pro-Castro sympathies to Carney in an effort to convince him that Castro was right. Carney refused to give this man any names.[85]

In summary, during the time when Oswald was in Russia, there are seven separate claims noted above of Oswald being impersonated. What is especially notable about many of these impersonation attempts is that they did not just use Oswald's name, but they also expressed support for Cuba, leaving one with the impression that there was an on-going intentional impersonation of Oswald.

In Mexico City

As previously discussed, two investigators for the House Select Committee on Assassinations, Dan Hardway and Edwin Lopez, wrote a report titled Analysis of Lee Harvey Oswald's Activities in Mexico City.[86] One of the specific questions this report, which came to be known as The Lopez Report, attempts to answer is whether Oswald was impersonated while visiting the Cuban and Soviet consulates in Mexico City during the fall of 1963.

After interviewing Mexican citizens who could have knowledge of Oswald's visit and reviewing documents provided by the CIA and FBI regarding Oswald's trip to Mexico City, The Lopez Report concluded that "[t]here is not enough evidence to firmly conclude that someone did impersonate Oswald in Mexico City. On the other hand, the evidence is of such a nature that the possibility cannot be dismissed."[87]

What led Lopez and Hardway to reach the conclusion that they could not determine whether or not Oswald had been impersonated?

---

[85] ALLEGATIONS BY RAYMOND B. CARNEY, NEWS DIRECTOR OF RADIO STATION KBEA, MISSION, KANSAS, THAT HE BELIEVED HE WAS IN CONTACT WITH LEE HARVEY OSWALD DURING MAY, 1961; Assassination Records Review Board Record Number 104-10004-10009

[86] The Lopez Report—https://historymatters.com/archive/jfk/hsca/lopezrpt_2003/pdf/LopezRpt_2003_7_Analysis.pdf

[87] Ibid., p 413

Oswald's signature is on an application for a Cuban in-transit visa. This fact points to Oswald's likely presence at the Cuban Consulate in Mexico City. However, the Cuban Consulate did not require that such applications were signed in person and allowed applicants to take blank applications with them to be returned later.[88]

Thus, even though Oswald signed the application, it is possible that he was not physically present to sign the document. Still, Silvia Duran, said that she was certain that Oswald signed the document in front of her.[89] But, according to the Lopez Report, "Oswald's signature on the Cuban visa application, however, does not by itself rule out the possibility that someone impersonated Oswald in contacts with the Cuban and Soviet Embassies."[90]

Someone, whom the CIA later identified as Oswald, visited the Cuban Consulate three times in Mexico City and the Soviet Consulate two times.

On September 27, 1963, at 4:05 p.m., the CIA intercepted a phone call via a tapped phone line from Silvia Duran to the Soviet Consulate. The call was about an American (who the CIA says was Oswald) who was seeking an in-transit visa to Cuba. We know that this American would have already been to the Soviet Consulate once at that point because Duran requested the name of the Soviet official who previously dealt with the American. Duran then received a call back from the Soviet Consular staff twenty minutes later who stated that Oswald did previously visit the Soviet Consulate.[91]

The next day, September 28, at 11:51 a.m., Duran called the Soviet Consulate again and this time put the American on the phone to speak to the Soviets. The American said he had just been to the Soviet Consulate but would be returning there again.[92]

There are several reasons to believe that Oswald was indeed impersonated in Mexico City and that the person who the CIA said was

---

[88] Ibid., p 405–406
[89] Ibid., p 406
[90] Ibid.
[91] Ibid., p 407
[92] Ibid.

Oswald, and who represented himself as Oswald to the Cubans and Soviets, may have been an impersonator.

First, Sylvia Duran's description of Oswald did not match Lee Harvey Oswald's true physical appearance. She said he had blonde hair. Her non-matching description of the physical attributes of the man she said was Oswald was deleted from later reports and never mentioned in the Warren Report.[93]

There were multiple CIA "pulse" cameras pointed at both the doors of the Cuban Consulate and the Russian Embassy. The CIA, through the testimony of David Atlee Phillips said that the cameras were not working at the time and that there were no photos to provide. However, after looking at all of the evidence provided by the CIA about the history of the cameras, the HSCA concluded, "The Committee believes that it is probable that the pulse camera was in operation on the days that Lee Harvey Oswald visited the Cuban Consulate."[94] Thus, according to Lopez and Hardway, the CIA's failure to turn over photographs from the cameras may demonstrate that the CIA was intentionally hiding the photos. The Lopez report says, "The committee notes the possibility, but does not conclude, that the missing production from the pulse camera and the LI/LYRIC base has something to do with the possibility that someone impersonated Oswald in Mexico City."[95]

Members of the HSCA spoke to Cuban leader Fidel Castro and obtained a photo from the Cuban Consulate of the person who identified himself as Oswald at the Cuban Consulate in 1963. This photograph looks nothing like Lee Harvey Oswald.[96] Further, there is another photograph that the CIA provided to the FBI on November 23, 1963, which shows a different man who looks nothing like Oswald or the person visiting the Cuban Consulate.

Second, the CIA intercepted a phone call on September 28, 1963, suggests that Oswald was impersonated. Duran insists that neither

---

[93] Ibid., p 408–409
[94] Ibid., p 138
[95] Ibid., p 410
[96] https://harveyandlee.net

Oswald nor any other American visited the Cuban consulate on September 28th—the day that the CIA overheard a call from the Cuban consulate to the Soviet consulate where the American purporting to be Oswald was put on the phone and actually spoke to the Soviets. This means that Duran was either lying or the person who visited the consulate on September 28th was not Oswald.[97]

However, there are reasons to believe that Duran was truthful—and that there was no actual visit made by Oswald to the Cuban Consulate on September 28th. First, the wiretapped conversation was linked to Oswald because of the notations of the CIA translator. The translator noted that the caller spoke, "terrible, hardly recognizable Russian." According to the CIA translator, that same man who spoke terrible Russian called the Soviet consulate again on October 1st and identified himself as Lee Oswald and said that he had previously spoken to them on September 28th (the call that Duran says didn't happen). The report of Oswald speaking poor Russian is inconsistent with what all of the other evidence shows about his Russian speaking, which is that he was a very fluent speaker of the Russian language having lived there for a few years.[98]

There were also three calls that appear to be from Oswald to the Soviet Consulate, which were completely in Spanish. However, Oswald most likely did not speak Spanish.[99]

The FBI heard the tape of Oswald speaking with the Soviet Consulate from the Cuban Consulate. It determined that Oswald was being impersonated and that the voice on the recording did not belong to Oswald. The tape that had this phone call recording later went missing.

The idea that Oswald was impersonated in Mexico City is supported by the FBI. A report written from Agent Belmont to the Deputy Director of the FBI, Clyde Tolson, said, "the Dallas Agents who listened to the tape of the conversation allegedly of Oswald from the Cuban Embassy to the Russian Embassy in Mexico and examined the photographs of the

---

[97] Lopez Report, p 410
[98] Ibid.
[99] Ibid., p 413

visitor to the Embassy in Mexico and were of the opinion that neither the tape nor the photograph pertained to Oswald."[100]

Additionally, a memo from J. Edgar Hoover to the chief of the Secret Service, James Rowley said, "The Central Intelligence Agency advised that on October 1, 1963, an extremely sensitive source had reported that an individual identified himself as Lee Oswald, who contacted the Soviet Embassy in Mexico City inquiring as to any messages. Special Agents of this Bureau, who have conversed with Oswald in Dallas, Texas, have observed photographs of the individual referred to above and have listened to his voice. These Special Agents are of the opinion that the above-referred-to-individual was not Lee Harvey Oswald."[101]

The day after the assassination, the head of the FBI, J. Edgar Hoover, spoke to President Johnson about Oswald's alleged trip to Mexico City. Hoover told Johnson that "[w]e have up here the tape and the photograph of the man who was at the Soviet Embassy using Oswald's name. The picture and the tape do not correspond to this man's voice, nor to his appearance. In other words, it appears that there was a second person who was at the Soviet Embassy down there."[102]

Thus, the FBI believed - and had evidence - that Oswald was being impersonated as of the day after the assassination.

Boarding a CIA Plane from Dallas, Texas to Roswell, New Mexico

Air Force Sergeant Robert G. Vinson claims to have a front seat to what became of the alleged Oswald lookalike after the assassination. Vinson was stationed in Colorado, but had business in Washington, at Andrews Air Force Base and was looking to catch a ride back to Colorado on a military plane on November 22, 1963. Vinson was notified to board a C54 cargo plane that was headed to Lowry Air Force Base in Denver. The

---

[100] The Lopez Report, Addendum to footnote 614
[101] Ibid., citing November 23, 1963, memo from Hoover to Rowley
[102] Phone Call between J. Edgar Hoover and President Johnson, November 23, 1963, 10:01 a.m.

plane was unmarked, except for a logo of an egg-shaped earth crossed by white grid marks, which Vinson later learned was a logo for the CIA.[103]

Vinson boarded the empty plane without signing a flight log, which was typically required. Two men with coveralls boarded the plane and walked to the front without speaking to Vinson. At 12:29, the pilot announced that the president had been shot.[104] Immediately after that announcement, the plane banked left and changed course to go to Dallas.

In Dallas, the plane landed in a rough, sandy area alongside the Trinity River. It was not a runway. Vinson thought it looked like a road that was under construction. The plane did a U-turn and kept the engines running. Then, the cargo door opened. Vinson saw two men running toward the plane from a jeep. One of the plane's pilots opened the passenger door. The two men boarded the plane, passing Vinson's seat without looking at or speaking to him.[105] The men carried nothing and sat right behind the cockpit. They did not speak to each other or the other pilots. The taller of the two men was 6 to 6'1', weighing 180 to 190 pounds and looked Latino. Vinson thought he was Cuban.

The shorter man was Caucasian between 5'7" to 5'9" and weighing 150 to 160 pounds. When Vinson later saw the video of Lee Harvey Oswald under arrest, he identified the man as being identical to Oswald.[106] The passengers quickly exited the plane when it landed. Vinson did not recognize where he was and was later told that he had landed at Roswell Air Force Base. He was not allowed to leave the base because it was on alert. Vinson was finally allowed to leave and returned to Colorado, where he told his wife about the incident. He didn't tell anyone else because he didn't believe it was safe after Oswald was killed by Ruby.

In the spring of 1964, Vinson's neighbors informed him that the FBI had been questioning them about what kind of people the Vinsons were and what they talked about. Shortly after that, Vinson was forced by his

---

[103] James P. Johnston and Jon Roe, Flight from Dallas: New Evidence of CIA Involvement in the Murder of President John Kennedy (2003), p. 19
[104] Ibid., pp 25, 28
[105] Ibid., p 26
[106] Ibid., pp 22–28

Air Force boss to sign a new secrecy agreement. Vinson's wife was also required to sign a secrecy agreement for the first time.[107]

On November 25, 1964, Vinson was ordered to go to Washington for a special project and call a phone number when he arrived there. This led to five days of psychological and physical tests that Vinson was subjected to at the CIA headquarters in Langley. CIA offered him a job, which Vinson turned down. He was then allowed to go home.[108]

Three months later, the Air Force assigned him to a top-secret CIA project at Area 51, the Blackbird SR 71 spy plane. Vinson did not have any special skills that would qualify him for this. He received a salary from the Air Force and monthly cash payments from the CIA during this time. No one from the Air Force or CIA ever spoke to Vinson specifically about the flight from Dallas. Nevertheless, the implication of him being sent to CIA for 5 days of questioning, then turning down a job with CIA, only to be assigned to CIA later, makes it appear that the CIA was employing Vinson to keep an eye on him, given the extremely damning information that he had.

CONCLUSION

In this chapter we have established clear and convincing evidence of numerous incidents of people impersonating Lee Harvey Oswald, a summary of the impersonation episodes is set out below.

- Dallas Deputy Sheriff, Roger Craig's under oath testimony of an "Oswald" running out of the back of the Texas Schoolbook Depository Building and getting into a Nash Rambler in Dealey Plaza;
- Shooting at the Sports Drome rifle range on multiple occasions;
- Being arrested out of the back door of the Texas Theater and later seen nearby in a Red Falcon with a license plate tied to a CIA contractor;

---

[107] Ibid., pp 32-33
[108] Ibid., pp 33-36

- Trying to charter a private jet for the afternoon of November 22, 1963;
- At the Texas Employment Commission with Laura Kittrell;
- In written letters to the Soviet Embassy;
- As a hitchhiker with curtain rods in a paper bag and questions about shooting the president driven from an area on the highway near Oswald's rooming house to the Texas School Book Depository Building two days before the assassination;
- Trying to buy vehicles on behalf of an anti-Castro Cuban group;
- In a memorandum from J. Edgar Hoover to the State Department while Oswald was in Russia;
- Visiting an anti-Castro Cuban with other anti-Castro Cubans,
- Mailing a Forwarding Notice from New Orleans when he was supposed to be in Dallas
- At a grocery store with Marina on a day when he was not in Irving,
- Applying for a job at the Southland Hotel Parking Garage a week before the Assassination
- In a phone call from J. Edgar Hoover to Lyndon Johnson after the assassination;
- In Washington D.C.;
- In Mexico City at the Soviet Embassy and the FPCC; and
- Flying from Dallas to Roswell on a CIA plane.

Without a doubt, Oswald was impersonated. The real question is why was Oswald being impersonated? In many of these instances, Oswald was being made to look unhinged and pro-Castro. Clearly, Oswald was not a drifter nor the lone nut the WC claims he was. Without any other plausible explanation being offered, one must ask, was Oswald being framed?

CHAPTER 4

OSWALD COULD NOT HAVE BEEN ON THE SIXTH FLOOR WHEN THE SHOTS WERE FIRED

BY MATT CRUMPTON

STATEMENT

ACCORDING TO THE Warren Report and those who defend it, Lee Harvey Oswald shot President Kennedy at 12:30 p.m. from the southeast corner of the sixth floor of the Texas School Book Depository Building. But there is ample evidence in the record and from later witness statements to demonstrate that Oswald could not have been in place to fire the shots.

EXECUTIVE SUMMARY

The two witnesses whom the Warren Commission claims saw Oswald (Howard Brennan and Charles Givens) do not establish that Oswald was on the sixth floor in the alleged Sniper's Nest at the time the shots were fired. Brennan was too far away and failed to identify Oswald at the police station and Givens only claims to have seen Oswald on the sixth floor thirty minutes before the shooting, and that was after he changed his original story. Other witnesses who saw a man in the window on the sixth—either saw multiple people or could not identify Oswald as the man in the window.

Officer Marion Baker's testimony and subsequent FBI reconstructions demonstrate that Oswald was on the second floor approximately one minute and eighteen seconds after the last shot was fired. Oswald likely had a coke bottle in his hand when he interacted with Baker, which would have taken even more time for him to purchase and keep the FBI's timeline. Carolyn Arnold claims that she saw Oswald on the first floor at 12:25. Also, after the shots were fired, Victoria Adams and Sandra Styles went down the same stairs Oswald would have had to traverse at the same time he would have been going down those stairs and they did not see him.

INTRODUCTION

First, let's discuss the background of what the School Book Depository was and what Oswald's job was there. The Depository, now known as the Dallas County Administration Building, is a 7-story brick building that looks out on Dealey Plaza—a large open park-like area where several roads come together. The purpose of the Depository was to act as a multi-floor warehouse for storing school textbooks and fulfilling orders for those books.

Oswald applied for a job at the School Book Depository on October 15, 1963, and began working as a temporary employee the next day.[1] He was an order filler, which meant that he reviewed orders of textbooks and then obtained those textbooks from wherever they were located within the School Book Depository.[2] The fifth, sixth, and seventh floors of the building housed the overflow stock of books. The orders that Oswald filled were mostly on behalf of publisher Scott, Foresman. The Scott, Foresman books were all on the first floor and the sixth floor. So, it would not have been out of the ordinary for Oswald to be seen on the sixth floor.

---

[1] Oswald's Job Application; https://texashistory.unt.edu/ark:/67531/met-apth190981/m1/3/
[2] Warren Commission Testimony of Roy Truly, WC Vol. 3, p 213

Howard Brennan and Charles Givens Do Not Establish
That Oswald Was in Place

If Oswald were firing shots on the sixth floor at 12:30 p.m., then there should be some witnesses that put Oswald in that position around the same time. On the other hand, if there are witnesses who say that Oswald was somewhere else around 12:30, that would support Oswald's innocence.

The Warren Report relies upon two key witnesses to place Lee Harvey Oswald on the sixth floor at 12:30: Howard Brennan and Charles Givens.

Pipefitter, Howard Brennan was leaning against a 4-foot-high retaining wall on the corner of Houston and Elm, directly across the street from the Schoolbook Depository Building. He checked his watch, and it was 12:18 when he arrived at that street corner.[3]

Several minutes later, Brennan noticed a man in the window of the southeast corner of the sixth floor. According to Brennan, when he looked up at the window from the street corner, he thought that the man was 5' 10", white, slender, with dark brown hair, and between 25 and 35 years old. When Brennan looked up after the first shot was fired, he said he saw the same man with a rifle.[4]

On the night of the assassination, at a lineup of suspects, Brennan said about Oswald, "He looks like the man, but I can't say for sure," failing to identify Oswald when given the chance.[5] Brennan had a good look at a man in the window, who he says took his time and fired the rifle. But when he was asked that night at the police station to identify the man, he could not identify Oswald as being the man he saw. Brennan later told the Warren Commission that he *could have* identified Oswald that night, but he just didn't.[6]

---

[3] Posner, Case Closed, p 248
[4] Ibid.
[5] Ibid.
[6] Ibid.

Brennan—who is the only witness in the Warren Report who puts Oswald specifically with a gun in his hands and on the sixth floor—was standing on the ground from across the street, looking up at a face he had never seen before on the sixth floor. It would be a challenge to reliably identify a person's facial features from that distance and height.

After Howard Brennan, the second witness that is heavily relied upon by the Warren Report to put Oswald on the sixth floor at the time of the shooting is Charles Givens—a co-worker of Oswald's. In Givens' sworn affidavit from the day of the assassination, he says that he worked on the sixth floor until 11:30. He then went downstairs to go to the bathroom and to have lunch. There was no mention of Oswald at all in Givens' original affidavit.[7]

Then on February 13, 1964, in an FBI report written by Special Agent Robert Gemberling, additional information was provided that Givens didn't mention in his affidavit on the day of the assassination. The report said, "[Givens] was on the sixth floor until about 11:30 a.m. when he used the elevator to travel to the first floor. As he was going down on the elevator, he stated an individual known to him as Lee, yelled to him to close the gates on the elevator so Lee could have the elevator return to him to the sixth floor."[8]

Givens' initial testimony to the FBI did not support Oswald's guilt because of Oswald asking for the elevator to be sent back up so that he could come down—which would mean that he wouldn't be on the sixth floor at 12:30 as far as Givens knew. When Givens was interviewed by the Warren Commission a few months later on April 8, 1964, he added that he forgot his cigarettes on the sixth floor and went back up around noon to get them. It was then that he saw Oswald near the southeast corner window of the sixth floor.

The final testimony from Givens to the Warren Commission was, "I came downstairs, and I discovered that I left my cigarettes in my jacket pocket upstairs. When I got back upstairs, [Oswald] was on the sixth floor ... in that vicinity ... toward the window up front where the shots were

[7] CE 2003, p. 27
[8] CD 735, FBI Gemberling Report of 10 March 1964

fired from. I was getting ready to get on the elevator and asked Oswald if he was coming downstairs. He said, "No."[9]

Givens' story to the Warren Commission is in conflict with what his co-worker, Bonnie Ray Williams, told the Warren Commission. Williams said that he heard Oswald ask Givens to send the elevator back up so Oswald could come down for lunch.[10] This makes a big difference. If Oswald is asking Givens to send the elevator down around 11:45, then he could plausibly be on the sixth floor at noon. But, if Oswald is asking Givens to send the elevator back up as Williams claims, that makes it less likely that Oswald could have gotten back into position on the sixth floor by 12:30.

One final, but important note on Givens: According to an FBI report of February 13, 1964, Lt. Jack Revill of the Dallas PD approached Robert Gemberling of the FBI and said that since he had dealt with Givens on a drug charge, he thought Givens may change his story for money.[11] On May 13, 1964, Revill told the Warren Commission that he encountered Givens on the day of the assassination and Givens said he saw Oswald on the *sixth floor*. Lt. Jack Revill named two corroborating witnesses Detective Brian and Captain Fritz of the Dallas PD—both of whom testified before the Warren Commission and were not asked about Givens seeing Oswald on the sixth floor around noon.[12]

To recap, the two primary witnesses who the Warren Report relies on to put Oswald on the sixth floor of the schoolbook depository are not very persuasive. Howard Brennan, the primary witness, who looked up from across the street and saw Oswald with a gun in the southeast corner of the sixth floor window, failed to identify Oswald in a lineup that day (even though he told the Warren Commission that he could have). Meanwhile, Charles Givens, Oswald's co-worker, told the Warren Commission he left Oswald alone on the sixth floor at 11:55, which is a change from

---

[9] *Warren Commission Testimony of Charles Givens, Vol. 6*, p 349
[10] Meagher, Accessories After the Fact at p 65; Warren Commission Testimony of Bonnie Ray Williams, 3H 168
[11] *CD 735, FBI Gemberling Report of 10 Mar 1964*, p 296
[12] Sylvia Meagher, The Texas Observer, 13 August 1971

his initial affidavit, and is hardly incriminating for Oswald, who still could have come downstairs at any time after 11:55.

Other Witnesses Saw either Multiple People or People Who Did Not Fit Oswald's Description

Amos Euins, who was 15 years old at the time, said he saw what looked like a pipe in a high window of the Schoolbook Depository near the southeast side. He then realized it was a gun after shots were fired. He could not identify the race of the man or any other characteristics, except that the man had a bald spot on his head.[13]

Carolyn Walther says she saw a man in a white shirt leaning out of the southeast corner window with a rifle in his hands pointed down. The man had blonde or light-brown hair and was looking down the street where the motorcade was about to come around the corner. She also says that she saw a second man behind the shooter in a brown suit coat.[14]

Another witness, Lillian Mooneyham, told the FBI she saw a man behind a sixth floor window of the Schoolbook Depository about 4 to 5 minutes after the shots were fired. According to the FBI Report, she, "observed the figure of a man standing in a sixth floor window behind some cardboard boxes. The man appeared to be looking out the window, but was standing slightly back from it.[15]

The police did not reach the depository to search for the assassin or evidence until around 1 p.m.—about 30 minutes after shots were fired.[16] This means that whoever it was that she saw would have likely been involved in the assassination. The Warren Commission did not interview Lillian Mooneyham.

Officer Baker's testimony helped to establish a timeline that, according to the Warren Report, put Oswald on the second floor within 1 minute

---

[13] Testimony of Amos Euins, WC, Vol. 2, p 204
[14] Douglass, JFK and the Unspeakable, at p 276
[15] FBI Report re Lillian Mooneyham, January 10, 1964
[16] Warren Report, p 79

and 18 seconds of the shots being fired. If Mooneyham is right, and there was—in fact—a man on the sixth floor four to five minutes after the shots were fired, we know that Oswald could not have been that man because he had already had his encounter with Officer Baker by that time and would have been on his way out of the building.

Arnold Rowland and his wife, Barbara, saw a light-skinned man with dark hair with a rifle on the sixth floor at 12:15.[17] But he saw the man in the southwest corner (the other side of the building from the sniper's nest). He also saw another man whom Rowland identified as being black and about 55-years old in the southeast corner of the sixth floor (where the sniper's nest was) who was there from 12:15 until about 12:25.[18] Rowland described the man as "practically bald."

If Oswald were the assassin, he would have to be on the sixth floor by 12:15. But, as we will see, there is a witness who puts Oswald on the second floor at 12:25, making it impossible for Oswald to have been in place.

Bonnie Ray Williams and the Planned Trade Mart Arrival Time

Bonnie Ray Williams finished his fried chicken lunch on the sixth floor minutes before the assassination. Williams said Oswald asked for an elevator to be <u>sent back up</u> when he saw Oswald on the fifth floor at 11:45 because Oswald was coming down for lunch (as Givens had also initially told the FBI). Williams had his lunch on the sixth floor in front of the 4th window, about 40 feet away from Oswald's alleged "sniper's nest." He says he could not see anything in the southeast corner because the books were stacked so high.[19]

The big question about Bonnie Ray Williams is "what time did his chicken lunch really end?" According to his FBI interview, he was done with lunch at 12:05.[20] Williams tells the Warren Commission (and they

---

[17] *Warren Commission Testimony of Arnold Rowland, Volume II, p. 176*
https://www.jfk-assassination.net/russ/testimony/rowland_a.htm
[18] Ibid.
[19] Meagher, p 35
[20] DiEugenio, Reclaiming Parkland, at p 97

accept) that the time was actually 12:20 when he was done with lunch.

What we know from Williams's testimony is that he did not see or hear anyone else on the sixth floor while he was eating. Assuming the Warren Report time of 12:20 for the end of Williams's lunch is correct, that means that if there was an assassin on the sixth floor, they must have arrived *after* Williams left—or the assassin must have been very sneaky, walked quietly, and hid behind boxes. But, if Oswald arrived on the sixth floor after Williams left, he would not have left himself much time to get set up for the shot.

The motorcade schedule called for the president to be at the Trade Mart by 12:15, which would have put him in Dealey Plaza around 12:10. If Oswald came up after Williams's lunch, that already makes him 3 minutes late to take the shots if the motorcade is on time.[21] If Oswald were really intent on killing JFK, he would not likely have risked the chance to miss his only shot at killing the President.

Officer Baker Demonstrates that Oswald Was on the Second Floor One Minute and Eighteen Seconds After the Shots Were Fired

After the shots were fired, Officer Marion Baker runs to the Schoolbook Depository building and encounters Oswald on the second floor. When asked whether Oswald appeared out of breath, he said, "No." When asked if Oswald was calm and collected, Baker responded, yes.[22] Truly, who was with Baker, said, Oswald, "didn't seem to be excited or overly afraid or anything."[23]

When the FBI ran tests to determine how long it would take Baker to get from where he was when the shots were fired to the second floor where he saw Oswald, they found it was 1 minute 18 seconds. When they did the same test for Oswald, the FBI found that Oswald would have

---

[21] Wikipedia Article About Timeline of Assassination—https://en.wikipe-dia.org/wiki/Timeline_of_the_John_F._Kennedy_assassination#President_Kennedy's_Texas_trip_schedule).

[22] DiEugenio, Reclaiming Parkland, p 193

[23] Douglass, JFK and the Unspeakable, p 286

had to do all he allegedly did and get to the second floor break room in 1 minute and 14 seconds.[24]

Baker says that Oswald appeared normal, calm, and collected—behavior you would not expect from someone who has just sprinted from killing the president on the other side of the sixth floor and had been standing there for only 4 seconds—the difference between the 1 minute 18 seconds it would take Baker and the 1 minute 14 seconds it would take Oswald.

Notably, Officer Baker's statement about the second floor interaction with Oswald did not appear in his initial affidavit. In the affidavit, Baker said, "As we reached the third or fourth floor, I saw a man walking away from the stairway. I asked Mr. Truly if he worked there and he said yes. It was a white man who was 5′ 9″, 165, about 30 years old.[25] To further confuse matters, Baker later told author Gary Savage that he actually saw Oswald on the first floor and that the investigator from Washington contacted him, but he guessed that they weren't interested in what he had to say.[26]

Witnesses Who Prove Oswald Was Not on the Sixth Floor at 12:30

In addition to Euins, Walther, and Rowland, there are other witnesses who tend to prove that Oswald could not have been in place in the southeast corner of the sixth floor to fire the shots, and then run back down to the first or second floor without being seen by any other co-workers.

Chief among those witnesses is Oswald himself. When Oswald was asked what part of the building he was in at the time the president was shot, he said that he was having his lunch about that time on the first floor. Oswald also said, "He went to the second floor where the Coca Cola machine was located and obtained a bottle of Coke for his lunch."[27]

---

[24] Meagher, Accessories After the Fact, p 70
[25] Affidavit of Marrion Baker, November 22, 1963—https://tex-ashistory.unt.edu/ark:/67531/metapth337201/m1/1/.
[26] *Gary Savage, JFK: First Day Evidence,* p 365
[27] Douglass at p 285

More importantly, Carolyn Arnold, a secretary at the School Book Depository, told the FBI on November 26, 1963, that on the day of the assassination, she saw Oswald standing in the hallway between the front door and the double doors on the first floor *a few minutes before 12:15*.[28] Arnold knew Oswald because he was in the habit of stopping by her desk on the second floor asking for change in nickels and dimes.[29]

Fifteen years later, Dallas reporter Earl Golz tracked down Arnold, who was still working at the School Book Depository. She told him that she "saw Oswald in the second floor lunchroom as she was on her way out of the Depository to watch the presidential motorcade."

When asked what Oswald was doing on the second floor when she saw him, Arnold said, "I do not recall that he was doing anything. I just recall that he was sitting there in one of the booth seats on the right-hand side of the room as you go in. He was alone as usual and appeared to be having lunch. I did not speak to him, but I recognized him clearly."[30]

To make things even more interesting, according to Golz, the FBI did not print the correct time she said she saw Oswald. She told the FBI that she saw Oswald on the *first floor* at about *12:25 pm*! She was surprised at what the FBI said her testimony was when she saw it.

Arnold's statement that she told the FBI she really saw Oswald on the first floor at 12:25 is a big deal. It would make it highly unlikely that Oswald shot the president on the sixth floor five minutes later. It was 15 years later when Golz approached Arnold. So, it's not a fresh statement after the event. But Golz, the reporter, was the one who approached Arnold. So, she was not out seeking attention or fame. Also, how does a person forget something like that? What reason would Arnold have to be lying? She had nothing to gain.

Warren Report defenders note that Arnold's co-worker, Virgie Rackley, says she accompanied Arnold outside the building and did not see Oswald any time that day. But this does not affect Arnold's testimony because all Rackley's testimony says is that she was outside with Arnold.

---

[28] Warren Report, CD 5, p 41
[29] Douglass, p 285
[30] Ibid.

Arnold says she saw Oswald before she went outside with Rackley and did not assert that Rackley also saw Oswald.[31]

Carolyn Arnold was never asked to testify before the Warren Commission.

Finally, let's look at what Victoria Adams and Sandra Styles have to add to what we know about Oswald's whereabouts within the book depository around the time JFK was shot. Adams was a book depository employee who testified that she went down the same stairs that Oswald would have had to traverse from the fourth floor to the first floor within one minute of the shooting and she did not see Oswald, Truly or Baker. The Warren Report concluded that Adams must have been mistaken about the details of her timing and ultimately discounted her testimony.[32]

According to Adams, she watched the motorcade from an open window on the fourth floor of publisher Scott, Foresman with her friend Sandra Styles, who was not interviewed by the Warren Commission.[33]

On its face, Adams's testimony tends to show that Oswald could not have come down the stairs from the sixth floor because Adams would have seen him or at least heard footsteps in the stairwell. But, because Adams did not see or hear Oswald on the stairs, her testimony puts a wrench in the official story because Oswald would be expected to be heard or seen as he descended the only stairs in the building.

Nevertheless, the Warren Report specifically addressed why it found Adams's testimony to be unreliable. It says that after Adams got down the stairs, she noticed employees Bill Shelley and Billy Lovelady and told them what she saw in the fourth floor window. Here's the kicker: the *Warren Report says the two men went to the rail yard after the shooting and then returned to the TSBD before Adams saw them.* So, if they had time to go to the rail yard, Adams must be mistaken in what she said because she would not have seen them immediately after since they were at the rail yard.[34]

---

[31] Commission Document 706, p 8

[32] *Warren Report* at 154

[33] *Testimony of Victoria Adams, WC, Vol. 6*, p 388

[34] *Warren Report at 154*

But, contrary to the Warren Report's theory of what happened, in Shelley and Lovelady's affidavits, there is no mention of them running to the railroad yards after the shots—which one would expect to be included. It wouldn't have been very hard for either man to write, "I went over to the railroad yards?" if they actually did go to the railroad yards.

In later interviews, both Victoria Adams and Sandra Styles say that they left the rear of the office within seconds, "before the limousine disappeared beneath the underpass." Neither Styles nor Adams saw Lovelady or Shelley when they got to the first floor.[35] Adams says that she did get a chance to correct her deposition and she did not remember the part about seeing Shelley and Lovelady being in there. "If it had been in there, since I didn't see them, I would have edited it out."[36]

There is even more confusion over Adams's affidavit and initial interview. In her November 25, 1963, FBI interview, Adams does not mention Lovelady or Shelley. And when writer Barry Ernest asked if Sandy Styles saw William Shelly or Billy Lovelady on the first floor, she said no she had not. But, in February 1964, Adams was visited by Dallas police officer, Jim Leavelle, who said there was a fire at the Dallas police department and her file was burned. He told her that the police needed to take her statement again. It was in this statement that Adams is first on the record as saying she saw Shelley and Lovelady.[37]

To recap, Adams and Styles both say that they went down the stairs immediately after the shots were fired. There is only one set of stairs in the building. So, they would have been going down the same staircase as Oswald at about the same time.

While Adams Warren Commission transcript does state that she saw Shelley and Lovelady, there are serious issues with the original documents to authenticate the legitimacy of her testimony. Researcher Barry Ernest went to the National Archives looking for the original stenographic copy of Adams's testimony that is consistent with the final Warren Report story. He found it. But the document is unsigned. Ernest asked the

---

[35] *Barry Ernest, The Girl on the Stairs,* pp. 36, 219
[36] Ibid., p 215
[37] Ibid., p 75-76

National Archives why it was not signed, and they said there are 2 versions of the documents and only the second version was signed after there were corrections. Then he asked for the tape recordings of the interview of Adams. Three weeks later he found out that *the Adams tapes are all missing and cannot be found.*[38]

One more thing on Adams, her story that she went downstairs immediately after JFK was shot is supported by testimony from Dorothy Garner, Adams' Supervisor. In a letter from Martha Jo Stroud, an assistant U.S. Attorney in Dallas , to its general counsel, J. Lee Rankin, it says "Miss Garner, Miss Adams' supervisor, stated this morning that *after* Miss Adams went downstairs, she (Miss Garner) saw Mr. Truly and the policeman come up."[39]

If the Warren Report's story had been correct, then Dorothy Garner would have seen Mr. Truly and Officer Marion Baker BEFORE Adams went downstairs. But Garner says it was the other way around—Adams went downstairs first.

The ultimate conclusion of the Warren Report was that Adams left the fourth floor "several minutes after Oswald."[40] This conclusion is inconsistent with what Adams, Styles, and Dorothy Garner have said. Additionally, the missing audio tapes call into question whether Adams actually said what the Warren Commission claims she did during her deposition.

Oswald With a Coke?

Oswald tells police during interrogations that he was on the first floor at the time of the shooting eating a Cheese sandwich (though he had gone up to the second floor to get a Coke). Oswald also said he was drinking a Coca Cola on the second floor in the lunchroom when the officer saw him.[41] But what does the record say about the Coke?

---

[38] DiEugenio at 95–96
[39] Letter from Martha Jo Stroud to J. Lee Rankin, June 2, 1964
[40] *Warren Report,* p 154
[41] *Oswald testimony summary, 11/22/63—Captain Fritz*

Almost a year after the assassination, on September 23, 1964—**Officer Baker** signed an affidavit that he "saw a man standing in the lunchroom drinking a coke." In the affidavit, Baker crossed out "drinking a coke" and initialed the change.[42] Mrs. R. A. Reid, a clerical supervisor, saw Oswald walk through the clerical office on the second floor at 12:32 holding a bottle of Coca Cola.[43] Warren Commission senior counsel, Albert Jenner Jr. said on WNYC TV on December 23, 1966, that Oswald was "drinking a bottle of Coke when the first policeman on the scene saw him."[44]

Would Oswald have time to get a coke after shooting the President and running down the stairs and not be out of breath? Why would he get a Coke if he had just shot the president? The Warren Commission decided Oswald had just barely enough time, after he shot the president to hide his rifle in the opposite corner of the sixth floor and then run down four flights of stairs into the lunchroom. Yet, according to Baker and Truly, Oswald was composed when they saw him—and, looking at the record, he likely had a Coke in his hand.

EVIDENCE

From an evidentiary standpoint, the only evidence that links Oswald to being in place on the sixth floor at the time shots were fired is the testimony of Howard Brennan to the Warren Commission (which is somewhat undercut by Brennan's failure to identify Oswald on the day of the assassination at the Police station).

The strongest evidence that exonerates Oswald is the FBI report stating that Carolyn Arnold saw Oswald at 12:15 on the second floor. Arnold later told reporter Earl Golz that she had told the FBI she saw Oswald at 12:25 on the first floor. Warren Commission testimony from Victoria Adams, which is supported by statements from Sandra Styles and a letter from Dorothy Garner tends to show that Oswald could not

---

[42] *CE 3076*
[43] *James Douglass, JFK and the Unspeakable*, p 286
[44] Meagher at p 226

have gone down the stairwell from the sixth floor to the second floor during the time the Warren Report alleges.

If a trial had been held each of these witnesses would have an opportunity to be examined and cross-examined under oath. All their statements would be accepted into evidence to be weighed by the finder of fact.

COUNTERPOINTS

The counterpoints put forth against the arguments presented in this chapter are as follows:

- Brennan was nervous about telling the truth at the police lineup because he thought there may have been other people involved who would have not been captured and would kill him. This argument does not change the distance from which Brennan viewed the person in the window or resolve the inconsistencies in Brennan's story about how he saw the man in the window standing.

- Fingerprints were found on 3 of the boxes in the sniper's nest. But Oswald worked in the building and specifically worked on the sixth floor. So, one would expect that his fingerprints would be on some of the boxes.

- Oswald's palm print was found on the rifle in evidence, which was found on the sixth floor, which shows that Oswald must have been the one who fired it. There are serious issues with the chain of custody of the palm print that was found on the rifle. The Dallas police officer who processed the rifle for prints, Lt. J.C. Day, took no action to protect the palm print when he sent it to the FBI. He did not tell the FBI that there was a palm print. The FBI firearms expert could not find a palm print. And then, days later, the palm print arrived at the FBI on an index card from Dallas. Lt. Day claimed that he lifted the print and then sent it to the FBI, but FBI agent Vincent Drain disputes Lt. Day's claim.

- Victoria Adams says she saw Bill Shelley in her affidavit. But, if she saw Shelley, he had gone to the train tracks according to what he and Billy Lovelady said. This would affect the timeline. Adams' Warren Commission testimony says that she did see Bill Shelley. She insists to author Barry Ernest that she did not see Bill Shelley and Billy Lovelady when she came down the stairs and that this was added to her transcript. However, she did sign the transcript.

CONCLUSION

Clearly, if Oswald were alive to stand trial for President Kennedy's murder, there would have easily been enough doubt raised through the testimony of Arnold Rowland, Carolyn Arnold, Victoria Adams, Sandra Styles, Dorothy Garner, that puts a reasonable doubt as to whether Oswald could have been in place on the sixth floor at 12:30.

The testimony of Adams was dismissed by the Warren Commission. Arnold and Styles were both completely ignored by the Commission. Their stories are at least as credible as the Warren Report. Even if you believe that Arnold was lying to Earl Golz and she saw Oswald at 12:15 and not 12:25, if that had been true, then Oswald could not have been the man Arnold Rowland saw holding a gun on the sixth floor at 12:15 because he was eating lunch on a lower floor.

Whether or not Oswald had a Coke in his hand when Baker saw him, the Warren Report testimony from Officer Baker and Truly was that Oswald was calm and not out of breath when standing on the second floor. It is unlikely that someone could shoot the President in one corner of the building, run to the other corner of the sixth floor to hide the gun, and then run down the stairs and be neither seen nor heard by a single witness (even though Styles and Adams were in the stairwell and Daugherty was next to it on the fifth floor)—only to encounter a police officer about 4 seconds later (according to the FBI's reconstructed timeline) and not be out of breath.

In addition, Baker later corrects what the Warren Report said and says that he saw Oswald on the *first floor* and saw someone else on the fourth floor who. Truly said worked there, which was ignored by the Warren Commission. Carolyn Arnold also says she saw Oswald on the first floor having lunch—though she says the Warren Commission changed her testimony to the second floor. The stories that Baker and Arnold say they told the FBI match what Oswald himself said he was doing at the time of the shooting—eating lunch on the *first floor*.

Charles Givens second story (as opposed to his initial story) merely puts Oswald on the sixth floor 30 minutes before the shooting. Howard Brennan did not identify Oswald when given the chance in a lineup and he was looking up 6 floors to see him. Brennan's testimony stands alone and is not enough to overcome the other witnesses putting Oswald on lower floors at the time, or at least not fleeing from the sixth floor.

The testimony of Rowland, and Walther establishes that there was someone with a rifle on the sixth floor of the School Book Depository building. But Walther and Rowland testified to seeing two men together at the same time and Lillian Mooneyham says there was someone on the sixth floor four or five minutes after the shots were fired. The HSCA's review of the James Powell photo also suggests that someone was moving the boxes shortly after shots were fired.

If these claims are true, then the Warren Report conclusion that Oswald was the lone gunman cannot be.

CHAPTER 5

JACK RUBY WAS ON A MISSION

BY PAUL BLEAU

STATEMENT

JACK RUBY'S CONNECTIONS, his behavior in and around the assassination, and his statements leave no doubt that his motive to kill Lee Harvey Oswald was to eliminate him so that he could not expose the conspiracy to kill President Kennedy. Ruby was connected to the Mafia. He stalked Oswald for two days before murdering him. He received assistance in getting to Oswald moments before the hit. The Warren Commission withheld information about Ruby.

INTRODUCTION

The Warren Commission concluded that the murders of JFK, Officer J. D. Tippit and Lee Harvey Oswald within 48 hours were perpetrated by two lone assassins: Lee Harvey Oswald and Jack Ruby.

Concerning Ruby, the Warren Commission stated the following:

The Commission has found no evidence that Jack Ruby acted with any other person in the killing of Lee Harvey Oswald;

The Commission believes that the evidence does not establish a significant link between Ruby and organized crime;[1]

The Commission concluded that Ruby entered the basement un-

---

[1] *WC Report appendix 16,* page 801

aided, probably via the Main Street ramp, and no more than 3 minutes before the shooting of Oswald;[2]

Ruby was never involved in pro- or anti-Castro Cuban activities;

Rumors of a relationship between Ruby and Oswald have proven groundless;

That testimony by Seth Kantor that he saw Jack Ruby and exchanged with him at Parkland Hospital right after JFK was taken there was not credible.

Over and above this, according to the Warren Commission, the motive for killing Oswald was limited to wanting to spare Jackie Kennedy the ordeal of going through a trial and later was shifted to temporary insanity caused by anguish over JFK's murder.

Later investigations and research into Jack Ruby completely dismantled the Warren Commission assessments of him and led to but one conclusion: Oswald could not be permitted to speak, and Jack Ruby was the guy chosen to take him out.

EVIDENCE

Burt Griffin and Leon Hubert Put a Fly in the WC Ointment

Lisa Pease, in an *August 1995 Probe article*,[3] gives a good summary of the memos written by assistant counsels to the Warren Commission Burt Griffin and Leon Hubert who were tasked with investigating Ruby:

---

[2] Ibid, page 219
[3] https://www.kennedysandking.com/john-f-kennedy-articles/gunrunner-ruby-and-the-cia

"The most promising links between Jack Ruby and the assassination of President Kennedy are established through underworld figures and anti-Castro Cubans, and extreme right-wing Americans."[4]

Two months later, Griffin and Hubert wrote another memo to the Commission, significantly titled "Adequacy of the Ruby Investigation," in which they warned, "We believe that a reasonable possibility exists that Ruby has maintained a close interest in Cuban affairs to the extent necessary to participate in gun sales or smuggling."

Ruby had talked about it himself while in jail, reportedly telling a friend, *"They're going to find out about Cuba. They're going to find out about the guns, find out about New Orleans, find out about everything."[5]*

Tales of Ruby running guns to Cuba abounded in the FBI reports taken in the first weeks after the assassination, yet neither the Warren Commission nor the House Select Committee pursued those leads very far. Griffin and Hubert expressed concern over this, saying that *"neither Oswald's Cuban interests in Dallas nor Ruby's Cuban activities have been adequately explored."*

Hubert and Griffin expressed in their memo of May 14 to Rankin that *"we believe that the possibility exists, based on evidence already available, that Ruby was involved in illegal dealings with Cuban elements who might have had contact with Oswald. The existence of such dealings can only be surmised since the present investigation has not focused on that area."* They expressed concern that *"Ruby had time to engage in substantial activities in addition to the management of his Clubs"* and that *"Ruby has always been a person who looked for money-making 'sidelines'."* They even

---

[4] Memo to Warren Commissioners dated March 20, 1964
[5] Appendix 10, Volume 8 HSCA report, p 162; Jack Ruby, in jail after a murder conviction, as reported by a visiting Carousel Club employee, Wally Weston

suggested that since the Fort Worth manufacturer of the famous "Twist Board" Ruby was demonstrating the night after the assassination had no known sales, and was manufactured by an oil field equipment company, that *"the possibility remains that the 'twist board' was a front for some other illegal enterprise."* But what Griffin and Hubert kept coming back to is that there was *"much evidence"* that Ruby *"was interested in Cuban matters"*, citing his relationship to Lewis McWillie; his attempted sale of jeeps to Castro, his reported attendance of meetings *"in connection with the sale of arms to Cubans and the smuggling out of refugees";* and Ruby's quick correction of Wade's remark that Oswald was a member of the Free Cuba Committee, a group populated with such notables as Clare Booth Luce, Admiral Arleigh Burke, and CIA journalistic asset Hal Hendrix: *"Bits of evidence link Ruby to others who may have been interested in Cuban affairs."*

Richard Schweiker and the HSCA Demolish the
WC Ruby Persona

Senator Richard Schweiker (Church Committee) indignantly expressed the following: *"J. Edgar Hoover writes, yes, we did have a relationship with Mr. Ruby and he acted as our informant. Now who said that at the time of the Warren Commission report? Did anybody ever imply that Jack Ruby was a confidential informant for the FBI? Nobody breathed that. That was classified."[6]*

One of the many takedowns of the Warren Commission by the HSCA was the following: The committee had other troubling conclusions: *Neither Lee Harvey Oswald nor Jack Ruby were the loners depicted by the Warren Commission, and were involved in relationships that could have matured into a conspiracy.[7]*

---

[6] *JFK Revisited,* page 22
[7] https://www.archives.gov/research/jfk/select-committee-report/part-1c.html (under page 180 section)

Ruby's Mob Connections

From his early days in Chicago to the time of the assassination, Ruby was always involved in illegal activities including narcotics, prostitution and gambling. He belonged to a Mafia group, known as the Yiddish Connection.[8] Dallas County Sheriff Steve Guthrie told the FBI that he believed Ruby *"operated some prostitution activities and other vices in his club"* since living in Dallas.[9]

While the Warren Commission did concede that Ruby was friendly *"with numerous underworld figures,"* the HSCA underscored a lot more, including his 1946-47 links to a group represented by Mafioso Paul Jones who attempted to use bribery of enforcement operatives to help a Chicago gang with links to Capone take over racketeering in Texas. Ruby, who may not have been significantly involved in the bribery attempt, does come across as a small-timer, eager to make inroads to the made men and well connected.[10] Ruby's links with the mob and aspirations to become a respected member seem to have strengthened somewhat over time.

Robert Blakey, who led the HSCA investigation, is one of numerous investigation insiders who believe there was a conspiracy. Up to recently he believed it to be strictly a mob job:[11]

ABC News: *In your book you point the finger squarely at Carlos Marcello and his organization. Why would he want to kill Kennedy?*

Blakey: *Carlos Marcello was being subject to the most vigorous investigation he had ever experienced in his life, designed to put him in jail. He was in fact summarily, without due process, deported to Guatemala. He took the deportation personally. He hated the Kennedys. He had the motive, the opportunity and the means in Lee Harvey Oswald to kill him. I think he did it through Oswald.*

---

[8] The Israel Times Nov. 2013— The Jew who Killed JFK's Killer.
[9] Warren Commission, Volume XXII:CE 1251—FBI report
[10] HSCA Appendix to Hearings—Volume IX-vi
[11] ABC News in 2003 interview of Robert Blakey

ABC News: *How central is Jack Ruby's murder of Oswald to your understanding of this case?*

Blakey: *To understand who killed President Kennedy and did he have help, I think you have to understand what happened to the assassin of President Kennedy, Lee Harvey Oswald. I see Jack Ruby's assassination of Lee Harvey Oswald as a mob hit.*

This is in direct contradiction to the Warren Commission. The Warren Commission portrayed, wrongly I think, Jack Ruby as a wild card who serendipitously got into position to kill Oswald. I think in fact he stalked him. I can show you from the Warren Commission's evidence that he tried to get into where he was being interrogated, number one. That he tried to get in where there was going to be a lineup, number two. That he was seen around the garage, where he was announced that he was going to be moved. And we know, from Jack Ruby himself, that he had a gun with him at the time of the lineup.

I believe that Ruby was able to get in to kill Oswald through the corrupt cooperation of the Dallas P.D. that he was let in through a back door and he was given an opportunity to kill Oswald. I see that, therefore, as a mob hit. And if that's a mob hit, there is only one reason for it, and that is to cover up the assassination of the president himself. You kill the killer.

ABC News: *Since you believe that Lee Oswald shot the president, and you also believe that Carlos Marcello was behind the assassination, what connections do you point to between Oswald and Marcello?*

Blakey: *I can show you that Lee Harvey Oswald knew, from his boyhood forward, David Ferrie, and David Ferrie was an investigator for Carlos Marcello on the day of the assassination, with him in a courtroom in New Orleans. I can show you that Lee Harvey Oswald, when he grew up in New Orleans, lived with the Dutz Murret family (one of Oswald's uncles). Dutz Murret is a bookmaker for Carlos Marcello.*

I can show you that there's a bar in New Orleans, and back in the "60s, bars used to have strippers and the strippers" circuit is from Jack Ruby's strip joint in Dallas to Marcello-connected strip joints in the New Orleans area. So, I can bring this connection. (Note: Dutz Murret had retired two years before the assassination).

Ruby and Trafficante

Since they did not know about the CIA-Mafia plots to kill Castro, maybe the Commission did not think Santo Trafficante, one of the leading mobsters of his era, was a person of interest. But Trafficante was one of the three Mafiosi the CIA contacted in order to do away with Fidel Castro (the other two were John Roselli and Sam Giancana). There were reliable reports, from more than one source (including British journalist John Wilson Hudson), that Ruby visited Trafficante while he was imprisoned by Castro at Tresconia Prison in late 1959. One eyewitness even said that he saw Ruby serving the mobster a meal.[12]

Another witness said that on this trip to Cuba, Ruby was also seen with Lewis McWillie. McWillie was a former manager of Trafficante's Tropicana gambling hotel in Havana. Ruby actually shipped handguns to McWillie in Cuba. By all accounts, Ruby idolized McWillie; and would do anything for him.[13]

The HSCA speculated that Ruby's trips to Cuba were as a courier for the mob: *"Based on the curious nature of the one-day trip to Cuba via Miami and the existence of a third trip to Cuba, vacationing was probably not Ruby's sole reason for traveling to Cuba,"* the committee concluded.

The HSCA was unable to positively link Ruby to Trafficante or the

---

[12] Michael Benson, Who's Who in the JFK Assassination, pages 455-56.
[13] Ibid., p 272

Tresconia camp, yet it stated, *"There was considerable evidence that a meeting did take place."[14]*

The chart below is used to *showcase Trafficante's links with CIA, Mafia and Cuban exiles of interest.* No fewer than six for certain and two plausibly are directly linked to Oswald and are also connected to Trafficante.

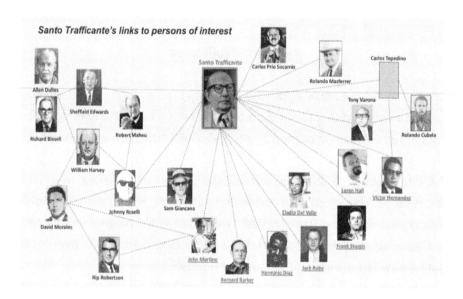

Santo Trafficante's links to persons of interest

Suspicious Phone Calls

The HSCA also analyzed Ruby phone calls during the weeks leading up to the assassination.[15] Not only do they expose a frenzy of growing activity... They reveal a number of suspicious calls.

Among calls that should of set off alarm bells: 6 calls in September to mobster and Trafficante contact Lewis McWillie; a twelve-minute October 26 call with powerful underworld bondsman, Irwin S. Weiner. Weiner was closely connected to Kennedy-hating Hoffa and Giancana; on October 30th he called Nofio Pecora who was a heroin smuggler and

---

[14] https://history-matters.com/archive/jfk/hsca/re-portvols/vol9/html/HSCA_Vol9_0086b.htm HSCA Appendix to Hearings—Volume IX, page 164

[15] HSCA Appendix to Hearings—Volume IX, pages 191 to 196

associate of Carlos Marcello; on November 7, he spoke for 17 minutes with Hoffa associate Barney Baker; On November 8 Ruby called Dusty Miller who was also connected to Hoffa and many other Mafiosi, and then again with Baker for fourteen minutes; Several days later he contacted San Francisco gambling kingpin Frank Goldstein; Eva Grant told the Warren Commission that Ruby contacted Mafia assassin and Giancana Lieutenant Lenny Patrick during the summer of 1963. Ruby's excuse was he had a union problem with dancers, but why would he be calling gangsters so far away if that was a local issue?

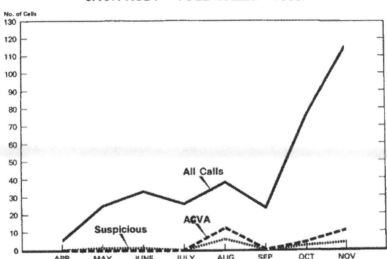

JACK RUBY - TOLL CALLS - 1963

One of Dallas's most notorious hoodlums according to the HSCA was ex-con James Henry Dolan who was connected closely to both Trafficante (for whom he performed an enforcement mandate) and Marcello. Dolan, ignored by the Warren Commission, was also friendly with Ruby since at least 1957 and a contact of Jim Braden, a crook who was detained for questioning in Dealey Plaza after the assassination.[16]

Here is just one of the HSCA's conclusions concerning Ruby's friend, Dolan: *Additionally, the committee found it difficult to dismiss certain Ruby associations with the explanation that they were solely related to*

---

[16] HSCA Appendix to Hearings—Volume IX, p. 422

his labor problems. For example, James Henry Dolan, a Dallas AGVA representative, was reportedly an acquaintance of both Carlos Marcello and Santo Trafficante.[17]

Another shady character who visited Ruby just two weeks before the assassination was Ruby's ex-roommate, Alex Gruber, who seemed to pop in out of nowhere. They spoke on November 17 and the day after JFK's murder as well as on November 24 before Oswald's murder. Gruber ended up taking care of one of Ruby's dogs. This important witness, according to the HSCA, received only cursory interest by the Warren Commission.[18]

On November 21, 1963, Ruby visited mobster Joe Campisi's Egyptian Lounge. Campisi was Ruby's first and most frequent visitor when he was jailed. This Mafioso, who the Warren Commission failed to question, was a close friend/associate to Joseph Civello head of the Dallas mob.[19]

The use of known mobsters (such as hitman Lenny Patrick) by the Warren Commission to vouch for Ruby not being linked to the mob is not reassuring, to say the least. The Warren Commission also propped up Ruby denials of wrongdoing with a rigged polygraph which was demolished by the HSCA.[20]

Ruby and Oswald

As noted by Robert Blakey, while speculative, both Oswald and Ruby have links to Marcello (indirect in the case of Oswald). Did Jack Ruby cross paths with Oswald before he stalked him during his weekend in jail?

Another link between Oswald and Ruby comes through their interactions with a gun smuggler and friend of Castro, Robert McKeown, who had been jailed for these activities. McKeown claimed at one time that

---

[17] https://www.archives.gov/research/jfk/select-committee-report/part-1c.html, page 156
[18] HSCA Appendix to Hearings—Volume IX
[19] Ibid., p. 336
[20] HSCA Volume VIII: The Analysis of Jack Ruby's Polygraph Examination (aarclibrary.org)

he got a call from Ruby who tried to use these ties in his efforts to convince the Castro regime to free Trafficante. McKeown did not want to get involved. In his website article, John Armstrong describes this stunning event:

> Robert McKeown watched as a car arrived, parked, and two men got out and walked toward his home. One of the men introduced himself to McKeown as Lee Oswald and said that he wanted to purchase rifles. McKeown, who was still on a 5-year probation for selling arms, refused to sell guns to Lee Oswald. The two men left but returned a few minutes later and again asked McKeown to sell rifles, but he refused. Lee Oswald's attempt to purchase rifles from Robert McKeown, who was a very close personal friend of Fidel Castro, was very significant and an obvious attempt by the conspirators to link Lee Oswald to Cuba.[21]

During a press conference by Dallas attorney Henry Wade, where he claimed that Oswald was part of the Free Cuba Committee, it was Ruby masquerading as a journalist who most vociferously corrected him by saying it was the Fair Play for Cuba Committee.[22]

Jack Ruby Informant and Cop Friendly

There have been many allegations about Ruby being closely connected to the Dallas Police Force: providing cops with women; helping some of them financially; traveling with the Chief of Police; making payoffs. Estimates of the number of officers he was acquainted with go from a minimum of 100 to over 600 to just about everybody, 1200.

The HSCA confirms that he did maintain a close relationship with the force and that he had a number of friendships with some of its members: providing sandwiches, paying for meals, waving cover charges at the Carousel Club; giving away whisky bottles, etc. At least one witness—

---

[21] https://harveyandlee.net/NID97.htm
[22] https://www.youtube.com/results?search_query=jack+ruby+henry+wade

Carousel employee Andy Armstrong—told investigators that Ruby knew Officer Tippit.[23]

Gerald Ford, in his otherwise uninformative book, *Portrait of an Assassin*, did reveal that Ruby had been an FBI informant. Before dying, Ruby made the claim that there was a high-level conspiracy.

Jack Ruby the Gunrunner

As a gunrunner for Cuban revolutionaries, Ruby's links were monitored by the CIA. Some of his gunrunning was done with a CIA operative called Donald Browder at a time when customs and the CIA were not opposed to Castro's revolution.[24]

Jack Ruby the Stalker

Seth Kantor was a journalist who knew Jack Ruby. He was in the press vehicle during the deadly JFK motorcade and encountered Jack Ruby at Parkland Hospital at 1:28 p.m. He is probably the writer who did the most research on Ruby. In 1978 he wrote the book, *Who was Jack Ruby* and revealed the following:

> "An hour after the shooting of President Kennedy I encountered Jack Ruby at Parkland Hospital. Ruby was someone I had known at the start of the Kennedy administration, when I had been a reporter on a Dallas newspaper. He sought me out at Parkland, called me by name and, later from jail, wrote me a warm, personal note. But he later denied that he had been inside Parkland Hospital at that critical time. As a result, the Warren Commission questioned both Ruby and me in June 1964, about the Parkland encounter. In the end, page 336 of the Warren Report declared that "Kantor probably did not see Ruby in Parkland Hospital."

---

[23] HSCA Appendix to Hearings—Volume IX, p. 128-29
[24] https://history-matters.com/archive/jfk/wc/wcvols/wh26/pdf/WH26_CE_3063.pdf

After reading Kantor's book, Burt W. Griffin, the Warren Commission attorney who developed these conclusions about Jack Ruby for the Warren Report, changed his mind about Ruby not appearing at Parkland soon after the President had been brought there. Griffin, who since has become a judge in Ohio, stated: "The greater weight of the evidence indicates he did see Ruby at Parkland."

In 1979, the House Select Committee on Assassinations reexamined Kantor's testimony and stated, "While the Warren Commission concluded that Kantor was mistaken (about his Parkland encounter with Ruby), the Committee determined he probably was not."

Between JFK's death and Oswald's murder, Ruby, masquerading at times as a Jewish journalist, was close to the action in and around Oswald. On November 22, 1963, at 4:30, he was seen on the third floor of the police station.[25]

On the evening of the assassination, Ruby brought sandwiches to officers who were on the job. He was also seen during the night and early morning, in the basement, third floor, assembly room and at a press conference. Then again on the 23rd, Ruby was seen several times by various people, day and evening in various places of the DPD building. This behavior got the attention of the HSCA:

> The committee noted that other Ruby activities and movements during the period immediately following the assassination—on November 22 and 23—raised disturbing questions. For example, Ruby's first encounter with Oswald occurred over 36 hours before he shot him. Ruby was standing within a few feet of Oswald as he was being moved from one part of police headquarters to another just before midnight on November 22. Ruby testified that he had no trouble entering the building, and the committee found no evidence contradicting his story. The committee was disturbed, however, by Ruby's easy access to headquarters and by his inconsistent accounts of his carrying a pistol. In an FBI interview on December 25, 1963, he said he had the pistol during the encounter with

---

[25] https://www.youtube.com/watch?v=sdAmZ0J9BOk

Oswald late in the evening of November 22. But when questioned about it by the Warren Commission, Ruby replied, "I will be honest with you. I lied about it. It isn't so, I didn't have a gun." Finally, the committee was troubled by reported sightings of Ruby on Saturday, November 23, at Dallas police headquarters and at the county jail at a time when Oswald's transfer to the county facility had originally been scheduled. These sightings, along with the one on Friday night, could indicate that Ruby was pursuing Oswald's movements throughout the weekend.[26]

And of course, November 24 was the day, when the security and protection of the world-leading villain should have been at its highest, Ruby eliminated the most important witness in U.S. history, gagging him forever.

... The committee was troubled by the apparently unlocked doors along the stairway route and the removal of security guards from the area of the garage nearest the stairway shortly before the shooting... There is also evidence that the Dallas Police Department withheld relevant information from the Warren Commission concerning Ruby's entry to the scene of the Oswald transfer.[27]

CONCLUSION

The claim that Oswald was a loner with no ties with intelligence agencies is one of the greatest deceptions put forth by the Warren Commission. The description of his murderer by the Warren Commission as another deranged person with no significant mob ties comes very close. For example, the phone calls that he was part of in the weeks leading up to the murder and that were analyzed by the HSCA revealed a frenzy of communications with known mobsters.

---

[26] https://www.archives.gov/research/jfk/select-committee-report/part-1c.html page 159 (see also pages 134–135)

[27] https://www.archives.gov/research/jfk/select-committee-report/part-1c.html page 157-158

Subsequent to his arrest, Ruby on a number of occasions said words to the effect that others at very high levels were involved, that he was forced into the position he was in.[28]

When he was accorded his appeal for a retrial, his mental evaluation was put into the hands of CIA/MKULTRA-linked Louis Jolyon West. Ruby claimed he was injected with cancer-causing cells and died shortly after of galloping cancer.[29]

The Warren Commission did not even want to question Ruby initially. When they finally did meet him, they were not very probing. When Ruby offered to say more if he were brought up to Washington, Chief Warren wanted none of it.

It is a matter of record that:

- Ruby was mob-connected
- Ruby was a gunrunner
- Ruby was an FBI informant
- Ruby was close to the DPD
- Ruby had easy access to Oswald during the 48 hours preceding his murder
- Ruby eliminated the most important witness to JFK's murder
- The head of the HSCA concluded that Ruby was an accomplice in the overall plot
- The Warren Commission did little investigation into Ruby and his connections
- The Warren Commission misrepresented Ruby and his behavior
- The HSCA, while torching the traditional narrative about Ruby and the WC fantasy used mild language in exposing the obvious

On that let's leave the final word to the HSCA:

"Ruby's shooting of Oswald was not a spontaneous act, in that it involved at least some premeditation. Similarly, the committee

---

[28] https://www.youtube.com/watch?v=mmUdtil8oOU
[29] https://en.wikipedia.org/wiki/Louis_Jolyon_West

believed it was less likely that Ruby entered the police basement without assistance, even though the assistance may have been provided with no knowledge of Ruby's intentions."[30]

---

[30] https://www.archives.gov/research/jfk/select-committee-report/part-1c.html page 157-158

CHAPTER 6

PRIOR PLOTS, THE FAIR PLAY FOR CUBA COMMITTEE, AND USEFUL IDIOTS

BY PAUL BLEAU

STATEMENT

SIMILAR CASE ANALYSIS demonstrates by clear and convincing evidence that Oswald was set up as a patsy in the murder of President Kennedy.

INTRODUCTION

Case linkage, also called linkage analysis or comparative case analysis, is an offender profiling process that helps investigators determine whether a series of crimes were committed by the same offender. The Warren Commission and the investigative agencies at their service never performed this type of standard research for the JFK assassination.

There were many subjects with personas similar to Oswald who were informants, provocateurs, communists and/or potential patsies during the year of the murder. These stratagems were coordinated centrally. As we will see, secrecy and obfuscation by intelligence forces around similar incidents were a recurring theme in 1963.

Normally, previous attempts to murder a victim should get a diligent sleuth's attention. In this case it would have led to investigating the plans and/or efforts in L.A., Chicago and Tampa and other suspicious precursor incidents that occurred within less than a year preceding November 22, 1963. Even similar events that took place after the crime should have been scoured over. There is not a whiff of any of these cases in the Warren Report or the accompanying 26 volumes of evidence.

Thomas Samoluk of the ARRB confirmed that the Secret Service in the mid-nineteen-nineties illegally destroyed the files pertaining to JFK travels in the fall of 1963 after they were legally required to make them available to the ARRB.[1]

In this section we will analyze similar cases that demonstrate stratagems around other subjects and incidents that occurred during the months preceding and succeeding the assassination of JFK that are revealing of a pattern that is indicative of central coordination.

What we can conclude from this analysis is that the peculiarities that one can find in many of the subjects' personas, associations and actions is hardly a haphazard collection of traits and behaviors.

EVIDENCE

Prior Plots and the Fingerprints of an M.O.

Springfield, Illinois, October 1962

At the height of the Cuban Missile Crisis, when JFK was at odds with his hawkish military advisors about how to solve the crisis, a serious threat to JFK took place which was buried for 54 years as reported by Stephen F. Knott, professor of National Security Affairs at the United States Naval War College, in *the Washington Post*.[2]

According to evidence declassified in 2017 found in the archives of the JFK Library, four days into the crisis, on October 19, JFK, in a motorcade on its way for a visit to Abraham Lincoln's tomb in Springfield, IL, was in the sights of a rifleman. A witness reported seeing a gun barrel of a rifle with a telescopic scope protruding from a second floor window. Two brothers-in-law, 20 and 16-years old, were taken in for questioning.

The report continued, "a .22-caliber semi-automatic rifle and a full

---

[1] DiEugenio, JFK Revisited, p 387
[2] https://historynewsnetwork.org/article/162604

box of .22 long rifle ammunition were seized." Both men admitted "pointing the gun out the window on the parade route. However, they claimed that they had merely been testing the power of the telescopic sight to determine if it would be worthwhile to remove it in order to get a better look at the President when the motorcade returned. As there was no evidence to the contrary, and neither man had any previous record, prosecution was declined."

Apparently, in 2019 when this story was first reported, at least one of the subjects was still living and questioned by the press but refused to comment.

The fact that none of the investigations had access to this information which prevented similar case analysis is a constant theme in this section and an indication of an ongoing intent to hide material facts.[3]

The Phantom Plot in Nashville, May 1963

Bill Adams in 1993 described a plot in Nashville for *The Fourth Decade*:[4]

In early 1992 I was shocked to see a tabloid print a story about an assassination attempt against JFK during the Nashville trip! Congressman Bob Clement of Tennessee had made a startling revelation. He said his father, the late Gov. Frank Clement (governor of Tennessee in 1963), told him of a strange incident while JFK awaited a helicopter after visiting the Governor. The tabloid quoted Congressman Bob Clement of Tennessee as stating, 'While the President waited for the helicopter, a man approached with a gun hidden underneath a sack. Secret Service agents spotted him and grabbed him.'"

I called and interviewed the congressman in the early summer of 1963. I also obtained actual Nashville news stories about the

[3] https://www.sj-r.com/story/news/2018/11/28/rifle-pointed-at-jfk-during/6579986007/

[4] Synopsis of Assassination Attempt Against JFK, May 18, 1963, in Nashville, TN

congressman's revelation in January of 1992. As a result of reading the news stories and talking to Congressman Clement, I have been able to piece together the following story.

President Kennedy arrived in Nashville on May 18, 1963. He rode in a motorcade to Vanderbilt University where he gave a speech outside in the football stadium. JFK left the stadium in another motorcade and drove to the governor's mansion. Somewhere between the governor's mansion and the helicopter landing site at Overton High School, a man approached JFK with a handgun under a sack. It is unclear whether JFK was in his limousine or not at the time. The Governor witnessed this event and the subsequent capture of the suspect by the Secret Service. The man was held at the High School for some time. Nothing more is known about the man. The Secret Service asked the Governor to keep the event out of the press for fear it would lead to more assassination attempts.

While the documented evidence about this failed plot is scant, it is worth noting for the following reasons:

1. A suspect was picked up and released without any trace: no names, fingerprints, photos, reports, etc.

2. The Nashville attempt, as was the case for all of the other failed plots, was revisited by neither the Secret Service nor the FBI after the JFK assassination, even though it was in the same year.

3. The Secret Service once again took steps to keep the media from publicizing it.

4. This failed plot as well as all others were not known to the Warren Commission.

5. The fact that the Secret Service destroyed many records related to the protection of President Kennedy's may have contributed to the dearth of evidence about this incident.

Los Angeles Attempt, June 1963, Vaughn Marlowe and Richard Case Nagell

Dick Russell in *The Man Who Knew Too Much* is perhaps the one who went the furthest in studying this plot to assassinate JFK, which would have culminated with his murder during the showing of *PT 109* in Beverly Hills.

Russell had two key sources. One was Richard Case Nagell who provided Jim Garrison with information about Oswald and the Dallas plot in his New Orleans case against Clay Shaw. Nagell talked to Russell about Vaughn Marlowe (his second source) who was the one who plotters were "considering" for recruitment as a shooter in L.A., or more likely a patsy who could be linked to Castro, according to Nagell. He also said he witnessed Cuban exiles, including one "Leopoldo," who may have been present during the Sylvia Odio incident, scouting Marlowe's store.

Nagell spoke fluent Japanese, Russian and some Spanish. His wife was Japanese. A Korean War hero who reached the level of multi-decorated captain Nagell had been posted in the Far East where he claimed to have met Oswald for the first time. Nagell stated that he had been trained in Army counterintelligence and then, he said, became a double agent for the CIA.

In the days leading up to the L.A. attempt, Nagell tried to get himself checked into a psychiatric ward so as to be isolated from the murder.

Nagell told Dick Russell that an anti-Castro Cuban exile group he was monitoring had set its sights on Kennedy and would make it look like Castro was behind it, and that David Ferrie, Clay Shaw, Guy Banister and Oswald were part of the conspiracy. Oswald, however, would be set up to make it look like Castro was behind him—and him alone.

Nagell, again fearing incrimination, faked a bank robbery in September of 1963 so as to be in jail when JFK's assassination occurred. After his arrest he stated that "all my problems are solved and now I won't have to go to Cuba… I can see this was going to be a frame, which is to be expected in our capitalistic system." Before this episode Nagell had spent some time in Mexico City. Nagell had apparently attempted to commit suicide just before the El Paso incident.

After his arrest, his cellmate stated that he said he tried to join the Communist Party. According to Russell who saw the arrest sheet or trial papers, the items in Nagell's possession when he was arrested are amazingly similar to items owned by Lee Harvey Oswald. They include:

1. One miniature Minox camera and developing kit.

2. Fair Play for Cuba leaflets.

3. The P.O. Box for the Fair Play for Cuba Committee in New Orleans, Louisiana. The committee had only one member. Lee Oswald.

4. Cuban and Communist literature, including *The Crime against Cuba* by Corliss Lamont, one of the documents also being used in New Orleans by Lee Oswald.

5. A notebook containing the unlisted telephone number of the Cuban embassy, the same number as one found in Oswald's notebook.

6. The notebook also contained names of individuals who would much later be identified as CIA personnel from its Los Angeles office. (The names were submitted by the FBI to CIA in October 63 and eventually verified by CIA as being names of actual employees.)

Existing documentary proof of Nagell's possessions can be found in a *December 10, 1968, D.C./CI/R&A Report: DEP* about the Nagell notebook that does refer to the Fair Play for Cuba Committee. This on its own should set off alarm bells, as it is a very particular trace that most other subjects discussed in this section share. It is not only Nagell's revelations about Oswald and possessions that are stunning: his own patsy persona similarities to Oswald are at a dead ringer level.[5]

In addition, the trial files for Richard Nagell also contain an identification card, the card being a military ID with Nagell's photo and the name and signature of Lee H. Oswald.

Courtesy of David Josephs

[5] https://www.archives.gov/files/research/jfk/releases/104-10305-10005.pdf see pp. 15 and 16

Though Nagell's mental competency has been put into question, Larry Hancock makes a strong case for his credibility in his <u>Man in the Middle</u> chronicle[6] about him, where he shows that his written warnings of the assassination, knowledge of Cuban exiles and CIA persons of interest, and referencing of specific documents could not have simply been made up by a charlatan.

Other researchers have speculated that Richard Case Nagell himself was also being maneuvered to be a potential patsy—something even he came to suspect, which is why he tried to get himself checked into a psychological ward during JFK's visit to L.A. (according to Russell) and got himself jailed before November 22, 1963.

Another interesting fact about Nagell is that one of his lawyers, William Martin, who Nagell describes as "a former member of the CIA's Dirty Tricks Division ... still on reserves" had his offices in the International Trade Mart managed by none other than Clay Shaw.[7]

Marlowe, also a Korean War vet, spoke with Russell. He acknowledged knowing Nagell, having the reputation of being a good shot and being part of the L.A. Chapter of the Fair Play for Cuba Committee (FPCC) and the Congress of Racial Equality (CORE) while having relations with the American Civil Liberties Union (ACLU) and Socialist Workers Party (SWP). Marlowe also traveled to Mexico on behalf of the FPCC in 1962, visited the Mexico City Cuban embassy to try and get a visa to travel to Cuba and met with Mexican communists while there. Even though the L.A. plot never materialized, the profile of the would-be patsy as well as the *framing of Castro* part of the said plan is intriguingly similar to Oswald's persona and what was planned for Dallas.[8]

Washington October 1, 1963

There is evidence that Oswald may have been set up as a patsy for a plot to kill JFK in Washington in and around September 26. Significantly,

---

[6] https://www.maryferrell.org/showDoc.html?docId=4886#relPageId=16
[7] The Garrison Files- Martin-Nagell correspondence
[8] *The Man Who Knew too Much, Dick Russell*

on October 1 there was a presidential motorcade with Ethiopia's leader Haile Selassie in the Capital.

Richard Case Nagell claimed to have tried to talk Oswald out of the Washington plot and how he typed up warning letters sent by registered mail in mid-September stating that "Lee Harvey Oswald of New Orleans" was currently taking part in a scheme "to shoot the president," probably "in Washington" and "in late September."[9]

This is important information to argue that there was a plan in the works, but this should be tempered by what researcher Dick Russell who met Nagell on a number of occasions, confirmed to this author a few years ago: "that these letters were never seen by researchers."

Oswald did write a series of letters at the end of August to the USA Communist Party (CPUSA) and SWP, maintaining he was moving to the D.C. area and offering his services, even volunteering to do photographic and layout work for publications, brochures, etc. Beyond that, he actually asked CPUSA for advice on going *underground.* Based on those letters we certainly know he was at least thinking about Washington.[10]

More corroboration of this set-up comes from the fact that in the very first FBI interview with Marina after the assassination, specific questions were asked about Oswald's travel to both Washington, D.C. and Mexico City. We have no concrete idea of what prompted the queries, but it may have been that they came from the FBI having obtained one of the letters as they were monitoring Oswald's mail.

Then there is a stunning piece of evidence discussed by Secret Service expert Vince Palamara in his book *Who's Who in the Secret Service.*[11] At around the time Oswald was supposedly in Mexico City, someone was impersonating him in the D.C./PA/Baltimore area.

---

[9] Russell, The Man Who Knew too Much
[10] Warren Commission H Vol. 20, p. 270 and Vol. 19, p. 577
[11] Vince Palamara, Who's Who in the Secret Service, p. 276

Chicago, November 2, 1963

Considering a number of these incidents left few traces in the months prior to the assassination, the contrary could be said of what happened in Chicago on November 2, 1963, despite attempts to keep it hidden. This incident was well covered by Edwin Black in his November 1975 article for *the Chicago Independent*,[12] and key information was added in James Douglass's *JFK and the Unspeakable.*

According to Edwin Black:

November 2, 1963, JFK was scheduled to attend the Army-Air Force game at Soldier Field. Plans called for him to arrive at O'Hare around 11 a.m., motorcade down what was then known as the Northwest Expressway to the Loop. At Jackson the caravan would lumber up the Jackson exit, make a slow, difficult left-hand turn onto the street and shuttle over to the stadium. The Jackson exit would be crowded with no fewer than 45 local schools and civic organizations anxious to see the President.

As in Dallas, JFK's limousine would pass through a warehouse district—which Secret Service advance men considered 10 times more deadly than any office building corridor.

As in Dallas, JFK's limousine would be forced to make a difficult 90-degree turn that would slow them to practically a standstill. As in Dallas, triangulation of fire would be simple because of the unobstructed view.

As in Dallas, the crowd would panic, allowing the assassins to escape unnoticed.

The article goes on to explain how the FBI received a tip from a person called "Lee" about an assassination attempt that would take place involving four assassins (at least one with a Latin name) with rifles and telescopic sights. Hoover ordered that the case be transferred to the Secret Service which was ill-equipped to do anything about the threat.

---

[12] The Plot to kill JFK in Chicago, November 2, 1963

Another tip came in on October 31, from a landlady who saw four rifles with telescopic sights and a sketch of the motorcade route in one of the rooms being used by out-of-towners. Because of botched surveillance, Secret Service agents chose to take in only two of the suspects without evidence. Following a weak interrogation, the suspects, who stonewalled the agents, were let go without even having had their identities retrieved.

Another suspect picked up for questioning was a would-be patsy. Black describes him as follows:

The man's name was Thomas Arthur Vallee, a 30-year-old ex-Marine classified as an extreme paranoid schizophrenic by military doctors. Vallee worked as an apprentice at IPP Litho-plate at 625 West Jackson. As the patsy, he was perfect—as perfect for the Chicago assassination plot as Lee Harvey Oswald was for the Dallas assassination plot.

444   *Documents*

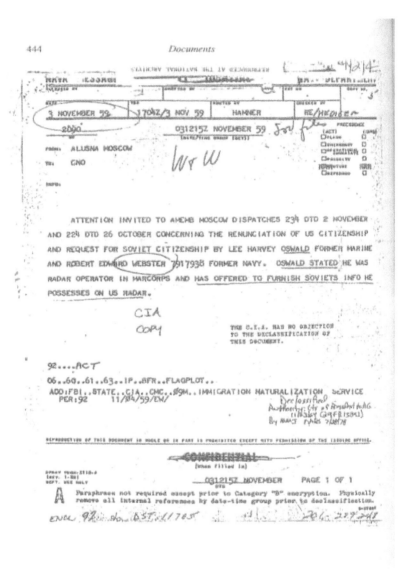

Courtesy of David Josephs

Vallee was born and raised in Chicago. Like Oswald, he joined the Marines in the mid-50s during the Korean War period. Like Oswald, Vallee was assigned to a U2 base in Japan (where he also worked as a radar operator—according to Jim Douglass). Oswald at Atsugi, Vallee at Camp Ōtsu. The cover reference for the U2 project at these bases was Joint Technical Advisory Group (JTAG). Since

CIA exerted a strong presence at these two bases, they were prime recruitment stations.

Both Vallee and Oswald appear to have been recruited by CIA for "black missions" or otherwise unsavory, personally discrediting assignments. In Oswald's case, at the height of the Cold War, he was instructed and helped to defect to Russia. With him he carried top secret radar codes. Oswald's mission, probably unbeknownst to him, may have been to reveal this disinformation for some complex CIA intelligence stratagem. Warren Commission testimony documents that all these radar codes had to be revised because of Oswald's defection.

Vallee was recruited about the same time to train members of a fiercely anti-Castro guerrilla group. Objective: the assassination of Fidel Castro. Training locale: in and around Levittown, Long Island.

Neither Vallee nor Oswald received money for their clandestine duties. The surreptitious nature of the business was ego-building to their personalities ... inherently rewarding. Both Vallee and Oswald had recently taken jobs in warehouses at the planned assassination sites. Oswald at the fifth floor book depository on Elm Street in Dallas. Vallee on the third floor IPP printing company looking out over the Jackson Street exit ramp where Kennedy's limousine would have been hit.

Both Vallee and Oswald could be shown to have extremist political views. Both owned rifles. Both were basically loners. Basically, drifters. Basically, lowlife. The dregs of society. Perfect for the work they were recruited. Perfect for a frame-up. They even resembled one another physically.

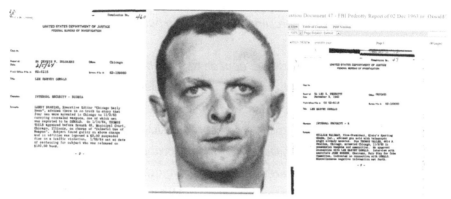

Courtesy of David Josephs—Vallee photo added

In the later part of the article Black describes the loss of evidence, the stonewalling he faced from investigators he interviewed and the embarrassment the FBI and Secret Service tried to avoid.

James Douglass in his well-researched book, *JFK and the Unspeakable*, adds strong evidence that the attempt in Chicago was intentionally kept off the radar which kept the door open for what did happen in Dallas. Douglass spoke to witnesses. He also visited the Dallas kill zone and compared it with what he found in Chicago. Interviewing Abraham Bolden, who had been hand-picked by JFK as the first Black person to join the Secret Service White House Detail, Douglass describes in detail the measures that were taken to strategically weaken the president's protection, as was also done in Dallas. Bolden was effectively silenced by framing him for a crime, getting him jailed and turning him into a pariah.

Douglass further adds these key observations: In August 1963 while Oswald moved from New Orleans to Dallas, Vallee moved from Long Island to Chicago where he got a job at IPP Litho-Plate in an eight-story building; When Douglass visited the building what he saw was a view that was a replica of what could be seen from the Texas School Book Depository and a motorcade route offering the same opportunities for the ambush that many witnesses described in Dallas.

When Bolden heard the news of the assassination, he brought up the parallels of what was attempted in Chicago to colleagues. From then on, his professional career went downhill. He was railroaded into jail after he was overheard trying to contact the Warren Commission. In 1967 he finally told a Garrison investigator and Mark Lane about his story, which got him placed in solitary confinement.

Douglass also described how Chicago Secret Service Chief Maurice Martineau took major steps to control the messaging by requiring that all agent reports about the incident not be in writing but funneled by dictation through his assistant thus eliminating all documentary trails. Only Martineau and Washington Secret Service chief James J. Rowley saw the top-secret report. In 1995, when the Assassinations Records Review Board (ARRB) ordered the copy released, the Secret Service destroyed it instead. Martineau also told his staff on November 22 what to believe: Lee Harvey Oswald was a lone gunman; There was no connection with Chicago; forget November 2 in Chicago. The only mention the press made about the Chicago plot at the time was that Vallee, like Oswald, was another gun-toting malcontent ... nothing about the other parallels described in this section.

By keeping silent about Chicago, the doors were kept wide open for what was to happen in Dallas or could have happened in Tampa a few days before the deadly ambush.[13]

Jim DiEugenio highlighted the following point in his <u>book review</u>[14] of the Douglass classic:

Interestingly, Dan Groth, the suspicious officer in on the arrest of Vallee, was later part of the SWAT team that assassinated Black Panthers Fred Hampton and Mark Clark in 1969. Groth took several lengthy leaves from Chicago to Washington for special training under the auspices of the FBI and CIA. Groth never had a regular police assignment, but always worked counterintelligence, with an early focus on the FPCC.

The House Select Committee on Assassinations (HSCA) knew little about the plot but did underscore the Secret Service's muteness around

---

[13] James Douglass, JFK and the Unspeakable, Chapter 5 Saigon and Chicago
[14] https://www.kennedysandking.com/john-f-kennedy-reviews/jfk-and-the-unspeakable-by-james-w-douglass

the Chicago incident and noted the significance of the similar back-grounds of Vallee and Oswald.[15]

Miami, November 18, 1963

As we have seen, the noose was getting very tight around JFK's neck during his last weeks. His morning in Miami, when he gave a speech before heading off for a motorcade in Tampa, was from all accounts very risky.

A person of interest, who has flown under the radar, is patsy candi-date: Santiago Garriga. The best source the writer of this section has found about this elusive character is Bill Simpich, author of *State Secret*.

Like with many of the others discussed in this article, Garriga's re-sumé was perfect for patsy recruiter/runners: It included interaction with Cuban associates in Mexico City; seemingly pro-Castro behavior, and his crowning achievement: Like Oswald in 1963, he opened the FPCC Miami chapter -a market deemed very hostile for such an enterprise.

Garriga is the potential fall guy who is the most clearly linked with intelligence, like Oswald and Nagell, he could be portrayed as a double agent by those who packaged them. While there is no concrete evidence that Garriga was being set up as a patsy, what makes Garriga so unique is that Simpich writes about his pseudonym and close links with CIA of-ficer William Harvey's team.

To cover this intriguing lead, it is best to cite a few excerpts from *State Secret*:[16]

> *It's pretty clear that one informant the HSCA did not know about was AMKNOB-1 aka Santiago Garriga. As we have seen, Garriga worked with both the CIA and with Cuban intelligence... During Oc-tober 1963 Garriga worked with other pro-Castro Cubans to set up a new chapter of the Fair Play for Cuba Committee in Miami... Alt-hough it appears that Garriga's ultimate loyalty was with the*

---

[15] House Select Committee on Assassinations Final Report, p. 232
[16] https://www.maryferrell.org/pages/State_Secret_Chapter3.html

Castro government, it's likely that Garriga's FPCC activity was designed by Anita Potocki (<u>Harvey's chief aide at the wiretap division known as Staff D</u>) (and colleague of David Atlee Phillips) to set up a flytrap for people like Oswald. Maybe even Garriga himself was considered as a possible fall guy.

CIA memos that identify Garriga were written by Anita Potocki.

As with all the other persons of interest identified in this essay, Garriga was not invented by a conspiracy theorist. Over and above his other patsy credentials, he represents yet another of many potential scapegoats that is linked to the FPCC.

Tampa, November 18, 1963

The chosen patsy for the Tampa attempt was a Cuban exile named Gilbert Policarpo Lopez who also had many similarities with Oswald: *links with the FPCC, being a former defector, a tie to Russia, getting into a fight over seeming pro-Castro sympathies, and an unusual trip to Mexico City.*

The Secret Service destroyed the Tampa attempt documents in 1995 in violation of the ARRB Act. Just like Allen Dulles kept the CIA-Mob association secret from his Warren Commission colleagues, the Secret Service added the Tampa and Chicago Plots to other suspiciously similar incidents as some of their dirty little secrets. Not even the Dallas Police were let in on this important information which could have affected security on November 22.

Existing Secret Service files in the *1970s made it clear that the Tampa threat was posed by a single mobile sniper who would fire from a tall building using a high-power rifle fitted with a scope.* Other accounts, however, describe the plot as multi-person.

The motorcade route in Tampa was very long and presented Dealey Plaza quality opportunities. Other researchers chronicled how Lopez moved from the Keys to Tampa shortly before the motorcade, echoing Vallee and Oswald's pawn-like pre-motorcade movements.

Another extremely important detail in an article in the *Tribune*[17] claims to have a source that places V. T. Lee (National Leader of the FPCC who was in frequent contact with Oswald) in Tampa on November 17, 1963, with Gilbert Policarpo Lopez. The FBI would easily know this based on the important number of informants at every FPCC meeting.

The HSCA described parts of what it called the Lopez allegation:[18]

> *Lopez would have obtained a tourist card in Tampa on November 20, 1963, entered Mexico at Nuevo Laredo on November 23 and flew from Mexico City to Havana on November 27. Further, Lopez was alleged to have attended a meeting of the Tampa Chapter of the FPCC on November 17... CIA files on Lopez reflect that in early December 1963 they received a classified message requesting urgent traces on Lopez... Later the CIA headquarters received another classified message stating that a source stated that "Lopes" had been involved in the Kennedy assassination ... had entered Mexico on foot from Laredo on November 13 ... proceeded by bus to Mexico City where he entered the Cuban embassy ... and left for Cuba as the only passenger on Flight 465 for Cuba. A CIA file on Lopez was classified as a counterintelligence case...*
>
> *An FBI investigation on Lopez through an interview with his cousin and wife as well as document research revealed that... He was pro-Castro and he had once gotten involved in a fistfight over his Castro sympathies.*
>
> *The FBI had previously documented that Lopez has actually been in contact with the FPCC and had attended a meeting in Tampa on November 20, 1963. In a March 1964 report, it recounted that at a November 17 meeting... Lopez said he had not been granted permission to return to Cuba but was awaiting a phone call about his return to his homeland... A Tampa FPCC member was*

---

quoted as saying she called a friend in Cuba on December 8, 1963, and was told that he arrived safely.

She also said that they (the FPCC) had given Lopez $190 for his return. The FBI confirmed the Mexico trip (Lopez's wife confirmed that in a letter he sent her from Cuba in November 1963, he had received financial assistance for his trip to Cuba from an organization in Tampa) ... information sent to the Warren Commission by the FBI on the Tampa chapter of the FPCC did not contain information on Lopez' activities ... nor apparently on Lopez himself. The Committee concurred with the Senate Select Committee that this omission was egregious, since the circumstances surrounding Lopez's travel seemed "suspicious."

Moreover, in March 1964 when the WC's investigation was in its most active stage, there were reports circulating that Lopez had been involved in the assassination... Lopez's association with the FPCC, however, coupled with the fact that the dates of his travel to Mexico via Texas coincide with the assassination, plus the reports that Lopez's activities were "suspicious" all amount to troublesome circumstances that the committee was unable to resolve with confidence.

San Antonio, November 21, 1963

Harry Power was yet another leftist, ex-marine with marital problems and a warped view of life, who checked into a Terre Haute House Hotel room in Indiana on November 25, 1963, with a long package. When he checked out, he left behind a rifle ... a Mannlicher-Carcano according to a retired Chief of Police Frank Riddle ... a Mauser according to another unidentified source.

A *United States Government Memo April 4, 1967—Alex Rosen to Deloach* describes the allegation.[19] Riddle claimed San Antonio authorities informed him that Power was a member of the Young Communist

---

[19] https://www.maryferrell.org/showDoc.html?do-cId=62410#relPageId=38&search=harry_and%20power%20and%20riddle

League and an expert rifle marksman. An ex-co-worker described him as anti-Kennedy. He held a job in San Antonio, Texas, in 1962.

Riddle stated that all information had been turned over to the Warren Commission and that the rifle was taken by Secret Service agents. The Secret Service claimed to have only found out about this incident in 1965. Their key source is none other than the head of the Washington Secret Service, Chief Rowley himself, whom you will recall played a key role in keeping the Chicago plot as secret as possible. The FBI did confirm, however, that the Terre Haute Police Department had in fact followed up on this lead around when Riddle claimed it happened … which would indicate further Secret Service and Warren Commission complacency.

According to Dick Russell, Richard Nagell told Jim Garrison that Power was a Trotskyite who had met Oswald. Given that JFK's motorcade is in San Antonio on November 21 and Power could easily be linked to that city, it is not a major leap to see similarities between Power, Oswald and the other scapegoat candidates that seem to have been lined up before the assassination.

The Indiana Rifle story had received little interest until journalist Sheldon Inkol researched it in 1993 *(The Third Decade, Volume 9, Issue 5: "The Indiana Rifle," by Sheldon Inkol)* and updated his findings in 1995 for *The Fourth Decade*. From his research and an FBI File, we can now add the following points:[20]

1. The rifle found in Indiana was most likely a Mauser and not a Mannlicher-Carcano.

2. Because of a bounced check written by Power, we know that at one time he was in New Orleans.

3. An ex-co-worker of Power the witness Riddle referred to was

---

[20] https://www.maryferrell.org/showDoc.html?docId=48768#relPageId=3 and https://www.maryferrell.org/showDoc.html?docId=48686#relPageId=16 and *FBI file 62–109060 JFK HQ*

Roger Dresch. He stated that Power was a hunter who sighted a rifle with a scope at a shooting range, that he had been a paratrooper complaining about his father being an alcoholic, and who occasionally talked about becoming a hermit in the wilderness.

According to Inkol, it was Dick Russell who first revealed the name of Harry Power in *The Man Who Knew Too Much* in 1992. There had only been insignificant articles about the incident before this. Inkol credits veteran researcher Larry Haapanen, who interviewed Riddle, for having confirmed the name of Power after following up on an article in 1970.

Dick Russell provided the following to the Harry Power profile:

A National Archives document about the affair was declassified in 1970 … a file reports that Power had been investigated in connection with the shooting attempt on General Walker in Dallas, a shooting that the WC falsely claimed to have been by Oswald and his Mannlicher-Carcano. Other files associated with the Power rifle claim that it was a 7.65 Mauser. CIA agent Richard Nagell told Garrison investigators in 1967 that Power was a Maoist or Trotskyite and "had known Lee Harvey Oswald and had been seen with him…"

According to Inkol, Frank Riddle insisted that Power was a suspect in the attempt on General Walker's life the previous April—something the Warren Commission tagged on Oswald. In 1964, Secret Service Chief James Rowley confirmed to Riddle that the FBI and the Secret Service had files on Power.

Inkol is not convinced that Power was even in the hotel. He argues that the description given (age, height and weight) of the person with the rifle in the hotel is very different from the San Antonio description of Power.

He believes one possibility that merits further investigation is that Power was being set up as an alternate patsy or part of a subversive pro-communist group intent on attacking the U.S. Government—Power could have been pinned as the shooter from the knoll if a frontal shot had been inescapable.

He also points out that had the assassination taken place in San Antonio where Kennedy's motorcade took place a day earlier, the patsy might have been Power instead of Oswald.

Was there a plan to kill JFK in San Antonio? According to David Lifton (interview with Paul Bleau) who researched a suspicious incident that took place on November 21, 1963, there could well have been:

> "I believe that it was the San Antonio papers—either the San Antonio Light, or the News—Express (there were only two San Antonio papers)—that carried stories about what happened on 11/21/63. About a 'mystery car' parked at a curb, and some remarks made by one of the occupants of that car, to the effect that 'he'll never get through this city.' Something like that. That led to the San Antonio Police dispatcher putting out a call for that vehicle to 'call in to your headquarters' or some such thing... That the San Antonio newspaper (one of them) reported after the assassination of JFK on Friday 11/22/63, that the 'mystery car' was a Secret Service vehicle. And that's what made the whole incident so very important."[21]

Prior Plots Observations

As we can clearly see, had case linkage analysis been found in the evidence, investigators would have certainly uncovered a template that would have been suggestive of a guiding hand. Even the HSCA found the omissions around the Tampa Plot to be **egregious.**

A number of clues could have been put in place to create an offender profile. Namely, the suspiciously timely movements or plans of a number of the potential patsies to be near the victim's whereabouts; potential patsies with similar profiles to Oswald; mutism and obfuscation by security and intelligence forces around these precursor events.

One particular trait a majority of the personalities above shared that

---

[21] Email exchange David Lifton—Paul Bleau : August 21, 2018

stood out like a sore thumb was their supposed sympathy toward Communism. Even more compelling is that five of the subjects were linked to the Fair Play for Cuba Committee: a quasi-statistical impossibility in 1963.

The FPCC

The analysis of the FPCC performed by the author of this section was presented in three parts for the Kennedysandking.com site, and it clearly showed that the FPCC was in a death spiral during the summer of 1963, and was heavily infiltrated by people with personalities similar to Oswald who would join to help identify communists or give themselves a track record for attempting to enter Cuba. It was also the best way to taint a patsy as pro-Castro.[22]

In Part 1 it is shown:

That the FPCC was in practically a dormant state when Oswald opened his chapter in New Orleans;

That the informants were known to and used by the FBI to target the FPCC under a program called AMSANTA in collaboration with the CIA and its high-ranking officer David Atlee Phillips;

That Oswald's choice of location for setting up his office at 544 Camp Street in a building populated by right-wing fanatics and anti-Castroites revealed he was a really a provocateur;

Oswald asked to meet the FBI after an arrest for disturbing the peace, revealing his informant role;

That Cuba invasion proponents used Oswald's FPCC links in a propaganda campaign to blame Castro.

---

[22] https://www.kennedysandking.com/john-f-kennedy-articles/exposing-the-fpcc-part-1 also follow links to parts 2 and 3

In Part 2 evidence was presented that: Oswald was paid $20 a day to distribute FPCC flyers; How other subjects' links to the FPCC were used to threaten or frame them; and David Atlee Phillips and George Joannides of the CIA should be viewed as persons of extreme interest.

Part 3 delves into Oswald's 544 Camp Street network that included Clay Shaw, David Ferrie, Guy Banister, Cuban exiles and others with which his universe was inexplicably intertwined.

By reading these thoroughly sourced essays, one will better understand the peculiarities around the prior attempts to assassinate JFK. All three articles share information on other subjects and suspicious events that clearly expose the FPCC in 1963 for what it was: a magnet for useful idiots, used by intelligence as pawns in their war against communism.

Miscellaneous FPCC Tainted Informants and Events

Harry Dean

Harry Dean is one of those characters who can be put into the category of unreliable witnesses who may have important knowledge, but who have made many statements that are easily contestable and that have had researchers chasing their tails. When researching the documentary trail about Harry Dean on the Mary Ferrell site, as well as on forums and websites that provide an in-depth analysis of Dean's statements and pertinent documents—we can find information about the FPCC, Dean himself and other characters that seem to be part of a model:[23]

Even though Dean does not seem like a highly prized asset for the FBI, the paper trail on Dean also confirms the following:

- Dean had been committed as a mental patient in Canada in 1948 and was sentenced at Chatham, Ontario;

- An OSI file[24] confirms that Harry Dean was in the U.S. Army in

---

[23] https://sites.google.com/site/xrt013/harrydean
[24] NARA Record Number: 104-10404-10041

1945 and then again in 1948 using the name George Robert Baker and that the Office of Naval Intelligence has three files on him. It also states that he had been arrested by the RCMP and the Detroit Police under the Registration Act;

- In 1958 he became a member of the 26th of July Movement, a group led by Fidel Castro;

- In late 1959 and early 1960, he received three letters from Juan A. Orta, the Director of the Prime Minister's Office of Cuba;

- He visited Cuba in June 1960;

- In August 1960, he was elected Recording Secretary, Chicago Chapter, FPCC. He soon after became a voluntary informant to the FBI (who nevertheless considered him a "*Fruitcake*");

- In 1961, he moved to Los Angeles, where he had casual contact with Edgar and Marjorie Swabeck, whom he had previously known in the Chicago area, and from them learned that Marjorie Swabeck is secretary of the LAX chapter of the FPCC at the present time. (Which perhaps brought him into the realm of Vaughn Marlowe and Richard Case Nagell;)

- In 1962, he joined the John Birch Society;

- After the assassination of JFK, In one of his forum posts, Dean states that the Swabecks may have been setting him up. The NARA documents do confirm a relationship that would have begun in 1960 when Harry met Edgar Swabeck during his trips to Cuba. According to Dean they played a role in getting him to set up the Chicago FPCC Branch;

It is also worth asking: If the murder had taken place in L.A., would a link to the cast of FPCC characters have also caused the downfall of the

SWP which was very close to the FPCC management in L.A. as well as at the national level?

John Glenn

Unlike most of the other potential fall guys that figure in this analysis, the case of John Glenn (not the astronaut) and his wife Marcia is quite well documented. This, however, has nothing to do with the FBI, CIA, or Warren Commission's efforts to scrutinize this Oswald semi-replica.

According to the WC, Oswald opening an FPCC chapter in New Orleans was a demonstration of his ego trip … period! Fortunately for researchers, the FPCC was under intensive scrutiny by the Internal Security Subcommittee of the Senate Judiciary Committee and the House Un-American Activities Committee (HUAC).

Through their reports and the writings in 1993 of Jerry Rose for The Third Decade,[25] we can paint a better picture of Glenn and the role the FPCC came to play in making our cast of puppets easy to frame for the crime of the century:

> The FPCC was characterized as "Castro's Network in the U.S.A." by the HUAC. Membership within this anti-U.S. organization was described during hearings as an effective door opener to enter Cuba via the Cuban Embassy in Mexico City and Cubana Airlines.
>
> Though the HUAC had been seriously rattled by the McCarthy era witch hunts, Castro was breathing some new life into this outfit for political showcasing of American patriotism. One area that got their attention was the trip to Cuba by American students despite a travel ban. On June 25, 1963, 58 students left New York and transited through Russia satellite Czechoslovakia on the way to Cuba where they were apparently well received by the Castro regime. This group had been infiltrated by an informant named Barry Hoffman who had gotten approval from agencies that were tied to the FBI, CIA, and State Department. During hearings in September of

---

[25] https://www.maryferrell.org/showDoc.html?docId=48773#relPageId=39

1963, he painted the students as pro-Cuba and anti-U.S.A. and talked about rumors that Cuba had not dismantled the nuclear installations on the island.

Evidently, he was a poor spy who was not trusted by the other students. He was "number 3 on their fink list." Numbers 1 and 2 were John Glenn and his wife Marcia.

On November 18, 1963—four days before JFK's assassination, the Glenns' testimony before the HUAC had the effect of smearing the FPCC. Transcripts of the hearings point out striking similarities with Oswald:[26]

John Glenn joined the U.S. Air Force in 1950.

While in the service, Glenn received training in the Russian language at Syracuse University and became a Russian linguist for Air Force Intelligence, with security clearance for secret, top secret, and cryptographic information. Meanwhile, he continued his regular college studies through night school and correspondence courses. Glenn, while still receiving regular military service pay, including food and housing allowances, returned to full-time studies at the Indiana University where he obtained a degree in business administration in January 1954.

He then resumed active duty with Air Force Intelligence for 2 more years, including 16 months overseas, before being discharged in January 1956, after reaching the rank of staff sergeant.

During the summer of 1958, he visited the Soviet Union, Czechoslovakia, and Poland for about 40 days as a guide for the Tom Maupintour Associates, an American travel agency. The next summer he toured the same countries, plus Yugoslavia and Romania, in a similar capacity for another travel organization.

The witness confirmed information obtained through an investigation by the Committee on Un-American Activities that he had traveled to

---

[26] https://archive.org/stream/violationsofstat04unit/violationsofstat04unit_djvu.txt

Mexico in the spring of 1962 in an attempt to get a Cuban visa. He was unsuccessful.

> It was at about this time, the fall of 1962, Glenn told the subcommittee that he joined the Fair Play for Cuba Committee. He had been a sympathizer of the group much earlier, he said. He admitted having written a letter printed in an Indiana University publication, dated February 10, 1962, in which he said that "the people in Fair Play are willing to argue to anyone who will listen that our government and our press are lying through their teeth (about Cuba)."
>
> The witness admitted that, without having applied for U.S. validation, he traveled to Cuba with the group of alleged students who departed from New York on a BOAC plane on June 25, 1963. Glenn acknowledged the accuracy of the subcommittee's information that on the return trip, after arriving in Spain with the main body of U.S. "students" on August 26, 1963, he left the group and traveled to Morocco.

Al Lewis Los Angeles FPCC

Oswald was not the only FPCC member who was slandered. According to Dick Russell, Al Lewis, executive director of the Los Angeles FPCC in 1963 and now a retired psychiatrist, remembered: "The FBI called me after Kennedy was assassinated, and apparently wanted to involve me in it in some way. They tried to pin a relationship with Oswald on me, because apparently, I'd been in Mexico at the same time he was, on my way to Cuba. Well, that was the first I heard about it. And I never heard of Oswald and the New Orleans Fair Play for Cuba Committee in the movement. That whole thing to me was a set-up of some kind by the intelligence services."[27]

---

[27] https://www.kennedysandking.com/john-f-kennedy-articles/exposing-the-fpcc-part-2#_edn8

Johnny Rossen Chicago and the National FPCC

Johnny Rossen,[28] who had been the head of the Chicago FPCC chapter and later became a National Chairman, was also the victim of wild rumors. An FBI report dated November 28, 1963, summarizes a slander campaign by an informant stating that he was a sex degenerate who slept with a Puerto Rican mistress named Carmen Osiokowski, who knew Oswald, who had sent money to him periodically and who hated Kennedy. His source was the mistress. When she was questioned, she denied everything. Upon re-questioning this informant's story completely fell apart.

Tony Perez,[29] an informant in Chicago, was qualified as a reliable source by the Chicago FBI. He was an anti-Castro Cuban and had provided dirt on Rossen. In a November 30, 1963, TELETYPE from SAC Chicago to Director and SAC Dallas,[30] the FBI is given the following information: That Johnny Rossen had held a number of late-night meetings in his Chicago Theater with FPCC subjects during the days leading up to the assassination. Some two years earlier, Perez, a representative of the Chicago Council for a Democratic Cuba, had debated Rossen at Northwestern University in opposition of his FPCC activities.

Like Oswald, Rossen was able to taint major organizations as he had always been an active pro-communist agitator having been the secretary of the U.S. Communist Party in St. Louis, where he ran for mayor for the party. Later, he would show Russian films in his Chicago Theater. He was active in the American Peace Crusade and Civil Rights Congress. He also used a number of aliases.

---

[28] https://archive.org/details/nsia-FairPlayforCubaCommittee/nsia-FairPlayforCuba-Committee/Fair%20Play%20Cuba%20Com%2022/page/n2/mode/1up

[29] https://maryferrell.org/showDoc.html?docId=10448#relPageId=31

[30] http://jfk.hood.edu/Collection/Weisberg%20Subject%20In-dex%20Files/F%20Disk/Fair%20Play%20for%20Cuba%20Committee/Item%2002.pdf

The Joseph Milteer Prediction

On November 9, white Nationalist Joseph Milteer was recorded by Miami Police informant William Somersett when the former claimed that there was a plot in the works to kill JFK with a high-power rifle from a tall building. On November 12, Miami intelligence provided the following transcript to the Secret Service: What follows is a partial transcript.[31]

> **Somersett**: Kennedy's coming here, I think, on the 18th or something like that to make some kind of speech…

> **Milteer:** You can bet your bottom dollar he is going to have a lot to say about the Cubans because there are so many of them here.

> **Somersett**: Yeah, well, he will have a thousand bodyguards. Don't worry about that.

> **Milteer**: The more bodyguards he has, the more easier it is to get him.

> **Somersett**: What?

> **Milteer**: The more bodyguards he has the more easier it is to get him.

> **Somersett**: Well, how in the hell do you figure would be the best way to get him?

> **Milteer**: From an office building with a high-power rifle…

> **Somersett**: They are really going to try to kill him?

---

[31] audio : https://www.maryferrell.org/audio/HSCA/Audio_hsca_Milteer_11-00-63_002228.mp3 transcripts: https://www.maryferrell.org/pages/Transcript_of_Milteer-Somersett_Tape.html

Milteer: "Oh, yeah. It's in the working...

Somersett: Hitting this Kennedy I'll tell you is going to be a hard proposition, I believe. Now you may have it figured out how to get him ... an office building and all that, but I don't know how them Secret Service ... they'd never cover all them office buildings and anywhere he's going. Do you know whether they do that or not?

Milteer: If they have any suspicion they will, of course. But without suspicion the chances are they wouldn't... You wouldn't have to take a gun up there ... take it up in pieces. All those guns come knock down and you can take them apart."...

Somersett: Boy, if that Kennedy gets shot we've got to know where we're at because you know that would be a real shake if they do that.

Milteer: They wouldn't leave any stone unturned there, no. No way.

Somersett: Oh, hell no.

Milteer: Hell, they'll pick up somebody within hours after, if anything like that would happen, just to throw the public off.

Somersett: Well, somebody is going to have to go to jail if he gets killed.

Milteer: Just like Bruno Hauptmann in the Lindbergh case, you know.

Given these threats, the HSCA noted how the poor security in Dallas was even more inexplicable.

Milteer's networking with violent right-wingers was also reported.[32]

---

[32] HSCA Final report, p. 261

Richard Taber National FPCC

The framing of Oswald and even the FPCC as a group were not the only lofty objectives of the anti-Castro forces. They planted the ridiculous story that the inaugural head of the FPCC, while in refuge in Cuba, had actually met a Lieutenant Lee Harvey Oswald in 1961 when he himself had "accompanied Castro during the Bay of Pigs Invasion."

TABOR'S COMPANION WAS DRESSED IN KHAKI TROUSERS AND BLUE DENIM SHIRT, AND WAS CARRYING A PORTFOLIO. TABOR WAS STILL ON CRUTCHES AS A RESULT OF HIS INJURY DURING THE INVASION. HE AND HIS COMPANION APPROACHED

Cuban

SOURCE, AND TABOR INTRODUCED HIS COMPANION TO LORENZO LUACES (SOURCE) AS LIEUTENANT HARVEY OSWALD. SOURCE RECALLS ASKING HIM TO SPELL OSWALD'S NAME INASMUCH AS SOURCE WAS NOT RPT NOT SURE WHETHER IT WAS SPELLED WITH A "D" OR "T" AT THE END. OSWALD DID NOT RPT NOT SAY WHAT HIS MISSION WAS IN HAVANA; HOWEVER, HE CLAIMED TO BE AN EXPERT IN ARMS, AND SHOWED SOURCE AN ACTUAL-SIZE EXPLODED PICTURE OF THE US M1 RIFLE, WHICH HE REMOVED FROM HIS PORTFOLIO. SOURCE CLAIMS THAT OS-WALD WAS PROB JUST "SHOWING OFF" BY SHOWING HIM THE PICTURE OF THE RIFLE. SOURCE WAS IN THE COMPANY OF TABOR AND OSWALD AT SLOPPY JOE'S BAR

Given that Oswald was in Minsk at this time, along with Taber's vehement denials, we can chalk this one up as another red herring designed to stimulate the invasion of Cuba.

Vincent T. Lee and Harrold Wilson National and Tampa FPCC

Vincent Theodore Lee, actually Army veteran Vincent Tappin, was elected Head of the Tampa FPCC Chapter in June 1961. On the Board was treasurer Harrold Wilson, who eventually replaced Lee when Lee took over from Richard Gibson as the national Chapter Chairman in 1962.

Oswald's actions in New Orleans parroted Lee's. Lee was heavily involved in leafleting, media coverage, and direct confrontations with anti-Castro Cubans featuring a near riot in November of 1961 in Marti

Park, where Sergio Arcacha Smith led CRC forces against the FPCC. Lee appeared on WBAI radio.

On December 26, 1962, Vincent T. Lee flew from New York City to Mexico City. From there, on December 28, he flew to Havana via Cubana Airlines[33] where he stayed for nearly one month. Oswald corresponded multiple times with Lee, reporting his FPCC agent provocateur coups. V. T. Lee, while providing him with advice, is the one who connected Oswald with Wilson so as to be better coached for his N.O. mission.

Other than this, not that much is known about V. T. Lee. As a witness during the Eastland Senate hearings, other than defending the FPCC and confirming his military record, he mostly took the Fifth Amendment. The Warren Commission did very little to go into his background during their typical probe light questioning. Lee also lied his head off by claiming he did not know Oswald. The HSCA never got him in as a witness despite obvious interest.

Based on newspaper articles and FBI intelligence,[34] there is compelling information that the FPCC National Chapter's V. T. Lee possibly met, at Tampa FPCC's Mary Quist's home on November 17, with FPCC tainted assassination suspect Policarpo Lopez, who, considering his Texas and Mexico travels, likely would also have been linked to Oswald had the pro-Castro conspiracy scenario not been deep-sixed. This also would have torn down the FPCC worldwide, if not the U.S. Communist Party, and could easily have stimulated the invasion of Cuba, given the direct link between Lee and Castro.

Robert Beaty Fennell San Francisco FPCC

On December 21, 1963, another Oswald-like character was arrested by the Secret Service in San Francisco for having on him notes containing

---

[33] https://www.maryferrell.org/showDoc.html?do-cId=109988#relPageId=8&search=Vincent_and%20theodore%20and%20lee
[34] https://www.kennedysandking.com/john-f-kennedy-articles/exposing-the-fpcc-part-2

threats to assassinate LBJ. Not much is known about Robert Beaty Fennell, but *this article*[35] reveals that he was said to be a member of the San Francisco FPCC, that he had mental problems, was involved in agitations and that he had received an honorable discharge from the Air Force five years earlier.

The Statue of Liberty Bombing Plot, February 1965

Here is the lead-in to the article on the Statue of Liberty bombing plot:

> "On 16 February 1965 three Americans and one Canadian were arrested in connection with a plot to destroy three of the United States' most treasured monuments: the Statue of Liberty, Liberty Bell, and Washington Monument. The Americans—Robert Steele Collier, Walter Augustus Bowe, and Khaleel Sultran Sayyed—were part of a small extremist organization known as the Black Liberation Front (BLF). The Canadian, a white woman named Michelle Duclos, was a member of a Quebec separatist party."

In an article in the Journal of Counterterrorism *(The Monumental Plot-Volume 16–2010)*, the reader will discover how some of the perpetrators visited Cuba, met Che Guevara who provided "technical information," and became involved in yet another major incident that would have favored the blaming of Cuba while tarnishing a "subversive" group. *(Click here to read)* One of them was part of the FPCC.

June Cobb

In the early 1950s, June Cobb was involved with a South American boyfriend in drug smuggling. She soon became an informant for the FBI.

In May 1960, while working for Castro in Havana as a translator, she was recruited by the CIA (KUBARK) and would report on Cuban

---

[35] https://archive.org/details/nsia-FairPlayforCubaCommittee/nsia-FairPlayforCuba-Committee/Fair%20Play%20Cuba%20Com%2030/

personnel. She was picked up by the Mexico City station where she would eventually work for David Atlee Phillips. After the assassination of JFK, contacts of Phillips in Mexico City made false claims about Oswald and him being in league with Castro, Cobb was one of these. She stated that she had seen Oswald at a twist party with known leftists.

Cobb also was active for the Fair Play for Cuba Committee, which was founded in March 1960, which strongly suggests she was a plant for the CIA whom she worked for in the spring of 1960.[36]

Victor Thomas Vicente

In 1960, the FBI penetrated three pro-Castro organizations including the FPCC National headquarters with Puerto Rican informant Vicente (T-3245-S). He played a key role in providing mailing lists and other valuable information. Vicente is the one who sent Oswald his original FPCC materials.

Aided by FPCC President Vincent Lee, and using his FPCC credentials, he entered Cuba by way of Mexico City around mid-July 1963 for espionage purposes as had done the head of the FPCC a year earlier. (Probably Richard Gibson.) CIA agents Louis De Santi, Henri Kitchens and Anita Potocki (who helped Santiago Garriga open a Miami FPCC chapter) helped prepare Vicente for his mission in which the FBI was also involved. A 1967 IG report states that a Puerto Rican claimed to have assisted Castro in the assassination of JFK. The CIA only says that they did not know if this person was Thomas Vicente.[37]

---

[36] https://documents.theblackvault.com/documents/jfk/NARA-Oct2017/2018/104-10218-10093.pdf and
https://history-matters.com/archive/jfk/wc/wcvols/wh26/pdf/WH26_CE_2953.pdf
[37] https://www.archives.gov/files/research/jfk/releases/2023/104-10308-10163.pdf

The Latin American Division/DDO 1977 Report and FPCC Pointing

This CIA document[38] adds weight to the whole FPCC patsy and Castro linking propaganda that was taking place in and around the assassination. Consider the following rumors that are underscored:

Page 33: A Cuban contact claimed that he received a letter in 1962 purporting to warn about a plot to assassinate JFK that linked the potential murderer to Richard Taber.

Page 54: Harry Dean is linked to a possible G2 officer named Frank Vega whom he would have met in Cuba prior to the assassination.

Combined with the vague suggestion about Vicente (see above), there seems to be traces that were left if *the Castro-was-behind-it* scenario had been favored.

HSCA Comments About the Secret Service and Prior Plots

While this section chronicles suspicious peculiarities around similar events and subjects pertaining to November 22, 1963, The HSCA commented on only three.

Concerning Vallee:

- That the Secret Service prior to the assassination possessed information that was not properly analyzed and disseminated.

- There is a November 27, 1963, notation on the similarities between Oswald and Vallee in terms of backgrounds.

- That even if Vallee remained a threat after November 2, information about Vallee was not forwarded to agents responsible for JFK's Texas trip… The Secret Service failed to make appropriate use of the information supplied about the Chicago threat in early November.

---

[38] https://www.archives.gov/files/research/jfk/releases/2023/104-10506-10028.pdf

Concerning Joseph Milteer:

- The Secret Service failed to follow up on the Miami threat out of Miami.

- The Milteer threat was ignored by Secret Service personnel in planning the trip to Dallas.

Both the Church Committee and the HSCA concurred when criticizing the lack of support by the FBI and the CIA to the Warren Commission by divulging nothing about a Tampa Plot to assassinate JFK and suspect Gilberto Policarpo Lopez:

- The Committee concurred with the Senate Select Committee that this omission was egregious, since the circumstances surrounding Lopez's travel seemed "suspicious."

The HSCA also stated that:

- The fact was, however, that two threats to assassinate the President using high-power rifles, both made in November 1963, were not relayed to the Dallas Region.

They go on to show how this led to deficiencies in the motorcade inspection and surveillance of buildings during the motorcade by security including the TSBD.

Based on only three incidents, the HSCA comments are blistering. One can only imagine what conclusions they would have come to, had the twenty plus incidents described in this section been delved into seriously.[39]

---

[39] https://www.maryferrell.org/showDoc.html?docId=800#relPageId=258

Similar Case Comparison Chart

The summary chart below compares 12 incidents (excluding the Milteer threats) and 15 subjects connected to these. Because the Secret Service destroyed or hid case files on these, and that almost all were not investigated by intelligence services, many questions around these cases remain unanswered.

From what we do know, there are peculiarities that come screaming out that cannot be explained by happenstance.

First let us look at some key points:

- Out of the twelve similar cases described in this section, only November 22 was the focus of any of the six governmental investigations.

- The HSCA and Church committees criticized the intelligence agencies in not passing on critical information to the Warren Commission. The HSCA singled out the Secret Service and FBI silence around Lopez, Milteer and Vallee cases as particularly questionable; The AARB highly criticized Secret Service destruction of JFK fall 1963 travel files just before they were to be made accessible to the ARRB. From the chart, we can see that risk management by the Secret Service should have been disseminated by data on at least ten key incidents that we know of that preceded the assassination.

- Another criticism of the HSCA was about how the Secret Service did not pass on prior plot data to the Dallas trip planners, which contributed to lapses in security. They stated that the risks of being fired on by a high-power rifle from a tall building in Dallas were not managed considering the Chicago plot and the Milteer threats, as well as JFK's own, expressed concerns about such a tragedy. The Springfield incident where a rifle was actually pointed at the President as well as the Tampa Plot represent at least two more killing M.O.s that fall in this category.

- Only one of the incidents is not connected to an area that is not mafia linked to Trafficante, Giancana, Marcello or Roselli (all Mafiosi of interest in the assassination of JFK).

- We know little to nothing about three subjects detained and questioned in the Springfield and Nashville plots as well as four likely assassins (two of whom were picked up for questioning) related to the Chicago threats.

- Six of the eight named murder-connected subjects served their country in the forces, up to five were posted in the far east like Oswald, one was a U2 radar operator like Oswald, two others were pro-Castro Cuban exiles. Vallée, Lopez and Oswald all moved to the cities where the threats were in play shortly before Kennedy's visits, a team of four suspected shooters traveled to Chicago to be there during a presidential motorcade. Oswald himself was linking himself and being linked to Washington for a September event.

- If we include the subjects in the Statue of Liberty bombing plot, we can see that at least nine out of twelve known subjects are FPCC linked; (note: Collier of the 1965 bombing threat was ex-Air force, Bowe was FPCC linked, Collier and Saulnier traveled to Cuba in 1964. Collier met Che Guevara during a United Nations event in the U.S.). Therefore at least fifteen of these characters were pro-Castro tainted. Only one of these, Arthur Vallée, cannot be confirmed to be plausibly communist. At least ten visited or attempted to visit Cuba. At least eleven have ties to subversive and/or communist associations (LBS, SWP, Communist Party, BLF, etc.).

Subject	Planned crime location	Date	Forces served	Intel link	Visit or Attempt to visit Cuba	Affiliations	Alleged instability	Secret Service file sharing
Lee Harvey Oswald	Dallas	Nov. 22, 1963	Marines	Likely Informant	Through Mexico Sept. 63	ACLU, CORE, SWP, FPCC	x	None
Lee Harvey Oswald	Wash.	Late Sept 63			alleged			None
Two Riflemen	Springfield, Illinois	Oct-62	Unknown	Unknown	Unknown	Unknown	Unknown	None
One shooter	Nashville	May 1, 1963	Unknown	Unknown	Unknown	Unknown	Unknown	None
Vaughn Marlowe	L.A.	Jun-63	Yes	Unknown	Through Mexico City	ACLU, CORE. SWP, FPCC	Unknown	None
Thomas Arthur Vallee	Chicago	Nov. 2, 1963	Yes	Unknown	No	JBS, Trained Cuban Exiles	x	None
Santiago Garriga	Miami	Nov. 18, 1963	No	Yes	Yes via Mexico City	FPCC/head Miami		None
Policarpo Lopez	Tampa	Nov. 18, 1963	Unknown	Unknown	Yes via Mexico City	FPCC	Yes	None
Harry Power	San Antonio	Nov. 21, 1963	Yes	Unknown		Young Communist League	Yes	None
Richard Case Nagell	Various	1963	Yes	Yes	Yes via Mexico City	FPCC and Communist Group	Yes	None
Robert Beaty Fernell	San Francisco Threats against LBJ	Dec. 21, 1963	Air Force			FPCC	Yes	None
Liberty Lobby Bombers -4 alleged terrorists	Several (Monument Destruction plans)	Feb. 16, 1965			Yes, met Che Guevara	Black Panthers		Unknown

Overall, the conclusions one can reach from all these related incidences are indefensible by backers of the Warren Report:

1. The crime of the century was extremely poorly investigated. The omission of doing case-linkage analysis is egregious.

2. The Secret Service was so deficient in both the protection of the president and the ensuing government inquiries as well as a proactive impediment to their investigation efforts, that at a minimum they should be guilty of being part of a cover-up.

3. The exponential increase in attempts to kill JFK in the fall of 1963 points to an end of 1963 drop-dead deadline to eliminate him.

4. An overwhelming number of subjects are ex-military and are FPCC/Castro-linked and cannot be explained by coincidence. The timely movements by some of the subjects so as to end up in strategic kill-Zone venues is further indicative of stratagems.

The subjects not in the chart but profiled in this section include Harry Dean, June Cobb, Victor Thomas Vicente, John Glenn, Vincent T. Lee, Harrold Wilson, Johnny Rossen, Al Lewis and Richard Taber. Though they cannot be definitely linked to attempts to kill JFK, there are definite similarities to Oswald in that they were all FPCC linked, many were likely or definite informants, visited Cuba and were ex-military, and number were connected with Castro—frame jobs after the assassination.

This cannot be explained by mere happenstance. There are too many peculiarities that point to an offender profile. The personas, connections, actions of the perpetrators profiled simply have too many similarities. The FPCC, deemed Castro's network in the U.S. by the Eastland Committee, was nationally in a vegetative state when the murder occurred with fewer than 1500 members on November 22, 1963, and infested by informants. Oswald's actions with the FPCC in New Orleans in the summer of 1963 were those of a provocateur on a mission that caused investigation insiders to have serious doubts about his true loyalties and credos. And the whole strategy, of selecting surrogates to commit a crime so shocking that the U.S. population would demand retribution, using paper trails and other markers as well as a patsy who could shift the blame on a foe, in this case Castro, comes right out of intelligence regime change and executive action playbooks code-named ZR/RIFLE[40] and Operation Northwoods.[41]

---

[40] https://spartacus-educational.com/JFKzrrifle.htm
[41] https://spartacus-educational.com/JFKnorthwoods.htm

CHAPTER 7

THE EVIDENTIARY MESS OF THE TWENTIETH CENTURY

BY JAMES DiEUGENIO

STATEMENT

JFK'S MURDER DEMANDED the best clinical investigation ever performed in U.S. history in order to help solve one of the nadiral crimes of the last century. Instead, his medical examination was one of the worst on record placed in the hands of order-taking incompetents. This alone would have seen a case against Oswald being thrown out of court and points to what can only be described as a rigged operation to prop up a lone nut scenario.

INTRODUCTION

In this chapter, we will look at three distinct episodes during the first hours following the assassination that strongly point to an active operation to obstruct both the investigation into the cause of death of President Kennedy and silence and suppress key expert medical personnel, whose eyewitness evidence differed from the developing lone-nut-shooter-from-behind narrative that was concocted to become the government's non-conspiracy theory. Those three episodes of obstruction and witness tampering/intimidation are as follows:

1. Dr. Malcolm Perry's determination of the anterior neck wound;

2. The failure to track President Kennedy's back wound at the autopsy;

3. The threats that were made to Dr. Malcolm Perry.

In terms of the evidentiary issues that arise from these clear indicators of hindrance and witness tampering, problems for the government's case would impact the admissibility of evidence, the weighing of evidence, and the potential for serious criminal charges resulting from the witness badgering.

EVIDENCE

Within 12 hours of John F. Kennedy being pronounced dead at Parkland Hospital, there is clear and convincing evidence that three acts were committed which would constitute obstruction of justice or witness tampering and intimidation in a court of law involving his murder. In a nutshell, these three incontrovertible facts each revolved around what today's law enforcement calls the determination of the "cause of death."

The court system relies entirely on the sanctity of evidence and on the reliable conduct of the officials involved in the investigation of a death and the determination of the cause of death. Establishing the precise cause of death is an absolutely necessary component of our justice system. Without such a determination, judges and juries would have an impossible job arriving at a verdict based on the criminal—beyond a reasonable doubt—standard of proof. To bring this into perspective, an example of the fundamental importance of accurately determining the cause of death could be drawn from a case where the police find a frozen body in a remote wooded area.

Understanding whether the death was the result of hypothermia or asphyxiation would dramatically change the course of the ensuing investigation, leading on one hand to a finding of a natural cause of death versus an unnatural cause of death. If police and medical pathologists concealed evidence of signs of asphyxiation, such as hemorrhaging in the eyes, edema in the skin and lungs, or bruising around the throat, the determination of hypothermia as the cause of death, would result in a horrible miscarriage of justice.

More than almost any other area of the Kennedy assassination, the medical evidence from Parkland Hospital in Dallas and the evidence from the autopsy that took place at Bethesda, Maryland, have been subjected to the greatest level of scrutiny and criticism from both the assassination research community and the American public in general.

The divergence of the evidence from Dallas and Bethesda has been responsible for the very large majority of the "American Jury" continuing to believe that Lee Harvey Oswald did not "act alone" or at all in respect to the murder. This divergence of the Dallas and Bethesda evidence strongly suggests that forces were at play to obstruct the investigation of the President's murder and to tamper with and intimidate critical witnesses whose evidence would challenge the Oswald did it alone from the sixth floor narrative.

Taking each of these incidents in isolation and examining the core pieces of evidence under the standard of proof of clear and convincing evidence, a clear picture emerges that the efforts to control the most important aspects of the determination of the cause of death and to silence key witnesses amounts to obstruction of justice and witness tampering/intimidation.

After President Kennedy was declared dead, Dr. Kemp Clark, who was the Director of Neurological Surgery at Parkland Hospital and the Chair of Neurological Surgery at the University of Texas, Southwestern Medical School and Dr. Malcolm Perry, General and Vascular Surgeon and then Assistant Professor at Southwestern Medical School—who both tried to save his life—held a press conference at Parkland Hospital.

Three times during that press conference, Dr. Perry stated that President Kennedy's anterior neck wound appeared to him to be an entrance wound.[1] Dr. Perry would have been in the best position to determine that since he performed the tracheotomy on the president which overlapped the entrance wound. This would mean that Kennedy was shot at from the front. Which, of course, would denote a conspiracy. Because the alleged assassin, Lee Harvey Oswald, was positioned behind the president at the Texas School Book Depository, and Kennedy was traveling

---

[1] Douglas Horne, Inside the ARRB, p. 645

away from the building. In the film, *The Parkland Doctors,*[2] it was revealed that, after that press conference, a well-dressed man grabbed Perry by the arm and told him, "Don't you ever say that again."

The scene of the autopsy on the evening of the assassination was the morgue at Bethesda Naval Center. Here, another obstruction took place. Since Kennedy was killed by gunshot wounds—through the back and through his skull—there should have been a dissection of bullet tracks: through his back and his brain. When the doctors were attempting to dissect the back wound, that proceeding was interrupted. At the 1969 trial of Clay Shaw in New Orleans, one of the pathologists, Pierre Finck, was placed on the witness stand by the defense. On cross-examination, he was asked this question by the assistant to DA Jim Garrison, Alvin Oser: *Why did you not dissect the path of the back wound in President Kennedy? Finck refused to answer, even though the question was repeated several times. Finally, the judge instructed Finck to reply. Finck said that he was told not to, but he did not recall by whom. Previously, Finck had testified that when Dr. James Humes, the lead pathologist asked, "Who is in charge here?" he heard an Army General say, "I am." After revealing this, Finck added, "You must understand that in those circumstances, there were law enforcement officials, military people, with various ranks and you have to coordinate the operations according to directions."*[3]

Later, there was a third obstruction of justice. About a week after the homicide, Malcolm Perry told reporter Martin Steadman that he was getting calls the night of the assassination from Bethesda. They had learned about what he said during his press conference at Parkland about the anterior neck wound. After the autopsy, a couple of the pathologists were now on the phone with him. They wanted him to take back what he said. Perry resisted. He had treated hundreds of patients with similar wounds, he therefore understood the difference between entrance and exit wounds. He was also a hunter, so he could ascertain the difference at a glance. He could only say that which he thought to be true.

---

[2] https://www.imdb.com/title/tt5536420/

[3] James DiEugenio, Destiny Betrayed, second edition, pp. 300-02

At this point, one or more of the doctors said he would be brought before a medical board if he continued to insist on his story. They threatened to take away his license. After Perry related this compelling story, Steadman asked him if he still thought the throat wound was one of entrance. Perry replied in the affirmative.[4]

Perry and Finck were doctors who were involved in the medical proceedings following a murder by gunshot wounds. This means they were material witnesses to the direct results of the outcome. Therefore, they would be called to testify at legal proceedings afterward. This is where the obstruction of justice and witness intimidation enters the picture. It is illegal for someone to interfere with a witness's statements before a legal proceeding has taken place. The incidents described above took place while Oswald was alive and therefore everyone involved assumed he would be standing trial for the crime of murder.

But in discussing proper legal procedure we should not leave out one other important element: Kennedy was killed in Dallas. Therefore, at that time, his autopsy should have been performed by the local medical examiner. That man was Dr. Earl Rose, and by all references and descriptions, he was a proficient forensic pathologist. His office was right in Parkland Hospital. So why was he not the examiner of record? He did try to carry out his duty. In fact, he intercepted the body as it was being escorted out by the Secret Service and Jacqueline Kennedy. He stopped it and said the following words: "There has been a homicide here. They won't be able to leave until there has been an autopsy."[5]

What happened next haunted Rose for months on end, maybe longer. Rose made it crystal clear that the law decreed that the body could not depart without him doing an autopsy. The Secret Service, particularly agent Roy Kellerman, said: "My friend, this is the body of the President of the United States, and we are going to take it back to Washington."[6]

The dialogue escalated into a loud argument, carried on by first

---

[4] "The Ordeal of Malcolm Perry," by James DiEugenio, at Kennedysandking.com
[5] William Manchester, The Death of a President, p. 297
[6] Ibid., p 298

Kellerman and then Admiral George Burkley, Kennedy's personal physician. Rose very acutely said, "You can't lose the chain of evidence."[7] Eventually there were close to forty people involved in what William Manchester justly called a melee. Rose was literally shoved aside. As we shall see, this fourth violation of the law would have momentous repercussions.[8] By all reports, Earl Rose would have given President Kennedy a professional autopsy. As the plane was in flight, Dr. Milton Helpern, the Medical Examiner in New York City, began packing his bags and contemplating who would be his assistants in this most important postmortem.[9] Helpern was the most famous, storied, illustrious forensic pathologist of that day. He is known today as the first superstar pathologist. If the autopsy was going to be done on the east coast, he was the natural choice to do it. He was surprised that no phone call came. As we shall see, the overrunning of Rose, and the failure to call Helpern, would spell enormous negative consequences for the Kennedy case.

When the body arrived at Andrews Air Force Base, there were three key events that occurred. First, since the autopsy would be done at Bethesda, the pathologists would be drawn from that institution. To typify the two men from that center as being a step down from Helpern does not do justice to what happened in that declension. As Russell Kent notes in his recent book, James Humes may have done one or two autopsies of gunshot victims at Tripler Hospital in Hawaii and the Naval Medical Center in San Diego. But his only exposure to forensic pathology was a one-week course he finished ten years prior to JFK's death.[10] In 1963, Humes was a senior administrator at Bethesda, not an active pathologist. He told the Warren Commission that he was "charged with the responsibility of the overall supervision of all of the laboratory operations in the Naval Medical Center."[11]

Thornton Boswell was Chief of Pathology at the National Naval Medical School. He was also not an active pathologist at this time. This can

---

[7] Ibid., p 299
[8] Ibid.
[9] Cyril Wecht, in Oliver Stone's film JFK Revisited
[10] JFK Medical Betrayal, p. 26
[11] Warren Commission Hearings, Vol. 2, p. 348

be imputed since on the autopsy face sheet, he did not write down Kennedy's name or sign his own document. Understanding they lacked some experience, they asked for an outside consultant. This request was denied.[12] Instead they were assigned, after the autopsy began, Dr. Finck, who was a forensic pathologist. Yet he had only been board certified for two years. And this came when he was not actively performing postmortem examinations. Since 1960, Finck had been at the Armed Forces Institute of Pathology (AFIP). His job was to review the works of other pathologists. At that, his office consisted of himself and a secretary.[13] Also, Finck was an army man in the midst of a Navy hospital.

Finck's presence that night would later result in the first inside view of what really happened in that autopsy room. As we have seen, this took place in 1969 at the trial of Clay Shaw in New Orleans.

The second important event that occurred as Kennedy's body was flying into Andrews was a phone call that Robert Knudsen received.[14] Knudsen was a White House photographer. Someone called him and told him to accompany Kennedy's body to Bethesda. This was odd since there was *already* an autopsy photographer at Bethesda, John Stringer. In 1977, Knudsen told a photography magazine that he had taken pictures of Kennedy's autopsy—and it was the hardest thing he did in his life.[15] This is a remarkable statement since he was never interviewed by the Warren Commission. In fact, his name is not in the Warren Report. Or perhaps it's not so remarkable, since Stringer was not interviewed either.[16] There are very real questions about the extant pictures of Kennedy from this autopsy. And Robert Knudsen belatedly adds a potentially significant piece to fill in that puzzle.

The third maneuver that took place at this time, and likely had an effect on the medical procedure, is something that was unknown for decades after Kennedy's death. It was only when a lost segment of the Air Force One Tapes were partly discovered that we learned some rather

---

[12] Dr. Gary Aguilar in Oliver Stone's JFK Destiny Betrayed
[13] Kent, p. 30
[14] Douglas Horne, Inside the ARRB, p. 249
[15] Ibid., p 247
[16] Walt Brown, The Warren Omission, pp. 99–100

surprising information about who was headed to Washington that night. In the recovered tapes, we learn that General Curtis LeMay was flying into town. Yet he would not respond to his aide-de-camp, Colonel George Dorman. Dorman tried to talk to LeMay at least three times. He did not reply to any of his attempts. As we shall see, there was a possible reason for that.[17]

Why is this important information? In his book *Dark Sun*, Richard Rhodes wrote that author Fletcher Knebel "said he got the idea for *Seven Days in May* while interviewing Curtis LeMay," the Air Force Chief of Staff. Knebel said that the general went off the record and accused President Kennedy of cowardice in his response to the failure of the Bay of Pigs invasion.[18] Needless to add, this had an inspirational impact on Knebel. *Seven Days in May* depicted an attempted overthrow of the American government by the Pentagon.

Why was LeMay flying into Washington at this particular time? And why would he not reply to Dorman? We will try to answer those questions later in this section.

One of the questions one has to pose is this: If the autopsy had been done by Helpern, would he have tolerated the surfeit of military brass, Secret Service and FBI agents at the proceedings? No one knows exactly how many were there. But Finck said under oath that the morgue was crawling with military men and the most current estimates range from 33 to 42.[19] The reason the number is indefinite is that the list that the FBI agents sent around was not signed by everyone.[20]

This influence may have impacted one of the most elementary processes which should have been made that evening, i.e., the weighing of Kennedy's brain. Officially, it was not done that night. But, complicating the matter, Thornton Boswell told the ARRB that it *was* weighed that evening.[21] It is difficult to understand which is worse: if the brain was not weighed that evening, or if it was and it was not recorded. The latter

---

[17] See "The New Air Force One Tapes" at the Mary Ferrell Foundation website.
[18] See Horne, p. 1743
[19] DiEugenio, Destiny Betrayed, p. 301
[20] JFK Revisited, by James DiEugenio, p. 189
[21] The Assassinations, edited by James DiEugenio and Lisa Pease, p. 253

alternative leaves the door open to all kinds of explanations as to why. It is almost impossible to imagine this would have happened under the stewardship of Earl Rose or Milton Helpern.

Why is this failure so important? In 1965, Finck stated that on November 29th, the brain weighed in at 1500 grams before the supplementary autopsy and brain examination. There are at least two serious problems with this. An extensive study of brain weight made in a Dutch medical journal established that the average brain for an adult male weighed about 1340 grams.[22] As Dr. Gary Aguilar and others have noted, how could Kennedy's brain weigh more than the average when anyone can inspect the photos and film during and after the shooting. Those images and witness testimonies all reveal a head explosion of blood and tissue into the air; brain being blasted out to the back of the car—which Jackie Kennedy retrieves; blood all over Jackie Kennedy; the back of the limousine imbued with more blood and tissue. And as Josiah Thompson noted in his book *Last Second in Dallas*, the motorcycle riders to Kennedy's left also said they had been hit with bits of brain, so hard that one of them thought he might have been hit by a projectile.[23] So how could Kennedy's brain weigh *more* than the average?

There is also a problem here with chains of possession. If Finck had recorded a weight on November 29th, then what is it that James Humes surrendered to George Burkley to be interred with Kennedy's body, with the interment done on November 25?[24] This mystery gets even more compelling when one looks at the records of the supplementary autopsy report. This report was supposed to include a separate brain exam. But it says that no sectioning took place "In the interest of preserving the specimen."[25] As many, including Cyril Wecht, have commented: Preserving the specimen for whom? And for what?

But this passage in the Warren Report was not explored to any consequential degree by Arlen Specter in his examination of the patho-

---

[22] JFK Revisited, by James DiEugenio, p. 298
[23] Thompson, Last Second in Dallas, pp 55-56
[24] DiEugenio and Pease, p. 255
[25] Warren Report, p 544

logists. To any real forensic pathologist—like Helpern or Rose—to fail to section the brain would, in reality, be unconscionable. After all, this was a murder by a gunshot case. If the brain is not sectioned, then how does one tell what the bullet path was through the skull, or even how many projectiles were fired through the head?[26]

The seeming break in the chain of possession of the brain that is outlined above, eventually led to a rather remarkable discovery. In 1972, Cyril Wecht was allowed to enter the National Archives and inspect the medical evidence housed there by deed of gift from the Kennedy family. He discovered that Kennedy's brain was not there.[27]

Therefore, if as James Humes said in the supplementary report, the brain was not sectioned, every review of the Kennedy case since the Warren Commission—the Ramsey Clark Panel of 1968, the Rockefeller Commission of 1975, the HSCA of 1976-78—has had to rely on the pictures and X-rays and not the (allegedly) preserved brain. So, the question becomes: are those pictures and X-rays reliable evidence?

As stated above, the Warren Commission did not interview either John Stringer or Robert Knudsen. The HSCA did question Stringer and Knudsen, but these were informal and were not published in their volumes of testimony and exhibits. It was the ARRB that finally began to excavate the probable reason that Knudsen was called in that day.

The ARRB did something that, rather strangely, had not been done before. They first interviewed Stringer about his preparation, routine, and techniques used in his photography. They then showed him the pictures he had allegedly taken of President Kennedy's brain.[28] The results of this exchange were striking. Stringer was quite surprised when he was confronted by the pictures.

ARRB employee Doug Horne was in the room during this deposition. Stringer's interview negated the autopsy pictures of Kennedy's brain from ever being introduced as evidence in any kind of legal proceeding. Because to be introduced as evidence, any picture, or illustration, must

---

[26] DiEugenio, JFK Revisited, p 298
[27] DiEugenio and Pease, p 269
[28] Horne, p 803

be attested to as being authentic by the person who produced it. Stringer identified five different ways in which the pictures in the archives differed from what he had taken.[29] Two of those five were because of the film process utilized in the extant pictures and the actual film stock used. This leaves the question: If Stringer did not take these pictures, then who did—and why?

As Doug Horne noted in his interview for Oliver Stone's film *JFK Revisited,* the HSCA did not publish Knudsen's statements, and they did not follow up on the information he offered. By the time the ARRB was up and running, Knudsen had already passed on.[30] It was the Board that caused an investigation into what he had said to the HSCA, and in private to his family. Knudsen had maintained to his wife and children that he had photographed the autopsy of President Kennedy, and he thought he was the only one who did.[31] His family also said he was gone from home for 72 hours from the time of the initiating phone call.

The observations made by Knudsen were contrary to where the HSCA was headed. For instance, Knudsen said he saw, and photographed probes inserted in the President's body which left little doubt about bullet trajectories. These do not exist today. Knudsen said that he did not recognize some of the photos the HSCA showed him of Kennedy's autopsy, and he thought one of them had been altered. He also saw a brain that was severely damaged, missing a significant amount of mass. Knudsen also claimed that the back of the head photo showing it to be intact was a forgery, there was a cavity there.[32]

Knudsen was not just backed up by his family or his photography magazine interview in 1977. His widow had located other Navy witnesses whom he also related his story to and worked with him in processing the Kennedy autopsy photos.[33] Further, Knudsen recalled his photos were taken in what was called a film pack or press pack.[34] This

---

[29] Ibid., p 810
[30] Ibid., p 248
[31] Ibid., pp 249-50
[32] Ibid., pp 251-53, 266
[33] Ibid., p 253
[34] Ibid., p 278

is a crucial distinction since it is this technique that Stringer said he *did not* use in his photography. Therefore, if Stringer did not take the pictures of the brain, did Knudsen?

The pictures and illustrations we have today depict not just a brain that is over the average weight, but one that is, except for some disruption on the right side—when seen from the bottom—almost intact.[35]

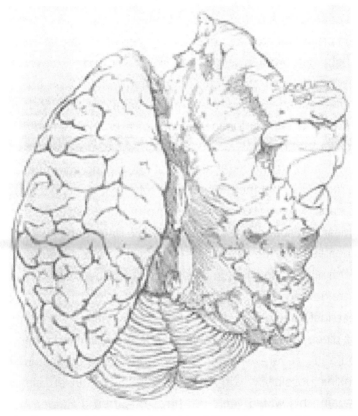

Again, how could this be in light of the photographic and film evidence to the contrary? But there is even more evidence defining this very severe evidentiary problem. That is in addition to the testimony of Stringer and Knudsen, plus the incomprehensible problem with the weight and shape of the brain, there is the fact that so many people saw a brain that did not look anything like what those pictures depict.

---

[35] https://history-matters.com/essays/jfkmed/How5Investigations/How5InvestigationsGotItWrong_tabfig.htm

To give some examples: Dr. Robert McClelland at Parkland said about a third of the brain and some cerebellar tissue had been blasted out.[36] Dr. Perry described a gaping wound in the back of the head "exposing lacerated brain." And he later added, "There was severe laceration of underlying brain tissue."[37] Nurse Diana Bowron packed Kennedy's head wound with gauze squares at Parkland. She later recalled that perhaps as much as half of the brain was gone.[38]

The descriptions of the brain at Bethesda also depict a very much damaged brain, not an intact one. Dr. Humes estimated as much as 2/3 of the right cerebrum was missing.[39] Dr. Thornton Boswell basically agreed when he said about half of one hemisphere was absent.[40] FBI agent James Sibert was very clear on this point. He noted that when one looks at a complete anatomical picture of a brain, Kennedy's was not anything like that.[41]

Boswell said something that is most compelling about this whole issue. He remarked that the brain was so torn up it would not have shown a bullet track.[42] James Curtis Jenkins, a morgue assistant said something similar. He stated that the brain was so damaged, it was difficult to induce needles into the blood vessels in order to perfuse the specimen with a formalin solution.[43] Humes essentially agreed with Jenkins about the severe damage creating perfusion problems.[44]

These last three observations are quite revealing as to the deception that took place at the autopsy about Kennedy's brain and related issues. How could the severely damaged brain described by Humes, Boswell and Jenkins possibly weigh 1500 grams and be in an almost intact state? Again, this would likely not have occurred if Helpern had been running things there. Or if the autopsy had taken place in Dallas under

---

[36] Robert Groden and Harrison Livingstone, High Treason, p. 226
[37] Ibid., p 247
[38] DiEugenio and Pease, p. 251
[39] Journal of the Medical Association, 5/27/92, p. 2798
[40] ARRB deposition, 2/26/96, pp. 42–43
[41] William Matson Law, in the Eye of History, p. 257
[42] ARRB deposition, p. 193
[43] DiEugenio and Pease, p. 251
[44] ARRB Deposition, 2/13/96, pp. 107-08

Earl Rose. These are strong indications that the shocking failure to weigh the brain at autopsy was purposeful. Or if it was weighed, the missing measurement was likely deep-sixed.

The photos of the brain revealed another anomaly, according to Doug Horne: "The review board had a consultant—a renowned forensic pathologist. He looked at the photographs and he said, this is a very well-fixed brain. It's all gray. It's not pink at all. It's been fixed for two or three weeks in formaldehyde. It's been fixed at least two weeks, maybe as long as three weeks. I looked back at Jeremy Gunn, and he looked back at me, and the hair stood up on the back of my neck, because I knew JFK's brain was examined less than three days after he was killed."[45]

If one needed any more evidence about this deception, there is a coda supplied by doctors David Mantik (radiologist) and Cyril Wecht (forensic pathologist). They were influenced by the revolutionary work on this matter by ARRB Chief Counsel Jeremy Gunn and Military Records Analyst Doug Horne. Therefore, they decided to explore this paradox by doing research and conducting experiments. Through the use of accurate medical reconstructions of what a brain should be made up of, and using optical densitometer readings to test that consistency, they came up with some rather surprising findings. These became manifest when they transferred the experiment to the National Archives and compared the readings against both the skull X-rays and brain photos. The X-ray readings did not match the pictures. To the two physicians, the OD readings showed that there was significant brain tissue absent in the pictures. The two professionals explain in detail where it was missing and why in their landmark essay.[46]

If you thought that this is as bewildering as it gets, take a deep breath. The official story has pathologist Jim Humes giving the medical exhibits, including the brain, to Admiral George Burkley—Kennedy's private doctor—for the internment. Two credible witnesses interviewed by the ARRB added a new twist to the JFK brain mystery. On April 1, 1997, Dave Montague, principal field investigator for the ARRB at this time, and

---

[45] DiEugenio, JFK Revisited, p. 161
[46] DiEugenio and Pease, pp. 264-66

Joan Zimmerman, who was the ARRB point person concerning the Se-cret Service, interviewed James M. Mastrovito. He was a 20-year vet-eran of the Secret Service: 1959 to 1979. He was on the White House detail from 1960 to 1962. After the murder of Kennedy, he was relocated from a field office to headquarters. Once the PRS—Protective Research Section—was reorganized into the Intelligence Division, he became a deputy there. He held this spot for about a decade. Then, for a few years before he retired, he became the director of that division.

During their exchange, Mastrovito revealed that he pared down five to six file cabinets of JFK files to just one. Stunning as this was, it is what he said about Kennedy's brain that can only be described as a bomb-shell: " ... he had received a piece of President Kennedy's brain." He continued by saying it was contained in a vial with the identifying label on it. And here he offered a very intriguing further detail. The vial, about the size of a prescription bottle, was from the Armed Forces Institute of Pathology (AFIP). When Zimmerman asked him who handed him the vial, he said that it was Walter Young, who was the first chief of the In-telligence Division. This was when Young retired and Mastrovito took over; he assumed it was given to Young from someone at AFIP. Unfor-tunately, Young had died a year before the interview. Incredibly, Mastrovito said he eliminated the content of the vial in a machine that destroys food.

Of course, naysayers will simply dismiss this as another mistaken witness, except that it corroborated another account given to the ARRB on November 12, 1996. *This one came from a man named Ken Vrtacnik who also worked at AFIP. Vrtacnik had been stationed at AFIP during the years 1964-65. He was interviewed by Montague and Horne. In a remarkable piece of testimony, what he had testified was consistent with Mastrovito's affirmations. He said that he had seen Kennedy's brain dur-ing the 1964-65 period, and he stated it had been kept in a locked room as part of the AFIP complex. Like Mastrovito, he said he knew it was Kennedy's brain since it was labeled as such. He also added that it was under very tight control. But he said an AFIP employee, Joyce Manus, who ran the Pathology Data Division, could produce a data sheet which would show when the specimen was received, from whom, and its current status there. This writer has not been able to find any ARRB interview with Manus.*[47]

CONCLUSION

The aim of this chapter has been to attempt to prove that there was a deception done at Bethesda the evening of the assassination involving President Kennedy's autopsy, especially his brain. This is why it was not weighed or sectioned, which should have been done almost by rote in this kind of death by gunshot wound case. The author has endeavored to prove this by multiple planes of evidence:

1. The testimony of autopsy photographers John Stringer and Robert Knudsen.

2. The comparison of normal weights of brain specimens with Kennedy's.

3. Statements made by eyewitnesses who do not recall a brain that looks like what the official renditions depict.

4. The optical densitometer readings which betray that the X-rays do not match the brain photos.

This would seem to the authors to supply a surfeit of evidence to prove this deception: namely that the brain photos extant at the National Archives are not the genuine pictures of President Kennedy's brain. According to Boswell, Humes and Jenkins, the apparent reason was that the actual brain revealed too much damage.

It is no wonder that Doug Horne was obviously bewildered by all of

---

[47] https://www.kennedysandking.com/john-f-kennedy-articles/the-mystery-of-kennedy-s-brain-deepens The Mystery of Kennedy's Brain Deepens J. DiEugenio, KennedysandKing, August 22, 2023

this when he stated: "So, the autopsy of John F. Kennedy is probably the evidentiary mess of the twentieth century."

But before concluding this work, we should add that this is not the only irregularity in the autopsy. Not even close. As noted above, the brain was not sectioned and therefore there was no path discerned to specify a bullet track or tracks. Well, the bullet wound in Kennedy's back was also not dissected. Therefore as Dr. Henry Lee told the author of this chapter, no missile trajectory can be adduced for this wound. Lee is likely the most experienced criminalist in America today.

But further, Dr. Humes wrote in his autopsy report that there existed a line of particles going from low in the rear of JFK's skull and ascending to a point high in the skull. When the ARRB questioned Humes, they asked him about this description. Namely did he see this particle trail that he described in the X-rays now placed before him. He admitted to the Board that it did not exist in these X-rays. The obvious question being: Where did that trail go? Or was it ever there in the first place?

There are the many quandaries that exist in this case to this day—60 years after Kennedy's death. Many of them are due to a completely unsatisfactory autopsy. Could it have been just by happenstance, or was it designed that way? After all, who was that man who warned Perry right after his press conference? And who was instructing the pathologists to call Perry and pressure him to change his story that night? In addition to failing to reply to Colonel Dorman, LeMay lied about where he was that day: he was not in Michigan, he was in Canada. He also broke orders by not landing at Andrews Air Force base.

A skilled attorney could conduct a cogent cross-examination of those issues. Why did LeMay lie about where he was that day? Why was he attempting to hide his plane's destination by not replying to Colonel Dorman? Why did he break orders about Andrews? Was it because he did not want anyone to photograph or film him landing there? These would have all been pertinent questions to pose to someone who genuinely disliked President Kennedy. To the point that a celebrated author wrote a best-selling book about an attempted coup because of him.

The attorney could have concluded that LeMay interrogation by reading the Air Force general some interesting testimony by morgue assistant Paul O'Connor. During the autopsy, Humes noticed someone smoking a cigar in the morgue gallery. He told Paul to tell the man to put out his cigar. But when the assistant got over to where the man was, he saw it was LeMay, who blew smoke at him. He reported this back to Humes, who understood the problem.

The above would have all made for a very interesting interview.

CHAPTER 8

THE SINGLE BULLET FABRICATION

BY JAMES DiEUGENIO

STATEMENT

THE SINGLE BULLET Theory cannot be correct which means that more than three shots were fired at JFK on November 22, 1963, which even the Warren Commission and its offspring recognize as impossible for a lone shooter to have accomplished. This, on its own, removes the whole foundation the Warren Commission conclusions rely upon ... which means that there were at least two shooters who fired at Kennedy ... which means there was a conspiracy.

INTRODUCTION

The Magic Bullet was the title given to Commission Exhibit 399. It was likely first bestowed with that sobriquet by Mark Lane in his 1966 critique of the Warren Report. The author gave several reasons for describing CE 399 as having magical properties. A few months later Raymond Marcus gave even more in his classic monograph, *The Bastard Bullet*. Today, in the light of the Assassination Records Review Board (ARRB), and the work of other researchers, we have a surfeit of reasons to characterize CE 399 as having magical properties.[1] In fact, the mode of its discovery is one reason for its shroud of mystery.

---

[1] Mark Lane, Rush to Judgment, p. 69

THE CASE AGAINST THE SINGLE BULLET

The Single Bullet became a creation of the Warren Commission out of a necessity to prop up the lone gunman. Video footage of the assassination and the limitations of the bolt action murder weapon constrained a single sniper to under six seconds to commit the crime according to the WC. The commission needed to explain an injury to a bystander, James Tague, JFK's head wounds and the remaining seven wounds to Kennedy and Governor Connally who was seated in front of him in the presidential limousine. Before having to admit to the Tague injury, on November 29, 1963, Hoover assertively told LBJ that two bullets struck JFK and one struck Connally.[2] Tague's injury changed all this and boxed the WC into a very small corner.

Arlen Specter, Assistant Counsel to the Warren Commission, was the leading architect of the Single Bullet Theory. During an exchange with a notorious Lone Nut scenario backer, Edward Epstein, Specter himself suggests it was a concoction. The following is what the writer of this chapter uncovered in Epstein's recent memoir:[3] "First, Epstein asks Specter: When the Secret Service did a reconstruction on December 7, 1963, why did they not arrive at the Magic Bullet concept? Specter replies like this:

> They had no idea at the time that unless one bullet had hit Kennedy and Connally, there had to be a second assassin.

In other words, Specter just confessed that the SBT was a matter of necessity, not evidence. But then, Specter tops that one. Epstein asks him how he convinced the Commission about this concept. This is Specter's reply:

> I showed them the Zapruder film, frame by frame, and explained

---

[2] LBJ and J. Edgar Hoover, 11/29/63. 1:40P. —YouTube
[3] https://www.kennedysandking.com/john-f-kennedy-articles/assume-nothing-about-edward-epstein

*that they could either accept the single-bullet theory or begin look-
ing for a second assassin.*

The case against the Single Bullet was unwittingly made by three
doctors at Parkland Hospital who saw JFK's neck wound before it was
altered by tracheostomy. They all described it as one of entry, which implied a frontal shot. One of them, Malcolm Perry, became one of many
Parkland doctors to be badgered and intimidated because of what he
saw.[4]

An early report about CE 399 stated that it had been found on President Kennedy's stretcher.[5] For reasons to be discussed later, this presented a serious evidentiary problem for the Warren Commission. Further, the man who discovered the bullet, Darrell Tomlinson, found it after
it rolled out from under a stretcher mat. It had rolled out when he moved
the gurney and was resting between the stretcher mat and its rim when
he first saw it.[6]

Tomlinson made his discovery at about 1:45 PM.[7] The story of CE
399 then shifted to O.P. Wright. Wright was the security officer at Parkland Hospital, where President John Kennedy and Governor John Connally had been taken for emergency treatment. Wright is a key witness
in the chain of possession of CE 399. Tomlinson brought him over to a
vestibule where the stretcher was located in front of a men's room.
Wright examined the bullet and then went looking for a federal officer to
take custody of the projectile.[8] Wright turned the exhibit over to Richard
Johnsen of the Secret Service.

But, right here, there will appear a problem in the chain of custody
for CE 399. O. P. Wright had a long history in law enforcement and therefore was familiar with guns and ammunition. So, there is no doubt he
was a key witness. Yet, amazingly, one will search far and wide to find
any indication that Commission lawyer Arlen Specter questioned him for

---

[4] JFK Revisited, DiEugenio, pp. 121, 122, 281, 304, 429, 430
[5] *New York Times*, November 27, 1963
[6] WCH, Vol. 6, p. 130
[7] Josiah Thompson, Six Seconds in Dallas, p. 156
[8] Ibid., p 156

the Warren Commission. This is incomprehensible, considering it was Wright who turned the bullet over to the Secret Service, and that agency was one of the main investigating arms for the Commission. As we shall see, there might have been a reason for this.

From Johnsen the bullet was then given to Chief James Rowley of the Secret Service. This occurred in Washington, and there was a receipt made out by Johnsen for this transfer. That receipt is contained in the Commission volumes. (*WCH, Volume 18*, p. 800.) The document reads as follows:

"The attached expended bullet was received by me about 5 minutes prior to Mrs. Kennedy's departure from the hospital. It was found on one of the stretchers located in the emergency ward of the hospital. Also on this same stretcher were rubber gloves, a stethoscope and other doctors' paraphernalia. It could not be determined who had used this stretcher or if President Kennedy had occupied it. No further information was obtained."

It then lists Wright's name and occupation, which was director of security, then Johnsen's name, and the time of transfer to Rowley, which was 7:30 PM on November 22, 1963. As we shall see, the description of what was on the stretcher—which Johnsen got from Wright—will prove to be central to the case.

From here, Rowley gave the bullet to an FBI agent, Elmer Lee Todd. Todd initialed it and then drove it to the FBI laboratory and delivered it to ballistics analyst Robert Frazier.[9] As we shall see there is something problematic about this transaction also.

As Josiah Thompson showed in his first-generation book, *Six Seconds in Dallas*, although Commission lawyer Arlen Specter does not appear to have questioned Wright—which is remarkable in itself—he did question Tomlinson. Specter seemed wholly preoccupied with trying to ascertain on which stretcher Tomlinson found the bullet. Probably because of that early *New York Times* story about the bullet being found on Kennedy's stretcher seems to have had an influence on the Commission. Commissioner Allen Dulles spoke of the bullet being found on

---

[9] WCH, Vol. 24, p. 412

Kennedy's stretcher.[10] This was on March 16, 1964, which was almost four months after the Commission had been appointed. This would mean that, at least some of the Commission was not yet aware of what their busy attorney, Mr. Specter, was devising: namely the Single Bullet Theory. And how that theory would make it mandatory for CE 399 *not to be found* on Kennedy's stretcher.

Upon Dulles saying this about the Kennedy stretcher, Specter chimed in. He said that he would be able to later produce evidence that would prove CE 399 was found on Governor John Connally's stretcher. Specter admitted they had been exploring the evidence along the lines that CE 399 was found on Kennedy's stretcher. But that scenario had been rejected, since the evidence would show that CE 399 was found on Connally's stretcher. What is astonishing about this statement is this: it was made four days *before* Specter examined Tomlinson.[11]

Specter clearly knew the direction he was now heading in before he could prove anything. Because it was Tomlinson who discovered the bullet, and it was Wright who took the bullet from the stretcher to Johnsen. Specter had already made up his mind not to examine Wright. Probably because he was a former Dallas Sheriff's deputy and now was a professional security officer. Which means he would be familiar with firearms and would be trained to recall such matters.

But further, the nurse, nurse's aide and the orderly who removed Connally's clothing in the emergency room before surgery were questioned by Specter or the FBI. As Don Thomas phrases it: "None saw a bullet in the Governor's clothing or a bullet on the stretcher or any bullet at all."[12] Same result with the doctors and attendants who lifted Connally onto the operating table.[13] The operating room nurse who removed the extraneous bandages and syringes and then removed the bloody sheets for laundry also failed to notice a bullet. All of this was before orderly

---

[10] WCH, Vol. 2, p. 368
[11] Ray Marcus, The Bastard Bullet, p. 26
[12] WCH Vol. 6, p. 116; Donald Thomas, Hear No Evil, p. 393
[13] WCH Vol. 6, p. 117

R. J. Jimison rolled the stretcher out of the emergency room and onto an elevator. He saw no medical instruments on the stretcher.[14]

In light of the above, Specter understood he had a problem, namely, where did this bullet come from? Almost any objective person who reads Specter's examination of Tomlinson would understand that it would have never been allowed in a court of law. The grounds being that Specter was clearly leading the witness. Even the late Gary Mack, who was later paid to support the official story by the Sixth Floor Museum in Dallas, admitted this to this writer.[15] Why did Specter break with legal ethics in his examination of Tomlinson?

Because what Tomlinson (and Wright) said would strongly indicate that CE 399 was *not* found on either Connally's stretcher or Kennedy's. Wright had told Johnsen that the stretcher the bullet was found on carried rubber gloves, a stethoscope and other doctors' paraphernalia.[16] In a clear, illustrated, witness backed demonstration, Thompson shows that Connally's stretcher did not match the description that both Tomlinson and Wright gave as to where they found the bullet. He also adds that the orderly, Jimison, who handled Connally's stretcher as it left the operating room, did not recall anything atop Connally's stretcher when he handled it.[17]

The true description matches the one that Tomlinson gave of a stretcher he brought off an elevator. After a two-page analysis, Thompson concluded that "The description of the Governor's stretcher given by Jimison matches Tomlinson's description of the stretcher he found on the elevator."[18] Thompson concluded that CE 399 was found on a stretcher belonging to neither Connally nor Kennedy, but to little Ronald Fuller, who was admitted right after Connally. It was his stretcher which fit the description of Tomlinson, and Wright in time, place, and the medical paraphernalia atop it. That Fuller's was the wrong stretcher will prove to be crucial to our later conclusion.

---

[14] WCH Vol. 6, p. 126
[15] Interview with Mack, August 1995
[16] WCH, Vol. 18, p. 799
[17] WCH, Vol. 6, p. 126
[18] Thompson, p. 160

The bullet that was supposed to come from Connally's thigh after having been found on Ronald Fuller's stretcher came to be the first break in the chain of possession of CE 399. Before describing the others, let us examine the weight and appearance of the bullet. According to the FBI, the maximum weight loss the bullet could have suffered was 2.4 grains.[19] Dr. Milton Helpern was the leading forensic pathologist of his day. He said he could not comprehend the idea that a bullet could have thrashed around in "all that bony tissue and lost only 1.4 to 2.4 grains."[20] The FBI's expert, Robert Frazier, told the Commission that the weight loss was hardly visible unless you looked at the base of the bullet.[21] Dr. Robert Shaw, who operated on Connally, was also surprised that the bullet had lost almost none of its substance.[22] He thought that there were more than three grains deposited just in Connally's wrist.[23] Dr. Pierre Finck, one of the autopsy doctors for Kennedy, said the same about the fragments in Connally's wrist.[24] James Humes, another JFK autopsist, agreed. Except he said there were too many fragments in Connally's thigh.[25]

This relates to the appearance of the bullet, which looks intact, with no flattening of the nose, even though it went through two bones in Connally. In fact, as noted by author Henry Hurt, bullets that went through nothing, but a bin of cotton wadding appeared to be more disrupted than CE 399.[26] Dr. Joseph Dolce, an illustrious battlefield surgeon who worked for the Commission, said that under no circumstances did he think a bullet that did this much damage could emerge as intact as CE 399.

---

[19] WCH, Vol. 3, p. 418, p. 430
[20] Marshall Houts, Where Death Delights, pp. 62–63
[21] WCH, Vol. 4, p. 121
[22] WCH, Vol. 4, p. 109
[23] Ibid, p. 113
[24] WCH Vol. 2, p. 382
[25] Marcus, p. 7
[26] Reasonable Doubt, p. 74

In fact, he said that just hitting Connally's wrist would visibly deform the bullet.[27] Dolce, using the original murder weapon, had a hundred bullets fired through cadavers' wrists (just one of the two broken bones), and in every instance the tip of the bullet was smashed. You will not find this expert's name in the Warren Commission report nor its 26 volumes.[28]

But it's even worse than that. Because Robert Frazier said that the bullet was clean; meaning it did not have any blood or tissue on it.[29] For a bullet that went through two men, making seven wounds, and smashing two bones, this would seem impossible. But the weight of the evidence would indicate such was the case since every man who carried

---

[27] DiEugenio, JFK Revisited, p. 30
[28] Ibid., p. 140
[29] WCH, Vol. 3, p. 428

the bullet was a law enforcement officer. And they would know not to alter the evidence in any way. This revelation by Frazier was so disturbing to the Commission that they tried to manipulate the testimony by confusing him with another exhibit: the bullet fragments found in the front seat of the limousine.[30]

Dr. Cyril Wecht, a very accomplished forensic pathologist who served on the House Select Committee on Assassinations (HSCA), also found the appearance of the bullet to be troubling. He implored his eight colleagues on the forensic pathology panel to produce evidence of any bullet they had ever encountered that did this kind of damage and came out virtually unscathed. None of them did so.[31]

The official story has two hits to Kennedy, both from behind. One went into his back and the other entered his skull. Therefore, another question one could ask about CE 399 is this: Why did the bullet that went into and out of Kennedy's brain break apart and fragment into scores of both larger and smaller particles, yet the Magic Bullet did not? After all, the former bullet allegedly went through two walls of the brain cranium. It broke into at least two large fragments that exited the skull, and, among others, numerous dust-like particles in the front of the brain.[32] This question is not addressed in the Warren Report, but it poses a disturbing dichotomy.

But there is even more professional testimony to renounce CE 399. In an interview that Thompson did with one of the doctors who operated on Connally, Dr. Charles Gregory, Gregory said that neither he nor Shaw could locate any cloth fibers in Connally's back wound. This contrasted with Connally's wrist wound which did contain them. This strongly indicates that the bullet that hit Connally 1.) did not hit Kennedy, and 2.) was not CE 399, since there were no such cloth markings on the Magic Bullet.[33]

Dr. Cyril Wecht seriously challenged the legendary trajectory of the

---

[30] Marcus, p. 45

[31] HSCA Vol. 1, p. 337

[32] DiEugenio, JFK Revisited, p. 169

[33] Thompson, p. 77; Donald Thomas, Hear No Evil, p. 392

Magic Bullet when he testified before the HSCA. He said that he could not understand how a bullet fired downward from the sixth floor of the Texas School Book Depository, hitting Kennedy in the back, could then deflect upward to exit at about the midline of his neck. And according to Dr. David Mantik, if one follows the official story, what is surprising is that the cervical vertebrae are intact?[34] Therefore the bullet was in all probability going through soft tissue. Yet this same bullet then entered Governor Connally at a downward trajectory of 25 degrees.[35]

Wecht's denial of the Magic Bullet is backed up by new physical evidence from reporter Jeff Meek. The name of Henry Heiberger is not in the Warren Report. He was the FBI technician who originally studied Kennedy's coat, shirt and tie for chemical composition. Meek recovered his lab notes which were supposed to be destroyed according to FBI procedure—from his daughter. The notes reveal that there was copper found around Kennedy's back wound. But none on the front neckband of his shirt or the necktie. (Note: Even though Connally's clothes were washed before ever being analyzed, belated tests showed traces of metal deposits.) As Meek writes: how could that be if the same bullet went through Kennedy's back and exited his throat?[36]

When asked about Meek's findings, Brian Edwards, member of the Lawrence, Kansas Police Force for twenty-two years and instructor in Criminal Justice at Washburn University had this to say: *"Is it possible that the tie and the front collar of JFK's shirt have no significant metallic deposits as reported by the FBI lab technician in his report…"*

He continued with, *"My thoughts are IF there were no significant metal deposits on JFK's tie or front collar, two possibilities exist:*

1. The copper jacket was completely destroyed on impact with a hard object PRIOR to it striking JFK's tie and front collar. What could have caused the entire copper cover to be instantly and completely destroyed—no idea.

---

[34] James DiEugenio, The JFK Assassination: The Evidence Today, p. 141
[35] HSCA Vol. 1, p. 344
[36] Hot Springs Village Voice, January 4, 2022

2. A projectile of an entirely different composition hit the tie and front collar—BUT, regardless of the composition of the projectile, it should have left some traces of metal, maybe not enough to be analyzed spectrographically."[37]

NOTE—Both alternatives render the SBT baseless!

Teletype was sent to Dallas 11/26

PC - 78282

Dir.

The fabric surrounding the hole in the back of the Q-22 coat and the fabric surrounding the hole in the back of the Q25 shirt were spectrographically examined. Foreign traces of copper were found. This copper could have been deposited by a copper coated bullet penetrating the cloth of these garments. It is to be noted that the bullets involved in this case are copper coated.

The fabric surrounding the hole in the front of the Q 24 necktie and the fabric surrounding the hole on the front of the Q25 shirt were also spectrographically examined. No significant deposits of metal were found in these pieces of fabric.

While we know that both Frazier and Hoover refer passingly to this report, the authors could find no traces of it in the Warren Commission Report, nor any attempts to elucidate its significance.

The HSCA desperately tried to revive the Magic Bullet concept in the late seventies. They largely did this through two tests. The first was by Dr. Vincent Guinn who was one of the fathers of Neutron Activation Analysis, which measures trace elements in bullet lead for comparison purposes. The HSCA used this to say that somehow CE 399 was related to other fragments recovered from the limousine, and this showed that these bullets came from the same assembly line batch.

There were always reservations about this test, and they were expressed by the late Wallace Milam at a critic's conference in Washington in the mid-nineties. As time went on, more and more people, like former FBI agent William Tobin, began to question the basis for Guinn's tests and also his findings. Until finally, the dam broke. In 2006, metallurgist Erik Randich and statistician Patrick Grant co-authored a paper on the subject blowing apart Guinn's foundational structure.[38] One was that the lead mixture used in Mannlicher Carcano ammunition—which Lee Oswald allegedly used—was somehow distinct from other mixtures. It was not.

Secondly, that the distribution of trace elements was uniform in these bullets. This was also false, as Randich showed with huge blow-ups of crystals traveling randomly throughout the chemical mixture. (For a thorough critique see Gary Aguilar's review of Vincent Bugliosi's *Reclaiming History* in *Federal Lawyer* Nov./Dec 2007.) The Randich/Grant work was so devastating to Guinn's test that the FBI stopped using this method in court, since it had been reduced to the level of "junk science".

Thomas Canning had worked at NASA on rocket trajectories for a number of years. The HSCA decided to have him explore whether or not CE 399 could have performed the miraculous flight path that the Warren Commission said it accomplished. To put it mildly, Canning had some serious problems in this assignment. Which led him into some questionable practices. For instance, the HSCA autopsy photograph clearly de-

---

[38] Journal of Forensic Science, July 11, 2016

notes that Kennedy was wounded in the back, not the neck. Well, Canning disregarded this and placed the wound back into the neck on a flat trajectory through Kennedy's body.[39] Further, Canning said that if his calculations were off on points of entrance and exit by just one inch, he would miss the originating firing point by anywhere from 30 to 40 feet.[40] As we have just noted, this was obviously the case. As the reader can see, the attempt by the HSCA to breathe life in the Magic Bullet was like using CPR on a corpse.[41]

In the end, what these two tests proved was the opposite of what they were designed to do. They showed there was no scientific method, no matter how ingenious, that would lend a shred of legitimacy to CE 399.

Let us conclude with another plane of evidence. This one showing how CE 399 either could never be admitted into a court of law, or if it was, it would explode the prosecution's case.

As we have outlined above once the bullet was turned over to Rowley in Washington, he gave it to FBI agent Elmer Lee Todd for transport to the FBI lab and analyst Robert Frazier. As with Johnsen and Rowley, they signed a receipt to certify the transaction. Todd wrote that he had received the exhibit from Rowley of the Secret Service at 8:50 PM.[42]

There is a serious problem with this. In Frazier's handwritten document titled "History of Evidence," he lists that he got the bullet from Todd at 7:30 PM.[43] He also listed the arrival of the stretcher bullet at 7:30 PM on the document entitled "Laboratory Worksheet."[44] Yet as we have seen, CE 399 was not turned over to an FBI agent until one hour and twenty minutes later. How could Frazier have a bullet that would not arrive until well over an hour later?

There is further evidence for this late delivery of a bullet. FBI officer

---

[39] HSCA Vol. 2, p. 170
[40] HSCA Vol. 2, p. 196
[41] For further demolitions of Canning see Thomas, pp. 421–450; and also Chapter 15: "The Tangled Web" at www.patspeer.com
[42] WCH Vol. 3, p. 428; Commission Document 320
[43] John Hunt, "The Mystery of the 7:30 Bullet" at JFK Lancer.com
[44] Ibid.

Alan Belmont wrote at about 9:18 PM that a Secret Service bullet was to be delivered at a future time. Todd was in receipt of such a bullet at the White House and he was about to hand deliver it to the FBI lab. All of this begs this question: What happened to Frazier's 7:30 bullet? This is a second break in the chain.

One particular document I ran across in the FBI Lab files at NARA purports to establish the "Todd-to-Frazier" portion of the bullet's chain of custody. Frazier titled the document, "History of Evidence." (See Figure 2.)

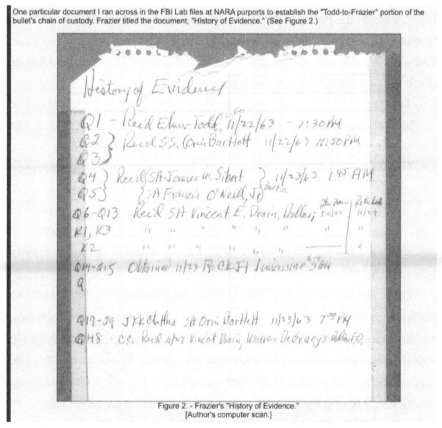

Figure 2. - Frazier's "History of Evidence."
[Author's computer scan.]

Reproduced from John Hunt's "The Mystery of the 7:30 Bullet" [2006]

There is yet another and this relates to what appears to be a falsity in an FBI document that was part of Commission Exhibit 2011. The pertinent pages attempt to verify identification of CE 399 by those who allegedly handled it or saw it on November 22, 1963. The document is dated July 7, 1964. It states that on June 12, 1964, FBI agent Bardwell Odum showed the bullet to Parkland employees Tomlinson and Wright. It then describes their reaction to seeing it as it "appears to be the same one" they originally found but that neither could "positively identify" it. In other words, maybe it was, but neither was sure. That would not suffice in a court of law.

Elsewhere in the document is recorded another set of strange comments on the bullet identification. On June 24th, FBI agent Todd showed the bullet to Johnsen and Rowley. They advised him they "could not identify this bullet as the one" they saw on the day of the assassination. This is quite odd since Rowley was the witness who gave the bullet to Todd. Should they not be reliving a mutual memory of identification? After all, there was a receipt for transfer between them.

To complicate matters even more, there was an FBI AIRTEL of 6/20/64 from the Dallas Special Agent in Charge to Director J. Edgar Hoover. It stated that neither Tomlinson nor Wright could identify the bullet. This was a modification (downward) from the June 12th hesitant identification. And the AIRTEL ignored what was supposed to be this previous judgment. What made this even more puzzling is that there were no further field reports—these are termed 302's by the FBI—to clarify matters. There were no field reports to support the alleged June 12th tentative identification.

Gary Aguilar was very puzzled by this (strange) pattern. He consulted with Thompson about it and Thompson, now a private investigator, said perhaps they should talk to Bardwell Odum about it. The PI located Odum in a suburb of Dallas and they wrote to him about this particular riddle. They then visited him in person. The result was shocking. As he had previously admitted on the phone, "He had never taken any bullet around to show to Parkland Hospital employees." And since he knew Wright, he would certainly never have forgotten doing that with his acquaintance. Further, if he had done so, there would be a 302 report in the files—which there was not.[45] In other words, none of the persons involved with the transfer of the projectile to the FBI—Wright, Tomlinson, Johnsen, Rowley—could recognize the exhibit for the Warren Commission. And somehow, someone wrote (falsely) that it was not really that negative.

---

[45] The Assassinations, edited by James DiEugenio and Lisa Pease, p. 284

One would think that creating a false event is about as bad as one can go in building a case. But perhaps this was a necessity, one that sheds light on Specter's failure to interview Mr. Wright—the man with experience in firearms and ammunition. Back in 1966, Thompson was working on his book *Six Seconds in Dallas*. He had been let go from a *Life* magazine investigative team on the JFK case. But he and his partner Ed Kern had uncovered much more evidence than that national magazine was willing to publish about the evidentiary problems with the Kennedy case—all of which were ignored by the Warren Commission. But further, the eventual article *Life* did publish on 11/25/66 greatly shortchanged the work those two had done. And the editors gave Specter an opportunity to reply. The article even said that the bullet angle through JFK's body matched up with Connally's, which was simply not true.[46]

Thompson decided to turn the unused portion of his work for *Life* into a book. Familiar with the Dallas witnesses, he decided to pay a visit to Mr. Wright. That visit is immortalized in *Six Seconds in Dallas*. Thompson brought with him a photo of Commission Exhibit 399. Wright was quite surprised by this, and his reaction further certifies that Odum never visited him. Because when Thompson asked him what the bullet looked like, Wright opened a drawer and showed him a pointed-tipped projectile very different from what the round-nosed CE 399 looks like. During the interview, Thompson came back to this point, and Wright stuck by his story. Wright even asked him if the picture he showed him of CE 399 was what the Commission said Tomlinson lifted it off the stretcher. The writer said it was. In other words, Specter and the Commission had kept Wright in the dark for not just months, but years. As attorneys in the trade say, this betrays "consciousness of guilt." As Thompson wrote in the footnotes to *Six Seconds in Dallas*, Wright's information would indicate that CE 399 was switched later in the chain. This could have only been done by some federal officer. Thus, indicating that the assassination conspiracy was an inside job.[47]

At this point we should complete a circle. As stated earlier, CE 399

[46] Thompson, Last Second in Dallas, p. 90
[47] Thompson, Six Seconds in Dallas, pp. 175-76

was, in all likelihood, not found on Connally's stretcher. In 1992, the late, excellent researcher Wallace Milam visited the widow of O. P. Wright. Her name was Elizabeth and she had been the director of nursing at Parkland. She liked Wallace and she told him something that, to my knowledge, no one involved with this case had ever revealed before. She said that they were finding bullets on stretchers for days after the assassination. To the point that ER nurse Doris Nelson said, "I wish they would stop putting bullets on stretchers."[48] The plotters never did find the right stretcher.

Decades ago, Ray Marcus began his fine monograph, *The Bastard Bullet,* with an explanation that was curtly phrased: WHY THE MAGIC BULLET?

Marcus wrote that the key to this question was in the Zapruder film and also in the alleged weapon used in the assassination, a bolt action Mannlicher Carcano rifle. The FBI had tested such a rifle and concluded it would take 2.3 seconds to work the bolt and recycle it for another bullet to be fired. That time span translated into 42 frames of the Zapruder film. Upon examining the film, the Commission concluded that the first frame at which alleged assassin Oswald could fire a clear shot—after the limousine had cleared the branches of an oak tree—was at frame 210. For them, the final shot came at frame 313. Once that is established, there could be no two hits in less than 42 frames of the film.[49]

President Kennedy was clearly reacting to a hit as he emerged from behind the Stemmons Freeway sign at frame 226. But Connally had not been hit. But he was reacting to a hit just prior to frame 240.[50] In other words, the film showed that the hits to Connally and Kennedy took place in less than 42 frames of film. This is something that the Commission could not tolerate. For as Commission lawyer Norman Redlich, assistant to Chief counsel J. Lee Rankin, declared: "To say they were hit by separate bullets is synonymous with saying there were two assassins."[51]

---

[48] Speech by Thompson at the 2003 Cyril Wecht Conference in Pittsburgh
[49] Marcus, p. 4
[50] Thompson, Six Seconds in Dallas, pp. 70–75
[51] Marcus, p. 5

Rather than accepting that, Specter came up with the Single Bullet Theory—one bullet through two men—with the preposterous CE 399 as the fulcrum point. What did Connally think of all this? Years later, when asked if he believed the Oswald did it/Magic Bullet scenario, Connally was unequivocal: "Absolutely not. I do not for one second believe the conclusions of the Warren Commission."[52]

Let us leave it at that.

Addendum – The Paul Landis Allegation

As this book went to press the new revelations by former Secret Service agent Paul Landis produced long stories in both Vanity Fair and the New York Times. The latter was exceptional since the Times has always supported the Warren Commission. Landis' story, if true, breaks down the fulcrum of the Warren Report, namely the Single Bullet Theory. What Landis is belatedly saying is that he found a bullet in the back seat of the presidential limousine as it arrived at Parkland Hospital. He was helping Jackie Kennedy out of the car and retrieving some of her things, like a purse. As he did so, he picked up a bullet. He later placed this on President Kennedy's stretcher.

This cannot be the Magic Bullet, CE 399. Because that projectile landed in Governor John Connally's thigh. Connally was sitting in front of Kennedy. It strains credulity that it would then, unprovoked, eject from that wound backwards. Second, CE 399 was allegedly found on Connally's stretcher, not Kennedy's. If this story is true, its an extra bullet. One bullet missed the car and struck the curb in front of bystander James Tague. One bullet hit Kennedy in the skull, and its fragments landed on the front seat floorboard. There was then the Magic Bullet.

But now we have the Landis bullet. Which makes four. But the Warren Report says Lee Oswald fired only three bullets. As there were three shells found at the Texas School Book Depository. So there was a second assassin. Further, this means that this bullet, since it was found in

---

[52] Joseph McBride, Into the Nightmare, p. 418

the back seat, likely dropped out of Kennedy's back. Because there was never any credible evidence that the back wound perforated Kennedy's body. In fact the FBI agents at the autopsy, Jim Sibert and Frank O'Neill, insisted it had not. If so, that eliminates the trajectory outline for the Magic Bullet going through both men.

But, in reality, if this is true, it's a fifth bullet. Because in Oliver Stone's four part film, JFK: Destiny Betrayed, Dr. Randy Robertson described his discovery of another bullet in the presidential limousine. (See the book JFK Revisited, p. 437) Dr. James Young was present at Kennedy's autopsy at Bethesda Medical Center that evening. He sent two assistants to pick up bone fragments from the limousine. They returned with fragments plus a bent bullet. With this new evidence from Robertson and Young, 60 years later, we can now pronounce the death of both the Lone Gunman and Single Bullet Theories.

CHAPTER 9

PROOF OF A FRONT SHOT IS OVERWHELMING

BY PAUL BLEAU

STATEMENT

EVIDENCE OF AT least one shot coming from the front of the JFK motorcade in Dealey Plaza, or from somewhere other than the Texas School Book Depository sixth floor where Oswald was said to have been, is overwhelming and proves that Oswald could not have acted alone, if at all, in the assassination of JFK.

EXECUTIVE SUMMARY

The Zapruder film of the assassination clearly shows JFK's head moving violently backward and to the left when it explodes from a gunshot that could have only come from in front of him. Attempts to explain this away by either the jet effect or a neuromuscular reaction have been thoroughly debunked. Oswald at the time of the murder was known to be behind the motorcade.

A majority of witnesses at Dealey Plaza, who spoke to where the shots came from, claimed that at least one came from either the front or the Texas School Book Depository (TSBD) or elsewhere versus those who only identified the TSBD as the only origin of the shots.

Almost all the witnesses, over eighty including almost all the medical personnel, who clearly saw the back of JFK's head injury, described what could only be an exit wound, which implies a shot from the front.

Three pathologists at Methodist Hospital who studied a skull-bone fragment picked up in Dealey Plaza confirmed it was occipital (from the back of the skull).

Spatter analysis shows that brain and blood debris splattered heavily behind Kennedy and to the left further confirming a front location origin of at least one gunshot.

Analysis of a particle trail from the X-rays confirms that small missile particles are mostly near the front of JFK's head and the larger ones are mostly near the back, once again indicating a front shot.

All the above, taken in its entirety, and more evidence we will discuss, make it impossible to conclude anything other than there was at least one shot fired at JFK on November 22, 1963, that came from in front of him, which provides powerful evidence that there was a conspiracy.

EVIDENCE

For this particular chokehold, it is important to keep in mind the concept of consilience. For some of the elements, there is some room for margin of error, particularly when it comes to statistics concerning the number of witnesses who made statements. In this area, both the Warren Commission and the HSCA were less than forthcoming, to say the least. Nevertheless, it is easy to conclude that witness testimony is a strong indicator of a conspiracy.

This factor taken alone, perhaps for some serious researchers, would not be enough to prove beyond a shadow of doubt that there was a multi-person plot. But seen in connection with one another and in their entirety, all the areas of evidence comprehensively and decisively demonstrate that there definitely was at least one frontal shot.

Dealey Plaza Witnesses

For this evidence, it is difficult to present accurate figures for many reasons: Depending on where one was in Dealey Plaza when the shots rang out, the types of weapons used, the observation and hearing acumen of the witnesses, the effect of echoes, and the level of pandemonium at the time. It is not surprising that witness testimony differed. There are a number of accounts of witnesses first saying that they felt shots came from the front, and later changed to say they came from the TSBD, some say they were pressured into saying shots came from the back. A significant number of witnesses were not even asked where they felt the shots came from and some who said they came from the front were not deposed. Other witnesses contest Dallas Police and FBI reports of what they claim these witnesses said.

Another key point is that what witnesses claim to have heard, does not negate the possibility that they were not able to identify the provenance of one of the shots. The real point indicating at least one front shot has nothing to do with the number of witnesses who felt that at least one shot came from the TSBD; rather, the only significant point should be whether there was at least one reliable witness who could confirm that at least one shot came from the front.

Our analysis is that despite attempts by the Warren Commission (WC) and House Select Committee on Assassinations (HSCA) to favor a TSBD provenance of the shots, there are simply too many reliable accounts of at least one shot coming from the front, providing at a minimum compelling evidence that there were multiple shooters.

To demonstrate this, we will refer to two websites that present analyses of witness data. One of the keys for both websites is that each witness that was accounted for in the research can be hyperlinked so as to see exactly what they are on the record as having said. Readers are encouraged to read this raw data and make their own judgments.

The Stewart Galanor Analysis

The Following chart is the Galanor breakdown of witness accounts:[1]

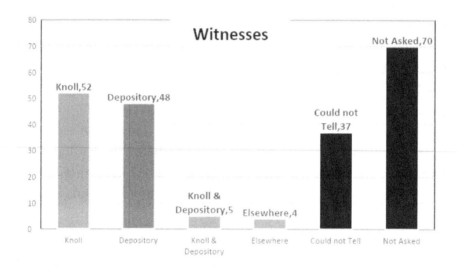

Of note in these numbers: a) The impressive total of those who thought shots came from somewhere other than the TSBD, 61 vs. 48 who only mention the TSBD. Another important stat is the number of 70 witnesses who were not even asked where they believed the shots came from. According to the analyst, there were between 325 and 400 witnesses total at Dealey Plaza at the time of the shooting.

Readers are encouraged to visit the website which provides the names of the witnesses with hyperlinks to what they are on the record of having said.Galanor also reveals the following:

Information not addressed by the HSCA. (Here we will give at least one example for each category, on the website one can find several more:)

---

[1] **https://www.history-matters.com/analysis/witness/index.htm**

1. ACCOMMODATING WITNESSES:

"Jesse Curry, the Dallas chief of police, told reporters on November 23 that although he was driving the lead car of the motorcade, he "could tell from the sound of the three shots that they had come from the book company's building near downtown Dallas."[2] However, when confronted with the transcript of the police radio transmissions, Curry admitted that just after the shots were fired, he broadcast over his car radio: "Get a man on top of that triple underpass and see what happened up there."[3]

2. ERRONEOUS REPORTS:

"Richard Dodd, a railroad track supervisor who was standing on the overpass during the assassination, was interviewed by two FBI agents. In their report to the Warren Commission, the FBI agents said that Dodd *"did not know where the shots came from."* (*22H835*) Several witnesses contradicted what was in their FBI reports, and Dodd was one of them. Dodd told Mark Lane in a filmed interview that he told federal agents that *"the shots, the smoke came from behind the hedge on the north side of the plaza."[4]*

3. DEFICIENT INTERROGATIONS:

Seymour Weitzman, a Dallas Police Officer, wrote in a statement made out the day after the assassination, *"I ran in a Northwest direction and scaled a fence toward where we thought the shots came from."[5]* The record shows that when Weitzman was interviewed by the FBI the next day and when he testified before

---

[2] The New York Times, 11/24/63

[3] Dorothy Kilgallen, *New York Journal American* (23 August 1964)

[4] Rush to Judgment Film, Mark Lane

[5] *24H, p 228*

counsel for the Warren Commission four months later, he was not asked where he thought the shots came from.

4. WITNESSES NOT CALLED:

According to the HSCA, 692 witnesses *"were present in the Plaza during the assassination."*[6] Most of them were never called to testify by either the Warren Commission or the HSCA.

Ed Johnson a reporter for the Fort Worth Star-Telegram who was riding in the motorcade, wrote for his paper the next day, *"Some of us saw little puffs of white smoke that seemed to hit the grassy area in the esplanade that divides Dallas' main downtown streets."* He was never interviewed by any government agency.

5. PUFF OF SMOKE WITNESSES:

At least seven witnesses (9, according to Josiah Thompson) saw a puff of smoke on the grassy knoll.

In May of 1966 Galanor spoke with railroad workers Thomas Murphy and Walter Winborn, who were standing on the triple overpass at the time of the assassination. Galanor asked Murphy, *"Could you tell me where you thought the shots came from?"*

Murphy. Yeah, they come from a tree to the left of my left, which is to the immediate right of the site of the assassination.

Galanor. That would be on that grassy hill up there.

Murphy. Yeah, on the hill up there. There are two or three hackberry and elm trees. And I say it comes from there.

Galanor. Well, was there anything that led you to believe that the shots came from there?

Murphy. Yeah, smoke.

Galanor. You saw smoke?

Murphy. Sure did.

Galanor. Could you tell me exactly where you saw the smoke?

---

[6] 8HSCA139

Murphy. Yeah, in that tree.[7] Walter Winborn told me he saw *"smoke that came out from under the trees on the right-hand side of the motorcade."* The FBI agents who interviewed Winborn for the Warren Commission, however, did not mention in their report that he had seen smoke on the knoll.

Galanor. Did you tell them about that, that you saw smoke on the grassy knoll?

Winborn. Oh yes. Oh yes.

Galanor. They didn't include it in their report.

Winborn. Well.

Galanor. Do you have any idea why they didn't?

Winborn. I don't have any idea. They are specialists in their field, and I'm just an amateur.[8]

S. M. Holland a railroad signal supervisor, was standing on the overpass watching the motorcade move toward him. *"I looked over toward the arcade and trees [the knoll] and saw a puff of smoke come from the trees."*[9] Later Holland told the Warren Commission, *"A puff of smoke came out about 6 or 8 feet above the ground right out from under those trees."*[10] The Warren Commission ignored Holland's testimony and never addressed the fact that five other railroad workers claimed to have seen smoke on the knoll at the time of the shots.

Galanor also makes the following observation:

"Thus, the tabulation of 216 witnesses (culled from the Warren Commission's 26 Volumes and from Commission Documents stored in the National Archives) does not constitute a random sample of the witnesses to the assassination. Hence, it cannot be the basis for an accurate statistical analysis of witness accounts. What happens if we separate out the 73 government employees from the 143 non-government employees?

---

[7] Coverup, p. 59
[8] Ibid., p. 60
[9] *19H480*
[10] *6H243*

143 Non-Government Employees	73 Government Employees
Depository 22	Depository 26
Grassy Knoll 44	Grassy Knoll 8

In the non-government group, the number of Knoll witnesses is two times larger than the Depository witnesses, while in the government group, the number of Depository witnesses is three times larger than the number of Knoll witnesses.

The HSCA's analysis of witness accounts is a disingenuous attempt to dismiss and discredit evidence that the shots were fired from at least two locations. The evidence of a shooter firing from behind the fence is staggering, not least of which is the testimony of witnesses who heard shots or saw smoke on the grassy knoll."

22November1963.or.uk Website

The above website[11] also offers an analysis that clearly points to a significant number of witnesses who stated that shots came from the front (over 40), as well as similar flaws and limitations in the WC investigation. It is also worth visiting by the reader.

The information at that website is corroborative of the Galanor analysis, and relies on fewer independent researcher investigations, even if a number of these were recorded. Once again, individual testimonies can be hyperlinked.

- Several witnesses gave statements that may be interpreted as evidence of shots from the grassy knoll.

- Four witnesses of varying degrees of credibility, Gordon Arnold, Cheryl McKinnon, Lee Bowers, and Ed Hoffman, also claimed to

---

[11] http://22november1963.org.uk/jfk-assassination-grassy-knoll-witnesses

have witnessed shots or other suspicious activity on the grassy knoll.

While lone-nut scenario believers have tried often to discredit witness testimony, it is simply not credible that so many people got it wrong and that there is not something more sinister that explains the obvious resistance by the WC and the HSCA to accept the testimony and what it meant.

Key Witnesses

Lee Bowers was interviewed by Mark Lane, filmed and recorded (at just past the 5-minute mark, notice how when interviewed during the investigation, the interviewer tries to deflect to another subject): "At the time of the shooting, in the vicinity of where the two men I have described were, there was a flash of light or, as far as I am concerned, something I could not identify, but there was something which occurred which caught my eye in this immediate area on the embankment. Now, what this was, I could not state at that time and at this time I could not identify it, other than there was some unusual occurrence—a flash of light or smoke or something which caused me to feel like something out of the ordinary had occurred there."[12]

Sam Holland: Sam Holland's account is also very compelling. Both are very indicative of a front shot: "I saw a puff of smoke still lingering among the trees in front of the wooden fence. The report sounded like it came from behind the wooden fence," Holland said.[13]

David F. Powers (presidential aide—riding in a follow-up car): My first impression was that the shots came from the right and overhead, but I also had a fleeting impression that the noise appeared to come from the front in the area of the triple overpass. This may have resulted from

---

[12] Lee Bowers interview. https://www.youtube.com/watch?v=k8H_DaL_tQk
[13] SM Holland interview. https://www.youtube.com/watch?v=NFVy6xxKKJU

my feeling, when I looked forward toward the overpass, that we might have ridden into an ambush.[14]

Ken O'Donnell (presidential aide—riding in a follow-up car):

Mr. O'DONNELL. My reaction (to the source of the shots) in part is re-construction—is that they came from the right rear. That could be my best judgment … looking at the manner of the President's movement, I would think you would have to feel the thrust of the shot was from the right rear.[15]

Mr. SPECTER. Now, what was there about the President's move-ment which leads you to that conclusion?

Mr. O'DONNELL. He was leaning out waving. He may have just been withdrawing his hand. And the shot hit him, and threw him to the left. He slumped on Mrs. Kennedy.

Tip O'Neill: I was never one of those people who had doubts or suspi-cions about the Warren Commission's report on the President's death. But five years after Jack died, I was having dinner with Kenny O'Donnell and a few other people at Jimmy's Harborside Restaurant in Boston, and we got to talking about the assassination. I was surprised to hear O'Don-nell say that he was sure he had heard two shots that came from behind the fence.

"That's not what you told the Warren Commission," I said.

"You're right," he replied.

"I told the FBI what I had heard but they said it couldn't have hap-pened that way and that I must have been imagining things. So I testified the way they wanted me to. I just didn't want to stir up any more pain and trouble for the family."

---

[14] *Affidavit 1964 : STATEMENT: May 18, 1964, 7H473 and full affidavit:* https://www.history-matters.com/ar-chive/jfk/wc/wcvols/wh7/html/WC_Vol7_0241a.htm
[15] O'Donnell WC Testimony

"I can't believe it," I said. *"I wouldn't have done that in a million years. I would have told the truth."*

"Tip, you have to understand. The family—everybody wanted this thing behind them."…

Dave Powers was with us at dinner that night, and his recollection of the shots was the same as O'Donnell's.[16]

Robert Blakey Confidences

One person who seems to have come around and has confirmed his confidence that shots came from the knoll area based on witness testimony is no other than HSCA Chief Counsel Robert Blakey himself:

During the AARC Conference in 2014[17] and on a 2015 *Black Op Radio* program he confirmed his belief in the Single Bullet theory, but also that a shot came from the grassy knoll due to witness testimony from several people whom the Warren Commission made every effort to undermine. This includes Secret Service agents, S. M. Holland, and presidential assistant Dave Powers. He said this caused him to lose confidence in the Warren Commission report. He said that *"It's not an investigation… It's a justification to assert that Oswald acted alone…"*

The Zapruder Film

Abraham Zapruder is one of three witnesses who are known to have movie-filmed the assassination. What was captured in his film was so compelling in 1) disproving the Single Bullet Theory and 2) demonstrating that the fatal head shot had to come from the front, that subsequent actions taken with regard to the film can only be interpreted as a total lack of transparency.

The film helped convince jurors at the Clay Shaw trial, and then audiences who finally saw it on national TV that there was a conspiracy.

---

[16] MAN OF THE HOUSE, by Tip O'Neill, Random House: 1987, page 178
[17] https://www.youtube.com/watch?v=6NTpmyYIeXE

This contributed to the forming of the HSCA and growing disbelief in the media and the government.

It also set off over the top attempts at trying to explain the violent backward thrust such as the "jet effect" and then a neuromuscular reaction which were debunked, most thoroughly by Gary Aguilar and Cyril Wecht.[18] Though some argue that JFK seems to have moved slightly forward before the violent back and to the left motion of his head, the sheer force of this motion simply cannot be explained by these concoctions that were belatedly pulled out of the hat to try and salvage a crumbling fairy tale.

The reader is encouraged to examine the Zapruder film and judge on his own. Three things should come jumping out 1) The delayed reaction between JFK holding his throat and Connally reacting to the alleged Single Bullet despite having had a number of his bones struck. 2) The violence of the backward and to the left motion of JFK's head on the fatal shot, and 3) Jackie Kennedy's instinctive actions to collect splatter debris on the rear of the limousine.[19]

Clark and the Throat Wound

Dr. Malcolm Perry performed a tracheotomy through Kennedy's wound in the throat and the autopsy pathologists did not analyze it and, furthermore, they did not perform proper trajectory analysis on any of the wounds during the autopsy. They simply tried to insert malleable probes through the back wound, which, according to more than one witness—including the two FBI agents, Jim Sibert and Frank O'Neill—did not appear to be able to connect all the way through.

Three Parkland doctors who did observe the small pencil size wound were Perry, Crenshaw and Dr. Carrico. Carrico described it as a small penetrating wound in his treatment notes and told Harold Weisberg that it was above the shirt collar. Dr. Perry stated three times during the Parkland press conference that it was an entry to the front. The Secret

---

[18] "Nova's Cold Case" by Gary Aguilar, 7/14/16 at Kennedysanking.com
[19] https://www.youtube.com/watch?v=jdwVUBlK-Y0

Proof of a Front Shot is Overwhelming

Service confiscated the videotapes of the newscast from numerous local TV stations, but the transcripts survived.[20]

While Perry, in his testimonies, did cooperate with those pushing a narrative of shots coming solely from the back... It seems clear that he was swayed to backtrack from his earliest, uncontaminated statements by a relentless attack from SS SA Elmer Moore. This is from a copy of the press conference transcript sent to Chief Rowley of the Secret Service.

> Q. Doctor, describe the entrance wound. You think from the front in the throat?
>
> DR. PERRY: The wound appeared to be an entrance wound in the front of the throat; yes, that is correct. The exit wound, I don't know. It could have been the head or there could have been a second wound of the head. There was not time to determine this at the particular instant.

Audrey Bell confirmed that Perry told her that he was pressured during the night following the assassination to change his mind about what he had confirmed to the press.[21] Secret Service agent Elmer Moore told Jim Gochenaur that he had been ordered to pressure Dr. Perry to change his mind.[22]

Dr. Donald Miller became a colleague of Dr. Perry's, and confirmed that, in 1977, Perry after operating with Miller confided to him while they were in the surgeon's lounge drinking coffee that it was an entrance wound, *"unquestionably an entrance wound"*... But later in front of the HSCA, he once again reverted publicly like he did with the Warren Commission.[23]

The intimidation of Malcolm Perry is corroborated by others—Taken verbatim from the The Ordeal of Malcolm Perry at KennedysandKing:[24]

"But it was not just Moore—and it was not just a couple of weeks later. As Horne stated during that FFF [Future of Freedom] conference, Nurse Audrey Bell testified that Perry told her he was getting calls that evening directing him to alter his testimony. This is now backed up by a startling piece of evidence surfaced by author Rob Couteau. Martin Steadman was a reporter at the time of the JFK assassination. Couteau discovered a journal entry by Martin that is online. Steadman was stationed in Dallas for several days after the assassination, gathering information. Some of it got in print and some of it did not. From all indications, the following did not.

One of the witnesses he spent some time with in Dallas was Dr. Malcolm Perry. Steadman was aware of what Perry had said at the press conference about the directionality of the neck wound. Steadman wrote that, about a week after the assassination, he and two other journalists were with Perry in his home. During this informal interview, Perry said he thought it was an entrance wound because the small circular hole was clean. He then added two important details. He said he had treated hundreds of patients with similar wounds and he knew the difference between an exit and entrance wound. Further, hunting was a hobby of his, so he understood from that experience what the difference was. And he could detect it at a glance.

Steadman went on to reveal something rather surprising. Perry said that during that night, he got a series of phone calls to his home from the doctors at Bethesda. They were very upset about his belief that the neck wound was one of entrance. They asked him if the Parkland doctors had turned over the body to see the wounds in Kennedy's back. Perry replied that they had not. They then said: how could he be sure about the neck wound in light of that? They

---

[24] https://www.kennedysandking.com/john-f-kennedy-articles/the-ordeal-of-malcolm-perry

then told him that he should not continue to say that he cut across an entrance wound when there was no evidence of a shot from the front. When Perry insisted that he could only say what he thought to be true, something truly bizarre happened. Perry said that one or more of the autopsy doctors told him that he would be brought before a Medical Board if he continued to insist on his story. Perry said they threatened to take away his license.

After Perry finished this rather gripping tale, everyone was silent for a moment. Steadman then asked him if he still thought the throat wound was one of entrance. After a second or so, Perry said yes, he did."

The Harper Fragment

The day after the assassination, a bone fragment was found in Dealey Plaza by pre-med student Billy Harper, which is why it is referred to as the Harper Fragment.[25]

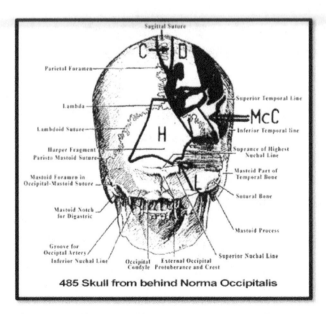

485 Skull from behind Norma Occipitalis

MANTIK'S RECONSTRUCTION OF THE JFK SKULL

---

[25] https://themantikview.org/pdf/The_JFK_Autopsy_Materials.pdf

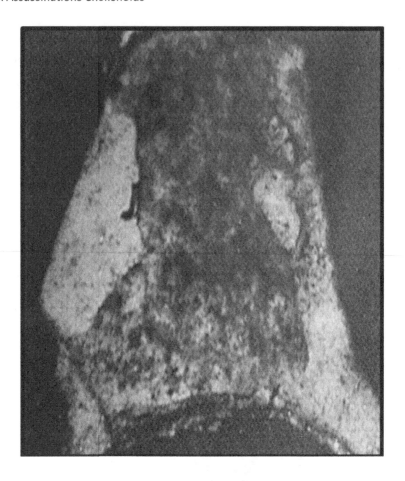

He brought it to his uncle, Jack Harper, a pathologist. He and two other pathologists (Dr. A.B. Cairns and Gerald Noteboom) looked at it and all three confirmed that it was a fresh piece of bone based on the condition of the blood on the two and half inch-wide bone and that it was occipital. They (and the FBI later) took pictures of it. Cairns was interviewed by the HSCA and insisted that it was occipital.[26]

The fragment became one of many key pieces of evidence to disappear. Admiral Burkley was the last to sign for it. Harper Fragment X-rays were inaccessible for many decades.[27] This bone fragment confirms eyewitness testimony of dozens of witnesses who saw the head injury.

---

[26] Doug Horne Presentation, The Medical Coverup minute 20.26
https://www.youtube.com/watch?v=iWWHBPy1bCk
[27] JFK's Head-Wounds-David Mantik

The Limousine Windshield

In what can only be described as destruction of evidence, JFK's limousine, the most important part of the crime scene, was quickly sent for repairs. At least nine people saw damage to and/or a hole in the windshield: Starvis Ellis D. P. D., H. R. Freeman D. P. D., Evalea Glanges—a medical student at Parkland Hospital, Joe Paolella Secret Service, Charles Taylor Jr. Secret Service, Richard Dudman and Frank Cormier St. Louis Post-Dispatch, Bill Greer Secret Service and George Whitaker Sr. —Supervisor at Ford Motor Company.

The most damning witness was Whitaker. Attorney Douglas Weldon interviewed him in August of 1993. Whitaker told Weldon that he had worked on replacing the damaged windshield. The damage was repaired on November 25 when most employers were given a holiday for JFK's funeral. He said the damage was 4 to 6 inches to the driver's side of the rear-view mirror. *(Altgens photo 6)*

He said that there was a bullet hole caused by a frontal shot.... *"It was a good clean hole right straight through from the front."* He also added that the interior of the limousine was completely stripped out … that the damaged windshield was destroyed.[28]

Mantik, Horne and Weldon all make a rather trenchant observation about the original windshield. Roy Kellerman and Morgan Geis of the Secret Service both said they saw the damaged windshield and the outside was smooth, the damage was on the inside. But safety glass only shows damage on the other side from which it's hit. Which means, what these observations show is that the impact was from the front.[29]

See the Weldon presentation here about his investigation around the limousine and the windshield.[30] You can hear audio excerpts of Whitaker interview in the following Weldon presentation starting 1:16:47.[31]

Spatter Analysis

It is important to preface the following rationale, by recognizing that blood spatter analysis has been often criticized for its lack of a scientific foundation and has been known to yield contradictory interpretation depending on many variables. However, in the case of JFK's assassination, certain observations about the debris from JFK should lead one to conclude that at least one shot came from the front.

Let us begin with what Jesse Curry, Dallas Chief of Police, believed about a gunshot origin. Curry, who was in the motorcade just in front of the president and interviewed Oswald after the assassination is on the record for saying: *"There is a possibility that one (a shot) came from in front of us… By the direction of the blood and the brains of the president from one of the shots, it just seems it would have to be fired from the front… I can't say that I could swear that there was one man and one man alone, I think that there is the possibility that there could be another man…"*[32]

---

[28] Inside the ARRB, Horne, p. 1446 and JFK Paradoxes, Essays and Reviews, David Mantik starting at p. 316

[29] Horne, p. 1449

[30] https://www.youtube.com/watch?v=idb_12I1uYQ

[31] https://www.youtube.com/watch?v=OACTLn75I30

[32] Spartacus Educational, The Killing of President Kennedy, 1978

Josiah Thompson, who has analyzed the case for over fifty years, in 2022 presented an <u>extremely strong case</u> that was recorded and should really be looked at in its entirety for researchers to fully grasp the stunning implications of this exposé.[33]

Josiah uses witness testimony of police officers and secret service agents who were trailing the presidential limousine on motorcycles and in the follow-up vehicle; witnesses who were between the vehicle and the infamous grassy knoll ahead and to the right of the limousine, witnesses who were beyond the knoll. He adds pictures taken near the moment of the famous headshot as well as video footage to accurately place the witnesses and those people and vehicles which were struck by splatter.

He argues correctly that the size of some of the debris as well as the powerful strength of much of the impact excludes any type of explanation around people or objects riding into some sort of blood mist that occurred.

Dr. Thompson was able to place people and vehicles just behind JFK around when he was first struck as such:

---

[33] https://vimeo.com/showcase/10132416

The key witnesses here are Officer Bobby Hargis (first back left [of JFK] motorcyclist) Officer B. J. Martin (second back left motorcyclist). Officers Jackson and Chaney (back right motorcyclists) Secret Service agents (Clint Hill standing on the left side of the follow-up vehicle and its driver Sam Kinney). (Note: Clint Hill was struck by debris at around frame 313 which coincides with JFK's head being propelled violently backwards.)

Here are some key statements and facts... *Officers Jackson and Chaney were not struck by debris. Bobby Hargis was hit hard: "As the president straightened back up, Mrs. Kennedy turned back toward him and that is when he got hit on the side of his head spinning it around. I was splattered with blood. Then I felt something hit me, it could have been concrete or something, but at first I thought I had been hit"... "I was splattered by blood and brain."*[34]B. J. Martin testified that he too had been struck by *"blood and matter,"* but just on his left side.[35]

Sam Kinney told Vince Palamara the following: *"Yeah, he had no brain left, it was blown out. Clint Hill and I unloaded him out of the car. There was nothing left. It was the whole back of the head as far as I'm concerned. I saw it hit and I saw his hair come out... I had brain matter all over my windshield and all over my left arm. That's how close we were. It was the right part of his head."*[36] *"I looked back at Mr. Kennedy and saw him hit in the head. He appeared to be hit just above the right ear. The top of his head flew away from me."*[37]

Thompson demonstrates that the reason Martin's right side was not struck is that Hargis was shielding that side of him. Kinney's left arm (likely hanging out the window), Clint Hill, the follow-up vehicle, the left side motorcycles and the trunk of the presidential limousine were all struck and tainted by debris. (Sources provided in Thompson seminar video.)

---

[34] *Hargis interview, NY Sunday News, November 24, 1963, and (Hargis testimony 6H294)*

[35] Martin testimony 6H292

[36] Survivor's Guilt, Vince Palamara, p. 253

[37] Officer Douglas Jackson, JFK First Day evidence, p. 363

This along with the Zapruder film footage and photos allowed Thompson to schematize the following:

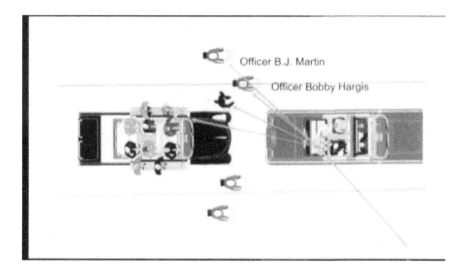

Thompson then shows that two bone fragments were found far to the left of the vehicle which is consistent with other splatter:

Next, Thompson shows how the witnesses (Bill Newman, Gail Newman and Emmet Hudson—who were part of a much thinner crowd of people) between JFK's vehicle at the time of the shot and the knoll believed the shots came from behind them, ergo to the right and in front of the president's limousine.

"Well, of course the President's being shot in the right side of the head by the third shot—I thought the third shot was fired from directly above and behind where we were standing. And that is what scared us because I thought we were in the direct path of gunfire." He also said that *"the shot had come from the garden directly behind me."*[38]

"The shots that I hear definitely came from behind and above me."[39]

Mr. SPECTER. When was it that Mrs. Kennedy made the statement which you have described, "My God, what are they doing?"

---

[38] WC Testimony, Bill Newman, 19H490

[39] WC Testimony, Emmet Hudson, 24H213

Mr. KELLERMAN. This occurred after the flurry of shots.

Mr. SPECTER. At that time you looked back and saw Special Agent Hill across the trunk of the car, had your automobile accelerated by that time?

Mr. KELLERMAN. Tremendously so; yes.

Mr. SPECTER. Now, to the best of your ability to recollect, exactly when did your automobile first accelerate?

Mr. KELLERMAN. Our car accelerated immediately on the time-at the time—this flurry of shots came into it.

Mr. SPECTER. Would you say the acceleration—

Mr. KELLERMAN. Between the second and third shot.

These witnesses narrow down the vicinity of the origins of the fatal gunshot considerably:

The witnesses who had a view from behind the knoll will help pinpoint the exact origin of the fatal shot, according to witness testimony.

One of these was Lee Bowers who was in a train yard tower. He actually saw commotion and suspicious activity in an area that corroborates the Newman and Hudson accounts.

Another was Sam Holland who was interviewed intensively by Josiah Thompson. Holland was considered extremely reliable by the HSCA and credited as being a very credible witness by Robert Blakey. Thompson in his presentation related that he and a colleague firmly interrogated Holland and that Holland reenacted for them his actions and related what he witnessed on January 22, 1963, in Dealey Plaza. He also stated that on multiple occasions intelligence agents tried to convince him to change his story.

He and eight other witnesses (according to Thompson) confirmed that they did see a puff of smoke emanating from a stockade fence, which with the sounds, brought Holland to explore where he thought the shots came from. He found several fresh footprints.

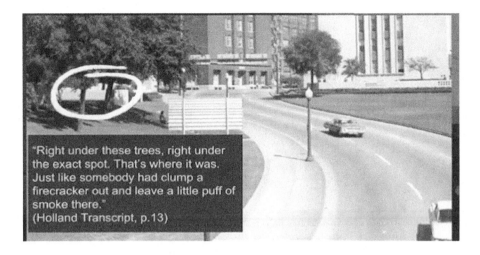

"Right under these trees, right under the exact spot. That's where it was. Just like somebody had clump a firecracker out and leave a little puff of smoke there."
(Holland Transcript, p.13)

Holland and Thompson then drew a diagram showing where Holland explored behind the picket fence:

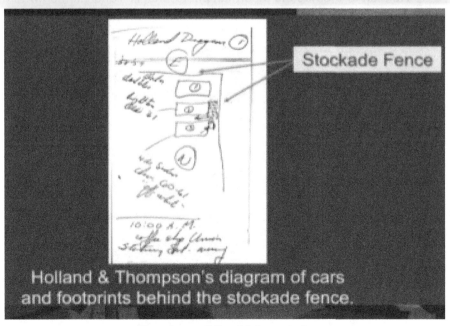

Stockade Fence

Holland & Thompson's diagram of cars and footprints behind the stockade fence.

(Courtesy of David Josephs)

Thompson then took a photo of Holland standing where these foot-prints were, which is where he thought the shots came from. *(Following photos from J. Thompson presentation)*

He then re-created the Moorman photo, with Holland situated where he said the shots came from:

Putting his recreation side-by-side with the Moorman photo, Josiah noticed a protrusion in the Moorman photo that is not normally there. Hmmm.

Thompson concludes the spatter analysis by showing that a shot emanating from this point of origin dovetails with witness testimony and debris trajectory.

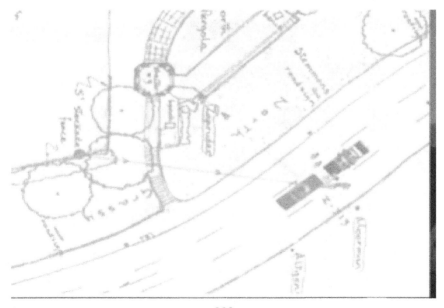

In concluding this element of evidence, it can be safely stated that while there can be some debate about the exact origin of the fatal front shot given margins of error, there can be no debate that the shot that caused the splatter described above did not come from the sixth floor of the schoolbook depository signifying that there were multiple shooters on November 22, 1963, in Dealey Plaza.

Particle Trails in X-ray

For this piece of evidence, let me quote from the following article: *"Peer Reviewed" Medical/Scientific Journalism Has Been Corrupted by Warren Commission Apologists—Part 2*.[40] We will also provide their sources.

> "Both authors Wecht and Aguilar have examined the still-secret, original, unenhanced X-rays at the National Archives and have seen that *"dust like"* fragments *are* present in the right front quadrant of Kennedy's skull X-rays. We are not the only ones who've noticed them. They were reported by Kennedy's chief pathologist, Dr. James Humes, by a Secret Service agent, as well as other government consulting, expert radiologists. The presence of minuscule fragments essentially rules out that Oswald's single, jacketed round hit Kennedy at frame 313 of the Zapruder Film.
>
> Why?
>
> For the good reasons, Larry Sturdivan gave: tiny fragments don't travel far in tissue, because of their low mass relative to their large surface area, their *"high drag"* in tissue. Tiny bullet fragments are quickly stopped in tissue. In contrast, larger fragments have proportionately less surface area compared with their mass than small fragments do, and so drive further through tissue before being stopped.
>
> Besides their presence, a telling detail is the location of the tiny

---

[40] https://www.kennedysandking.com/john-f-kennedy-articles/peer-reviewed-medical-scientific-journalism-has-been-corrupted-by-warren-commission-apologists-part-2

fragments. They sit in the right front quadrant of JFK's skull, which, to borrow from Sturdivan, is likely *"very near the entrance wound."* This evidence has largely lain unrecognized and unappreciated in the record since 1964.

- During his Warren Commission testimony in 1964, Dr. Humes said: *"(JFK's X-rays) had disclosed to us multiple minute fragments of radio-opaque material … these tiny fragments that were seen dispersed through the substance of the brain in between were, in fact, just that extremely minute, less than 1 mm in size for the most part."* A few moments later, Dr. Humes was asked, *"Approximately how many fragments were observed, Dr. Humes, on the X-ray?" "I would have to refer to them again (the X-rays),"* he answered, *"but I would say between 30 or 40 tiny dust-like particle fragments of radio-opaque material, with the exception of this one I previously mentioned, which was seen to be above and very slightly behind the right orbit."*
- Secret Service Agent Roy Kellerman, an autopsy witness, testified that the fragments in JFK's skull X-ray, *"looked like a little mass of stars; there must have been 30, 40 lights where these pieces were so minute that they couldn't be reached."*
- Russell Morgan, MD, the chairman of the department of radiology at Johns Hopkins University, was the Clark Panel's radiologist. *"Distributed through the right cerebral hemisphere are numerous, small irregular metallic fragments,"* the Panel reported, *"most of which are less than 1 mm in maximum dimension. The majority of these fragments lie anteriorly and superiorly. None can be visualized on the left side of the brain and none below a horizontal plane through the floor of the anterior fossa of the skull."* (Emphasis added)
- Cook County Hospital Forensic Radiologist, John Fitzpatrick, MD, examined JFK's X-rays in consultation for the ARRB and agreed, writing: *"There is a 'snow trail' of metallic fragments in the lateral skull X-rays which probably corresponds to a bullet*

track through the head, but the direction of the bullet (whether back-to-front or front-to-back) [sic] cannot be determined by anything about the snow trail itself."

Authors Wecht and Aguilar concur: There are myriad *"dust like"* fragments visible on JFK's lateral X-ray, a *"snow trail,"* if you will. The vast majority are confined to the right front quadrant of Kennedy's skull, which is where, as per Sturdivan, a non-jacketed bullet struck.

Practicing neurologist Michael Chesser, MD examined the original, unenhanced JFK X-rays and came to the same conclusion: *"This location, on the intracranial side of the bony defect, is highly suggestive of an entry wound,"* he wrote. *"One of the principles of skull ballistics is that the largest fragments travel the furthest from the entry site, with the smallest traveling the least distance, and that is exactly what is seen on this right lateral skull X-ray. Tiny fragments are seen on the inner side of this right frontal skull defect, and the largest fragments were noted in the back of the skull..."*

The trail of small, but not minuscule, fragments that are visible runs along the top of JFK's skull in both the enhanced and unenhanced lateral X-rays. It does not align with the supposed low entrance wound specified by the autopsy surgeons in occipital bone, although the autopsy surgeons said it did. Nor does it line up with the higher entrance wound the Clark Panel identified, although the Clark Panel said it did. In fact, as anyone can see the fragment trail in JFK's lateral X-ray is about 5 cm above where both the Clark Panel and the HSCA said it was. (See pictures below.) That high fragment trail offers evidence there was a second head shot, from behind, with a jacketed round, a possibility that is also suggested by the "jiggle" evidence in the Zapruder film, by Professor Barger's acoustic analysis, and by JFK's rapidly forward-moving skull after frame 328, as explored by Thompson in *Last Second in Dallas*.[41]

---

[41] Warren Commission testimony of James H. Humes, MD, Vol. 2:353; Warren Commission testimony of Secret Service Agent Roy Kellerman. Vol. 2, p. 100. "Inside the

The following is from *JFK's Head-Wounds by David Mantik)*[42] and shows the lateral autopsy X-ray. Note the trail of metallic debris across the top of the skull, at least 10 cm above the occipital wound that the pathologists identified.

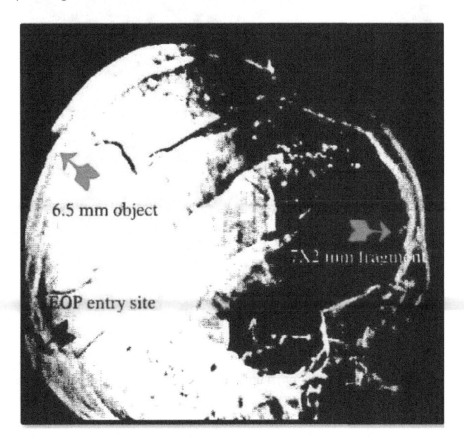

ARRB: Appendices—Current Section: Appendix 44: ARRB staff report of observations and opinions of forensic radiologist Dr. John J. Fitzpatrick, after viewing the JFK autopsy photos and X-rays," p. 2. Chesser, M. A Review of the JFK Cranial X-rays and Photographs. DiMaio, VJM. Gunshot wounds—Practical Aspects of Firearms, Forensics, and Ballistics Techniques, Third Edition, p. 166.
[42] https://themantikview.org/pdf/The_JFK_Autopsy_Materials.pdf pp. 35, 36

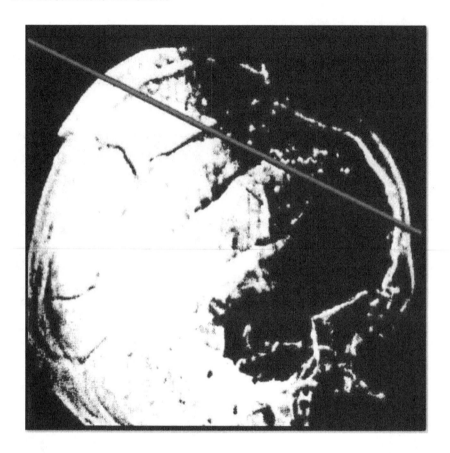

Although no proposed posterior entry site matches this trail of metallic debris, on the other hand, a bullet that entered the right forehead, near the hairline, directly over the outer edge of the right eye socket, would match this bullet trail with remarkable precision.

What Professional, Medical Personnel Witnesses at Parkland and Bethesda Saw

So far, we have seen that three Parkland doctors who observed Kennedy's throat wound concluded that it was one of penetration implying a shot from the front. Bethesda doctors did not analyze this wound.

One of the biggest mysteries to hover around the JFK case was the supposed difference in what was observed at Parkland, where doctors tried to save Kennedy's life, and Bethesda where the autopsy was performed. A very large number of witnesses at Parkland said they saw an egg-sized exit wound in the back of Kennedy's head in the occipital, parietal area on the right side. Some claimed it was a little higher on the back of the head.

According to the Warren Commission and the HSCA—relying on the autopsy, photographs of Kennedy's skull, and witness accounts—there was no such injury in the back of the head.

It took the ARRB to clear up this very confounding situation when they looked at classified documents and questioned witnesses and checked out other evidence.

It ends up that what the Parkland doctors saw was correct; that a large number of witnesses at Bethesda concurred, and that the JFK photographs at the autopsy appear to be manipulated to back the lone-nut scenario. Another deception that was exposed was the information published by the autopsy doctors that stated that Kennedy's brain weighed 1500 grams, a full 150 grams more than the average brain, despite it having been pulverized. (See the film *JFK Revisited* for an examination of this issue.)

ARRB employee Doug Horne also explained that contrary to other depositions done of the autopsists during other investigations, the ARRB questioned Dr. Humes and Dr. Boswell separately. This yielded a stunning result: "While Humes contended under oath that there was no bone missing in the back of JFK's skull, Boswell said there was bone missing in the rear skull and actually made a sketch on a three-dimensional skull model (now at the archives) showing missing bone skull from the top of the head, part of the right side, and the entire right rear of the cranium."[43]

When Jeremy Gunn of the ARRB showed Saundra Spencer, the Navy Warrant Officer who processed the autopsy film, the official photos from the National Archives <u>during her deposition in 1997</u>, she said they were not the pictures she remembered processing. What's more, the official pictures weren't anything like the ones she remembered. *"The*

---

[43] JFK Revisited, pages 299 to 314

prints that we printed did not have the massive head damage that is visible here," she told Gunn.[44]

Crenshaw Blows the Whistle

One of the most compelling medical witnesses wrote a book about his experience as one of the Parkland Doctors who treated JFK. Dr. Charles Crenshaw in *JFK Conspiracy of Silence* explained what he saw about JFK wounds, and the intimidation Parkland doctors faced to toe the line.

"I noticed immediately that almost the entire right hemisphere in the back of his brain was missing…" "Part of his cerebellum was hanging by a single strand of tissue"… "I also identified a small opening about the diameter of a pencil at the midline of his throat to be an entry bullet hole. There was no doubt in my mind about that wound."[45] He also pointed out, as others did, to where the entry shot was.

These three short sentences, and images, from a doctor who had more experience with gunshot wounds than the three autopsy pathologists provides strong evidence that there was a shooter who was not on the sixth floor of the TSBD. And the narrative coming out of Bethesda was in clear contradiction to what was observed closely by many at Parkland. Corroboration of Crenshaw's account and proof of deception in the official investigations would be compelling, to say the least.

Let's go on: "Clint Hill, the Secret Service agent who had pushed Jacqueline back into the car, was rambling around the room in a wild-eyed, disoriented fashion, waving a cocked and ready *to fire .38 caliber pistol. There we were, getting ready to work on a man who had just lost half his head from a bullet, and we had a crazed man running around with a loaded gun."*[46]

"*I walked to the President's head to get a closer look. His entire cerebral hemisphere appeared to be gone. It looked like a cratered—an empty cavity. All I could see there was mangled, bloody tissue. From the*

---

[44] https://www.jfk-assassination.net/russ/testimony/spencer.htm

[45] JFK Conspiracy of Silence, pp. 78–79

[46] Ibid., p 80

damage I saw, there was no doubt in my mind that the bullet had entered his head through the front, and as it surgically passed through his cranium, the missile obliterated part of the temporal and part of the parietal and occipital lobes before it lacerated and exposed the cerebellum."[47]

Crenshaw describes the scuffle in the hospital after JFK was pronounced dead, when Secret Service agents with guns ignored pleas by Parkland doctors to perform an autopsy in Dallas as per Texas law, and aggressively confiscated the corpse. *"My impression was that someone, who had given explicit instructions to these men, wanted Kennedy's body out of Texas in a hurry."*[48]

During a press conference shortly after JFK was pronounced dead, White House Press Secretary, Malcolm Kilduff described the cause of death while pointing to his forehead: *"Dr. Burkley told me it's a simple matter ... of a bullet right through the head."*[49]

---

[47] Ibid., p 86
[48] Ibid., p 99
[49] Ibid., p 110

When Crenshaw saw pictures taken of JFK's throat at Bethesda, he noted it had been enlarged and *"It looked to be the work of a butcher."*[50]

Other highly incriminating information one can find in Crenshaw's book include:

1. His outright dismissal of the Single Bullet theory *(p. 114)*

2. He points out that at Parkland, observers saw considerable damage to the back of JFK's head while at Bethesda this part of his head *was said* to be intact. *(p. 132)*

3. The stretcher bullet was a plant (no residue, dismissed by some who handled it, too little damage to it, too many fragments connected to Connally's injuries, etc.). *(pp. 133–136)*

4. He sensed pervasive corruption *(p. 152)*

5. How Drs. Perry and Clark believed the shots came from the front *(p. 153)*

He concludes with the following: *"In the case of the medical personnel at Parkland Hospital, the conspiracy of silence was a mixture of fraternal doctrine, naiveté, fear and career mindedness." (p. 201)*

Law Enforcement in Dallas, Doctors and Medical Personnel at Parkland and Bethesda who Made Descriptions of Wounds Indicating a Front Shot:

1. Parkland doctors: Robert Mclelland, Charles Crenshaw, Paul Peters, William Zedlitz, Ronald Jones, Richard Dulany, Charles Carrico, Ken Salyer, Kemp Clark, James Duke, Malcolm Perry, Charles Baxter, Don Curtis, Marion Jenkins, Robert Grossman, Adolph Giesecke, Fouad Bashour, William Midgett, Jackie Hunt,

---

[50] Ibid., p 111

David Stewart; Nurses: Diana Bowron, Audrey Bell, Doris Nelson, Phyliss Hall, Pat Hutton, Margaret Hinchliffe Other Parkland personnel and onlookers—Justice of the Peace Theron Ward, Ambulance driver Aubrey Rike, Darrell Tomlinson

2. Bethesda Personnel: Dennis David, Jerrol Custer, Floyd Riebe, Paul O'Connor, James Curtis, James Humes, Dr. Thornton Boswell, Saundra Spencer, Godfrey McHugh, Joe O'Donnell, Dr. John Ebersole, John Stringer, Dr. Robert Karnel, James Metzler, Chester Boyers, Joseph Hagan, Tom Robinson, John Van Hoesen, Robert Knudsen, James Sibert, Frank O'Neill

3. Law enforcement: James Courson D. P. D. Police Officer, Milton Wright, Texas, Highway Patrolman, Vincent Drain FBI Special Agent, Samuel Kinney Secret Service Agent, Joe Cody DPD Police Officer, Clint Hill Secret Service, Bill Greer Secret Service, Roy Kellerman Secret Service[51]

L-R: Dr. Robert McClelland, Dr. Paul Peters, and Dr. Kenneth Salyer, all of Parkland Hospital.

L-R: Dr. Charles Crenshaw, Dr. Richard Dulaney, and Nurse Audrey Bell, also all of Parkland Hospital.

[51] *JFK Absolute Proof,* pages 149 to 156

Dr. Charles Carrico:
"There was a large — quite a large — defect about here [pointing] on his skull."

Aubrey Rike
"You could feel the sharp edges of the bone at the edge of the hole in the back of his head."

(Pictures from: https://www.kennedysandking.com/john-f-kennedy-articles/parkland-doctors)

More Important Parkland Hospital Medical Personnel Statements:[52]

PAUL PETERS, MD: "... I noticed that there was a large defect in the occiput... It seemed to me that in the right occipital/parietal area that there was a large defect."[53]

MALCOLM PERRY, MD: "I looked at the head wound briefly by leaning over the table and noticed that the parietal occipital head wound was

---

[52] Source of photos, quotes and sketches taken from:
https://paulseaton.com/jfk/boh/parkland_boh/parkland_wound.htm
[53] WC-V6:71

largely avulsive and there was visible brain tissue in the macard and some cerebellum seen..."[54]

CHARLES CRENSHAW, MD: It extended from the approximate center of the skull in the back to just behind the right ear, utilizing a left to right orientation and from a position a couple of inches above the right ear to the approximate middle of the right ear utilizing a top to bottom orientation.[55]

CHARLES JAMES CARRICO, MD: "The (skull) wound that I saw was a large gaping wound, located in the right occipital/parietal area, I would estimate to be about 5 to 7 cm. in size, more or less circular, with avulsions of the calvarium and scalp tissue. As I stated before, I believe there was shredded macerated cerebral and cerebellar tissues both in the wounds and on the fragments of the skull attached to the dura."[56]

NURSE DIANA HAMILTON BOWRON: " ...there was blood all over this neck and shoulders. There was a gaping wound in the back of his head."[57]

GENE AIKIN, MD: "The back of the right occipital/parietal portion of his head was shattered with brain substance extruding."[58]

CHARLES RUFUS BAXTER, MD: " ...the right temporal and occipital bones were missing (emphasis added) and the brain was lying on the table..."[59]

AUDREY BELL: "there was a massive wound in the back of his head...
— She said she could see brain and spinal fluid coming out of the wound, but could not tell what type of brain tissue it was."

---

[54] HSCA-V7:302-interview with Purdy 1-11-78
[55] FBI file # 89 A-DL-60165-99
[56] *WC Testimony, Carrico 6H6*
[57] *Livingstone, Killing the Truth, p. 180*
[58] *WC-V6:65*
[59] *WR: (532)*

Dr. McClelland's Drawing

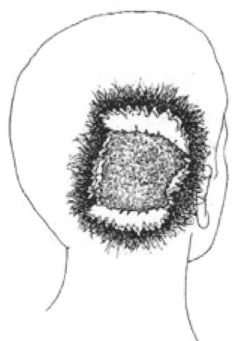

bowron

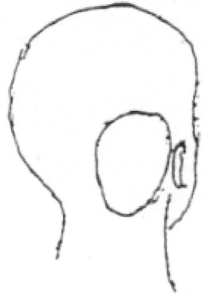

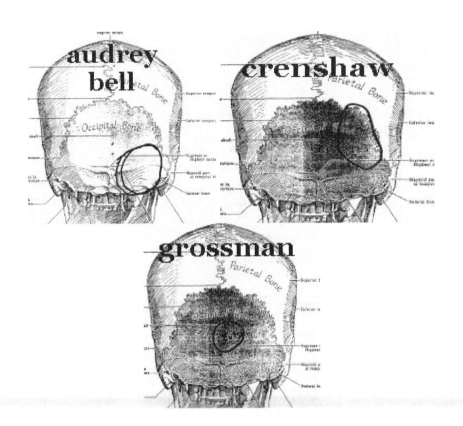

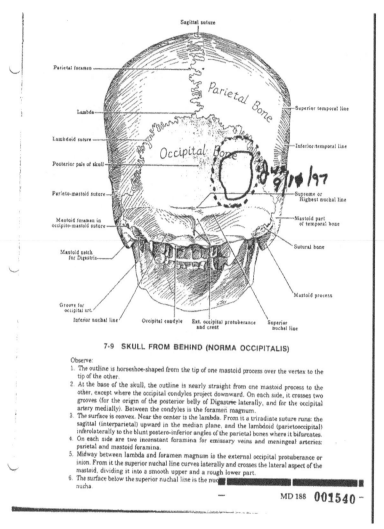

7-9 SKULL FROM BEHIND (NORMA OCCIPITALIS)

MD 188—Sketch Made by James W. Sibert on Anatomical Drawing of Wound in President Kennedy's Head (Executed on September 11, 1997)

Cerebellum Blown Out

Many witnesses confirmed that cerebellum was blasted out of JFK's brain which confirms the occipital defect and a frontal shot. This is from the sworn testimony of Dr. McClelland from the ARRB:

1 that? Come over Monday morning and I'll let you
2 look at them.
3   And so that's what he did. He
4 looked at them and he's the one who told me he
5 wasn't sure the cerebellum had been injured as I
6 had testified that I thought it was. And having
7 viewed the pictures at the National Archives, I
8 still feel it was. It was certainly displaced,
9 if not lacerated.
10   DR. McCLELLAND: Well, I know it
11 was. I don't often say that but I didn't just
12 glance at it. I looked at it for several
13 minutes, and it was clearly cerebellum. There's
14 no question about it, and I could look down into
15 the skull. In fact, I made that point there.
16   DR. PETERS: Right.
17   DR. McCLELLAND: There was
18 nothing in the -- in the area where the
19 cerebellum usually sits.
20   And as I said, most of it was
21 probably gone when I first began to look down
22 into the wound, and then as I stood there,
23 probably just maybe a minute after I came in,
24 another large portion of it, which I thought -- I
25 remember thinking now, well, that's the rest of

1 the cerebellum oozed out into the table. So it's
2 not, well, I kind of think it was. It was.
3   MR. GUNN: I'd like to hand out
4 a document to each of you that first appeared in
5 a book by Josiah Thompson, which I assume that

Bethesda Witnesses[60]

TOM ROBINSON: In an HSCA interview released in 1993 with mortician Tom Robinson, conducted by Andy Purdy and Jim Conzelman, Purdy asked Robinson: "Approximately where was this wound (the skull wound) located?" Robinson: "Directly behind the back of his head." Purdy: "Approximately between the ears or higher up?" Robinson, "No, I would say pretty much between them."[61] Purdy and Conzelman signed

---

[60] https://paulseaton.com/jfk/boh/beth/beth.htm
[61] *HSCA rec # 189-10089-10178, agency file # 000661*, p. 3

a diagram prepared and also signed by Robinson. The sketch depicts a defect directly in the central, lower rear portion of the skull.[62]

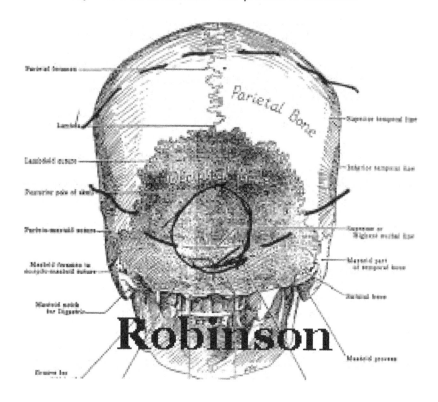

PAUL O'CONNOR: one of two laboratory technologists present during JFK's autopsy at Bethesda, he has repeatedly insisted that the skull wound extended on the right side well into the rear of the skull. O'Connor was shown the autopsy photographs and he said, "No, that doesn't look like what I saw… A lot worse wound extended way back here, and he demonstrated with his hand to the back of the head."[63] O'Connor has consistently maintained that opinion in interviews since that time. (This was also confirmed by Radiologist Ebersole and Cpt. Canada)

---

[62] *HSCA doc # 180-10089-10179, agency file # 000662*

[63] Groden & Livingstone, High Treason, p. 451

Paul O'Connor
"[There was] an open area
all the way across int., the
rear of the brain."

JAMES JENKINS was the other laboratory technologist who worked with the autopsy team on JFK. Jenkins was, at that time, in a Ph.D. program in pathology. The HSCA's Jim Kelly and Andy Purdy reported that Jenkins said he saw a head wound in the " ... *middle temporal region back to the occipital.*"[64]

EDWARD REED: one of two X-ray technicians who worked with Jerrol F. Custer taking X-rays told author David Lifton that he formed an opinion the night of the autopsy that JFK had been shot from the front because the skull wound was *"more posterior than anterior."*[65]

JAN GAIL RUDNICKI: Dr. Boswell's lab assistant on the night of the autopsy, Rudnicki was interviewed by HSCA's Mark Flanagan on 5/2/78.

[64] *HSCA interview with Curtis Jenkins, Jim Kelly and Andy Purdy, 8-29-77. JFK Collection, RG 233, Document #002193, p. 4) and High Treason II, p. 226*
[65] *Lifton, David, Best Evidence, p. 619*

Flanagan reported Rudnicki said the *"back-right quadrant of the head was missing."*[66]

JERROL CUSTER:

Q: Now, on the drawing that you have made, and with the bones as they're identified here, none of the principal part of the missing wound goes into the occipital bone; is that correct?

A: The hole doesn't. but this is all unstable. A lot of this bone was out. It would flap out.

Q: And when you say this bone, you're referring to the—A: The occipital region.

Q: — The parietal—A: Right… And part of the lambdoidal, and down through the posterior of the occipital protuberance. This was all unstable material I mean, completely.[67]

JAMES METZLER: he was a hospital corpsman, third class who helped transport the body from the casket to the autopsy table in the morgue. Author David Lifton reported, *"It was also his impression, from the way the wound was located toward the back of the head, that President Kennedy must have been shot in the head from the front."*[68]

"Metzler recalled a wound situated in the 'right side of the head behind the right ear, extending down to the center of the back of the skull.' Metzler mentioned that pieces of brain extended outward from the defect, which measured at least four inches long."[69]

JOHN EBERSOLE, MD: was Assistant Chief of Radiology and head of the Radiology Division at Bethesda and was the radiologist who evaluated the X-rays in close cooperation with the autopsists on the night of the autopsy. He was not called to testify before the Warren Commission. However, he was called to testify by the HSCA on March 11, 1978.

---

[66] *HSCA rec # 180–10105–10,397, agency file number # 014461, p. 2*
[67] *Custer, ARRB deposition*
[68] *Best Evidence, Lifton pp. 633–634*
[69] *HSCA telephone interview Apr 21, 1978*

Ebersole's deposition was not published by the HSCA causing it to be sealed for 50 years under congressional rules. (Due to pressure, however, the transcript of his interview was released in October 1993.)

A brief wire service account appeared regarding his appearance before the HSCA claiming that he agreed with the Warren Commissions' conclusions. However, in an interview with reporter Gil Dulaney published two days before his HSCA appearance Ebersole said of the head wound, *"When the body was removed from the casket there was a very obvious horrible gaping wound to the back of the head"*, and *"The front of the body, except for a very slight bruise above the right eye on the forehead, was absolutely intact. It was the back of the head that was blown off."*[70]

Dr. Boswell also Confronts the Photo Deception

His ARRB testimony:

Q. So you're saying that on the fourth view, which are the photographs that are in your hand right now, the scalp has been pulled back and folded back over the top of the head in a way different from the way that they appeared in the third view, the superior view of the head?

A. Yes.

Q. Is that fair?

A. In the previous one, it was permitted just to drop. In this one, it's pulled forward up over the forehead, toward the forehead.

Q. Who, if you recall, pulled up the scalp for the photograph to be taken?

A. There are about three of us involved here, because there are two right hands on that centimeter scale. I think that I probably was pulling the scalp up.[71]

---

[70] Lifton, p 543, 546
[71] Boswell ARRB

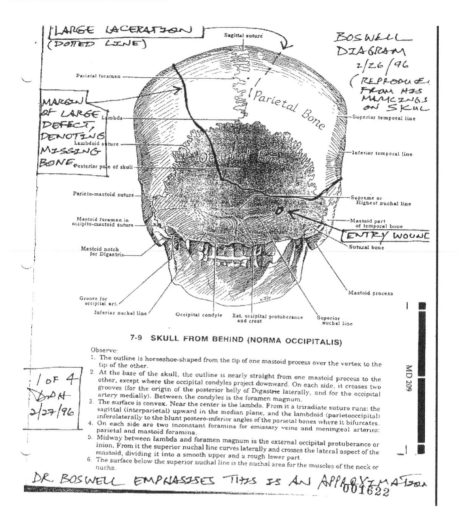

7-9 SKULL FROM BEHIND (NORMA OCCIPITALIS)

Observe:

1. The outline is horseshoe-shaped from the tip of one mastoid process over the vertex to the tip of the other.
2. At the base of the skull, the outline is nearly straight from one mastoid process to the other, except where the occipital condyles project downward. On each side, it crosses two grooves (for the origin of the posterior belly of Digastric laterally, and for the occipital artery medially). Between the condyles is the foramen magnum.
3. The surface is convex. Near the center is the lambda. From it a triradiate suture runs: the sagittal (interparietal) upward in the median plane, and the lambdoid (parietooccipital) inferolaterally to the blunt postero-inferior angles of the parietal bones where it bifurcates.
4. On each side are two inconstant foramina for emissary veins and meningeal arteries: parietal and mastoid foramina.
5. Midway between lambda and foramen magnum is the external occipital protuberance or inion. From it the superior nuchal line curves laterally and crosses the lateral aspect of the mastoid, dividing it into a smooth upper and a rough lower part.
6. The surface below the superior nuchal line is the nuchal area for the muscles of the neck or nucha.

DR. BOSWELL EMPHASISES THIS IS AN APPROXIMATION

001622

MD 209

320

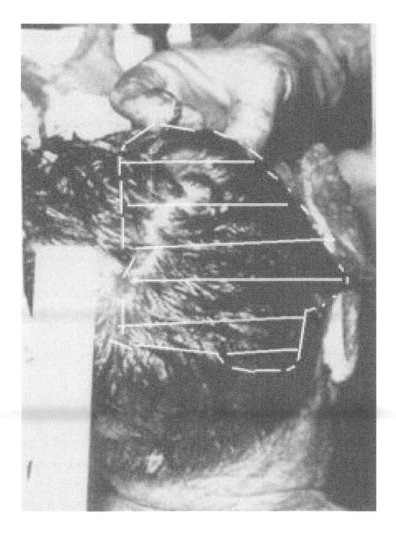

Color autopsy photo. The yellow hashed area marks the approximate location of the skull defect according to a skull Boswell marked for the ARRB.

"Well, this was an attempt to illustrate the magnitude of the wound again. And as you can see, it's 10 centimeters from right to left, 17 centimeters from posterior to anterior. This was a piece of 10-centimeter bone that was fractured off of the skull and was attached to the under surface of the skull… There were fragments attached to the skull or to the scalp and all the three major flaps."[72]

---

[72] Boswell, interviewed by the HSCA FPP

Boswell is explicit that the skull is missing beneath the scalp in the autopsy picture, above:

Q. Now I'd like to ask you a question about what is underneath the scalp of what we are looking at now. Let's take the marking that appears toward the hairline right at the base of the neck, or where the hairline meets the neck. If we take the point above that, where would you say that the scalp is or that the skull will be missing underneath the scalp that we can view there?
A. Probably right about here.
Q. So you're—
A. Just about the base of the ear.
Q. So you're pointing to approximately halfway up the ruler that we can observe and to the right of that small fragment, so the skull is missing?
A. Right.[73]

Compare this to Humes' ARRB testimony:[74]

Q. Okay. Let me try another question. Can you describe generally where there was any missing bone from the posterior portion to the best of your recollection?
A. There basically wasn't any. It was just a hole. Not a significant missing bone.
Q. So a puncture hole—
A. Puncture hole.
Q. And no bone missing
A. No.

NOTE: THIS IS A FLAGRANT DISAGREEMENT WITH BOSWELL AC-COUNT. SEE SKETCH ABOVE

---

[73] Boswell ARRB Testimony
[74] https://paulseaton.com/jfk/boh/beth/beth.htm

Q. Anywhere in the occipital

A. No, no. Unless maybe—you know, these drawings are always strange. Unless the part of this wound extended that far back. I don't think it did, really. Most of it was parietal temporal.

Q. So on the scalp of President Kennedy here, still in View No. 4, [above] that underneath the scalp the bone was all intact with the exception of the puncture wound—

A. Yeah.

Q. *and perhaps some fragment—[Ed. Note: Gunn should have finished this sentence. Presumably, he was going on to say "fragmentation."]*

A. In the back of the skull, back, yes, sir.

Q. Are you able to identify whose arm that is holding the President's head?

A. No.

Q. When that photograph was taken, was the scalp being pulled forward, that is, toward the eyes of the President, in order for that photograph to be taken?

A. It's possible. I'm not sure. It looks like that's what's happening. The edge of the defect is up there. *The edge of the defect is adjacent to where the fingers and thumb of the person appear on the photograph.*

Q. I asked you a similar question with another view, but I'd just like to try the same question again. Looking at the posterior skull here, the portion that is below the ear—so if we were to draw a line from between the top of the ear and the top of the ruler down, is it your understanding that the skull behind that scalp would be intact?

A. **Reasonably intact.**[75]

To see a sample of how the Parkland doctors contested the JFK back of the head photo read the following ARRB Sworn testimonies:

---

[75] Humes, ARRB Testimony

```
 7   picture --
 8              DR. McCLELLAND: This one
 9   here --
10              MR. GUNN: -- on Exhibit 264.
11              DR. McCLELLAND: There was no
12   hole on that picture that looked like that. And
13   I said, Well, I think I know why that is. I
14   think it may be because if you'll notice there
15   are some fingers at the top of the photograph
16   apparently pulling a flap of scalp forward, and I
17   think the flap was being pulled over that opening
18   when they took the pictures.
12              DR. PETERS: Well, I would
13   certainly agree with what Bob said. It was my
14   thought exactly that they just kind of pulled
15   that flap back into place and took a picture so
16   they could show how it looked with things
17   restored as much as possible and it just -- a
18   flap just kind of -- had been torn back and now
19   they were just kind of putting it back and
20   snapping a picture. For what reason, I don't
21   know.
22              But I'm certain there was a hole
23   there, too. I walked around right and looked in
24   his head. You could look directly into the
25   cranial vault and see cerebral injury to the
```

```
 1   cerebral cortex and I thought at the time to the
 2   cerebellum. So I know the hole was big enough to
 3   look into. I estimated it at seven centimeters
 4   at that time, and I don't know what the actual
 5   measurements were when they took the radiographs,
 6   but I thought just exactly what Bob did. They
 7   were probably making a series of pictures and
 8   they had just pulled that flap back up there to
 9   cover it up and took a picture of that to show
10   the head with the flap restored, so to speak, for
11   whatever reason. I'm sure there were many other
12   pictures that were made at the same time.
```

Doug Horne Exposes the Deception by the HSCA:

Multiple witnesses refuted the following picture (also see above)... Including Humes himself: *"I did not see the red spot, and I did not wash his hair. The large hole extended into the OCCIPUT as I stated."*[76]

---

[76] JFK Head Wounds, page IV

Verbatim Comments,
Under Oath, by FBI
Agents Sibert and O'Neill,
and Dr. Ebersole

• <u>Sibert</u> (to ARRB, 1997):
"Well, I don't have a recollection of it being that intact...I don't recall anything like this at all during the autopsy...it looks like it could have been reconstructed or something."

• <u>O'Neill</u> (to ARRB, 1997):
"This looks like it's been doctored in some way...Like the stuff has been pushed back in, and it looks like more towards the end than the beginning [of the autopsy]...quite frankly, I thought there was a larger opening...in the back of the head."

• <u>Ebersole</u> (to HSCA, 1978):
As he recalled, JFK had "<u>more of a gaping occipital wound than this</u>," and that the autopsy photos depict a head wound "<u>more superior and lateral</u>" than what he remembered on the body. Ebersole testified: "<u>The back of the head was missing</u>...later in the evening, a large fragment of <u>occipital bone</u> was received from Dallas."

Autopsy Photos
42, 43 (Color)
Figure 65

The HSCA Tells a "Big Lie" About the Autopsy Photos; The "Big Lie" is Exposed by Early Release of Its Own Records by the JFK Records Act

• **The HSCA wrote in Volume VII:**
   "In disagreement with the observations of the Parkland doctors are the 26 people present at the autopsy. **All of those interviewed** who attended the autopsy corroborated the general location of the wounds as depicted in the photographs; **none had differing accounts.**" [emphasis added]

• The HSCA sealed Dr. Ebersole's deposition and most of its medical witness interview reports for 50 years, until 2029.

• However, the 1992 JFK Records Act mandated the immediate release of all assassination records unless certain stringent criteria could be met (sources and methods, etc.).

• Accordingly, the HSCA's sequestered medical files were released in 1993.

• THE RESULT: Twelve autopsy witnesses interviewed by the HSCA staff **CONTRADICTED** the "Big Lie" in Volume VII of its report <u>by recalling serious damage to the rear of President Kennedy's head</u>.

₄₅

Boswell contradicts his early depiction of head-wound claiming that only the top of JFK's head had missing bone as well Humes' similar claims.

The ARRB Asked Dr. Boswell to Render A Three-Dimensional
Interpretation of His Autopsy Sketch <u>On a Human Skull
Model</u> at His 1996 Deposition:
(Shown Here in 4 Drawings: Slide 1 of 2)

Note the Missing Bone in the Right Rear of the Skull	Much of the Right Side of the Skull Was Missing Also
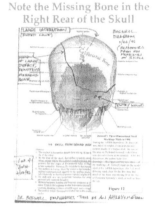	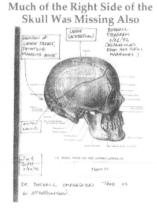

The Cerebellum Damage and Splatter (Near Occipital Area) Prove a Front Shot

Recall that the spatter analysis showcased numerous witnesses of cerebellum or brain matter being propelled backwards. This dovetails with testimony from many of those who saw the brain wounds including Audrey Bell, Frank O'Neill, Tom Robinson, Dr. Robert McClelland, Dr. Charles Crenshaw, Dr. Charles Carrico, Dr. Charles Baxter, Dr. Marion Jenkins, Dr. Kemp Clark, Doris Nelson, Dr. William Midgett... Photographers Knudsen and Stringer and photo developer Saundra Spencer testified that the photos they were shown were not representative of the damage they had seen with respect to the real autopsy photos. This proved that the intact brain photographs in the archives are not JFK's.

CONCLUSION

Witness accounts strongly indicate that at least one shot came from the front. The HSCA was impressed by Sam Holland, Powers, O'Donnell and others whom they found to be very credible. Many investigation insiders stated that they believed that there was at least one front shot:

Robert Blakey, FBI agents Sibert and O'Neill, Dallas Police Chief Jesse Curry, Doug Horne of the ARRB and many others.

The Zapruder Film shows JFK's head pushed backwards and to the left. This film was suppressed and misrepresented for many years because it contradicts the official narrative. Attempts to explain this revealing movement such as the jet effect and a neuromuscular reaction are not credible.

Numerous witnesses who saw or received hard-flying debris moving backward and to the left prove that at least some of the splatter's direction could only be explained by a frontal origin of at least one gun shot.

The Harper Fragment, last seen by Dr. Burkley, came from JFK's occipital bone and later went missing.

There can be seen a trail of particles in one of the X-rays that are best explained by a shot entering JFK's forehead and exiting from the back of his skull. The three doctors who saw JFK's throat wound up close described it as an entry wound.

Testimony from over 50 witnesses—many from both Dallas and Bethesda—who saw Kennedy's wounds, sketches drawn by many of these, damage to the cerebellum, contradictory statements made by the autopsy pathologist, all strongly indicate that there was massive damage to the back of Kennedy's skull. This, plus the extensive damage that so many witnesses saw to Kennedy's brain reveal just too much damage for one bullet from behind. The HSCA misled the public in its report by claiming that Bethesda witnesses refuted the back of the head damage seen by over twenty people in Dallas, including many medical personnel. Which matches the declassified record at Bethesda—as assembled by Gary Aguilar among others.

The only conclusion one can draw from all of this is that there was at least one shot that came from the front, which Oswald could not have fired.

CHAPTER 10

SIXTY YEARS OF OBSTRUCTION OF JUSTICE

BY PAUL BLEAU AND ANDREW ILER

STATEMENT

THE OBFUSCATION AND outright sabotage of investigations into the JFK assassination combined with propaganda efforts to suppress evidence, spread disinformation and counter any criticism has been omnipresent from the time immediately after the murder to today's unlawful delays in the declassification of assassination records as mandated by the John F. Kennedy Assassination Records Collection Act of 1992. The official history clearly indicates that powerful interests, including intelligence agencies, are hiding the truth behind what happened on November 22, 1963.

Definition of Obstruction of Justice[1]

18 U.S.C. § 1503 defines "obstruction of justice" as an act that "corruptly or by threats or force, or by any threatening letter or communication, influences, obstructs, or impedes, or endeavors to influence, obstruct, or impede, the due administration of justice."

Someone obstructs justice when that person has a specific intent to obstruct or interfere with a judicial proceeding. For a person to be convicted of obstructing justice, that person must not only have the specific intent to obstruct the proceeding, but that person must know (1) that a proceeding was actually pending at the time; and (2) there must be a

---

[1] https://www.law.cornell.edu//uscode/text/18/1503

connection between the endeavor to obstruct justice and the proceeding, and the person must have knowledge of this connection.

§ 1503 applies only to federal judicial proceedings. Under 18 U.S.C. § 1505, however, a defendant can be convicted of obstruction of justice by obstructing a pending proceeding before Congress or a federal administrative agency. A pending proceeding could include an informal investigation by an executive agency.

INTRODUCTION

The overall picture of what the official investigations into JFK's assassination reveal, for those who are attentive enough to read and analyze what the official historical record actually states, is that a conspiracy to both kill President Kennedy and cover up the true nature of the assassination, its purposes and perpetrators, is now beyond any reasonable doubt.

These conclusions can be reached not because of the efforts of the intelligence and law enforcement organizations involved in the investigations, but because much of the truth has been revealed, painstakingly, in spite of them. This is not only the supposition of independent researchers, but also, as we will see, a matter of official record.

We will also see how definite rigging and communications were driven by guiding hands.

EXECUTIVE SUMMARY

The Warren Commission from the get-go was set up in a way to stifle rumors about conspiracies and parallel investigations into the assassination. Lyndon Johnson, by including a person of interest in Allen Dulles who despised the Kennedys and was well connected, became a driving force on the obfuscation that followed. Gerald Ford and John J. McCloy were two other commissioners who could be counted upon to follow a game plan for painting Oswald as a lone nut. LBJ intimidated chairman

329

Earl Warren into doing his patriotic duty in avoiding a nuclear war by agreeing with the concoction the trio later peddled.

Considering that we are talking about perhaps the most impactful murder of the twentieth century, the investigation of the crime scene (including the limousine), the autopsy, the interrogation of witnesses and tampering with their statements, the lack of respect of the chain of custody guidelines, the manufacturing of false evidence, the intimidation of witnesses, the lack of similar case analysis provides clear and convincing evidence of not only incompetence but also subterfuge.

In 1967, when the Garrison case against Clay Shaw (a.k.a. Bertrand) became threatening to the official narrative, the CIA created a team to take the District Attorney for Orleans Parish, Jim Garrison down. As proven by writers like William Davy and Joan Mellen, the use of infiltration, espionage, slander by some of their media assets and support of Garrison adversaries has been demonstrated with conclusively clear and convincing evidence.[2]

Gerald Ford in the early 1970s created the biased Rockefeller Commission which was steered by the Warren Commission's own lawyer with clear biases, David Belin.

When the HSCA in the mid-seventies was making headway, particularly with respect to Oswald's alleged trip to Mexico City and his connections to anti Castro Cubans, it was sabotaged by the removals of attorneys Richard Sprague and Robert Tanenbaum and the insertion of George Joannides as the CIA liaison, about whom the HSCA leaders were told had no links with what happened in 1963. This was a lie, as he supervised the DRE right out of New Orleans. Of course, he put the brakes on all CIA cooperation with the House committee.

When the ARRB got under way in the mid 1990s, the ONI and the Secret Service went into file destruction mode and the other intelligence agencies were most uncooperative when it came to complying with the Act.

---

[2] "The Obstruction of Garrison", in *The Assassinations* edited by James DiEugenio and Lisa Pease, pp. 17–50

Today, 60 years after the assassination, after all files were supposed to be released in 2017, two successive presidents, Donald Trump and Joe Biden, have broken the law by stalling, if not halting, the declassification.

Intelligence even came up with their talking points to counter those who had found strong evidence of conspiracy and used their vast contacts that emanated out of Operation Mockingbird to control the press.

All the time the mainstream media and history book authors have been complicit in toeing the line: It was they who promoted the Warren Commission fairy tale, kept the Zapruder film hidden for over a decade, who claimed that Kennedy's head moved violently forward after being struck in the head, planted false stories about Garrison, ignored the conclusions of the HSCA that there was a likely conspiracy and so on.

These sixty years of secrets, media manipulation, and gaslighting can now be seen for what they really signify: That there has been and still is a massive cover-up of a conspiracy and ultimately undeniable obstruction of justice in respect to the investigations into the murder of President John F. Kennedy.

THE ASSASSINATION AND THE WARREN COMMISSION

November 22 to November 24, the Keystone Cops

Despite Oswald's checkered past—the FBI had files and information on Oswald's treasonous behavior in Russia, links to the SWP, FPCC, a controversial trip to Mexico City and threats he made to the FBI—he was not on the FBI Security Index on November 22, 1963. He was given a free pass to be on the Dallas motorcade route. Hoover wrote in a memo to FBI official William Sullivan that the Bureau personnel who failed to include Oswald on the Security Index, "could not have been more stupid … and now that the Bureau has been debunked publicly, I intend to take additional administrative action."[3]

---

[3] Final Report, Church Committee, Book 5, p. 52 https://www.intelligence.senate.gov/sites/default/files/94755_V.pdf

Thus, even though both the Dallas and New Orleans FBI field offices (and the CIA) were aware that Oswald had allegedly been in contact with the Soviet Embassy in Mexico City, there is no evidence that either of these field offices intensified their "efforts" to locate and interview Oswald.

Most surprising, however, is that the "Soviet experts" at FBI Headquarters did not strengthen their efforts in the Oswald case after being informed that Oswald had met with Vice Consul Valeri Kostikov at the Soviet Embassy in Mexico City. Not only were these specialists familiar with Soviet activities in general, but they knew that Kostikov was a member of the KGB. Further, the Bureau's Soviet experts had reason to believe he was an agent within the KGB's department which carries out assassinations and sabotage.

Ironically, the teletype which informed the Bureau of Oswald's Mexico City activities was sitting on a pile of documents on a Headquarters supervisor's desk awaiting initial action on November 22, 1963. That portion of the Gale memorandum which discusses Oswald's Mexico City trip reads as follows: The SOG [Seat of Government] supervisor failed to take any action on the teletypes, stating it did not appear to him any action was warranted. Inspector (i.e., Gale) feels … the field should have been instructed to intensify the investigation, and Oswald placed on Security Index 4.[4]

The Warren Commission—Rigged from the Start:

LBJ Manipulated Warren

Newly ascended President Lyndon Johnson convinced Earl Warren, Chief Justice at the time, to head the commission and advanced to him that it was important that the American public be satisfied that Oswald was a lone assassin. Any links of Oswald to Cuba-friendly conspirators

---

[4] Book 5 Church Committee report, p. 92

could lead to a nuclear holocaust and should be dismissed. Warren reluctantly took on the mandate.[5]

Stacking the Deck of the WC

The malleable Warren was joined by McLoy and Dulles, two Kennedy haters and Gerald Ford who became the FBI's inside man to know what was going on with the Committee. The Dulles/Ford/McCloy trio attended the most meetings and asked, by far, the most questions.[6]

Cooperative Liaisons

It is known that LBJ and Hoover enjoyed a very friendly, cooperative relationship. As recorded during a November 29 phone conversation, they quickly agreed on getting Dulles, McLoy and Ford on a blue-ribbon commission that would be focused on approving an FBI report and would also serve to stifle any other investigation. During this discussion, Hoover clearly contradicts the Single Bullet theory.[7]

John Whitten was assigned by Richard Helms to be the CIA liaison to the Warren Commission. Though he initially posited that Oswald acted alone, he learned of hidden evidence by the CIA and argued for more examination.

Whitten testified to the HSCA that his team of thirty agents was provided with no details about "Oswald's political activity in the United States, especially the 'pro-Castro activity' and autobiographical sketches … found among his effects." … that if he had known about Oswald's activities in New Orleans and contacts with the DRE Cubans, he would have focused his investigation on the "possible involvement of the CIA Miami station."

---

[5] https://www.history-matters.com/archive/jfk/lbjlib/phone_calls/Nov_1963/audio/LBJ-Russell_11-29-63_2nd.htm
[6] Walt Brown, The Warren Omission, pp. 83–87
[7] LBJ and J. Edgar Hoover, 11/29/63. 1:40P. —YouTube

Whitten also knew nothing about William Harvey (a madman according to him) and the CIA's executive action programs.[8]

Richard Helms replaced Whitten with Dulles loyalist James Angleton, who was now responsible for investigative matters in the assassination. Ray Rocca served as liaison for the FBI and Paul Paterni for the Secret Service. All three of these served on the OSS at the same time in Milan during World War II. Combined with Hoover, Rankin, Dulles, Ford, LBJ and McCloy ... control by the like-minded was ensured.[9]

Dulles Tries to Silence Truman

Suspicions of a conspiracy were also omnipresent in the U.S. after the murder. In an article written for the Washington Post, and published exactly one month after the assassination, former president Harry Truman, who had established the CIA in 1947, opined that the CIA was basically out of control: "For some time I have been disturbed by the way the CIA has been diverted from its original assignment, ... This quiet intelligence arm of the President has been so removed from its intended role that it is being interpreted as a symbol of sinister and mysterious foreign intrigue—and subject for cold war enemy propaganda." He said the CIA's "operational duties" "should be terminated." Allen Dulles, then sitting on the Warren Commission, tried unsuccessfully to get Truman to retract the story. Some have speculated that the timing of the writing of the article is linked to the assassination.[10]

Nicholas Katzenbach and Hoover's Slips Were Showing

On November 25, 1963, the day after Oswald was eliminated, the Deputy Attorney General delivered a memo dictated by J. Edgar Hoover for Mr. Bill Moyers, stating among other things: "The public must be satisfied that Oswald was the assassin, that he did not have any confederates...

---

[8] Whitten Deposition to HSCA, ARRB
[9] Who's who in the Secret Service, pp. 28–29
[10] http://www.maebrussell.com/Prouty/Harry%20Truman's%20CIA%20article.html

Speculation about Oswald's motivation ought to be cut off..."[11] The fix was in. The Commission was to rely almost entirely on FBI investigative resources, led by Hoover, head of the FBI and a very close friend of President Johnson's, ergo restricting WC autonomy and independence. Within a matter of weeks, the FBI tabled a report claiming that Oswald was a lone nut.

The Church and HSCA Committees revealed just how biased the Warren Commission was:

- On December 9, 1963, Katzenbach wrote each member of the WC recommending that the Commission issue a press release stating that there was no international conspiracy and that Oswald was a loner.

- Almost directly after the assassination, Hoover, the Justice Department and the White House exerted pressure on senior Bureau officials to complete their investigation and issue a factual report supporting the conclusion that Oswald was the lone assassin.[12]

- The pressure to issue a report that would establish Oswald as the lone assassin is reflected in internal Bureau memoranda. On November 24, 1963, Assistant FBI Director Alan Belmont informed Associate FBI Director Clyde Tolson that he was sending two headquarters supervisors to Dallas to review the written interview and investigative findings of our agents on the Oswald matter, so that we can prepare a memorandum to the Attorney General ... setting out the evidence showing that Oswald is responsible for the shooting that killed the President.[13]

- On December 3, 1963, the UPI wire carried a story reported in

---

[11] 105–82555 File (Headquarters Lee Harvey Oswald)

[12] Book 5 Church Committee report, p. 32

[13] Ibid., p 33

various newspapers under the following lead: an exhaustive FBI report now nearly ready for the White House will indicate that Lee Harvey Oswald was the lone and unaided assassin of President Kennedy, government sources said today. When he was informed of these news articles, Director Hoover wrote, "I thought no one knew this outside the FBI." According to William Sullivan, Hoover himself ordered the report "leaked" to the press in an attempt to "blunt the drive for an independent investigation of the assassination."[14]

- Hoover may have succeeded in intimidating the Commission by employing one of his favorite dirty tricks. "Derogatory information pertaining to both Commission members and staff was brought to Mr. Hoover's attention," the Church Committee discovered.[15]

- During an appearance before the HSCA in 1977, no less than Warren Commission chief counsel J. Lee Rankin sheepishly conceded, "Who could protest against what Mr. Hoover did back in those days?"[16]

- On December 9, the FBI's 5-volume report on the assassination was completed. Deputy Attorney General Katzenbach writes the Warren Commission and recommends that the Commission immediately state that the FBI report clearly shows Oswald was a loner.[17]

- In a telephone conversation with White House Aide Walter Jenkins immediately following Oswald's murder, Director Hoover stated: "The thing I am most concerned about, and so is Mr. Katzenbach, is having something issued so we can convince the

---

[14] Ibid., p 34
[15] *Final Report of the Select Committee to Study Governmental Operations, Book V,* p. 47
[16] HSCA, vol. 11, p. 49
[17] Book 5 Church Committee report, p. 104

public that Oswald is the real assassin. The pressure to issue a report that would establish Oswald as the lone assassin is reflected in internal Bureau memoranda."[18]

- William Sullivan, former Assistant Director in charge of the Domestic Intelligence Division, stated that "on November 29, 1963, the FBI had no data to support the conclusion that there was no foreign conspiracy."[19]

- The FBI was very conflicted according to the Church Committee: Bureau officials were continually concerned with the possibility that the FBI might be regarded as "responsible for negligence that resulted in the assassination of President Kennedy because of pre-assassination investigative deficiencies in the Oswald case."[20]

- Former FBI Assistant Director Alex Rosen told the Church Committee that the FBI was not actively investigating a conspiracy, but was "in the position of standing on the corner with our pockets open, waiting for someone to drop information into it…"[21]

Warren Lays Down the Law

In the first executive session on December 5, 1963, Warren enumerated the following policies:

- He did not want the Commission to employ its own investigators;

- He wanted to rely on evidence produced by the FBI and Secret Service;

---

[18] Ibid., p 33
[19] Staff interview of William C. Sullivan, 4/21/76
[20] Book 5 Church Committee report, p. 53
[21] Mary Ferrell Foundation: TESTIMONY OF ALEX ROSEN, 30 APR 1976

- No public hearings. No subpoena powers;

- No calling of witnesses by the Commission, since it "would retard rather than help our investigation."

The real objective of the Warren Commission was set forth in Melvin Eisenberg's memo.

MEMORANDUM   February 17, 1964
TO: Files
FROM: Melvin A. Eisenberg
SUBJECT: First Staff Conference (January 20, 1964)

On January 20, 1964, Chief Justice Warren met with the staff. After brief introductions, the Chief Justice discussed the circumstances under which he had accepted the chairmanship of the Commission.

When the position had first been offered to him he declined it, as the principle that Supreme Court Justices should not take this kind of role. His associate justices concurred in this decision. At this point, however, President Johnson called him. The President stated that rumors of the most exagerrated [sic] kind were circulating in this country and overseas. Some rumors went as far as attributing the assassination to a faction within the Government wishing to see the Presidency assumed by President Johnson. Others, if not quenched, could conceivably lead the country into a war which could cost 40 million lives. No one could refuse to do something which might help to present such a possibility. The President convinced him that his was an occasion on which actual conditions had to override general principles.

The Chief Justice then discussed the role of the Commission. He placed emphasis on the importance of quenching rumors, and precluding future speculation such as that which has surrounded the death of Lincoln. He emphasized that the Commission had to determine the truth, whatever that might be.

Warren told the young lawyers about Johnson's warnings about a nuclear holocaust, and how Johnson convinced him that this was an occasion on which actual conditions had to override general principles. *(Ed. Note: The Commission did eventually call witnesses, but one can see that the Commission was reluctant to investigate thoroughly on its own.)*

Dulles and McCloy Set the Mood

At the very first meeting of the Commission on December 5, 1963, John McCloy, truncating a commonly used expression, said: "This Commission is set up to lay the dust, dust not only in The United States but all over the world ... everybody is looking for it to come forward promptly, unfortunately, with an objective, comprehensive report which will lay all the dust..."[22]

Then on December 16, 1963, Allen Dulles handed out paperback copies of a book about previous assassinations (backing lone nut scenarios). Said Dulles: "It's a book written about ten years ago giving the background of seven attempts on the lives of the President... It's a fascinating book, but you'll find a pattern running through here that I think we'll find in the present case. I hate to give you a paperback, but that's all there is." Said Chairman Warren: "Paperback is good enough. Thank you very much."

Then Dulles again brought up the subject, stating that except for the Truman assassination attempt, " ... these other cases are all habitual, going back to the attack on Jackson in 1835."

During these two sessions McCloy and Dulles, corralled Warren into accepting J. Lee Rankin as Chief Legal Counsel, over his choice, Warren Olney. This enabled two Kennedy opponents to control the Commission.[23] After a rump meeting including Dulles, McCloy and Ford, McCloy came up with a list and their first choice was J. Lee Rankin. One of the initial things Rankin did was to deprive the accused, but deceased, Lee Oswald of any representation before the Commission. This was in January of 1964.[24]

Rankin's appointment pleased the FBI: In a memo recounting the December meeting, where an inspector was briefed on his new assignment, the Director wrote: "I told him that I wanted him to establish the

---

[22] Minutes of WC executive session Dec. 5, 1963

[23] https://www.maryferrell.org/php/showlist.php?docset=1007 (in Executive sessions transcripts Jan 5–6) and (Gerald McKnight, Breach of Trust, pp. 41–43)

[24] Commission Exhibit 2033

closest and most amiable working relationship with Mr. Rankin. I told him that I had personally known Mr. Rankin quite well since he had served as Solicitor General under Attorneys General Brownell and Rogers."[25]

Ford: The FBI's Spy

According to William Sullivan, Hoover was delighted when Gerald Ford was named to the Warren Commission. The director wrote in one of his internal memos that the bureau could expect Ford to "look after FBI interests," and he did, keeping us fully advised of what was going on behind closed doors. He was our man, our informant, on the Warren Commission.[26]

The CIA's Passive Investigation

The Church Committee said this about the CIA: Moreover, SAS (Special Affairs Staff) capabilities to obtain information from Cuba, and from Cuban exiles, were not fully utilized... Indeed, all the evidence suggests that the CIA investigation into any Cuban connection, whether pro-Castro or anti-Castro, was passive in nature... Apparently, neither the Warren Commission as a body nor its staff was given details of CIA Cuban operations. Although CIA manpower in Florida far surpassed the FBI, the Warren Commission and its staff relied completely on the FBI for reports about the Cuban exile community in Florida. In any event, the Warren Commission did not pursue with the CIA the questions of Oswald's pro-Castro and anti-Castro contacts... During its investigation, the Select Committee noted several instances where detailed knowledge of the intelligence agencies' operations with respect to Cuban matters would have been of assistance to the Warren Commission in its investigation.[27]

---

[25] Book 5 Church Committee report, p. 33
[26] William C. Sullivan-assistant director of the FBI's Intelligence Division—in his book The Bureau: My Thirty Years in Hoover's FBI [1979]
[27] Book 5 Church Committee report, pp. 58–60

Concerning the AM/LASH project to kill Castro in 1963: "In hindsight, the AM/LASH operation seems very relevant to the investigation of President Kennedy's assassination. It is difficult to understand why those aware of the operation did not think it relevant and did not inform those investigating President Kennedy's assassination of possible connections between that operation and the assassination ... the conduct of the AM/LASH operation during the fall of 1963, should have raised major concerns within the CIA about its possible connection with the Kennedy assassination."[28]

Allen Dulles Keeps His Colleagues in the Dark

CIA-Mafia plots to kill Castro as well as Operation Mongoose were kept hidden by Allen Dulles and the CIA. So were Dulles' links with Oswald contacts George de Mohrenschildt, Ruth and Michael Paine, as well as Mexico City operations, false defector programs, FPCC infiltration operations, Cuban exile—CIA relations etc.[29]

Key Witnesses not Questioned

Key witnesses were not called: JFK's physician Admiral Burkley, who signed the face sheet of the death notice and who was at both Parkland and Bethesda; FBI agents Sibert and O'Neil who wrote an FBI report about the autopsy and who would have wrecked the Single Bullet theory; David Atlee Phillips, who committed perjury during his HSCA testimony with regard to Oswald's alleged Mexico City sojourn; Elsie Dorman, Sandy Styles and Dorothy Garner who would have corroborated Victoria Adams movements after the assassination thus providing Oswald with an alibi; John Stringer and Robert Knudsen (autopsy photographers) and Saundra Spencer (photo developer for the autopsy photos) who would have confirmed photo tampering and created suspicion around the photos in the archives; Dr. Joseph Dolce who worked for the Warren Com-

---

[28] Ibid., p 71-74
[29] Ibid., p 68

mission and who conducted experiments, by test-firing Mannlicher-Carcano ammunition on cadavers wrists demonstrating the lack of damage to CE399 (the Magic Bullet) was impossible; White House Physician James Young who witnessed a projectile found in the back of the presidential limousine.

According to Doug Horne, Arlen Specter lied and said they (FBI agents Sibert and O'Neill) did not take any notes at the autopsy. Presumably because he did not like what they had to say.[30]

The depositions of the three autopsists were taken from all three present at the same time, as was the case in other investigations, which ensured that they would not contradict one another. This was not the case with the ARRB when at least one major contradiction between Humes and Boswell took place.[31]

According to the HSCA, 692 witnesses "were present in the Plaza during the assassination." Most of them were never called to testify by either the Warren Commission or the HSCA.[32]

Ed Johnson a reporter for the Fort Worth Star-Telegram who was riding in the motorcade, wrote for his paper the next day, "Some of us saw little puffs of white smoke that seemed to hit the grassy area in the esplanade that divides Dallas's main downtown streets." He was never interviewed by any government agency.[33]

Leading Questions

Questions were often asked in a way for the WC interrogators to get the answer they wanted rather than seeking the truth. The following is but one example:

SPECTER: And have you noted in the autopsy report the reference to the presence of a wound on the upper right posterior thorax just

---

[30] JFK Revisited, p. 107
[31] Ibid.
[32] 8HSCA139
[33] https://www.history-matters.com/analysis/witness/artScience.htm

above the upper border of the scapula, being 7 by 4 mm. in oval dimension and being located 14 cm. from the tip of the right acromion process and 14 cm. below the tip of the right mastoid process?

Dr. PERRY. Yes; I saw that.

Mr. SPECTER. Assuming that was a point of entry of a missile, which parenthetically was the opinion of the three autopsy surgeons, and assuming still further that the missile which struck the President at that spot was a 6.5-mm. Jacketed bullet shot from a rifle at a distance of 166 to 250 feet, having a muzzle velocity of approximately 2,606 feet per second, and that upon entering the President's body, the bullet traveled between two strap muscles, through a fascia channel, without violating the pleural cavity, striking the trachea, causing the damage which you testified about being on the interior of the President's throat, and exited from the President's throat in the wound which you have described in the midline of his neck, would your findings and observations as to the nature of the wound on the throat be consistent with the set of facts I just presented to you?

Dr. PERRY. It would be entirely compatible.

Note: Perry, during a press conference after JFK passed, stated three times that the wound in the throat of JFK appeared to be an entrance wound.

Questions Not Asked

About Larry Crafard: "Crafard had worked at Jack Ruby's Carousel Club before he was seized by FBI men as he was hightailing it out of town the day after the assassination, having told someone, "They are not going to pin this on me!" In the interview, Warren asks Crafard what he did before he was a bartender. "I was a master sniper in the Marine Corps," Crafard answered. The next question that Warren immediately asked was: "What kind of entertainment did they have at the club?"[34]

Stenographer Hanky-Panky[35]

There is strong evidence that Rankin set up a stenography charade when Commissioner Russell expressed dissenting views during a WC meeting:

> "More sinister was Rankin's treatment of the record of September 18 meeting. Although a stenographer appeared to be present, the official written record of the meeting did not take the form of a verbatim transcript, as was the case with the other sessions, but was merely a list of trivial procedural items.[36] No hint was given of Russell's and Cooper's arguments with Rankin and Earl Warren, or of the discussions that, according to Russell's conversation with Johnson, took place about the wording of the *Report*'s conclusions. Russell had prepared two written statements, neither of which found their way into the record.
>
> This was not the only example of manipulation of the records of the Warren Commission. After the 22 January 1964 meeting that dealt with the rumors that Oswald was associated with the FBI or the CIA,[37] the stenographer's notes were destroyed. It is possible that the stenographer at the September 18 meeting was not even genuine; Ward and Paul, the firm that had supplied stenographers for all the Warren Commission's witness hearings and executive sessions, did not submit an invoice for the final session."

---

[34] Gaeton Fonzi, speech on receiving the Mary Ferrell-JFK Lancer Pioneer Award [21st November 21, 1998], https://spartacus-educational.com/JFKcrafard.htm

[35] http://22november1963.org.uk/richard-russell-warren-report#warren-commission-meeting

[36] Ibid.

[37] http://22november1963.org.uk/memo-was-oswald-an-fbi-agent

The Botched Autopsy

The surgeon in charge of JFK's autopsy was an anatomic pathologist, Navy Commander James H. Humes, MD. So was his second in charge, Commander J. Thornton Boswell, MD. Thirty minutes after the autopsy had begun, a properly credentialed, Army forensics pathologist, Colonel Pierre Finck, MD, arrived from the Armed Forces Institute of Pathology to lend a hand. During the previous two years prior to examining JFK, Finck had performed no autopsies. His job at the AFIP was to do arm-chair reviews of autopsies others had done. These are some of the relevant points Finck revealed in his under oath questioning at the trial of Clay Shaw.

Pierre Finck stated that senior non-medical military officers had taken an active part in the proceedings, and he implies that they were in charge of the autopsy.

He admitted, after trying hard to avoid the question, that the pathologists were forbidden to dissect the president's back and throat wounds and the connecting tissue.[38]

Those in charge of the autopsy would surely have been aware that President Kennedy's wounds may have been caused by more than one gunman, and that dissecting the wounds was likely to resolve the question one way or the other. Their refusal to allow the dissection can only reasonably be interpreted as a fear of discovering definitive evidence of conspiracy.

The room in which they worked was crowded with a variety of non-medical onlookers, several of whom were giving orders to the pathologists.

The famed New York City coroner Milton Helpern, MD, has laid out the problem particularly well: "Colonel Finck's position throughout the entire proceeding was extremely uncomfortable. If it had not been for him, the autopsy would not have been handled as well as it was; but he was in the role of the poor bastard Army child foisted into the Navy family

---

[38] (State of Louisiana vs. Clay L. Shaw, Criminal District Court, Parish of Orleans, State of Louisiana, 198–059 1426 [30] section C, transcript, pp.51f) and (Ibid., pp. 114–8)

reunion. He was the only one of the three doctors with any experience with bullet wounds; but you have to remember that his experience was limited primarily to 'reviewing' files, pictures, and records of finished cases. There's a world of difference between standing at the autopsy table and trying to decide whether a hole in the body is a wound of entrance or a wound of exit, and in reviewing another man's work at some later date in the relaxed, academic atmosphere of a private office ...."[39]

The HSCA concluded the following about the medical evidence and autopsy:

1. The President's body was taken out of the hands of those legally responsible for the investigation of the death and autopsy - Texas authorities.

2. Those performing the autopsy had insufficient training and experience to evaluate a death from gunshot wounds.

3. Physicians who treated the President were not consulted before commencing the autopsy.

4. Circumstances at the time of the autopsy were not controlled by the pathologists.

5. Proper photographs were not taken.

6. The President's clothing was not examined.

7. The autopsy was incomplete because: a) External examination failed to accurately locate wounds. b) Bullet tracks were not dissected to determine their course through the body. c) The axis of the bullet tracks were not measured relative to the body axis. d) The brain was not properly examined and sectioned. e) The head

---

[39] Quote cited in: Josiah Thompson. Six Seconds in Dallas. New York: Bernard Geis Associates for Random House, 1967, p. 198

wound location was incorrect. f) Other wounds of the president's body were not localized with reference to fixed body landmarks so as to permit reconstruction of trajectories.[40]

Doug Horne of the ARRB said this of the autopsy of JFK "The evidentiary mess of the twentieth century. It's the worst thing imaginable."[41]

As of today, the real story is that the precise cause of death of President Kennedy has not ever been established and that the "best evidence" to determine with certainty the cause of death, lies beneath the eternal flame in Arlington Cemetery, Virginia. If forensic science can determine the identity and cause of death of KingRichard III, who died at the battle of Bosworth on August 22, 1485, was thrown naked into an unmarked hole in the ground behind the friary of a cathedral, and not discovered until 2013, some five hundred and twenty-seven years later, we should have no trouble putting to rest for once and for all, President Kennedy's cause of death.

X-rays and Photographs Kept Hidden and a 10 CM Correction

"The Commission accepted at face value the pathologists' claim that JFK had a right-sided, 'parieto-temporo-occipital' skull wound. In layman's terms, this is a wound that involves the right rear side of the head. The controversies began in 1968, with the Clark Panel's determination that the fatal bullet had struck JFK's skull 10-cm higher than reported in the original autopsy report. Given that, from top to bottom, the back of the skull measures only 12 cm., it is difficult to dismiss a 10 cm discrepancy as unremarkable, negligible. The controversy might have surfaced in 1964 if the Commission had examined JFK's autopsy photographs and X-rays, an inexcusable omission noted early on by Sylvia Meagher and others."[42]

---

[40] Conspiracy of Silence, p. 131 and https://history-matters.com/archive/jfk/hsca/reportvols/vol7/html/HSCA_Vol7_0004a.htm

[41] JFK Revisited, p. 302

[42] https://www.history-matters.com/essays/jfkmed/How5Investigations/How5InvestigationsGotItWrong_1b.htm

Autopsy Photos, X-rays and other Autopsy Evidence
Altered or Disappeared

From: HOW FIVE INVESTIGATIONS INTO JFK'S MEDICAL/AUTOPSY EVIDENCE GOT IT WRONG *by* Gary L. Aguilar, MD and Kathy Cunningham May 2003:[43]

"From both public and once-secret files, we have learned that each of JFK's three pathologists and both autopsy photographers later repeatedly testified under oath that photographs they took on the night of the autopsy were missing from the official inventory they had signed off as complete in 1966.

For example, in a once-secret memo, HSCA counsel, D. Andy Purdy, JD, reported that during an interview, chief autopsy photographer," (John) STRINGER (sic) said it was his recollection that all the photographs he had taken were *not* present in 1966 (when Stringer saw the photographs for the first time). Among the missing pictures are those taken of the interior of JFK's chest. None survive in the current inventory. Yet every autopsy participant who was asked recalled that photographs were taken of the interior of JFK's body, as indeed they should have been to document the passage of the non-fatal bullet through JFK's chest.

John Stringer told the HSCA he recalled taking, "at least two exposures of the body cavity." (A. Purdy)

James Humes, MD was reported in an HSCA memo to have, " ... specifically recalled photographs ... were taken of the President's chest ... (these photographs) do not exist." As already discussed, Humes had told the Warren Commission in 1964 that he had taken pictures of the interior of Kennedy's chest.

J. Thornton Boswell, MD, the second in command, backed Stringer and Humes. The HSCA recorded that, " ... he (Boswell) thought they photographed ' ... the exposed thoracic cavity and

---

[43] https://www.history-matters.com/essays/jfkmed/How5Investigations/How5InvestigationsGotItWrong_2.htm

lung ... ' but (he) doesn't remember ever seeing those photographs."

Robert Karnei, MD, a Navy pathologist who assisted but was not a member of the official autopsy team, told the HSCA, "He (Karnei) recalls them putting the probe in and taking pictures (the body was on the side at the time)."[44]

Doug Horne reviewed the military records, including the military autopsy for the ARRB. What he found was revealed during interviews as well as the book he wrote, *Inside the ARRB*, published in 2009. Its contents are fascinating and would surprise students of American history who base their beliefs on many of the history textbooks.

Numerous persons the ARRB deposed or interviewed—FBI agents Jim Sibert and Frank O'Neill, photo technician Sandy Spencer—essentially disowned the autopsy photographs showing the back of JFK's head intact. O'Neill said the photos of the back of the head looked "doctored" (by which he meant that he thought the wound had been repaired—put back together—not that the photo looked altered), and Sibert said the back of the head looked "reconstructed." Tom Robinson of Gawler's funeral home said there was a large hole in the back of the head where it looks intact in the photos. Pathologist J. Thornton Boswell said that there was a lot of bone missing in the right rear of the head behind where the scalp looks intact, but did not explain how the scalp could be intact if the bone in the right rear of the skull was missing![45]

But perhaps Horne's most stunning conclusion was that the photographs of "the President's brain" in the autopsy collection are really photographs of someone else's brain ... a major deception in this case. These images, which appear to show damage consistent with a shot from above and behind, were disowned under oath to the ARRB by John

[44] HOW FIVE INVESTIGATIONS INTO JFK'S MEDICAL/AUTOPSY EVIDENCE GOT IT WRONG
Gary L. Aguilar, MD and Kathy Cunningham May 2003

[45] The ARRB deposition transcripts of Frank O'Neill, James Sibert, and J. Thornton Boswell, as well as the unsworn report of the ARRB interview with Tom Robinson.

Stringer, the photographer who took the official brain photos at JFK's supplementary autopsy. He disowned the images because of the angles at which they were shot, and because they were taken on the wrong film—film he did not use. Plus they were done in a photographic technique, a press pack, that he did not use. These photos have been used for years by supporters of the Warren Commission's conclusions to support their shooting scenario, and to discount those who claim there were shots from the front or right front.

Doug Horne also stated that there are also photographs taken that don't reflect what anyone saw. Most particularly the back of the head photographs. The photograph showing the back of the head intact is something that no witness saw at either Parkland or Bethesda. He stated that there were at least eighteen views missing ... (including some with probes in the body)[46]

Finally, regarding JFK's still-controversial skull wound, in formerly secret testimony taken 24 years ago, Dr. Finck described to the Select Committee how he had photographed the beveling in JFK's skull bone to prove that the low wound in occipital bone was an entrance wound. In the following exchange, Dr. Finck was being asked by the Select Committee's forensic consultants whether the official images were those Dr. Finck had claimed were missing.

Charles Petty, MD: "If I understand you correctly, Dr. Finck, you wanted particularly to have a photograph made of the external aspect of the skull from the back to show that there was no cratering to the outside of the skull."

Finck: "Absolutely."

Petty: "Did you ever see such a photograph?"

Finck: "I don't think so and I brought with me a memorandum referring to the examination of photographs in 1967 ... and as I can recall

---

[46] JFK Revisited, p. 303

I never saw pictures of the outer aspect of the wound of entry in the back of the head and inner aspect in the skull in order to show a crater although I was there asking for these photographs. I don't remember seeing those photographs."

Petty: "All right. Let me ask you one other question. In order to expose that area where the wound was present in the bone, did you have to, or did someone have to dissect the scalp off of the bone in order to show this?"

Finck: "Yes."

Petty: "Was this a difficult dissection and did it go very low into the head so as to expose the external aspect of the posterior cranial fascia (sic—meant 'fossa')?"

Finck: "I don't remember the difficulty involved in separating the scalp from the skull but this was done in order to have a clear view of the outside and inside to show the crater from the inside … the skull had to be separated from it in order to show in the back of the head the wound in the bone."

Add to this, Kennedy's lost brain, and skin tissue slides that were deep-sixed, and we can conclude either total incompetence or that someone had something to hide.

The WC Misleading Description of the Zapruder Film

Nowhere in the report will you find a description of JFK's violent back and to the left motion when struck by the headshot, as one can clearly see in the Zapruder film. Here is the actual description from the report:[47]

The Subsequent Bullet That Hit

After a bullet penetrated President Kennedy's neck, a subsequent shot entered the back of his head and exited through the upper right portion of his skull. The Zapruder, Nix and Muchmore films show the instant in the sequence when that bullet struck. (See Commission Exhibit No. 902, p. 108.) That impact was evident from the explosion of the President's brain tissues from the right side of his head. The immediately preceding frame from the Zapruder film shows the President slumped to his left, clutching at his throat, with his chin close to his chest and his head tilted forward at an angle.[325] Based upon information provided by the doctors who conducted the autopsy, an artist's drawing depicted the path of the bullet through the President's head, with his head being in the same approximate position.[326]

109

"The Warren Commission Report itself never addressed the backward motion of the president's head, thus sparing itself the burden of having to explain it. This omission was facilitated by the reversal of the two frames following the explosive frame 313 in the Warren Commission's published volumes, which considerably confused the issue by making it seem as if the head jerked forward. J. Edgar Hoover later blamed the switch on a *printing error*."[48]

Humes Burns His Notes and First Draft of the Autopsy Report

On August 2, 1998, the *Associated Press* reported an important new ARRB finding that raised questions about the original autopsy record: "Under oath (before the ARRB), Dr. Humes, finally acknowledged under persistent questioning—in testimony that differs from what he told the Warren Commission—that he had destroyed both his notes taken at the autopsy and the first draft of the autopsy report."[49] The Review Board had extracted Humes' sworn admission of something that had long been known: He had burned *both* a preliminary draft of the autopsy report, which he had told the Warren Commission about, and he had also

---

[48] https://www.kennedysandking.com/john-f-kennedy-articles/jfk-how-the-media-as-sassinated-the-real-story

[49] Mike Feinsalber, *"JFK Autopsy Files Are Incomplete." Associated Press, August 2, 1998, 11:48 a.m.*

destroyed original autopsy notes taken on the night of the autopsy, something Humes had kept from the Warren Commission, if not one of the Commission's lawyers.

Connally's Clothes Travels[50]

The chain of custody of Connally's clothes does not allow us to rely on the clothing as evidence.

1. Connally's suit jacket and shirt, but evidently not the trousers, were mysteriously hand-carried in bloody paper bags to Washington, D.C. by Congressman Henry Gonzalez, who stored them in his office closet for an estimated two weeks.

2. Two Secret Service agents then took the garments, but not to the FBI. Evidently on orders from the White House, the clothes were sent back to Texas and Mrs. Connally. The Governor's wife might have washed the shirt in a tub of cold water, but more likely sent the clothes to professional cleaning service.

3. Then, possibly, the shirt and coat and other garments, were sent to the Texas Archives in Austin, Texas, although this is not verified.

4. The Governor's clothes were then sent back to Washington and to the Warren Commission offices on April 1, 1964, where they were examined.

5. The Connally assassination-day clothes were then finally sent on eight days later to the FBI lab, also in Washington.

---

[50] *From: November 20, 2021 The Strange, Strange Story of Governor Connally's Shirt & Coat and Congressman Henry B. Gonzalez, Kennedysandking, Benjamin Cole*

Further confusing matters are the conflicting accounts of Mrs. Connally: Mrs. Connally related to *Life* magazine, she had the shirt and suit jacket in her possession for "seven weeks." Then she decided to dip the shirt into cold water several times, remove flesh and blood, and to "preserve it."

Investigators were not concerned about Connally's clothes, as she recalled, in her interview with *Life* magazine. "I told the Secret Service, and I guess the FBI, that I had the clothes, but nobody seemed interested." After that, she related, "Someone finally came to pick up his clothes."

By Mrs. Connally's 1966 account, she did *not* have the clothes or jacket laundered or dry-cleaned.

And so, for decades, there was something of a mystery of who had professionally cleaned and pressed Connally's shirt and jacket before their arrival at the Commission in Washington. Maybe there still is.

But four decades later, and further confusing matters, Mrs. Connally also provided a second version of what happened to Connally's assassination-day clothes. This was on the 40th anniversary of her husband's shooting, in her book, *From Love Field*, published in 2003:

> Much later (after November 22), I received his clothes in the mail, unpressed and uncleaned, in exactly the same condition as when they had been cut from him at Parkland. I couldn't bear to look at the blood, nor did I feel right about destroying them, so I told the cleaner to remove the stains as best he could but do nothing to alter the holes or other damage, which is exactly what he did.[51]

The spectrographic analysis of Connally's clothing was not performed during the WC investigation. This critical, standard step would have helped reveal facts around the composition and provenance of the bullet [or bullets] that struck Governor Connally.

---

[51] "From Love Field: our final hours with President John F. Kennedy," 2003, Nellie Connally

The Murder Scene Investigation Screw-ups

The limousine was hastily tampered with: Two days after the assassination, Agent Vaughan Ferguson went to the White House garage and cleaned the upholstery. One day later, Carl Renas, head of the Dearborn Division of the Ford Motor Company, drove the limousine from Washington to Cincinnati for repairs. The windshield and chrome molding, where a number of witnesses describe bullet damage, were replaced. (*See Doug Weldon 1999 windshield cover-up video.*)[52] Later on the 25th of November, the limousine was flown back to Andrews Air Base. One witness stated that Ferguson ordered the limousine cleaned in case he wanted to use it for the funeral.[53]

The Texas School Book Depository seems to have experienced some of its own artistic recreation activities: "The shells looked like they were placed in some sort of pattern on the floor. They did not look like they were ejected from the rifle. They were very close together... Much later people started questioning, you know, I've shot a rifle and I couldn't even find my shells... It became important because it looked like the scene was staged..."[54]

Hosty's Note

The Church Committee report sheds light on a note that was written by Lee Harvey Oswald to James Hosty and later destroyed by the FBI.

"Finally, it should be noted that facts publicly disclosed by the Bureau in October 1975, establish that some two weeks prior to the assassination, Lee Harvey Oswald visited the FBI's Dallas Field Office and left a note for Special Agent James P. Hosty, Jr., and that the note was subsequently destroyed... The Bureau's initial file

---

[52] https://www.youtube.com/watch?v=cxeqAXCOzKg
[53] The Assassination Paradoxes Essays and Review, David Mantik, p. 329
[54] Debra Conway JFK Revisited, Through the Looking Glass, p. 426

review failed to develop any information indicating that Oswald had ever visited the FBI field office in Dallas or that he had left a note.

FBI interviews with personnel assigned to the Dallas field office in 1963 established that: (1) Lee Harvey Oswald did visit the office some two or three weeks prior to the assassination; (2) Oswald asked to see S. A. James Hosty, and upon being informed that he was not in, left a note for Hosty; (3) the note was destroyed after the assassination.

The evidence developed by the Bureau contained sharp conflicts. The investigation failed to establish: (1) whether the note was threatening in nature; and (2) at whose instruction the note was destroyed...

According to the receptionists, the note read as follows: "Let this be a warning. I will blow up the FBI and the Dallas Police Department if you don't stop bothering my wife. Signed-Lee Harvey Oswald."

Sometime later in the day the receptionists personally gave the note to Hosty. Hosty recalled the note's wording as: "If you have anything you want to learn about me, come talk to me directly. If you don't cease bothering my wife, I will take appropriate action and report this to proper authorities."

Hosty's supervisor said he recalled that the note contained some kind of threat but could not remember specifics. Aside from the receptionist, Agent Hosty, and the supervisor, no one else interviewed by the FBI recalled having seen the note. Some other individuals indicated that from conversations they had had with the receptionist after the assassination, they understood that the note contained a threat...

William Sullivan, who was an Assistant Director of the Bureau at the time of the assassination, has stated that he discussed the Oswald case many times with Shanklin; and that Shanklin stated, "he had an internal problem involving one of his agents who had received a threatening message from Oswald because the Agent was investigating Oswald."[55]

This incident magnifies the suspiciously weak security during the motorcade in that the already communist-tainted Oswald was allowed to be in the TSBD after brazenly issuing threats to the FBI right in the hospices of the Dallas Bureau directed at the agent in charge of the Oswald dossier!

The HSCA on Ruby's WC Polygraph

Oswald's murderer, Jack Ruby, was polygraphed for the Warren Commission. It has been referred to by many to negate conspiracy in the removal of the most important witness in JFK's murder. The U.S. Government reached a conclusion through the HSCA about this all-important evidence: IT IS USELESS!

The following is from the *HSCA REPORT OF THE POLYGRAPH PANEL* on crucial factors affecting the examination:

"The panel noted the four factors mentioned ... as having a detrimental effect on the examination: The time elapsed since the shooting; Ruby's extensive prior interrogation; the many people present during the examination; and the great number of relevant questions asked. The panel believed these factors had a serious negative impact on the validity and reliability of the polygraph examination. Because Ruby had been extensively interrogated previously, [FBI technician Bell] Herndon should have been sure that the polygraph examination was very carefully conducted... Numerous instances in the transcript of the Ruby polygraph examination indicate that Herndon completely lost control over the examination. The problem most often stemmed from the ad hoc participation of the observers in the conduct of the polygraph examination. (Of

---

[55] Book 5 Church Committee report, pp. 93–98

course, the panel found the number of observers itself to be detrimental to the examination.)

In addition to the factors discussed above which impaired the Ruby polygraph examination, the panel concluded that 10 additional factors, of perhaps less importance, further reduced the validity and reliability of the examination. These are as follows:

1. It is generally agreed that the best time to examine is in the morning, because then the great majority of people are both physically and mentally "fresh." As the day progresses, a person normally tires. Since the polygraph mainly records physical change induced by mental stimulation, a tired person does not react to stimulation as well as a rested person does. Although Ruby most likely was a night-oriented person as a result of his occupation as a nightclub owner, by July 18, 1964, normal prison routine no doubt had changed his orientation. The panel therefore concluded that the examination should have started early in the day, perhaps around 8 a.m. As it was, the examination started at 2:23 p.m., with the first test beginning at 3:10 p.m.

2. When administering an extremely difficult examination, most experts advocate reexamination on a later date to check the reliability of the first examination, that is, will the same reactions be obtained on the reexamination? Ruby was never given a second polygraph examination, nor is there any indication that one was ever considered. After reviewing the charts, each panel member believed strongly that a reexamination was absolutely essential for at least three reasons. a. It is a basic and commonly accepted polygraph procedure. b. Herndon did not repeat relevant questions, thereby providing no possible corroboration of the results. c. All of the adverse factors working against the

orderly conduct of the examination made the results of the examination suspect, at best.

3. The panel concluded that the polygraph instrument was either improperly adjusted, or defective, or both... The panel found the galvanic skin response (GSR) tracing to be of minimal help in analyzing Ruby's charts. The main problem with the GSR in the first session (before the break) is a lack of sensitivity due to Herndon's setting the sensitivity at one fourth of the maximum. He decreased it to one fifth for the third series of questions. The panel noted that it should have been tried at a maximum sensitivity prior to the first test, where it probably should have remained for the entire examination.

4. Herndon's definition of a "control" question goes far beyond the generally recognized definition, as discussed in the leading book of the day by Inbau and Rend. The "control" question, developed by Reid in 1943, is one similar but unrelated to the crime being investigated to which the expert knows the correct answer and to which the person will probably lie. If the person's reaction to a properly worded control is more pronounced than to the relevant questions, he is considered to be truthful. On the other hand, if his reaction to the relevant questions is more pronounced, he is considered to be lying to the relevant questions.

5. What Herndon considers to be irrelevant questions often do not meet the criteria for an irrelevant question.

6. It is customary to repeat every question at least on a second test. This is done in order to establish the consistency (reliability) of the polygraph reactions. This was not done

in the Ruby examination. Therefore, there was no way for Herndon to establish the reliability of the relevant questions.

7. Between tests, a polygraphist should not tell a person if the tracings indicate truthful or lying responses to the relevant questions. This is particularly important in case a liar has some method of "beating the lie detector. "If he believes he is coming across as truthful, he is reassured that his method is working. Thus, he will feel less uneasy when he lies, producing less dramatic reactions... Herndon finished the discussion of series 1 with the comment: 'Mr. Ruby, you are now a veteran of the first series. You did real well. You cooperated very fine.'

8. A great deal of thought and preparation is necessary to conduct a quality polygraph examination. When a case is complicated or the examination conditions adverse, more pre-examination preparation is necessary. In the panel's opinion, Herndon appeared largely unprepared to conduct the Ruby examination.

9. The panel concluded that Herndon often used techniques in conducting the polygraph examination which did not conform to generally recognized principles of polygraphy. An example is test series 3A, which apparently was a 'searching peak-of-tension test.'

10. It is generally agreed that the more a person is tested, the less responsive he becomes. If a liar is tested enough times, sooner or later, his reaction to lies will be no more intense than to control and relevant questions. He therefore will appear truthful when lying: For this reason, the great majority of the recognized polygraph techniques limit the

number of test groups to five or less, with no more than two different series of questions. Most call for the entire examination to be concluded within 2 hours. Panel member Richard Arther, for example, uses just one series of four relevant questions, asked in three separate test groups. The Ruby examination consisted of 13 groups of questions, with the actual examination starting at 2:23 p.m. and ending at 8:59 p.m. Even though there supposedly was a break of 100 minutes, the testing should never have been resumed that day."[56]

Other Prosecutorial Abuse

The Church Committee Destroys the Warren Commission

"The Committee has developed evidence," the Church Committee concluded, "which impeaches the process by which the intelligence agencies arrived at their own conclusions about the assassination, and by which they provided information to the Warren Commission. This evidence indicates that the investigation of the assassination was deficient and that facts which might have substantially affected the course of the investigation were not provided the Warren Commission or those individuals within the FBI and the CIA, as well as other agencies of Government, who were charged with investigating the assassination."[57]

Senators Schweiker and Hart who co-chaired the subcommittee both drove a stake right through the heart of the WC investigation with the following comments: *Hart, "Who Oswald really was—who did he know? What affiliation did he have in the Cuban network? Was his public identification with the left-wing a cover for a connection with the anti-Castro right-wing?"*

---

[56] https://history-matters.com/archive/jfk/hsca/reportvols/vol8/pdf/HSCA_Vol8_RubyPolygraph.pdf

[57] https://www.history-matters.com/essays/jfkmed/How5Investigations/How5InvestigationsGotItWrong_1b.htm#_ednref119

Hart believed that Oswald was a double agent, which was one of the reasons why the FBI and CIA had made *"a conscious decision to withhold evidence from the Warren Commission."*[58]

Schweiker: *"The most important thing was that the intelligence agencies did all the wrong things if they were really looking for a conspiracy or to find out who killed John Kennedy…The Warren Commission has in fact collapsed like a house of cards and I believe it was set up at the time to feed pablum to the American people for reasons not yet known, and one of the biggest cover-ups in the history of our country occurred at that time."*[59]

The HSCA and Blakey Concur

Regarding the FBI's endeavors, the House Select Committee was blistering: "It must be said that the FBI generally exhausted its resources in confirming its case against Oswald as the lone assassin, a case that Director J. Edgar Hoover, at least, seemed determined to make within 24 hours of the assassination."[60]

The following are some of its conclusions:

1. The Federal Bureau of Investigation failed to investigate adequately the possibility of a conspiracy to assassinate the President.

2. The Federal Bureau of Investigation was deficient in its sharing of information with other agencies and departments.

3. The Central Intelligence Agency was deficient in its collection and sharing of information both prior to and subsequent to the assassination.

---

[58] Interview Hart gave to the Denver Post
[59] BBC documentary, the Killing of President Kennedy
[60] The Final Assassinations Report—Report of the Select Committee on Assassinations, U.S. House of Representatives

4. The Warren Commission performed with varying degrees of competency in the fulfillment of its duties.

5. The Warren Commission failed to investigate adequately the possibility of a conspiracy to assassinate the President. This deficiency was attributable in part to the failure of the Commission to receive all the relevant information that was in the possession of other agencies and departments of the Government.

6. The Warren Commission presented the conclusions in its report in a fashion that was too definitive.[61]

ARRB Investigators on the Warren Commission

Judge John Tunheim, Chairman of the ARRB: "Angleton took control of the CIA's investigation into the assassination and compiled a large series of records. Those records, when we tried to find them, existed in various parts of the agency. Most were no longer maintained as part of a collection. I think it is pretty clear Angleton destroyed records before he was dismissed from the CIA."... "It (the autopsy) surely was a mess."[62]

Jeremy Gunn—Executive counsel, on November 10, 2013, made the following *remarks for NPR*: "There were many things that were disturbing... I can recite a litany of other unresolved questions surrounding the Kennedy assassination—ones the Warren Commission failed to answer. For example, in New Orleans in 1963, Oswald came in contact with the FBI. When he was arrested after a scuffle at a demonstration, he asked to meet with the FBI. Why would Oswald ask to see someone from the FBI?" Gunn asks. "But an FBI agent went and interviewed Oswald, came back and wrote a memo on it, put it in the file."

For the Warren Commission, transparency had its own difficulties. "There are serious problems with the forensics evidence, with the ballistics evidence, with the autopsy evidence," Gunn says. "And, in my opin-

---

[61] Ibid.
[62] JFK Revisited Through the Looking Glass, pp. 343–345

ion, if they had said that openly, it would have not put the issue to rest." "If the president had been killed as part of a conspiracy, that needed to be known," he said. "The institution that had the opportunity to best get to the bottom of this, as much as it was possible, was the Warren Commission, and they didn't do it." He adds: "Now it's too late to do what should have been done originally."[63]

The CIA and FBI Break Their Promise

Before the Warren Commission issued its report on the assassination of President Kennedy on September 24, 1964, both the CIA and the FBI had assured the Commission that they would never close the case. When appearing before the Warren Commission, CIA Deputy Director for Plans Richard Helms stated:

> Q. After the Commission completed its report you would keep the matter open if there was anything new that developed in the future that could be properly presented to the authorities?

> A. Yes. I would assume the case will never be closed.

FBI Director Hoover made a similar statement before the Warren Commission: ... "so far as the FBI is concerned, the case will be continued in an open classification for all time."[64] The Church Committee report goes on to explain how these pledges were dishonored.

---

[63] https://www.npr.org/2013/11/10/243981006/inconsistencies-haunt-official-record-of-kennedys-death

[64] Book 5 Church Committee report, p. 77

THE GARRISON CASE AND RAMSEY CLARK

The CIA Forms the Garrison Group and Counters Garrison

The Garrison Group at CIA headquarters was created by order of Director Richard Helms. It was designed to calculate the implications of what Garrison was doing in New Orleans before, during, and after the trial of Clay Shaw. At the first meeting, Counterintelligence Chief James Angleton's first assistant predicted that, if left alone, Garrison would attain a conviction of Clay Shaw.[65]

The CIA used infiltrators to spy on Garrison. Bernardo De Torres was the first and began filing reports on Garrison with the Miami CIA almost immediately.[66] William Gurvich and Gordon Novel soon followed. Gurvich was fired by Garrison for lack of loyalty and theft and Novel, who knew Allen Dulles, wired Garrison's office.[67]

As the documents then show, task forces were designed and there was much interference in the Shaw legal proceedings.[68] This interference continued all the way up to and during the actual trial itself. It included the actual physical harassment of Garrison's witnesses (e.g., Richard Case Nagell and Aloysius Habighorst).[69] At a talk he gave in Chicago in 1992, Deputy Chief Counsel of the House Select Committee on Assassinations, Robert Tanenbaum, said he saw the CIA documents describing these kinds of actions. They came out of Helms' office.[70] James Angleton spied on Garrison witness John Nichols (concerning Single Bullet theory debunking by Garrison).[71]

---

[65] James DiEugenio, Destiny Betrayed, Second Edition—CIA Memorandum for the Record of James Garrison Sept. 20, 1967

[66] DiEugenio 1995 Interview with Al Gonzalez HSCA investigator

[67] Destiny Betrayed, pp. 229–233

[68] Ibid, pp. 271-78

[69] Ibid, p. 294

[70] Probe Magazine, Vol. 3, No. 5

[71] 28 FEB. 1969 [Microfilmed Apr 4, 1969] MEMORANDUM FOR: Director Federal Bureau of Investigation Attention: Mr. S. J. Papich SUBJECT Garrison and the Kennedy Assassination Dr. John M. Nichols)

Attorney General Ramsey Clark Joins the Fray

In March 1967, Clark made the claim that Clay Shaw (defendant in the Garrison case) had been investigated in 1963 by the FBI and that Garrison's case was baseless. This was a slip that most of the press did not pounce on… Why would a supposedly outstanding citizen like Shaw need to be investigated was the question. A subordinate tried to rectify by stating that "The Attorney General has since determined that this was erroneous."[72] As authors like William Davy have shown, it was not in error. The FBI had gathered information on Shaw in December of 1963.

Horne goes into a discussion of what the panel appointed by Attorney General Ramsey Clark did in its review of the medical evidence in February of 1968. This panel met for only a short period of time, less than a week.[73] Yet, its findings were held back from the public until January 16, 1969, for about ten months. Ramsey Clark and the Justice Department decided to announce the findings right on the eve of the Clay Shaw trial. This was part of the huge effort waged by Washington and aimed at 1) Burying the Garrison investigation in a tidal wave of propaganda, and 2) Capsizing his inquiry by subversion.

The following is taken directly from Lisa Pease's excellent *Probe Magazine* article on the Clark Panel: *The Formation of the Clark Panel: More of the Secret Team at Work? Friday, 15 December 1995:*

"The Clark Panel was the medical panel convened almost immediately after Ramsey Clark had been approved for his appointment as Attorney General in 1967. The panel was clearly convened to put to rest the growing doubts caused by the exposures of Mark Lane, Harold Weisberg, other researchers and even in late 1966 *LIFE* magazine itself. All of the above talked about the evidence of conspiracy, and the implication is that the medical evidence would either show conspiracy, or else, signs of tampering. What brought it to a crux was Jim Garrison's all-out investigation of the assassi-

---

[72] New York Post March 2, 1967, and New York Times June 3, 1967
[73] Doug Horne, Inside the ARRB, p. 344

nation, which, in 1967, was making official story proponents very nervous. One of the key questions raised by the New Orleans DA was this: Why hadn't the Warren Commission members examined the autopsy photographs and X-rays?"

In the article, she makes a strong case that those who nominated doctors for the Clark Panel had strong links to intelligence: One such person was CIA-linked John Hannah: In April of 1966, *Ramparts* magazine revealed that Michigan State University had been running a police training program for the CIA, a program which also provided cover for key CIA officers. Hannah, then President of Michigan State University, denied all knowledge of CIA involvement in the program. But the CIA's Inspector General, Lyman Kirkpatrick, said the university had signed the $25,000,000 contract knowing full well that the program belonged to the CIA.

"Knowledge of the background of men like Russell Fisher who (found the death of John Paisley to be a suicide), when indications are he was killed: Lincoln Gordon (involved in a CIA organized coup in Brazil), and Hannah, make it increasingly difficult to swallow the comment from the Clark Panel's report that *'each has acted with complete and unbiased independence, free of preconceived views as to the correctness of the medical conclusions reached in the 1963 Autopsy Report and Supplementary Report."*[74]

More recently, in a thoroughly researched book by Russell Kent, even more of the shenanigans to stock the odds in favor of the WC narrative are described in the review of Kent's book *JFK Medical Betrayal: Where The Evidence Lies by Russell Kent* (Review by James DiEugenio at Kennedysandking.com)

---

[74] https://www.kennedysandking.com/john-f-kennedy-articles/the-formation-of-the-clark-panel-more-of-the-secret-team-at-work

For example, Kent delves into the creation of the Single Bullet Theory. The FBI concluded that there were 3 shots, and 3 hits: one to Kennedy's back, one to his head and one to Governor Connally's back. "They discounted the bullet strike to James Tague on Commerce Street and Kennedy's anterior neck wound. J. Edgar Hoover never bought the Single Bullet Theory."

"...Dr. Robert Shaw, who worked on Connally at Parkland, testified twice. He could not find one bullet in Connally, he also was reluctant to accept CE 399, the Magic Bullet. *(p. 57)*

Concerning the Clark Panel: "Deputy Attorney General Carl Eardley now asked Thornton Boswell to write a letter sanctioning an independent panel. Eardley tried to create an illusion that this was Boswell's idea, but the evidence indicates the letter was written by the DOJ and sent to Boswell to sign. *(p. 70)*. This was the beginning of the creation of the Clark Panel: a panel of four men allegedly independently appointed from academia to review the autopsy at Bethesda. But as with the letter, Kent advances a case that this was not really accurate. That it was really Attorney General Ramsey Clark who appointed this panel."

... "The four men chosen, likely by Ramsey Clark, were: Doctors William Carnes (pathologist), RussellMorgan (radiologist), Alan Moritz and, most importantly, Russell Fisher (the last two qualified as forensic pathologists). A high point of the book is Kent's analysis of the backgrounds of these four men, indicating that Clark did not want an honest review, which is why he chose them. *(pp. 72–76)* This section seemed to me to be original and well-reasoned. For instance, Moritz taught Fisher at Harvard, Fisher was very reliant on government funding, and Fisher knew both Humes and Boswell."

... "Kent also adds that their report on damage to JFK's brain differs from what the original autopsy report depicts. First, the panel reported significant damage on the left side of the brain which the original report did not, and second, was that the corpus callosum was widely torn down the midline. *(p. 83)* In fact, eventually Fisher admitted that Kennedy's brain was not sectioned, which he characterized was really a crucial step." *(p. 84)*

"In their description of the now infamous 6.5 mm fragment on the X-rays of the skull, there is no mention that this measurement matches the caliber of the alleged bullet fired at Kennedy. Neither do they say that the dust-like particles in the front of Kennedy's skull are above the posterior entrance wound. This would suggest an entrance wound. Further, the fact that the larger particles are located near the back of the skull would also suggest this origin, as Dr. Vincent DiMaio wrote." *(p. 91)*

"Another deception was that the report described 'a track between two cutaneous wounds,' presumably between JFK's back and neck. But as Kent notes this was an imputation: there was no proven track. *(p. 92)* The main reason being that this wound—as well as the skull wound—was not dissected."

Mike Chesser had this to say about X-ray evidence; "The fragment trail does not fit the conclusions of the Clark Panel or the HSCA…So, it's impossible for a shot here, in the back of the skull, to result in all the tiniest bullet fragments in the frontal region…"

About the 6.5 mm fragment in an X-ray only notice in 1968 by the Clark Panel (no doctor noticed it at the autopsy): "The bright object (supposed bullet part) suddenly shows up between the Bethesda autopsy and the Clark Panel. I think it was most likely … placed there shortly after the autopsy…"

Chesser explains later that it is not credible that this had been missed, and also that Ebersole (the radiologist) refused to talk about this.[75]

Clark further kibitzed in the Garrison Case according to autopsist Dr. Boswell. Both in *JAMA* and under oath to the ARRB, Boswell explained the rest of the story. He said that the Justice Department was "really upset" when Pierre Finck had testified that a general, and not chief pathologist Humes, was in charge of JFK's autopsy. "So," Boswell

---

[75] JFK Revisited, Through the Looking Glass, pp. 292–296

testified, "(Justice) put me on a plane that day to New Orleans." "They (the Justice Department) ... talked to me and tried to get me to agree that (Finck) was very strange ...." Then, Boswell explained, "They showed me the transcript of Pierre (Finck's) testimony for the past couple of days, and I spent all night reviewing that testimony." The Justice Department's obvious purpose, Boswell admitted, was to prepare him "to refute Finck's testimony."

Ultimately, however, Boswell was never called to the stand. Nevertheless, it is worth asking, as ARRB's counsel Gunn astutely put it to Boswell under oath in 1996, "What was the United States Department of Justice doing in relationship to a case between the district attorney of New Orleans and a resident of New Orleans?" After all, Shaw was on trial in a state court on state, not federal, charges.[76]

Humes, Boswell and Finck Undermine the Clark Panel

At their private conference (HSCA) with select members of Dr. Baden's medical panel, all three autopsy doctors—Humes, Pierre Finck, and J. Thornton Boswell—mightily resisted this new location (as put forth by the Clark Panel) for the head wound: four inches up from where they had originally placed Kennedy's fatal head shot. In the newly declassified HSCA files, Finck argues that he had the body right in front of him and that should be the strongest evidence.

Humes also argues that what the HSCA is now calling a bullet hole does not even look like a wound to him. Humes said about the small red dot that the HSCA called an entrance wound, "I just don't know what it is, but it certainly was not any wound of entrance." This argument went on until one of the HSCA pathologists interjected. "We have no business recording this," said Dr. George Loquvam. "This is for us to decide between ourselves; I don't think this belongs on this record... You guys are nuts. You guys are nuts writing this stuff. It doesn't belong in that damn

---

[76] ARRB testimony J. Thornton Boswell, College Park, Maryland, 2/26/96, p. 211. (Pierre Fink testimony Shaw trial) and https://www.history-matters.com/essays/jfk-med/How5Investigations/How5InvestigationsGotItWrong_2.htm#_edn172

record." *(Vol. 7, p. 255)* (Loquvam ended up writing the draft report of the medical panel.)

Suffice it to say, what the HSCA presented *to the public* was not an accurate portrayal of the dispute between Humes and the medical panel. Humes himself dramatized this years-later when after Oliver Stone's *JFK* came out, he reverted back to his original position for the head wound, four inches downward on the skull, for the publication *Journal of the AMA.*[77]

Subpoenas Not Honored

Garrison subpoenaed Sandra Moffet (girlfriend of important witness Perry Russo), Sergio Arcacha Smith, whom he attempted to extradite back to New Orleans, Richard Helms, photographs of Oswald in Mexico City, Allen Dulles, Jim Braden (who had been picked up for questioning in Dealey Plaza on the day of the assassination), as well as Oswald's tax records... all were refused.[78]

Coordinated Media Slander Campaign

As the declassified files reveal, before Garrison's probe was exposed, he was making a lot of progress. Afterwards, it was open season on him. And he was targeted by the big guns of the media. NBC sent in Walter Sheridan, *Newsweek* sent in Hugh Aynesworth, and the *Saturday Evening Post* sent down James Phelan. Many writers have shown how these men obstructed Garrison once his inquiry was out in the open. Sheridan got very involved in slandering and/or flipping Garrison witnesses and appears to have some intel links.[79]

---

[77] https://www.kennedysandking.com/john-f-kennedy-articles/the-sins-of-robert-bla-key-part-2
[78] *Destiny Betrayed, DiEugenio* p. 271
[79] Destiny Betrayed, Chapters 11 and 12

Garrison Vindicated, Intelligence Agencies Panned

Despite having lost the trial, Garrison was largely vindicated in later investigations.

The Lopez report, as we have seen, shows that he was correct in suspecting something sinister took place in Mexico City. The HSCA concluded that Oswald had a relationship with David Ferrie and, likely, with Guy Banister. Clay Shaw, contrary to his denials, was a well-paid CIA contract agent with a security clearance.

In a previously noted interview HSCA Deputy Counsel Robert Tanenbaum did with Jim DiEugenio, he said he saw documents proving the CIA was monitoring and harassing Garrison's witnesses. He was also interested in the connection between New Orleans and the CIA station JM/WAVE in Miami and exactly what was the connection between Clay Shaw and the Agency.

THE ROCKEFELLER COMMISSION[80]

Ford Loads the Dice

Gerald Ford was highly criticized for his work, or lack thereof, on the Warren Commission. His appointed Rockefeller Commission is generally regarded as a whitewash and was superseded by the Church Committee.

Its flaws begin with its very narrow scope: *It also conducted a narrow study of issues relating to the JFK assassination, specifically the backward head snap as seen in the Zapruder film (first shown publicly in 1975), and the possible presence of E. Howard Hunt and Frank Sturgis in Dallas.*

According to Russell Kent, Ford stacked the Commission with mouthpieces: "Incredibly, Warren Commission lawyer David Belin was appointed the chief counsel to this body." He tried to neutralize the issue

---

[80] https://history-matters.com/archive/contents/church/contents_church_reports_rockcomm.htm

of bias by having Robert Olson run the JFK inquiry. But as Kent writes, "Belin showed up during the medical review and took the testimony of two doctors…"

Making it worse was that one of the doctors, Richard Lindenberg, worked with Finck at the Armed Forces Institute of Pathology. He was also an odd choice in that most of his papers dealt with aviation accidents. Perhaps this was because he was in the medical corps for the Luftwaffe and came to the U.S.A. as part of Operation Paperclip. *(p. 114)* Needless to say, he later wrote a paper with Fisher. Werner Spitz was also on the panel, and he worked with Fisher for a number of years from the late fifties and during the sixties. *(p. 123)*. Another dubious choice on the panel was Alfred Olivier, since he showed some prejudice working for and testifying in front of the Warren Commission.

Finally, the Rockefeller Commission misrepresented Dr. Cyril Wecht's testimony. He was asked to testify, and he did so for five hours in May of 1975. He was critical of the autopsy and the Magic Bullet. His testimony was reduced to three paragraphs in the report, and one would never know how critical he was. Misrepresenting his testimony, it looked like Wecht supported the Rockefeller Commission conclusions. This dispute reached the pages of the *New York Times*. Wecht asked to see his transcript. He was denied. *(p. 135)*[81]

Kissinger Stifled Belin

As of mid-April 1975, Belin expected to have the assassination portion of the panel report complete by the end of the month. He so informed White House officials. However, the CIA dragged its feet on providing materials, and Secretary of State Henry Kissinger, who initially promised cooperation, provided little. Kissinger became a major actor in the struggle to suppress the Rockefeller assassinations report. When Belin scheduled a press conference to announce the panel's assassination findings, deputy assistant to the president Dick Cheney (eventual VP of

---

[81] KennedysandKing JFK Medical Betrayal: Where the Evidence Lies by Russell Kent article 20 January 2023

George W. Bush) and White House Counsel Philip Buchen, citing Kissinger's concerns, intervened to induce Belin to cancel it.[82]

Ford Made Certain the Report was Heavily Edited

- White House officials of the Ford administration attempted to keep a presidential review panel—the Rockefeller Commission—from investigating reports of CIA planning for assassinations abroad.

- Ford administration officials suppressed the Rockefeller Commission's actual report on CIA assassination plots. (Note: This would have opened doors to the CIA mafia plots to kill Castro and links to Dulles and the Kennedy assassination.)

- Richard Cheney, then the deputy assistant to the president, edited the report of the Rockefeller Commission from inside the Ford White House, stripping the report of its independent character.

- The Rockefeller Commission remained silent on this manipulation.

- Rockefeller Commission lawyers and public relations officials warned of the damage that would be done to the credibility of the entire investigation by avoiding the subject of assassinations.

- President Ford passed investigative materials concerning assassinations along to the Church Committee of the United States Senate and then attempted—but failed—to suppress the Church Committee's report as well.

---

[82] https://nsarchive.gwu.edu/briefing-book/intelligence/2016-02-29/gerald-ford-white-house-altered-rockefeller-commission-report

- The White House markup of the Rockefeller Commission report used the secrecy of the CIA budget as an example of excesses and recommended Congress consider making agency spending public to some degree.[83]

THE CHURCH COMMITTEE

In 1975, dubbed *The Year of Intelligence*, The Church Committee began investigating abuses of U.S. intelligence agencies. It and other committees uncovered a multitude of scandalous operations including mind control, press and academia influencing, assassinations of foreign leaders, illegal mail opening and use of telecommunications companies for illegal spying.

Helms Lies to the Church Committee

Even Wikipedia says that Helms lied to the Church Committee. "After Nixon's 1974 resignation, information uncovered in 1975 by the Church Committee hearings showed that Helms' February 1973 statements (about secret CIA activity during 1970 in Chile) were clearly in error. He had misled Congress. Helms was prosecuted in 1977. Later that year, Helms pled nolo contendere to two lesser, misdemeanor charges that he had not 'fully, completely and accurately' testified to Congress. He received a two-year suspended sentence and a $2,000 fine. Helms, nonetheless, continued to enjoy the support of many in the CIA, both active officers and retired veterans, including James Angleton. 'He was sworn not to disclose the very things that he was being requested by the [Senate] Committee to disclose,' Edward Bennett Williams, Helms' defense attorney, told the press. Williams added that Helms would 'wear this conviction like a badge of honor, like a banner,' a sentiment later seconded by James Schlesinger, who had followed Helms as DCI in 1973. After his court appearance and sentencing, Helms attended a large gathering

---

[83] https://nsarchive.gwu.edu/briefing-book/intelligence/2016-02-29/gerald-ford-white-house-altered-rockefeller-commission-report

of CIA officers in Bethesda, Maryland, where he received a standing ova-
tion. A collection was taken, netting enough to pay his fine."[84]

Enter Poppy Bush

Gerald Ford, already assisted by Donald Rumsfeld and Dick Cheney,
recruited George H. W. Bush to head the CIA in 1976. His mission: Because of the harm done to its image with the Watergate Scandal and the
investigations, Ford wanted Bush to repair the image of the CIA.[85] In the
HBO documentary, *41*, George H.W. Bush admits that he put a stop to
the investigations of the fine, loyal people of the CIA.

Carl Bernstein Reveals Influence Peddling

In his milestone 1977 Rolling Stone article about the CIA and the press,
Bernstein reveals the following on how the Church Committee was tampered with:

> *"DESPITE THE EVIDENCE OF WIDESPREAD CIA USE OF JOURNAL-
> ISTS, the Senate Intelligence Committee and its staff decided
> against questioning any of the reporters, editors, publishers or
> broadcast executives whose relationships with the Agency are de-
> tailed in CIA files:*
>
> *According to sources in the Senate and the Agency, the use of
> journalists was one of two areas of inquiry which the CIA went to
> extraordinary lengths to curtail. The other was the Agency's contin-
> uing and extensive use of academics for recruitment and infor-
> mation-gathering purposes.*
>
> *In both instances, the sources said, former directors Colby and
> Bush and CIA special counsel Mitchell Rogovin were able to con-
> vince key members of the committee that full inquiry or even limited
> public disclosure of the dimensions of the activities would do*

---

[84] https://en.wikipedia.org/wiki/Richard_Helms
[85] Meacham 2015, pp. 189–193

irreparable damage to the nation's intelligence-gathering appa-
ratus, as well as to the reputations of hundreds of individuals. Colby
was reported to have been especially persuasive in arguing that dis-
closure would bring on a latter-day "witch hunt" in which the vic-
tims would be reporters, publishers and editors...[86]

THE HSCA

Established in 1976, under star prosecutors Richard Sprague and Bob
Tanenbaum, the HSCA began re-investigating the murders of JFK and
Martin Luther King aggressively and independently of the intelligence
agencies. Great progress was being made ... which would not be tolerated.

The Ousting of Sprague and Tanenbaum

Richard Sprague and Bob Tanenbaum had excellent careers as tough
attorneys. They were selected to lead the HSCA investigation into the
assassination. They were making great progress. Much of what we know
today about Miami links and the Mexico City incidents, we owe to them
and to investigators Al Gonzalez and Gaeton Fonzi.

This is why steps were taken to oust Tanenbaum and Sprague. The
obfuscators knew they had to do several things to turn the situation
around and keep the American public in the dark. Here is what they had
to do:

- Remove Chief Counsel Richard Sprague;
- Remove Committee Chairman Henry Gonzalez;
- Remove Sprague's key men and keep them away from more in-
  criminating CIA evidence;

---

[86] THE CIA AND THE MEDIA How America's Most Powerful News Media Worked Hand
in Glove with the Central Intelligence Agency and Why the Church Committee Covered It Up BY CARL BERNSTEIN https://www.carlbernstein.com/the-cia-and-the-me-
dia-rolling-stone-10-20-1977

- Install their own chief counsel to control the investigation;
- Nominate a new HSCA chairman who would go along, or who could be fooled;
- Limit Sprague's investigations of CIA people. Make sure some of the people aren't found or, if necessary, dispose of CIA people who might talk;
- Create a new investigative environment whose purpose would be to confirm all of the findings of the Warren Commission and divert attention away from the who-did-it-and-why approach;
- Control the committee staff in such a way as to keep any of them separate from other teams and silent by signing nondisclosure agreements;
- Control the media by not holding any press conferences.

These things all happened, fundamentally altering the temperament and goals of the HSCA.

It simply was not the same once Sprague and Tanenbaum left. As many observers think, this was the last, best chance to solve the JFK case.

Robert Tanenbaum, when interviewed by Jim DiEugenio, said the following:

"In my opinion, Congress never wanted to go forward with these investigations at all. That's just based upon my having spoken with a lot of the membership of the House as I was asked to do by the Committee, in order to get funding. That's something I never thought would be an issue before I went down there. They sort of politicized into it with some very distinguished members of Congress who were retiring in 1976, requesting that the Kennedy portion be investigated because they had seen Groden's presentation of the Zapruder film and were very persuaded by it. Then the Black Caucus got involved and said well, investigate the murder of Dr. King. It was an election year and they said, 'OK, why not? We'll do that.' But there was no commitment to really do it, unfortunately, which regrettably we found out while we were in the midst of investigating the case. They pulled our budget, they pulled our long-distance phone privileges, our franking privileges, we couldn't even send out mail. And all of this was happening at a time when we were making some significant headway. .... Tip O'Neill, who was the Speaker, was never committed to it. Only many, many years later did he realize that he'd made a tragic mistake."

According to Gaeton Fonzi in *The Last Investigation*:

"The key factors that drove Richard Sprague to resign as Chief Counsel of the Assassinations Committee appeared, at the time, to be apparent and on the surface. His proposed use of certain investigative equipment, his demand for an expensive, unrestricted investigation, his refusal to play politics with Chairman Gonzalez—all were apparent grounds for the vociferous criticism which, in the long run, was debilitating to the Committee's efforts to get on with its job."

Sprague himself had this say to Probe: In a <u>2000 interview for Probe Magazine</u>[87] with John Williams, he described his being fired this way:

SPRAGUE: *We were just going to do that type of thorough thing. I demanded the records from the CIA, and now there was an abrupt refusal, and I subpoenaed them. At that point, Gonzalez, who was Chairman of the Committee, ordered the CIA, or told the CIA that they need not respond to my subpoena, and fired me, and ordered the U.S. Marshals come in and remove me from my office.*

WILLIAMS: Oh, so that firing was directly after you had subpoenaed the records from the Central Intelligence Agency.

SPRAGUE: *Right. But there's more involved in it than the timing*

WILLIAMS: Right.

---

[87] https://www.kennedysandking.com/john-f-kennedy-articles/interview-with-rich-ard-sprague

SPRAGUE: ... *if you checked the record. That came up after that. He ordered my firing. He ordered marshals to remove me from my office in what I'm sure was the first and only time in the history of the United States Congress. The rest of the Committee backed me to a man and overrode the Chairman, and ordered that I remain, and the marshals were directed to get off. Of course, that led to Gonzalez taking it up in the House of Representatives, and the House backed the rest of the Committee. And he resigned and Stokes came on. [Louis Stokes was the representative from Ohio. Eds. Note] I'm sure that's the only time in the history of the United States Congress that in a fight between the Chairman and the Director, that the Chairman got bounced. But there's a terrible price paid for that. Every Congressman dreams of being chairman of a Committee and being all powerful. It ultimately did not sit well with the Congress that a chairman got ousted...*

The Blahut Affair

Regis Blahut was a CIA liaison with the Committee. In late June of 1978, one of the security officers for the Committee discovered that some of the autopsy materials stored in the safe had been taken out, looked at, and one of the color photos had been removed from its plastic sleeve. The Committee conducted an internal inquiry and found through fingerprint matches on the safe that the culprit was Blahut. Blakey conducted three separate interviews with him. The first two were taped. Blakey concluded that in both interviews, Blahut's responses conflicted with the facts.[88]

---

[88] https://www.kennedysandking.com/john-f-kennedy-articles/the-sins-of-robert-blakey-part-2

Goodpasture and Phillips Both Lied

The CIA claimed that tapes of Oswald in Mexico City were destroyed (as they routinely do after a week or so)… The Lopez report states the following:[89]

10) The CIA telephone surveillance on the Soviet Embassy taped several calls of a man using the name "Lee Oswald." These tapes were retained for a routine two week period and were most likely erased shortly after 16 October 1963. These tapes were probably existence at the time of the assassination.

Hoover confirmed that FBI agents heard at least one of these tapes when they were interrogating Oswald after the assassination and that the voice on the tape was not Oswald's.[90]

Plans were taken to charge Phillips (2 counts) and Goodpasture (1 count) with perjury, which were discarded after the investigators found out the committee members had no real interest in doing so.

George Joannides Derails the HSCA

In 2014, for an ARRC conference, both Hardway and Lopez talked about their experience on the HSCA and the report.[91] A lot of focus was put on how they had been making progress in the HSCA investigation until the CIA placed George Joannides as their resource person in charge of supervising the CIA's interaction with the HSCA. Despite claims that

---

[89] https://history-matters.com/archive/jfk/hsca/lopezrpt_2003/html/LopezRpt_0022a.htm *The Lopez Report HSCA*
[90] Nov. 23 1963: The aftermath and a curious phone call> JFK Facts and Oswald, the CIA, and Mexico City | FRONTLINE (pbs.org)
[91] https://www.c-span.org/video/?321703-2/oswald-cia-mexico-city

Joannides was impartial, it was confirmed that he was directly involved with the Cuban exile organization called the DRE in 1963. Oswald had direct interaction with the DRE in events that became very public and were used to paint him as a communist. Hardway concludes his speech with "The CIA has something to hide; Joannides knew what they had to hide. The CIA knew he knew and knew we did not know who or what he was hiding; Joannides hid what he had to hide."

Edwin Lopez confirmed the stonewalling and gave examples on how they were being spied on. He referred to the continued holding back of documents as a mess we all needed to work on together.

As noted in Chapter 1 of this book, Robert Blakey finally admitted how he and the HSCA were deceived by the CIA:

I am no longer confident that the Central Intelligence Agency coop-erated with the Committee... We also now know that the Agency set up a process that could only have been designed to frustrate the ability of the committee in 1976-79 to obtain any information that might adversely affect the Agency.

Many have told me that the culture of the Agency is one of pre-varication and dissimulation and that you cannot trust it or its peo-ple. Period. End of story.

I am now in that camp.

During his appearance for the *AARC Conference in 2014,* Blakey's reiterated his views: It was also discovered subsequent to the HSCA hearings that Joannides was acting as an undercover agent in his deal-ings with the HSCA.[92] He also said that FBI agent Regis Kennedy de-scribed Marcello as a tomato salesman who was not part of the mob.

---

[92] https://www.youtube.com/watch?v=6NTpmyYIeXE

Neuromuscular Reaction Malarkey

As had the Rockefeller Commission, the HSCA peddled a neuromuscular reaction pushed by Larry Sturdivan, to explain JFK's violent backward motion seen in the Zapruder film.

Gary Aguilar and Cyril Wecht have debunked this argument.

The first point worth noting is that, though properly credentialed pathologists, none of the Rockefeller or HSCA experts were neurophysiologists, or neurologists, or neurosurgeons, or even trauma surgeons familiar with what actually happens to living humans who suffer brain trauma. They were forensic pathologists whose work was supplemented by consulting radiologists. They worked on dead people, using X-rays, microscopes and lab data. In other words, when opining on the somewhat obscure neurophysiological phenomena in the JFK case, they weren't speaking on the basis of any professional expertise; they were like orthopedists offering their "expert" opinions on a pediatric problem.

That is made plain by the fact that JFK's recoil differs from any kind of recognized "neuromuscular" etiology the pathologists had specified, both in timing and manifestation, whether decorticate or decerebrate. Rather, there are multiple, independent avenues of evidence that converge in support of author Wecht's minority "suspicion" that it was a non-jacketed, soft-pointed shell that struck JFK from the right front, driving him back and to the left.

Decorticate posturing has been well described. The back arches rearwards, the legs extend and the arms flex inward. In decerebrate posturing the back arches and the legs extend, as they do in decorticate posturing. But the arms extend downward, parallel to the body. If one compares his posture at Zapruder frame 230, or in any frame after the back shot but before the head shot, Kennedy is reacting to the first shot. His elbows are raised and abducted *away* from his body, and his arms and hands are flexed inward toward his neck.[93]

Zapruder frame 230, Kennedy is reacting to the first shot. His elbows are raised and abducted away from his body. His wrists are flexed inward across his mouth and neck.

In the frames following the head shot, there is no "violent straightening and stiffening of Kennedy's entire body," as Rockefeller Commission experts claimed. JFK's head moves backward, but his back does not arch, nor do his upper arms move toward his body (adduct), but instead fall limply toward his side. And although not visible in the film, there's no jerking motion of his body to suggest that

---

[93] 22 November 2021 Peer Reviewed Medical/Scientific Journalism Has Been Corrupted by Warren Commission Apologists—Part 1 Written by Gary Aguilar, MD and Cyril Wecht, MD, KennedysandKing)

his legs extend. Nor do his arms flex inward or extend inferiorly. They instead fall limply toward his lap. His upper body, likely paralyzed from the spinal injury caused by the first shot, passively follows his blasted cranium "back and to the left."[94]

The HSCA Misrepresents Bethesda Witnesses on JFK Head Wound

According to ophthalmologist Gary Aguilar: "They said that all the witnesses at the autopsy, they all agreed to those autopsy photographs (showing no damage to the back of JFK's head). But they suppressed the witness statements themselves. When the ARRB came along, and out come those witness statements, out come the diagrams. And lo and behold, it turns out that the witnesses at the autopsy all agreed with the doctors at Dallas: That the defect involved the rear of the head. They basically lied about what was there..."[95] (See Chapter 9)

---

[94] https://www.kennedysandking.com/john-f-kennedy-articles/peer-reviewed-medical-scientific-journalism-has-been-corrupted-by-warren-commission-apologists
[95] JFK Revisited, p. 283 (See sections: Proof of a front-shot; What Investigation insiders confirmed)

THE ARRB

Intelligence Agency Resistance

Thomas Samoluk (Deputy Director and Press Officer of the ARRB): " ... the intelligence agencies kind of adopt that approach, that they (the ARRB) will eventually go away. The Review Board will not last forever. We'll still be here."

He also revealed that the Secret Service destroyed files about JFK's 1963 travels and how the FBI and CIA attempted stonewalling when the ARRB tried to access some of their files.[96]

John Tunheim—Chairman of the ARRB, confirmed CIA attempts to resist transfers of files and how George H. W. Bush tried to oppose the bill before it became law, and then moved very slowly to cooperate once he was elected. Finally, he stated that the CIA misled the ARRB, as they had the HSCA, about the HSCA CIA liaison to that investigation: George Joannides, by hiding his involvement with the CIA Miami Station at the time of the assassination.... They have been fighting the release of his file. Which Tunheim feels is terribly misguided because the information should have been released a long time ago.

About New Orleans DA Harry Connick: "He (Connick) was embarrassed because he said all the files (Garrison) had been preserved and turned everything over to us. When in fact he had ordered the records to be destroyed. And they weren't destroyed... Connick even sued the ARRB to try and prevent the release of the Garrison files."

Tunheim also noted the destruction of autopsy records and Secret Service files, how the Secret Service was very difficult to work with, how they destroyed files without an explanation, how the CIA and President H. W. Bush opposed the release of classified the documents and how Trump did not respect the law by stalling declassification, and finally how the CIA is resisting the release of the Joannides files. He said that his experience with the CIA is that they did not want any records released at all.

---

[96] Ibid., pp. 383 to 389

Judge Tunheim said that the information (non-declassified documents) was intended to be released in 2017. Only under extreme circumstances was a president in 2017 supposed to continue to protect records. And they didn't, as near as I can tell, they didn't provide that certification.[97]

The Office of Naval Intelligence Squashes Lieutenant Commander Terri Pike

The following is taken verbatim from *JFKcountercoup Monday, October 17, 2011, The Railroading of LCDR Terri Pike, William Kelly Post:*[98]

"On November 14, 1995, the ARRB requested a large number of files from ONI, pertaining to the assassination of JFK. The Director of ONI responded on Nov. 27 by letter stating that "the Office of Naval Intelligence holds no records responsive to the tasking of 14 Nov.," but that didn't satisfy the ARRB. Then months went by without a response and eventually some ONI records officers were assigned the task of responding to the ARRB requests, including LCDR Florence "Terri" Pike and LCDR Paul Doolittle... "For reasons not entirely clear to either the ONI team or ARRB," Barger notes, "the tasking for this project only trickled down to them on Friday, March 7, 1997.

Pike got straight to work: "Despite the fact that they had only learned of this tasking on Friday, they had located and designated approximately 125 cubic feet of documents that directly relate to subjects we mentioned in our letter to the Navy. These will be reviewed page by page. She anticipated being able to complete the review by the stated deadline set by the Navy and ARRB of April 30, 1997.... "In addition, she said that ONI had identified about 950 cubic feet, or approximately 2.4 million pages of records which might

---

[97] Ibid., pp. 341–350

[98] https://jfkcountercoup.blogspot.com/2011/10/railroading-of-lcdr-terri-pike-over.html?m=1

be related to the topics we were interested in, but that we had not specifically mentioned..."

Pike was very much appreciated by the ARRB: In summary, the ARRB meeting report notes, "In closing, it should be reported that this team and LCDR Pike in particular, are very impressive, they appear very much to have their act together on this project...

After a progress note, Pike seems to have been targeted for removal: LCDR Pike Faxed the ARRB, indicating that she had finished a declassification review of the .8 cubic feet of defector records, and had prepared a page-by-page index of the same. She indicated that transmittal of these documents would occur in the near future.

That appears to be the beginning of the end of such cooperation and the end of LCDR Terri Pike.

A Chronology of Key Events in ARRB-ONI Interface notes that on "... ARRB staffer Doug Horne called Terri Pike and requested that ONI look for '119 Reports' covering an alleged ONI investigation of Lee Harvey Oswald's October 1959 defection to the Soviet Union. LCDR Pike accepted the tasking, but ARRB never received any feedback on its results."

One of the key liaisons between the ARRB and ONI, at least in the eyes of the Review Board staff, had simply disappeared.

A Memo Terri Pike sent to ARRB Military unit member Doug Horne amplified the situation when she wrote to them that, "... I was relieved from the leadership position on this project in late August (1997) by the ONI Reserve Directorate Head... As you know, it was my responsibility to identify all records required under 44 U.S.C. 2107. I felt a personal commitment to ensure this effort was conducted 'with vigor' and as thoroughly as possible..."

Another memo from Pike dated 10 Nov. 97 notes that, "In its questioning to date, the ONI IG has narrowly focused on my travel requirements and has declared that the taskings of... The Kennedy review did not include the requirement for searches for all records regardless of physical location, just those available locally."

She was charged with "fraudulent" official travel because her "tasking did not say to search regional record centers." She was accused of work and travel "fraud" in regard to the travel from D.C. to the remote ONI records storage centers…

The new point of contact was the FOIA office Staff Judge Advocate (ONI-OCB) LCDR. R. Bastien. An ARRB staffer who dealt with Bastien said he, " … was a real bastard, the nastiest individual I encountered within the military structure. He seemed actively opposed to what we were doing at the ARRB… He was a Navy legal officer, a military attorney, acting as the pit bull guard dog protecting the ONI family jewels."

An ONI document says directly that the department " … strongly objects to Pike's cooperation in the investigation being conducted by Mr. Jeremy Gunn of ARRB. ONI is unaware of any unauthorized investigation regarding this issue. If Mr. Gunn wishes to conduct an investigation or inquiry, such an effort should be coordinated through the Office of Naval Intelligence. Your objections are noted."

One member of the ARRB staff met with Pike and her counsel, and part of the meeting was with the attorney alone, at his request, when he said that she had received psychiatric testing and, "Her attorney was somewhat disloyal, speaking of her diagnosis as 'bipolar' as if she were somewhat unstable or unreliable (though) she seemed completely lucid and under control when I spoke with her at this meeting

From a review of the documents, it is clear that Pike was removed from her job, reprimanded, demoted, and wrongly disciplined under trumped up charges. Her career was effectively ended because she took the initiative to retrieve and catalog ONI records pursuant to the John F. Kennedy Assassination Records Review Act."[99]

---

[99] Ibid.

MEDIA COMPLICITY

CIA Attacks Critics

Released in 1977 after a FOIA demand, the following CIA document[100] presents the CIA playbook on how to counter critics:

To: Chiefs, Certain Stations and Bases

From: Chief WOVIEW

Our Concern. *From the day of* President Kennedy's assassination *on, there has been speculation about the responsibility for his murder. Although this was stemmed for a time by the Warren Commission report (which appeared at the end of September 1964), various writers have now had time to scan the Commission's published report and documents for new pretexts for questioning, and there has been a new wave of books and articles criticizing the Commission's findings. In most cases the critics have speculated as to the existence of some kind of conspiracy, and often they have implied that the Commission itself was involved. Presumably as a result of the increasing challenge to the Warren Commission's Report, a public opinion poll recently indicated that 46% of the American public did not think that Oswald acted alone, while more than half of those polled thought that the Commission had left some questions unresolved. Doubtless polls abroad would show similar, or possibly more adverse results.*

This trend of opinion is a matter of concern to the U.S. government, including our organization. The members of the Warren Commission were naturally chosen for their integrity, experience and prominence. They represented both major parties, and they and their staff were deliberately drawn from all sections of the country.

---

[100] CIA document 1035–960 is available at the National Archives: NARA RIF no. 104–10009–10022

Just because of the standing of the commissioners, efforts to impugn their rectitude and wisdom tend to cast doubt on the whole leadership of American society. Moreover, there seems to be an increasing tendency to hint that President Johnson himself, as the one person who might be said to have benefited, was in some way responsible for the assassination. Innuendo of such seriousness affects not only the individual concerned, but also the whole reputation of the American government. Our organization itself is directly involved: among other facts, we contributed information to the investigation. Conspiracy theories have frequently thrown suspicion on our organization, for example, by falsely alleging that <u>Lee Harvey Oswald</u> worked for us. The aim of this dispatch is to provide material countering and discrediting the claims of the conspiracy theorists, so as to inhibit the circulation of such claims in other countries. Background information is supplied in a classified section and in a number of unclassified attachments.

__Action__. We do __not__ recommend that discussion of the assassination question be initiated where it is not already taking place. Where discussion is active, addressees are requested:

To discuss the publicity problem with liaison and friendly elite contacts (especially politicians and editors), pointing out that the Warren Commission made as thorough an investigation as humanly possible, that the charges of the critics are without serious foundation, and that further speculative discussion only plays into the hands of the opposition. Point out also that parts of the conspiracy talk appear to be deliberately generated by Communist propagandists. Urge them to use their influence to discourage unfounded and irresponsible speculation.

To employ propaganda assets to answer and refute the attacks of the critics. Book reviews and feature articles are particularly appropriate for this purpose. The unclassified attachments to this guidance should provide useful background material for passing to assets. Our play should point out, as applicable, that the critics are (i) wedded to theories adopted before the evidence was in (ii) politically interested (iii) financially interested (iv) hasty and inaccurate in their research, or (v) infatuated with their own theories. In the course of discussions of the whole phenomenon of criticism, a useful strategy may be to single out Epstein's theory for attack, using the attached Fletcher Knebel article and Spectator piece for background. (Although <u>Mark Lane</u>*'s book is much less convincing than Epstein's and comes off badly where confronted by knowledgeable critics, it is also much more difficult to answer as a whole, as one becomes lost in a morass of unrelated details.)*

In private to media discussions not directed at any particular writer, or in attacking publications which may be yet forthcoming, the following arguments should be useful:

No significant new evidence *has emerged which the Commission did not consider. The assassination is sometimes compared (e.g., by Joachim Joesten and Bertrand Russell) with the Dreyfus case; however, unlike that case, the attacks on the Warren Commission have produced no new evidence, no new culprits have been convincingly identified, and there is no agreement among the critics. (A better parallel, though an imperfect one, might be with the Reichstag fire of 1933, which some competent historians [Fritz Tobias, A. J. P. Taylor, D. C. Watt] now believe was set by Van der Lubbe on his own initiative, without acting for either Nazis or Communists; the Nazis tried to pin the blame on the Communists, but the latter have been more successful in convincing the world that the Nazis were to blame.)*

Critics usually overvalue particular items and ignore others. They tend to place more emphasis on the recollections of individual witnesses (which are less reliable and more divergent—and hence offer more hand—holds for criticism) and less on ballistics, autopsy, and photographic evidence. A close examination of the Commission's records will usually show that the conflicting eyewitness accounts are quoted out of context, or were discarded by the Commission for good and sufficient reason.

Conspiracy on the large scale often suggested would be

impossible to conceal in the United States, esp. since informants could expect to receive large royalties, etc. Note that Robert Kennedy, Attorney General at the time and John F. Kennedy's brother, would be the last man to overlook or conceal any conspiracy. And as one reviewer pointed out, Congressman Gerald R. Ford would hardly have held his tongue for the sake of the Democratic administration, and Senator Russell would have had every political interest in exposing any misdeeds on the part of Chief Justice Warren. A conspirator, moreover, would hardly choose a location for a shooting where so much depended on conditions beyond his control: the route, the speed of the cars, the moving target, the risk that the assassin would be discovered. A group of wealthy conspirators could have arranged much more secure conditions.

Critics have often been enticed by a form of intellectual pride: they light on some theory and fall in love with it; they also scoff at the Commission because it did not always answer every question with a flat decision one way or the other. Actually, the make-up of the Commission and its staff was an excellent safeguard against overcommitment to anyone theory, or against the illicit transformation of probabilities into certainties.

Oswald would not have been any sensible person's choice for a co-conspirator. He was a "loner," mixed up, of questionable reliability and an unknown quantity to any professional intelligence service.

As to charges that the Commission's report was a rush job, it emerged three months after the deadline originally set. But to the degree that the Commission tried to speed up its reporting, this was largely due to the pressure of irresponsible speculation already appearing, in some cases coming from the same critics who, refusing to admit their errors, are now putting out new criticisms.

Such vague accusations as that "more than ten people have died mysteriously," can always be explained in some natural way e.g.: the individuals concerned have for the most part died of natural causes; the Commission staff questioned 418 witnesses (the FBI interviewed far more people, conducting 25,000 interviews and re-interviews), and in such a large group, a certain number of deaths are to be expected. (When Penn Jones, one of the originators of the "ten mysterious deaths" line, appeared on television, it emerged that two of the deaths on his list were from heart attacks, one from cancer, one was from a head-on collision on a bridge, and one oc-curred when a driver drifted into a bridge abutment.)

Where possible, counter speculation by encouraging reference to the Commission's Report itself. Open-minded foreign readers should still be impressed by the care, thoroughness, objectivity and speed with which the Commission worked. Reviewers of other books might be encouraged to add to their account the idea that, checking back with the Report itself, they found it far superior to the work of its critics.

CLAYTON P. NURNAD DESTROY WHEN NO LONGER NEEDED

1 April 1967 (CIA no. 1035–960)

Mockingbird

Set up in 1950 by the CIA's Frank Wisner, Operation Mockingbird (also known as the Mighty Wurlitzer), was a CIA stratagem to coordinate press, academia and other communications players to use propaganda in their favor. Frank Wisner developed a relationship with the Washington Post's Phillip Graham to coordinate with the Press Industry. In 1951 Allen Dulles chose Cord Meyer of the CIA to be its principal operative.

"One of the most important journalists under the control of Opera-tion Mockingbird was Joseph Alsop, whose articles appeared in over 300 different newspapers. Other journalists willing to promote the views of the CIA included Stewart Alsop (New York Herald Tribune), Ben Bradlee (Newsweek), James Reston (New York Times), C. D. Jackson (Time Magazine), Walter Pincus (Washington Post),

Walter Winchell (New York Daily Mirror), Drew Pearson, Walter Lippmann, William Allen White, Edgar Mowrer (Chicago Daily News), Hal Hendrix (Miami News), Whitelaw Reid (New York Herald Tribune), Jerry O'Leary (Washington Star), William C. Baggs (Miami News), Herb Gold (Miami News) and Charles L. Bartlett (Chattanooga Times). According to Nina Burleigh, the author of A Very Private Woman (1998) these journalists sometimes wrote articles that were commissioned by Frank Wisner. The CIA also provided them with classified information to help them with their work."

"After 1953 the network was overseen by Allen W. Dulles, director of the Central Intelligence Agency. By this time Operation Mockingbird had a major influence over 25 newspapers and wire agencies. These organizations were run by people such as William Paley (CBS), Henry Luce (Time Magazine and Life Magazine), Arthur Hays Sulzberger (New York Times), Helen Rogers Reid (New York Herald Tribune), Dorothy Schiff (New York Post), Alfred Friendly (managing editor of the Washington Post), Barry Bingham (Louisville Courier-Journal) and James S. Copley (Copley News Services)."[101]

Media and the JFK Assassination

Jim DeBrosse in his book *See No Evil* presents an analysis of how the media is likely to write about the JFK assassination. Some of his findings are revealing:

"The author sectioned off the years 1988–2013 and then searched Lexis/Nexis in order to find rubrics like book reviews of the JFK case. One of the things he discovered was that pro-Warren Commission books are five times more likely to be reviewed than anti-Commis-

---

[101] https://spartacus-educational.com/JFKmockingbird.htm and https://www.carl-bernstein.com/the-cia-and-the-media-rolling-stone-10-20-1977

sion books.[102] 1) And of those reviews, about 65% of the former were positive, while over 90% of the latter were negative. That does not sound like a random pattern, does it? To give one example of why it doesn't: Jeff Morley was an MSM journalist for over 20 years, writing for publications like The New Republic, The Nation, and The Washington Post. Yet the author could not find an MSM review of his Our Man in Mexico, the only biography about Winston Scott, the CIA station chief in Mexico City in 1963."[103]

"Under every rubric the author searched for, published news stories, TV broadcasts, TV stories on JFK theories, etc., this statistic held strongly. For example, the ratio in news stories was 3–1 in favor of pro Commission stories. (Ibid, p. 53) In TV news broadcasts, it was 2–1. DeBrosse also notes that the major networks were worse than the cable channels."

"Addressing the two-week period in 2017, when President Donald Trump tweeted about releasing the last of the classified JFK documents, the author notes who the main televised interview subjects were. Philip Shenon made 23 appearances, Larry Sabato did 17, and Gerald Posner did 16. There was simply no balance, as Jeff Morley did 4 and John Newman did 1."[104] "With this kind of media bias, why does most of the public still think Kennedy was killed in a conspiracy? One of the most common techniques used to explain that divergence is the mantra that the reason the public does not buy the Warren Report is because Americans cannot accept the notion that someone as inconsequential as Oswald could end the life of someone as glamorous and powerful as President Kennedy. DeBrosse found this idea cited over 20 times in his studied time frame."[105]

---

[102] DeBrosse, pp. 50 – 5 and https://www.kennedysandking.com/john-f-kennedy-reviews/how-the-msm-blew-the-jfk-case-part-one
[103] Ibid., p 52
[104] Ibid., p 66
[105] Ibid., p. 69 and https://www.kennedysandking.com/john-f-kennedy-reviews/how-the-msm-blew-the-jfk-case-part-one

The following is an example of media manipulation:

Dan Rather, reported shortly after seeing the Zapruder Film that Kennedy's head could be seen moving violently forward.

In 1975, Seth Kantor learned that the records of one of his phone calls on the the day of the assassination was classified for reasons of national security. So he filed a Freedom of Information Act (FOIA) request and obtained the records to find out the big secret. He discovered that after talking to his editor, he was told to call another Scripps Howard news correspondent in Florida, Harold "Hal" Hendrix. From Florida, Hendrix supplied Kantor with detailed background information on Lee Harvey Oswald, who had just been arrested and named as the chief suspect in the assassination. Hendrix had more information in Florida than Kantor did at the scene of the crime. We later learned why Kantor's call to Hendrix was considered worthy of being classified for reasons of national security. Hal Hendrix, who won the Pulitzer Prize for his reporting on the Cuban Missile Crisis, was just one of many working journalists that David Atlee Phillips used as an asset in the course of coups and covert operations, from the Dominican Republic to Chile. And the Scripps-Howard News Service (SHNS) served as a network that distributed designated disinformation on behalf of the government intelligence agencies as part of the so-called "Mockingbird" network.[106]

One of the first international crises that faced Lyndon Johnson as President was a coup in the Dominican Republic, where David Atlee Phillips had just been assigned the new CIA Chief of Station. In September 1963 Hendrix had written about a regime change in a story that came out before it actually happened, and a scoop that earned Hendrix his nickname, "Spook."

After covering Latin American affairs for SHNS, Hendrix took a job in public relations with International Telephone and Telegraph (ITT), and was sent to Chile where another coup transpired, and where David Atlee Phillips was once again working on CIA operations in the country where

---

[106] https://spartacus-educational.com/JFKhendrixH.htm and https://spartacus-educational.com/JFKmockingbird.htm

he was originally recruited into the CIA while working as a newspaper publisher.

While it is today difficult to retrace what became public record and when, back in 1963, Hendrix's innate ability to be ahead of his colleagues and special contacts have raised many eyebrows.

New York Times coverage, was epitomized by the definitive headline of November 25, 1963, "President's Assassin Shot to Death in Jail Corridor by a Dallas Citizen." Thus, the *Times* required no Warren Commission to tell it what it had already assumed three days after the President's assassination: that Lee Harvey Oswald, the official suspect, was the assassin... Nor were Jack Ruby's motives any mystery to the *Times* as was demonstrated the same day by the headline, "Kennedy Admirer Fired One Bullet."[107]

"On 29th November, *Life Magazine* published a series of 31 photographs documenting the entire shooting sequence from the Zapruder film. It was only later discovered that the critical frames that depicted the rearward motion of Kennedy's head were transposed to indicate a forward motion."[108]

The following information is from "*A New Look at the Enigma of the Backyard Photographs*", Parts 1–3, Written by Jeff Carter at KennedysandKing "In early 1964, the backyard photo identified as 133-A was sold and/or released to several newspapers and magazines, resulting in wide public dissemination, most notably on the cover of Life Magazine's February 21 issue. The release of the photo was considered a serious breach of the Warren Commission's confidentiality, and the FBI was tasked with investigating 'how the press got hold of the photo.' The FBI responded energetically, focusing resources in numerous cities"... "The cover of the February 21 issue of Life single-handedly stamped the image of Oswald brandishing a rifle and militant socialist literature into the consciousness of millions of persons (several Warren Commission witnesses refer to 'the picture published in Life' when discussing a backyard

---

[107] New York Times, November 25, 1963, pp. 1–10—https://ratical.org/ratville/JFK/PA-NYT.htma#fn7
[108] https://spartacus-educational.com/JFKzapruderF.htm

photo). In Life's accompanying nine page 'clinical study' of Lee Oswald's biography, lone nut behavior patterns are emphasized, and left-wing connections identified."[109]

On June 1, 1964, the *New York Times* ran a Page One exclusive, "Panel to Reject Theories of Plot in Kennedy's Death." This amounted to an extensive preview of the Warren Report nearly four months, prior to its official release.

When the Warren Commission's report was issued on September 27, 1964, its most vocal advocate was The New York Times. The lead story said that "the commission analyzed every issue in exhaustive, almost archeological detail." A Times editorial said that "the facts—exhaustively gathered, independently checked and cogently set forth—destroy the basis for conspiracy theories that have grown weedlike in this country."[110]

The New York Times followed the March 1, 1969, acquittal of Clay L. Shaw—charged by New Orleans D.A. Jim Garrison with conspiring to assassinate the late President—with a renewed offensive against previous criticism of the Warren Report. An editorial on March 2 referred to Garrison's "obsessional conviction about the fraudulent character of the Warren Commission" as a "fantasy."

The News of the Week in Review that day carried a piece by Sidney Zion, "Garrison Flops on the Conspiracy Theory," which maintained, in essence, that Garrison had "restored the credibility of the Warren Report." The Times ignored the fact that the jury had been charged solely with the duty of determining the guilt or innocence of Mr. Shaw, not with determining the validity of the Warren Report.

"While the *Times* was busy selling the Warren Commission story, *Life* magazine went one step beyond that, actively intervening to spirit away crucial physical evidence in the case. Aside from swooping down on Oswald's wife and mother and sequestering them in a hotel room to protect *Life's* exclusive interviews, *Life* was in Dallas making arrange-

---

[109] https://www.kennedysandking.com/john-f-kennedy-articles/a-new-look-at-the-enigma-of-the-backyard-photographs-parts-1-3
[110] https://ratical.org/ratville/JFK/PA-NYT.htma#fn7

ments to buy the original Zapruder film only four hours after the assassination... According to Richard Stolley, who was the editorial director of Time Inc. and who handled the Zapruder transaction for *Life,* the order to acquire the film and 'withhold it from public viewing' came from Life's publisher, C. D. Jackson... The critical Zapruder film was kept exclusively in the hands of Time Inc. and out of the public's reach for the next 12 years, allowing Life to take the American people on one of the longest rides ever in American journalism... *Life's* December 6, 1963, edition gave a simple and conclusive explanation, based on the Zapruder film, an answer only *Life* could provide. Wrote *Life:* 'The 8 mm [Zapruder] film shows the President turning his body far around to the right as he waves to someone in the crowd. His throat is exposed to the sniper's nest just before he clutches it.' This description of the Zapruder film went a long way toward allaying fears of conspiracy in those early days, for it explained away a troublesome inconsistency in the lone assassin scenario. There was only one problem: The description of the Zapruder film was a total fabrication. Although the film shows Kennedy turning to the right—toward the grassy knoll, that is—at no time does he turn 180 degrees toward the book depository. Indeed, by the time he is hit, he is once again turning toward the front..."[111]

"For its 1966 documentary, in trying to determine whether Oswald could possibly have fired all the rounds believed to have been squeezed off in Dealey Plaza, CBS used a rifle that was faster than Oswald's: capable of three shots in 4.1 seconds as opposed to 4.6 seconds for Oswald's. The 11 CBS marksmen fired 37 firing runs of three shots each; of those, an amazing 17 of the 37 runs were disqualified as Cronkite said, 'because of trouble with the rifle.' And, even with their faster guns and time to practice, the 11 marksmen averaged 5.6 seconds to get off their three shots, with an average of 1.2 hits. Oswald, a notoriously bad shot firing with a slower gun, is alleged to have done much better—three shots and two direct hits in 5.6 seconds, with no warm-up. CBS neglected to inform its viewers of the poor total average hit ratio. How did

---

[111] https://www.kennedys-storyandking.com/john-f-kennedy-articles/jfk-how-the-media-assassinated-the-real

CBS interpret these rifle tests? 'It seems reasonable to say that an expert could fire that rifle in five seconds,' intoned Walter Cronkite. 'It seems equally reasonable to say that Oswald, under normal circumstances, would take longer. But these were not normal circumstances. Oswald was shooting at a president. So our answer is: probably fast enough.'... The article goes on to show how Warren Commissioner McLoy and his daughter Ellen (who worked for CBS), played a role in influencing CBS..."[112]

Writers Jerry Policoff and Robert Hennelly continued with:

"Even Johnny Carson was coached to attack Garrison: What Carson did was what Mort Sahl would not do on his show: a premeditated attack to prevent any elucidation and education of the public on the issues surrounding Kennedy's death. Carson had been thoroughly briefed, and NBC lawyers had interviewed Garrison in advance. The lawyers furnished Carson with cue cards as to how to question Garrison. But still, Garrison did fairly well and Carson came off like the hatchet man he was prepped to be. The host was very angry with Sahl for getting him into this sticky situation. Afterwards, he yelled at him: 'You will never be on my show again.'[113]

Carson kept his word. Sahl paid a stiff price for backing Jim Garrison. His career went into a steep decline."[114]

According to Gaeton Fonzi, author of *The Last Investigation,* Dick Sprague had made it obvious that he wanted to conduct an honest and independent investigation that would uncover the truth—whatever that may be. He knew that he could not rely on the same agencies that the Warren Commission had (i.e., the FBI and the CIA) as his investigators, since those very agencies might themselves be under suspicion. So he insisted on hiring his own

---

[112] https://www.kennedys-storyandking.com/john-f-kennedy-articles/jfk-how-the-media-assassinated-the-real

[113] See television appearance here -
https://www.youtube.com/watch?v=EZN2FGHKzQI

[114] https://www.kennedysandking.com/videos-and-interviews/mort-sahl-1970-interview

investigators. Pretty quickly the CIA began stonewalling the Committee's requests for information—especially those relating to Lee Harvey Oswald's alleged Mexico City sojourn—and insisting that Sprague sign a secrecy agreement which he refused to do, asking how he could "possibly sign an agreement with an agency I'm supposed to be investigating."[115] Instead, Sprague responded that he would subpoena the CIA for all relevant materials. What followed, predictably enough, was a media smear campaign led by Agency assets that essentially resulted in congress refusing to reauthorize the committee until Sprague was removed.

The HSCA quietly concluded there had, in fact, been at least one other gunman involved in the shooting and that this suggested a conspiracy of unknown order. Even though this meant that at least one assassin had gotten away scot-free, the report was not acted upon. No arrests were ever made. No further investigatory or judicial action was taken. The media reaction was, by now, predictable.

The Washington Post offered the following "likelihood" in response to the commission's findings of a "possible conspiracy" and evidence of a second gunman: *Could it have been some other malcontent whom Mr. Oswald met casually? Could not as many as three or four societal outcastes with no ties to any one organization have developed in some spontaneous way a common determination to express their alienation in the killing of President Kennedy? It is possible that two persons acting independently attempted to shoot the President at the very same time.*[116]

When Oliver Stone's 1991 film, *JFK* debuted. Jack Valenti of the Motion Picture Association of America compared the film to the Nazi propaganda classic *Triumph of the Will*. The assaults came from all angles. In fact, the *New York Times* published 30 articles during the first month the film was shown.[117]

---

[115] Gaeton Fonzi, The Last Investigation, p 217

[116] https://www.washingtonpost.com/archive/politics/1979/01/06/the-evidence-of-conspiracy/05e42933-23f4-4c60-a3b2-f7e0ea40a7ad/

[117] https://www.latimes.com/archives/la-xpm-1992-04-04-ca-175-story.html

The Sixth Floor Museum, for anyone who has visited it, including the authors of these writings, is known for its bias toward backing the lone-nut scenario despite all of the records we have described throughout our exposés. The late Gary Mack, who in 1994, became an archivist and later curator of the Sixth Floor Museum at Dealey Plaza in Dallas, was a vociferous backer of the Warren Commission findings.

As of November 2022, the museum presents a false graphical/video reproduction of the supposed view of what the motorcade would like from Oswald's alleged sniper's nest: It presents only two motorcycles adjacent to the presidential limousine that end up ahead of it when the deadly headshot hits Kennedy, which is in complete contradiction of the Zapruder film and ignores the blood spatter evidence that struck two of the motorcyclists who were to the left and behind the vehicle when this shot took place.

The CIA actually had a TDSB Sixth Floor Museum liaison (intelligence officer Charles A. Briggs) to help with its launch, according to his obituary.[118]

History Book writers are also pushing the lone nut scenario as well as painting JFK with an unfair Cold Warrior persona. Researcher, Paul Bleau, analyzed how history books present the assassination and interacted with the authors and here is some of what he discovered:

- Out of nineteen of the most popular North American History books;

- Four of the sources simply say that JFK was assassinated;

- One says that he was killed by a lone shooter;

- One only states that "it seemed unworthy that one misfit was involved";

---

[118] https://www.legacy.com/us/obituaries/washingtonpost/name/charles-briggs-obituary?id=6058654

- Six state that Lee Harvey Oswald assassinated the president;

- One states that Oswald most likely killed the president;

- Five do mention that some believe in a conspiracy. However all but one of these end up supporting the Lone Assassin scenario. Some of these make conspiracy backers out to be part of a fringe group or simply misguided;

- Two state that there is a lot of debate over the Warren Commission's conclusions;

- One history book states that Oswald went to Cuba;

- There is one critique of the Oliver Stone movie;

- The only investigation referred to by any of the history books is that of the Warren Commission (seven times).

History books are therefore clearly skewed toward portraying Lee Harvey Oswald as the lone assassin. There exists no evidence of analysis of post-Warren Commission investigations.

Answers to the author's questions revealed the following: it is clear that most are influenced by proponents of the lone assassin point of view: five mention the Warren Commission, four *Case Closed* by Posner, two Bugliosi's work, and three *A Cruel and Shocking Act* by Philip Shenon (which states that Oswald was a lone shooter but that he may have received guidance from Castro agents).

The Church Committee, HSCA and ARRB findings, and work by independent authors who present a case for a conspiracy and uncertainty around Oswald's involvement, these are clearly not referenced. In fact, they are nowhere to be found. Which is a bit surprising, if not startling.

For it seems to indicate that these authors do not go beyond the corporate press for their information.[119]

TODAY: TRUMP AND BIDEN BREAKING THE LAW

In 1992, the American public and assassination researchers worldwide experienced a watershed event on transparency and declassification of government assassination records. The U.S. Congress unanimously passed the John F. Kennedy Assassination Records Collection Act of 1992. Throughout this part of the chapter, we will refer to this law as the JFK Records Act.

The JFK Records Act officially became the law of the United States on October 26, 1992. Why did Congress take such strong action, and why was this a watershed moment for citizens seeking the truth about the Kennedy assassination?

Oliver Stone's 1991 film "JFK" was the driving force. That is putting it mildly. Stone's film focused on a conspiracy based out of New Orleans, investigated by Orleans Parish District Attorney Jim Garrison. The film was, of course, heavily criticized by the mainstream media and researchers who still held on to the Warren Commission's "lone nut" conclusion. The film was also applauded by millions worldwide and it sparked a renewed interest in the assassination. The film's ultimate theme was that JFK was killed because he refused to capitulate to the CIA, the Joint Chiefs and the Pentagon and refused to go to war in Cuba and Vietnam, and ultimately war against the Soviet Union. Kennedy refused to invade Cuba during the Bay of Pigs debacle, and he discovered the manipulation by the CIA in that operation. He refused to invade Cuba during the Cuban Missile Crisis. Kennedy refused to engage in nuclear war with the Soviet Union, and in fact had established a way to communicate with Khrushchev to avoid nuclear Armageddon. The film certainly got the attention of the American public and citizens worldwide, and its cinematic

---

[119] https://www.kennedysandking.com/john-f-kennedy-articles/the-jfk-assassination-according-to-the-history-textbooks-part-1

effect is undeniable. But the biggest impact is found in the film's epilogue.

In the final scenes of the film, Stone re-creates the trial against Clay
Shaw, the CIA asset who was allegedly involved in the conspiracy to
frame Lee Harvey Oswald for the assassination of President Kennedy.
Immediately following that scene, there was a powerful epilogue where
Stone discusses the status of assassination records at the time. Here
are excerpts from the epilogue that are most pertinent to this chapter:

> "In 1979, Richard Helms, Director of Covert Operations in 1963, ad-
> mitted under oath that Clay Shaw had worked for the CIA."
>
> "A congressional investigation from 1976 to 1979 found a prob-
> able conspiracy in the assassination of John F. Kennedy and recom-
> mended the Justice Department investigate further. As of 1991,
> the Justice Department has done nothing. The files of the House
> Select Committee on Assassinations are locked away until the
> year 2029."

The JFK film, and more importantly the epilogue, put tremendous
pressure on the U.S. Congress to take action. Within a year, Congress
passed the JFK Records Act in unanimous fashion. Even Oliver Stone
testified before the Congressional Committee. President Joe Biden, a
senator at the time, voted in favor of the JFK Records Act. President
George H. W. Bush signed the JFK Records Act into law.

Why would Congress act so strongly and swiftly in 1992, almost 30
years after the Kennedy Assassination? As discussed above, the epilogue in Stone's film mentioned the House Select Committee on Associations (HSCA). The HSCA concluded in early 1979 that there was a
probable conspiracy to assassinate President Kennedy. The HSCA referred the matter to the U.S. Justice Department for further investigation. As discussed above, regarding Stone's film, the Justice Department
did nothing. The film's epilogue also confirmed a staggering fact—that
records from the HSCA investigation would not be available to the public
until at least the year 2029.

So, it is obvious that Congress had to do something in response to the public outrage created by Stone's film. Its own committee (the HSCA) found that there was a probable conspiracy in the assassination. The Justice Department did nothing really. Technically, they referred the acoustic evidence developed by the HSCA to a panel which included, of all people, Luis Alvarez, an inveterate Warren Report supporter. The Ramsey Panel consequently attempted to debunk that evidence. (For an expose, See Josiah Thompson, *Last Second in Dallas*, p. 287) But more importantly, there was no congressional oversight after 1979 to ensure that the matter was properly investigated by the DOJ) In 1979, and even in the 1980s with a proper criminal investigation, the murder of John Kennedy could have been solved. Many key witnesses were still alive, and the HSCA took sworn statements from many persons suspected to have been involved in the assassination—or at least had knowledge of what happened.

As discussed above, Congress finally took strong action in 1992. That action would not have happened without Stone's "JFK" film and the public outrage that ensued. Why is the JFK Records Act so important for the public, why is it still a problem today, and why is it a chokehold?

On reading the JFK Records Act, one does not have to go past the first page of the statute to see what Congress declared and how strong the language is. The key provisions from Section 2 of the JFK Records Act are the following:

Section 2(a)(2), JFK Records Act: "all Government records concerning the assassination of President John F. Kennedy should carry a presumption of immediate disclosure, and all records should be eventually disclosed to enable the public to become fully informed about the history surrounding the assassination."

Section 2(a)(3), JFK Records Act: "Legislation is necessary to create an enforceable, independent, and accountable process for the public disclosure of such records."

407

Section 2(a)(4), JFK Records Act: "Legislation is necessary because congressional records related to the assassination of President John F. Kennedy would not otherwise be subject to public disclosure until at least the year 2029."

Section 2(a)(7): "most of the records related to the assassination of President John F. Kennedy are almost 30 years old, and only in the rarest cases is there any legitimate need for continued protection of such records."

This is what your Congress declared in 1992, 30 years ago, and with the strongest of language. Congress declared that records pertaining to the JFK assassination had already been unreasonably withheld from the public for 30 years. Even the CIA felt the JFK Records Act was a different breed of declassification law, that had the teeth to go much further than FOIA (Freedom of Information Act) or any previous effort to shed light on deep government secrets. In a 1998 internal CIA Memorandum titled *JFK Records Review—Lessons Learned*,[120] the CIA stated that, "The level of evidence required by the Board [the Assassination Records Review Board or ARRB] to postpone what was generally considered protectable information was extremely high and usually required documentation of 'current harm.' Defenses based on general principles such as official cover or sources and methods were not acceptable."

In 2022, after *another* 30 years, and in spite of the strongest possible legislation, the President and responsible agencies were still withholding almost 15,000 records that were relevant to the JFK Assassination. Many records are still withheld in full. Others have been "released" with significant redactions.

The JFK Records Act established and created the Assassination Records Review Board (ARRB). Upon the creation of the JFK Records Act, agencies and government offices were ordered to deliver all assassination records to the National Archives and Records Administration

---

[120] https://www.maryferrell.org/showDoc.html?do-cId=162816#relPageId=1&search=cia_lessons%20learned

(NARA). An assassination record is defined as any record related to the assassination of President Kennedy that was "created or made available for use by, obtained by, otherwise came into the possession of" (i) the Warren Commission; (ii) the Rockefeller Commission; (iii) the Church Committee; (iv) the Pike Committee; (v) the House Select Committee on Assassinations (HSCA); (vi) any executive agency; and (vii) and other office of the Federal Government, or any state or local law enforcement office that performed work in connection with the federal inquiry in the Kennedy assassination. For anyone looking to understand the full scope of the JFK Records Act and the work of the ARRB, the ARRB's Final Report is essential reading.[121]

The above-defined assassination records became known as the JFK Records Collection, or the "Collection." It was then the job of the ARRB, an independent body, to review the Collection and make legal determinations on which records might still qualify for classification under the standards of the JFK Records Act.

What are those standards? For an agency or government office to request continued classification, section 6 of the JFK Records Act put the burden of proof on the objecting agencies. The burden of proof is not on researchers and the American public to demonstrate why an assassination record(s) should be released. For agencies and government offices to make a proper legal case for continued classification and secrecy, they were required to provide the ARRB with *clear and convincing evidence* that:

a) the threat to the military defense, intelligence operations, or conduct of foreign relations posed by the public disclosure of the assassination (record) is of such gravity that it outweighs the public interest, and such public disclosure would reveal (i) an intelligence agent whose identify *currently* requires protection; (ii) an intelligence source or method; or (iii) any other matter *currently* relating to the military defense or intelligence operations, the disclosure of which would *demonstrably* impair national security.

[121] https://www.archives.gov/research/jfk/review-board/report

b) the disclosure of the record would reveal the identity of a *living person* who provided confidential information to the United States;

c) the disclosure of the record could constitute an unwarranted invasion of privacy;

d) the disclosure of the record would compromise the existence of a confidentiality agreement between a U.S. government agent and a cooperating individual or foreign government; or

e) the disclosure would reveal a security or protective procedure *currently* utilized by the Secret Service or other agency responsible for protecting government officials.

In other words, any agency still seeking classification (the CIA, FBI or Secret Service, to name a few) was required to provide the ARRB with demonstrably clear and convincing evidence based on the above standards from the JFK Records Act. If they did not, the ARRB had the legal authority to order the declassification of the assassination record. If there was some evidence warranting continued classification, the ARRB issued a final order recommending a date for final declassification. These Final Orders from the ARRB were contained in a form document called a "Final Determination Notification, under its statutory authority. These documents provided the unclassified reasons for postponement for each assassination record that disclosure was postponed in whole or in part, along with the ARRB's recommended date or triggering event for the release of said record.

To its credit, the ARRB did a tremendous amount of work from 1994 to 1998, releasing more than 2 million pages of assassination records. In 1998, however, the ARRB's authority had run its course according to its congressional mandate and the ARRB was dissolved in late September of 1998. NARA, and the American public, were then left with a Collection that still contained tens of thousands of classified records, totaling hundreds of thousands of pages. Agencies were required under the JFK Records Act to perform *periodic review* pursuant to the recommendations and Final Determinations of the ARRB in order to ensure timely declassification and release of the assassination records.

What happened after 1998? Virtually nothing. Without the independent ARRB to ensure that agencies and government offices continued their periodic review obligation, it was up to NARA to hope that agencies and government offices would finish the work on declassification. The intent of Congress is that maybe 1% (or less) of the Collection could plausibly still require classification as of 2017; again, "most of the records related to the assassination of President John F. Kennedy are almost 30 years old, and only in the rarest cases is there any legitimate need for continued protection of such records." That declaration was made in 1992! Reflect on that for a moment.

October 26, 2017, was in fact the deadline for final declassification. Section 5(g)(2)(d) of the JFK Records Act required the President (Trump at the time) to take specific action to ensure that Congress's mandate to release all assassination records by the deadline was completed. We are all aware of Trump's tweets in which he committed to the final release of all assassination records on the eve of this deadline in 2017.

The President only has authority to authorize continued classification of an assassination record if he certifies that "each" specific record continues to pose an *identifiable harm* to the military defense, intelligence operations, law enforcement, or conduct of foreign relations, *as required by the Act*; and that such identifiable harm is of such gravity that it outweighs the public interest in disclosure. In other words, the President is required to make decisions with regard to each assassination record under the same constraints and authority as the ARRB. The President was therefore required to finish the ARRB's job by October 26, 2017, or provide published unclassified reasons, based on clear and convincing evidence **for each assassination record** under the criteria set out in section 6 of the JFK Records Act, as outlined in detail above.

What happened instead? President Trump initially issued an <u>Executive Memorandum</u>[122] on October 26, 2017, delaying the release of assassination records. This order was illegal and did not comply with the clear standards of the JFK Records Act. Trump's first order in October 2017 authorized a 6-month delay for agencies and governments to continue their review of assassination records and make recommendations to Trump by April 2018. Then it got even worse. On April 26, 2018, President Trump issued another Executive Memorandum authorizing another delay of over three (3) years.[123]

Trump's Executive Memorandum prompted reactions by Thomas Samoluk and Judge John Tuenheim of the ARRB:

Samoluk: "It is really frustrating what has happened. Because the law said that anything that was not released ... needed to be released under the law by October 26, 2017. Now there is a clause that says if the president certifies, under certain conditions, that the records would not be released. I don't think the process under the law was followed. The records have not been released in total, and I don't think any good reasons have been given."

Judge John Tunheim: "The information (non-declassified documents) was intended to be released in 2017. Only under extreme circumstances was a president in 2017 supposed to continue to protect records. And they didn't, as near as I can tell, they didn't provide that certification."[124]

In October of 2021, President Biden continued the trend of his predecessor, which is extremely troubling. President Biden issued another <u>Executive Memorandum</u> giving agencies and government offices until December 15, 2022, to make final decisions on the release of assassination records.[125] In his Memorandum, President Biden has empowered agencies and government offices to make their <u>own</u> decisions on declassification. This is exactly the <u>opposite</u> of how the JFK Records Act was

---

[122] https://public-inspection.federalregister.gov/2017-23795.pdf

[123] https://public-inspection.federalregister.gov/2018-09392.pdf

[124] DiEugenio, JFK Revisited, pp. 341–350

[125] https://public-inspection.federalregister.gov/2021-23563.pdf

intended to work. Like both of President Trump's Memoranda, President Biden's Executive Memorandum is also unlawful. But things would get even worse.

In the waning hours of the evening of Friday, June 30, 2023, long after the filing deadlines of the media elite in Washington, D.C., and even longer after the most dedicated talking head had left to celebrate their July 4th independence from tyranny in the Hamptons, the Biden Administration issued an Executive Memorandum that is a flagrant and illegitimate attempt to terminate an Act of Congress and usurp congressional authority over its own processes and records.[126] A copy of President Biden's Executive Memorandum is here.[127]

It is unclear what truly prompted President Biden to take a flamethrower to an Act of Congress that he himself voted for in 1992 as a member of the Senate, due to bipartisan public pressure to release records related to the 1963 assassination of President John F. Kennedy. It is further perplexing that Biden has chosen to continue to deny the American public transparency into the death of a much admired predecessor since he has chosen to surround himself in the White House with artwork memorializing the Kennedys e.g., the bust of Robert F. Kennedy in the Oval Office and the famous portrait of JFK by Jamie Wyeth that President Biden specifically requested to be borrowed from the Museum of Fine Arts in Boston to hang in his private White House study.

Congress was abundantly clear that the purpose of the JFK Records Act was to publicly disclose all records related to the assassination of President Kennedy through an enforceable process of downgrading and declassification. In all but the "rarest of cases" was any assassination record to be kept secret beyond the final deadline for release on October 26, 2017. It therefore defies both reason and Congress that two presi-

---

[126] https://www.kennedysandking.com/john-f-kennedy-articles/the-biden-cia-attempt-to-usurp-congress-authority-over-jfk-records The Biden/CIA Attempt to Usurp Congress's Authority Over JFK Records, KennedysandKing, July 2023, Written by Andrew Iler

[127] https://www.whitehouse.gov/briefing-room/presidential-actions/2023/06/30/memorandum-on-certifications-regarding-disclosure-of-information-in-certain-records-related-to-the-assassination-of-president-john-f-kennedy-2/

dents, the Archivist, NARA, and a number of executive agencies have determined that the standards for continuing postponement of the with-held assassination records have somehow become less onerous now after that deadline for release and after 60 years have passed.

The government continues to operate under the findings of the War-ren Commission, which is that Lee Harvey Oswald acted alone in the assassination and with no confederates. That Commission also con-cluded that Jack Ruby assassinated Oswald on his own and with no as-sociates. The House Select Committee on Assassinations (HSCA) con-cluded in 1978 that there was a probable conspiracy in the Kennedy as-sassination and referred the matter to the U.S. Justice Department for further investigation. However, the Justice Department has done nothing to further investigate the murder of the 35th President of the United States. If Oswald did act alone, or even if he acted with other alleged "pro-Castro sympathizers," why the continued secrecy? One can only assume that the thousands of withheld records will show a U.S. Intelli-gence connection to Oswald, which was covered up immediately after the assassination and is still being covered up.

There is no reasonable or legal reason to continue the sixty (60) years of government secrecy regarding the Kennedy assassination. That is why this issue is a chokehold. The more that time goes on, it becomes more and more obvious that, in all probability, the government is cover-ing up a domestic intelligence operation that backfired in Dallas, or even worse, a calculated plan by intelligence assets and the Pentagon to re-move President Kennedy from office in a way that would deter future presidents from trying to actually manage U.S. domestic and foreign pol-icy.

CONCLUSION

This chapter is by far the longest of the whole book. Despite attempts by the authors to summarize, it was impossible to cover the obfuscation, media and history book manipulation and breaches in the law over sixty years, taking place through multiple investigations in a shorter exposé.

414

For this chokehold, the most vocal objectors are the investigators themselves. The ARRB, HSCA and Church Committee all lambaste the job done by the intelligence agencies as well as the Warren Commission performance and they shred the reliability of its conclusions. Since the impeached Warren Commission investigation was the only one to conclude that Oswald alone was responsible for the murder of President JFK, backers of the lone nut theory do not have a leg to stand on. History book writers use the Warren Commission final report as their go to source to back up the writings. Written in 1964, superseded by many other government investigations that followed over 60 years that impeached it, the Warren Commission Report and its 26 Volumes are not even worth the paper it was written on.

The questions readers should ask themselves are:

1. Why are young students, sixty years later, still being fed this contrived demonstrably false whitewash of a narrative that dishonors the U.S. Fourth Estate and takes its citizens for fools?

2. What is there to hide?

3. Who are these people still propping up a factually unsupported official narrative?

Critical thinking can only lead to one inescapable conclusion: The fact that there was a conspiracy in the JFK assassination that has been covered up for sixty years!

CONCLUSION

BY JAMES DiEUGENIO

THIS BOOK IS not a narrative style book about the John Kennedy assassination. That is, it does not try to tell the reader who killed the president, how they did it, and why. This is a book about the most current and strongest evidence in the case and how for sixty years powerful individuals and agencies have actively obstructed justice and intentionally suppressed critical evidence from entering the public domain – and have done so without consequences, thereby participating in a massive cover up.

In the Introduction, lawyer Andrew Iler sketched out different standards of proof in the law. He then explained how the "beyond a reasonable doubt" standard originated, and why it is used in criminal cases like homicides, which the Kennedy case was. As Andrew notes, one reason it is the highest standard in the law is that the public should not be left in doubt about innocent men having their rights, liberty and, perhaps their lives, taken away unjustly. Andrew also noted that this high standard has to be sustained about "every fact necessary to constitute the crime...." That is, there cannot be any breaks in the chain of custody or that evidence will be declared inadmissible. Without standards of proof, the legal process becomes ersatz, not being able to "withstand the mildest level of public scrutiny."

Neither the Warren Commission nor the House Select Committee on Assassinations (HSCA) employed such a "reasonable doubt" standard. Or, in fact, any legal standard. And neither allowed the accused, Lee Oswald, any representative to provide for a defense. Oswald was convicted in absentia and without legal representation.

This book has ten chapters, each dealing with a defined subject.

Each chapter, taken as a whole, would provide a strong basis for a reasonable doubt of Oswald's guilt, or on the flipside would demonstrate the existence of clear and convincing evidence of a conspiracy. For instance, in chapter 9, we present Malcolm Perry's conversation with reporter Martin Steadman, in which the Parkland doctor describes a clear case of attempted witness intimidation, one which would remove evidence of Oswald's innocence. That chapter also contains Josiah Thompson's blood spatter analysis, which clearly indicates that Kennedy was hit from the front and to his right. Third, we present evidence that the fragmentation pattern in Kennedy's skull is representative of a shot from the front. We do this based on a forensic rule put forth by the Warren Commission and HSCA's own expert, Larry Sturdivan. This chapter, in and of itself, provides both reasonable doubt of Oswald's guilt and clear and convincing evidence of at least another shooter from the front in this case. For how could Oswald shoot Kennedy from the front, if he was behind the motorcade. This is why we call this a chokehold.

But taken as whole, the book shows that the case against Oswald holds more than reasonable doubt. That current JFK case consists of a virtual tidal wave of doubt, and on more than one level. Let us describe each chokehold, as there is more than one way such strangulation by evidence can be performed.

Chapter 1 shows a formidable list of investigatory insiders who either disagreed with the official story at the time or came into disagreement. These disagreements were based on significant evidentiary issues. This included FBI agents Jim Sibert and Frank O'Neill, autopsy photographer John Stringer, Warren Commissioners Richard Russell, John Sherman Cooper, Hale Boggs and Gerald Ford, senators Gary Hart and Richard Schweiker, Dallas Police Chief Jesse Curry, the HSCA's first Chief Counsel Richard Sprague and his Deputy Bob Tanenbaum, HSCA Mexico City investigators Dan Hardway and Ed Lopez, ARRB investigators Jeremy Gunn and Doug Horne, plus the intelligence branches of the governments of Cuba, France and Russia. Which makes quite an impressive list.

Chapter 2 deals with the evidence that Oswald was not a communist, but some kind of intelligence asset. Again, we do this with insiders. This includes CIA officials Jane Roman and William Kent; the latter termed Oswald a "useful idiot". But thirdly, we refer to the revolutionary work of HSCA investigator Betsy Wolf, which had to wait for the declassification process of the ARRB to be exposed to the light of day. That work indicates that Oswald's CIA file was being rigged at the time he left for Russia. If Oswald was an intelligence agent this alters the whole equation of his life—and death.

Chapter 3 explains, in a comprehensive manner, how Oswald was impersonated numerous times – all the way up *to the day of Kennedy's assassination*. This includes supporting witnesses to Deputy Sheriff Roger Craig, like Marvin Robinson and Roy Cooper. In the weeks up to the assassination, we examine credible witnesses to someone impersonating Oswald at shooting ranges, gun shops, car purchase transactions, and at Red Bird Airfield south of Dallas. Why would such systematic events be happening?

Chapter 4 presents the case that Oswald could not have been on the 6th floor of the Texas School Book Depository at the proper time to kill President Kennedy. This chapter shows the problems with witnesses Howard Brennan and Charles Givens, both of whom testified before the Commission. It then presents the exculpatory evidence of Lillian Mooneyham, Carolyn Arnold, Victoria Adams, Sandy Styles and Dorothy Garner. Four of those five *did not* testify before the Commission. Why not?

Chapter 5 describes the life, character and the highly suggestive actions of Jack Ruby on the weekend of the assassination. For example, the HSCA analyzed a long series of phone calls Ruby made in the months leading up to Kennedy's murder, none of which seemed consistent with Ruby's excuse of a local union dispute. In fact, one was hit man Lenny Patrick out of Chicago. There was credible evidence Ruby met with Santo Trafficante, one of the Dons the CIA hired to kill Castro; further he tried to free Trafficante from Cuba with help from gunrunner Robert McKeown. There was also credible evidence Ruby was running guns into Cuba with CIA operative Donald Browder.

Chapter 6 details some of the prior plots to kill Kennedy and how neither the Warren Commission nor the FBI took note of these for a comparative case analysis. The repeated use of the Fair Play for Cuba Committee was quite obvious. And the plot to kill Kennedy in Chicago pretty much screamed out for this kind of comparison, and in more than one way, since it so closely resembled what happened in Dallas.

Chapter 7 goes over some of the very serious questions about Kennedy's autopsy. Dr. Pierre Finck's stunning testimony at the trial of Clay Shaw revealed who really controlled the proceedings at Bethesda that night. We also deal with the controversy of who took the official autopsy photos, was it Robert Knudsen? And in one of the strongest pieces of evidence, we declare the very high improbability that the official weight of Kennedy's brain—1500 grams—cannot be feasible.

Chapter 8 deals with the mythology of CE 399, commonly called the Magic Bullet. We include Arlen Specter's confession to Edward Epstein that he created it, not from the evidence, but out of necessity. The FBI clearly lied about agent Bardwell Odum showing the exhibit to various witnesses for identification purposes for the Warren Commission – since he denied doing this to Gary Aguilar and Josiah Thompson. Third, we show that the official record reveals that the exhibit was at the FBI lab well over an hour before it was even delivered to the Bureau in Washington.

Chapter 10 deals with the wide variety of attempts to obstruct investigations in the case. This began with President Johnson's Doomsday warning to Chief Justice Earl Warren about the specter of atomic holocaust due to a war with Russia – which clearly influenced Chief Justice Warren and his conduct of the Commission's work. It also deals with how the FBI fixed the polygraph test of Jack Ruby. And third, how HSCA investigators wanted to indict David Phillips and Anne Goodpasture for perjury due to their false testimony about Oswald in Mexico City before that committee. These are all examples of how the evidence in this case has been seriously compromised and justice obstructed. How can justice be served under these conditions? Does this not necessitate the need for a new inquiry? A president was killed in broad daylight, amid hundreds of witnesses, yet the wheels of justice were stalled from the start.

And these are just highlights in a larger mosaic. Taken as a totality, this presentation goes beyond raising a reasonable doubt of Oswald's guilt or demonstrating clear and convincing evidence of a conspiracy. It raises serious questions about how the American Establishment simply cannot deal with the true facts of the Kennedy assassination. Oswald did not have a lawyer when he was alive. He was refused one during the Warren Commission. (See Commission Exhibit 2033) The HSCA did not provide him one. What this meant was that, for all intents and purposes, for the first 16 years of the JFK case, no one in the mainstream media presented Oswald's case to the public or was in a position to question the government's lop-sided pre-determined script. Combined with the obstructions, is that not a disgraceful record?

Major challenges to the government's narrative happened in 1975 when the Zapruder film was first shown to the public on Geraldo Rivera's Good Night America and again in 1991 with the release of Oliver Stone's JFK.. Once these challenges started, the resulting forces have caused a seismic shift in the public perception of its government. By the time Oliver Stone's film *JFK* opened in December of 1991, it had been attacked in the press continually for seven months previous. This was unprece-dented in the history of cinema. For how can one criticize a film without seeing it? This indicated not an aesthetic or intellectual judgment, but a socio-political one, one designed to maintain the status quo. The Powers That Be had sold their souls to the Warren Report back in 1964,and they did not notice that a bit over three months after the Commission volumes were issued, President Lyndon Johnson sent the first combat troops to Vietnam. Something Kennedy had repeatedly refused to do. Stone's film not only undermined the Warren Report, it also pointed out that Johnson reversed Kennedy's Vietnam policy, leading to an enormous military de-bacle in Indochina. To put it mildly, the establishment did not like that. Rather than admit they were wrong, which they were, they decided to pillory Stone.

But there was one point in Stone's film that no one could argue about.

During the film's end titles, a caption appeared which stated that the files of the last inquiry into Kennedy's murder, the HSCA, were locked away until 2029. That message ignited a firestorm of public outrage. Why would the government do such a thing? This provoked hearings on Capitol Hill, during which several luminaries—including Oliver Stone—testified before congress. Legislation was passed, which we refer to in this book, and the Assassination Records Review Board was set up and operated from 1994-98.

The ARRB declassified about 2 million pages of documents. They even did their own inquiry into the Kennedy autopsy. Some of the things they uncovered—which the authors discuss-- should have been front page news. But as Chairman John Tunheim noted in Stone's documentary *JFK Revisited,* they worked in relative anonymity.

If that were not bad enough, things got worse after the ARRB disbanded. That Board did not have enough time to fulfill its mandate. There were literally thousands of records still classified. According to the JFK Act there was supposed to be a periodic review with the passage of time as to when they could be opened to the public. There was very little of that done. But, as everyone knew, the final disclosure date was in October of 2017. Everything was to be let go then. President Trump even tweeted about this in advance, it was an event he was looking forward to.

On the day this was supposed to occur—Thursday, October 26, 2017—Trump backed down. He then set up a 6-month hiatus that put everything on hold. In direct defiance of the law, he failed to issue any explanation as to why he was refusing to declassify the rest of the documents.[1] Trump then did something worse. He now added on a 3-year extension, which would actually extend past his presidency.

When Joe Biden was in the senate, he voted for the JFK Records Collection Act in 1992. It is almost unfathomable as to why he has now chosen to pretty much vitiate the act he voted for. As Mark and Andrew Iler described in a landmark article, on the evening of June 30, 2023, in

---

[1] See "JFK Assassination Records—the Picture is Getting Clearer" by Mark Adamczyk, 8/04/2021 at *Kennedysandkingcom*

a Friday night news dump, the White House announced that it was, for all intents and purposes, doing away with the JFK Act of 1992.[2]

With this executive order Biden stated that *he* had made "final certi-fication". And such was "the last required under the Act". As attorney Andrew Iler has demonstrated, what Biden did was a complete ransacking of the JFK Act. Neither he nor Trump provide any identification aids to the documents they were withholding. Neither man provided a written, unclassified rationale for that withholding, which was to be published in the Federal Register. President Biden even wants to control documents not produced by the executive branch, for example those involving congressional inquiries.

But further, Biden now changed the standard of proof, and the actual process for withholding the last documents—which is now thought to be about 4,000 in number. The JFK Act stated that to withhold a document one must provide "clear and convincing evidence" that the document will endanger national security. Biden changed this to "except when the strongest possible reasons counsel otherwise". Which is not a standard of proof recognized anywhere. Finally, Biden is trying to dodge the final declassification process of the last documents by turning those decisions over to a panel called the National Declassification Center under the advice of plans proffered by the executive intelligence agencies. (See Section 5 of Biden's June 30, 2023 executive order.) This is where we are in 2023, six years after the law stated everything on the JFK case was to be opened to the public.

Somehow President Biden is supposed to be unaware of how this turns the law he voted for in 1992 upside down. Or that what he is proposing is how this problem of secrecy in the JFK case originated in the first place. Six decades later, this is just the latest cover up and obstruction of justice in the rather sickening legacy of President Kennedy's assassination.

This is why this case cries out for a new investigation.

---

[2] "The Biden /CIA Attempt to Usurp Congress' Authority over JFK Records", July 21, 2023, *Kennedysandking.com*

INDEX

544 Camp, 3, 94, 105, 106, 107, 115, 116, 219, 220

Adams, Bill, 199

Adams, Victoria, 165, 174, 175, 177, 179, 341, 418

Aguilar, Gary, 35, 244, 246, 267, 270, 286, 300, 302, 327, 348, 349, 383, 384, 385, 419

Albert Schweitzer College, 95

Alpha 66, 60, 66, 89

Alsop, Joseph, 394

Alsop, Stewart, 394

Alvarez, Luis, 407

AM/LASH, 341

American Historical Association, 1, 92

Andrews, Dean, 116

Angleton, James, 43, 44, 82, 334, 363, 365, 375

Area 51, 162

Arlen Specter, 7, 30, 32, 33, 38, 66, 246, 257, 258, 259, 342, 419

Arnold, Carolyn, 165, 173, 174, 177, 179, 180, 418

ARRB (Assassination Records Review Board), 10, 17, 23, 24, 32, 33, 35, 38, 43, 44, 53, 79, 80, 81, 82, 84, 85, 86, 90, 91, 101, 198, 211, 213, 234, 240, 244, 245, 247, 248, 250, 251, 252, 253, 254, 256, 292, 301, 303, 305, 314, 318, 319, 321, 322, 323, 327, 330, 334, 342, 347, 349, 352, 363, 366,369, 370, 385, 386, 387, 388, 389, 404, 408, 409, 410, 411, 412, 415, 417, 418, 421

Arther, Richard, 361

Arthus, James, 107

Ashkenasy, Ernest, 64, 65

Atsugi, 95, 96, 208

Aynesworth, Hugh, 371

Baggs, William C., 395

Bagley, Peter, 94

Baker, Barney, 189

Baker, Marion, 3, 164, 165, 169, 170, 171, 172, 174, 176, 177, 179, 180, 221

Banister, Guy, 53, 63, 94, 105, 106, 107, 108, 115, 118, 119, 120, 124, 154, 201, 220, 372

Bartlett, Charles L., 395

Bashour, Fouad, 34, 308

Bastien, R., 389

Bates, Paulina Virginia, 123

Baxter, Charles, 34, 308, 311, 326

Bay of Pigs, 66, 150, 228, 245, 405

Belin, David, 8, 31, 54, 64, 330, 372, 373, 374

Bell, Audrey, 34, 287, 288, 309, 311, 326

Belmont, Alan, 269, 335

Bertrand, Clay, 48, 108

Bethesda, 7, 32, 34, 35, 36, 47, 81, 240, 241, 243, 244, 250, 253, 274, 288, 304, 305, 306, 308, 309, 315, 316, 318, 327, 341, 350, 368, 369, 376, 385, 419

Biden, 1, 4, 5, 331, 406, 412, 413, 421, 422

Bingham, Barry, 395

Bishop, Maurice, 60, 66

Black Op Radio, 68, 78, 285

Black, Edwin, 206

Blackmer, Jonathan, 50

Blahut, Regis, 380

Blakey, Robert, 65, 66, 73, 75, 78, 122, 143, 185, 186, 190, 285, 296, 327, 362, 380, 382

Bleau, Paul, 1, 2, 5, 1, 79, 124, 147, 218, 266, 403

Blunt, Malcolm, 3, 94, 97, 99, 100, 104

Bogard, Albert, 141, 142

Boggs, Hale, 42, 114, 147, 417

Bolden, Abraham, 210

Bolton Ford, 154

Boring, Floyd, 153

Boston, 284, 413

Boswell, Thornton, 33, 34, 84, 85, 243, 245, 250, 253, 305, 309, 317, 319, 321, 322, 325, 342, 345, 348, 349, 368, 369, 370

Bowe, Walter Augustus, 230

Bowers, Lee, 282, 283, 296

Bowron, Diana, 34, 250, 309

Bowron, Diana Hamilton, 311

Boyers, Chester, 34, 309

Braden, Jim, 189

Bradford, Dewey, 140

Bradlee, Ben, 394

Brady, Surell, 121

Breckinridge, Scott, 76, 77

Brennan, Howard, 164, 166, 167, 168, 177, 180, 418

Briggs, Charles A., 403

Bringuier, Carlos, 114, 123, 124, 125, 126

Brown, Oran, 141

Buchen, Philip, 374

Bugliosi, Vincent, 6, 267

Burke, Arleigh, 184

Burkley, George, 36, 38, 243, 246, 251, 290, 307, 327, 341

Burleigh, Nina, 395

Burroughs, Butch, 144, 145

Bush, George H.W., 82, 376, 386, 406

Butler, Ed, 124, 126

Cairns, A.B., 290

Campisi, Joe, 190

Canning, Thomas, 267

Capote, Truman, 103

Carcano, 31, 138, 140, 215, 216, 217, 267, 272, 342

Carney, Ray, 155

Carrico, Charles, 34, 286, 308, 311, 326

Carson, Johnny, 401

Carter, Jeff, 398

Castro, Fidel, 9, 40, 44, 53, 54, 56, 57, 60, 62, 66, 69, 75, 76, 78, 86, 88, 89, 103, 105, 106,

108, 114, 115, 118, 119, 121,
126, 127, 149, 150, 155, 156,
158, 163, 182, 183, 184, 187,
190, 191, 192, 201, 204, 209,
212, 213, 214, 219, 221, 222,
225, 228, 229, 230, 231, 232,
235, 237, 330, 333, 340, 341,
361, 374, 404, 414, 418
Cheney, Dick, 54, 376
Cheramie, Rose, 50, 51, 52
Chesser, Michael, 302
Chesser, Mike, 369
Chicago, 57, 105, 118, 185, 197,
206, 207, 208, 210, 211, 212,
213, 216, 221, 225, 232, 234,
235, 365, 395, 418, 419
Chile, 9, 375, 397
Church Committee, 9, 38, 54, 55,
56, 58, 59, 66, 93, 115, 184,
233, 331, 332, 335, 336, 337,
340, 355, 357, 361, 364, 372,
374, 375, 376, 377, 404, 409,
415
Church, Frank, 9, 54, 124
CIA, 3, 8, 9, 10, 40, 41, 42, 43,
44, 53, 54, 55, 56, 57, 58, 59,
60, 64, 65, 66, 67, 68, 69, 71,
72, 74, 75, 78, 80, 81, 82, 86,
88, 89, 94, 96, 97, 98, 99, 100,
101, 102, 105, 106, 108, 115,
118, 123, 125, 126, 127, 146,
156, 157, 158, 159, 160, 161,
162, 163, 184, 187, 188, 192,
195, 201, 202, 204, 209, 211,
212, 213, 214, 217, 219, 220,
222, 230, 231, 232, 233, 330,
332, 333, 334, 340, 341, 344,
361, 362, 363, 364, 365, 367,
372, 373, 374, 375, 376, 377,
378, 379, 380, 381, 382, 386,
390, 394, 396, 397, 401, 403,
405, 406, 408, 410, 413, 418,
422
Cincinnati, 355
Civello, Joseph, 190
Civil Air Patrol, 107
Clark Panel, 247, 301, 302, 347,
366, 367, 368, 369, 370
Clark, Kemp, 34, 240, 308, 326
Clark, Mark, 211
Clark, Ramsey, 247, 366, 368
Clement, Bob, 199
Clement, Frank, 199
Cobb, June, 230, 237
Cody, Joe, 34, 309
COINTELPRO, 105
College Park, Maryland, 33, 83,
147, 370
Collier, Robert Steele, 230
Communist Party, 116, 117, 118,
202, 205, 225, 229, 235
Congo, 9
Connally, John, 29, 30, 33, 35,
38, 41, 42, 45, 65, 257, 258,
260, 261, 262, 263, 264, 265,
271, 272, 273, 286, 308, 353,
354, 368
Connick, Harry, 81, 386
Conzelman, Jim, 315
Cooper, John, 42, 130, 131, 344,
417, 418
Copley, James S., 395
Corbin, Michael, 66
Cormier, Frank, 291
Cornwell, Gary, 70
Courson, James, 34, 309
Couteau, Rob, 288
Crafard, Larry, 343
Craig, Roger, 20, 30, 31, 125,
129, 131, 132, 162, 418

Crenshaw, Charles, 34, 286, 306, 307, 308, 326
Cronkite, Walter, 46, 400, 401
Cuba, 9, 11, 53, 58, 64, 86, 88, 89, 92, 94, 97, 100, 102, 103, 104, 105, 106, 107, 108, 109, 114, 117, 118, 119, 121, 130, 142, 148, 149, 150, 154, 155, 156, 157, 183, 184, 187, 191, 201, 202, 204, 212, 214, 215, 219, 221, 222, 224, 225, 228, 229, 230, 231, 232, 235, 237, 332, 340, 404, 405, 417, 418, 419
Cuban Revolutionary Council, 105, 106
Curry, Jesse, 31, 279, 292, 327, 417
Curtis, Don, 34, 308
Curtis, James, 34, 250, 309
Custer, Jerrol, 34, 309
Czechoslovakia, 222, 223
Dabbs, Charlie, 153
Dale, Alan, 100
Dallas, 7, 2, 18, 21, 25, 30, 31, 33, 34, 35, 50, 51, 52, 61, 62, 67, 76, 87, 88, 89, 94, 105, 118, 123, 124, 130, 132, 133, 134, 136, 139, 140, 142, 144, 145, 146, 148, 149, 151, 152, 153, 155, 159, 160, 161, 162, 163, 165, 168, 173, 175, 178, 183, 185, 186, 187, 189, 190, 191, 192, 194, 201, 204, 206, 207, 209, 210, 211, 213, 217, 225, 227, 233, 234, 240, 242, 246, 250, 258, 259, 260, 261, 270, 271, 272, 277, 279, 280, 288, 292, 302, 307, 308, 327, 331, 332, 335, 342, 346, 355, 356, 357, 372, 385, 398, 399, 403, 407, 414, 417, 418, 419
David, Dennis, 34, 309
Davis, Benjamin, 116
Davy, William, 330, 366
Day, J.C., 178
de Gaulle, Charles, 86
de Mohrenschildt, George, 72, 124, 125, 341
De Santi, Louis, 231
Dealey Plaza, 30, 66, 79, 130, 131, 141, 148, 162, 165, 171, 189, 213, 275, 276, 277, 278, 289, 296, 300, 371, 400, 403
Dean, Harry, 103, 220, 232, 237
Dearborn, 355
DeBrosse, Jim, 395
DeBrueys, Warren, 114, 115
Del Valle, Eladio, 53
Detroit, 118, 221
Dick Cheney, 373
Diem, 9
DiEugenio, James, 4, 96, 114, 211, 372, 378
DiMaio, Vincent, 369
Dobbs House, 135, 136
Dobrynin, Anatoly, 147
Dodd, Richard, 279
Dolan, James Henry, 189, 190
Dolce, Joseph, 262, 341
Dominican Republic, 9, 397
Doolittle, Paul, 387
Dorman, Elsie, 341
Dorman, George, 245, 254
Douglass, James, 102, 131, 132, 133, 134, 142, 144, 146, 169, 171, 172, 173, 177, 206, 208, 210, 211
Dowling, Mary, 136
Drain, Vincent, 34, 178, 309

DRE (Student Revolutionary Directorate), 44, 67, 69, 75, 76, 77, 94, 114, 123, 125, 126, 330, 333, 382

Dresch, Roger, 217

Duclos, Michelle, 230

Dudman, Richard, 291

Duke, James, 34, 308

Dulany, Richard, 34, 308

Dulles, Allen, 7, 9, 18, 42, 54, 55, 68, 125, 213, 259, 260, 329, 333, 334, 339, 341, 365, 371, 374, 394, 395

Duran, Sylvia, 157, 158

Ebersole, John, 34, 309, 316, 318, 319, 369

Einspruch, Burton, 150, 151

Eisenberg, Melvin, 338

Eisenhower, Dwight, 90

El Chico Restaurant, 145, 146

Ellis, Starvis, 291

England, 95

Epstein, Edward, 257, 419

Ernest, Barry, 175, 179

Escalante, Fabian, 88, 89

Euins, Amos, 169, 172

Fair Play for Cuba, 104, 107, 114, 130, 154, 191, 224

Fannin, Gary, 31

FBI, 9, 28, 30, 32, 34, 38, 40, 41, 42, 44, 45, 46, 51, 54, 55, 56, 57, 59, 67, 70, 71, 74, 81, 82, 84, 85, 91, 93, 94, 96, 100, 103, 104, 105, 106, 107, 108, 114, 115, 118, 125, 127, 130, 133, 134, 135, 136, 140, 142, 143, 146, 148, 149, 150, 151, 152, 154, 155, 156, 158, 159, 160, 161, 164, 167, 168, 169, 170, 171, 173, 175, 177, 178, 179, 180, 183, 184, 185, 192, 193, 195, 200, 202, 205, 206, 210, 211, 214, 215, 216, 217, 219, 220, 221, 222, 224, 225, 229, 230, 231, 233, 234, 245, 250, 259, 260, 262, 265, 267, 268, 269, 270, 272, 274, 277, 279, 281, 284, 286, 290, 309, 311, 327, 331, 332, 333, 334, 335, 336, 337, 339, 340, 341, 342, 343, 344, 349, 353, 354, 355, 356, 357, 361, 362, 363, 364, 366, 368, 381, 382, 386, 393, 398, 401, 410, 417, 419

Fennell, Robert Beaty, 229, 230

Fenton, Cliff, 60

Ferrell, Mary, 38, 39, 66, 126, 220, 245, 337, 344

Ferrie, David, 7, 52, 53, 56, 63, 94, 107, 108, 119, 124, 186, 201, 220, 372

Finck, Pierre, 46, 47, 241, 242, 244, 245, 246, 262, 345, 350, 351, 369, 370, 373, 419

Finland, 95

Fisher, Russell, 367, 368

Fitzpatrick, John, 301

Flanagan, Mark, 317

Florida, 6, 51, 340, 397

Fonzi, Gaeton, 61, 66, 74, 123, 143, 344, 377, 379, 401, 402

Ford, Gerald, 8, 18, 37, 38, 43, 44, 54, 73, 138, 192, 329, 330, 333, 334, 339, 340, 372, 374, 376, 393, 417

Forrest, Helen, 129, 131

FPCC
    Fair Play for Cuba Committee, 88, 94, 102, 103, 104, 105, 108, 109, 113, 114, 115,

116, 118, 119, 121, 125,
126, 127, 129, 147, 163,
204, 211, 212, 213, 214,
215, 219, 220, 221, 222,
223, 224, 225, 228, 229,
230, 231, 232, 235, 237,
331, 341
France, 43, 86, 92, 417
Frazier, Buell Wesley, 132, 134
Frazier, Robert, 259, 262, 263, 268
Freeman, H. R., 291
Friendly, Alfred, 395
Fritz, John William, 31, 132, 168, 176
Fruge, Francis, 50, 51, 52
Fuller, Ronald, 261, 262
Galanor, Stewart, 278
Galveston, 52
Gambino, Robert, 99
Gannaway, W.P., 145
Garner, Dorothy, 176, 177, 179, 341, 418
Garner, Jesse, 119
Garriga, Santiago, 104, 212, 213, 231
Garrison, Jim, 8, 46, 48, 50, 51, 52, 53, 63, 72, 79, 81, 86, 95, 108, 119, 125, 201, 204, 211, 216, 217, 241, 330, 331, 365, 366, 369, 371, 372, 386, 399, 401, 405
Gaudet, William, 124
Gawler's Funeral Home, 84
Gemberling, Robert, 148, 167, 168
Gerald Posner, 6, 91, 396
Giancana, Sam, 57, 187, 188, 189, 235
Gibson, Richard, 103, 228, 231
Giesecke, Adolph, 34, 308
Gill, G. Wray, 53
Giscard d'Estaing, Valérie, 43
Givens, Charles, 164, 166, 167, 168, 170, 180, 418
Glanges, Evalea, 291
Glenn, John, 104, 222, 223, 237
Gold, Herb, 395
Goldsmith, Michael, 98
Goldstein, Frank, 189
Golz, Earl, 173, 177, 179
Gonzalez, Henry, 353, 377
Gordon, Lincoln, 367
Gosse, Van, 103
Graham, Phillip, 394
Grant, Patrick, 267
Greer, Bill, 34, 291, 309
Griffin, Burt, 39, 40, 182, 183, 184, 193
Groden, Robert, 21, 34, 43, 64, 65, 70, 250, 316, 378
Grossman, Robert, 34, 308
Groth, Dan, 211
Gruber, Alex, 190
Guevara, Che, 230, 235
Guinn, Vincent, 267
Gunn, Jeremy, 53, 82, 83, 84, 251, 305, 306, 323, 363, 370, 389, 417
Gurvich, William, 365
Guthrie, Steve, 185
Haapanen, Larry, 217
Habighorst, Aloysius, 48, 49, 365
Hagan, Joseph, 34, 309
Haggerty, Edward, 49
Haire, Bernard, 144, 145
Hall, Gus, 116
Hall, Phyliss, 34, 309
Hampton, Fred, 211
Hannah, John, 367

Hardway, Dan, 67, 68, 80, 94, 98, 118, 126, 156, 158, 381, 382, 417

Hargis, Bobby, 294

Harper, Billy, 289

Harper, Jack, 290

Hart, Gary, 9, 55, 56, 57, 58, 124, 361, 362, 417

Harvard, 368

Harvey, William, 44, 68, 69, 212, 334

Havana, 89, 187, 214, 229, 230

Helms, Richard, 43, 98, 101, 333, 334, 364, 365, 371, 375, 376, 406

Helpern, Milton, 243, 246, 262, 345

Hendrix, Hal, 184, 395, 397

Hendrix, Harold "Hal", 397

Hickey, Edward, 155

Hill, Clint, 34, 294, 306, 309

Hill, Gary, 97

Hinchliffe, Margaret, 34, 309

Hoboken, 101

Hoch, Paul, 85, 86

Hoffman, Barry, 222

Hoffman, Ed, 282

Holland, S. M., 78, 285

Holland, Sam (S.M.), 281, 283, 296, 297, 298, 326

Holmes, Harry, 152

Hoover, J. Edgar, 40, 42, 44, 45, 64, 71, 87, 130, 133, 155, 160, 163, 184, 206, 257, 267, 270, 331, 333, 334, 335, 336, 340, 352, 362, 364, 368, 381

Horne, Doug, 84, 85, 240, 244, 245, 247, 248, 251, 252, 253, 287, 288, 290, 292, 305, 324, 327, 342, 347, 349, 350, 366, 388, 417

Hosty, James, 40, 355, 356

Houston, 52, 133, 166

HSCA (House Select Committee on Assassinations), 10, 15, 21, 22, 23, 24, 28, 34, 38, 40, 44, 50, 51, 52, 53, 54, 60, 61, 64, 65, 66, 67, 68, 69, 70, 75, 81, 82, 88, 89, 91, 93, 94, 97, 98, 99, 105, 106, 108, 121, 122, 126, 130, 131, 143, 147, 151, 158, 180, 183, 184, 185, 187, 188, 189, 190, 191, 192, 193, 194, 195, 211, 212, 214, 218, 226, 227, 229, 232, 233, 234, 247, 248, 264, 265, 267, 268, 276, 277, 278, 280, 282, 283, 285, 286, 287, 290, 296, 302, 305, 311, 315, 316, 317, 318, 319, 321, 324, 326, 327, 330, 331, 333, 334, 335, 336, 341, 342, 346, 347, 348, 349, 357, 361, 362, 365, 369, 370, 371, 372, 377, 378, 381, 382, 383, 385, 386, 402, 404, 406, 407, 409, 414, 415, 416, 417, 418, 419, 420, 421

HT/LINGUAL, 9, 55

HUAC (House Un-American Activites Committee), 103, 222, 223

Hubert, Leon, 39, 153, 182, 183, 184

Hudson, Emmet, 295

Hudson, John Wilson, 187

Humes, James, 34, 35, 83, 85, 241, 243, 246, 247, 250, 251, 253, 254, 255, 262, 300, 301, 302, 305, 309, 322, 323, 324,

325, 342, 345, 348, 352, 353, 368, 369, 370, 371

Hunt, E Howard, 8, 10, 54, 79, 125, 126, 268, 308, 372

Hunt, Jackie, 34

Hunt, John, 269

Hurt, Henry, 262

Hurt, John, 121, 123

Hutchison, Leonard, 151, 152

Hutton, Pat, 34, 309

Indiana, 118, 215, 216, 223, 224

Inkol, Sheldon, 216, 217

Jackson, C. D., 394, 400

Jaffe, Steven, 79, 86

January, Wayne, 142

Japan, 89, 95, 96, 124, 208

Jenkins, James, 317

Jenkins, Marion, 34, 308, 326

Jenkins, Walter, 336

Jenner, Jr., Albert, 177

JFK Records Act, 17, 24, 405, 406, 407, 408, 409, 410, 411, 412, 413

JFK Records Collection Act, 1, 5, 421

Jimison, R. J., 261

JM/WAVE, 66, 123, 372

Joannides, George, 44, 67, 68, 69, 75, 76, 77, 82, 121, 123, 220, 330, 381, 382, 386

John F. Kennedy Assassination Records Collection Act 1992, 6, 24

Johnsen, Richard, 258

Johnson, Ed, 280, 342

Johnson, Lyndon, 7, 18, 28, 29, 45, 46, 146, 155, 160, 163, 329, 332, 335, 338, 344, 391, 397, 419, 420

Johnson, Priscilla, 124

Jones, Dempsey, 133

Jones, Paul, 185

Jones, Ronald, 34, 308

JURE, 149

Kantor, Seth, 182, 192, 397

Karamessines, Tom, 101

Karnei, Robert, 349

Karnel, Robert, 34, 309

Katzenbach, Nicholas, 29, 334

Kellerman, Roy, 34, 242, 243, 292, 301, 302, 309

Kelly, William, 387

Kennedy, Jackie, 86, 182, 246, 273, 286

KennedysandKing, 5, 1, 86, 100, 253, 288, 373, 384, 398, 413

Kent, Russell, 243, 367, 372, 373

Kent, William, 94, 123, 418

Kern, Ed, 271

KGB, 90, 332

Khrushchev, Nikita, 86, 87, 88, 90, 405

Kilduff, Malcolm, 307

King, Dr. Martin Luther, 10, 22, 61, 377, 378

Kinney, Samuel, 34, 294, 309

Kirkpatrick, Lyman, 367

Kissinger, Henry, 373

Kitchens, Henri, 231

Kittrell, Laura, 129, 143, 163

Knebel, Fletcher, 245, 392

Knott, Stephen, 198

Knudsen, Robert, 34, 244, 247, 253, 309, 341, 419

Kostikov, Valeri, 332

La Frontera, 143

Landis, Paul, 4, 90, 273

Lane, Mark, 8, 10, 46, 79, 96, 97, 211, 256, 279, 283, 366, 392

Leavelle, Jim, 31, 175

Lee, Vincent T., 104, 117, 228, 229, 237
LeMay, Curtis, 245
Levittown, 209
Lewis, Al, 224, 237
LI/LYRIC, 158
Liberty Lobby, 10, 79
Liebeler, Wesley, 116, 119, 152
Life Magazine, 64, 395, 398
Lifton, David, 218, 317, 318
Lindenberg, Richard, 373
Lippmann, Walter, 395
Lopez, Edwin, 64, 67, 68, 80, 126, 156, 157, 158, 159, 160, 214, 229, 235, 372, 381, 382, 417
Lopez, Gilbert Policarpo, 213
Lopez, Policarpo, 103, 214
Loquvam, George, 370
Los Angeles, 118, 201, 202, 221, 224
Lovelady, Billy, 174, 175, 179
Luce, Clare Booth, 184
Luce, Henry, 395
Lumumba, 9
Mack, Gary, 261, 403
Mafia, 41, 54, 57, 58, 64, 69, 78, 86, 89, 181, 185, 187, 188, 189, 341
Magic Bullet, 35, 65, 256, 257, 264, 265, 267, 268, 273, 274, 342, 368, 373, 419
Mailer, Norman, 103
Mantik, David, 251, 265, 290, 292, 303, 355
Marcello, Carlos, 39, 53, 108, 185, 186, 187, 189, 190, 235, 382
Marcus, Raymond, 256
Markham, Helen, 39

Marlowe, Vaughn, 103, 201, 221
Martin, B. J., 294
Martin, William, 96, 204
Martineau, Maurice, 211
Massicotte, Miles, 86
Mastrovito, James, 252
Mather, Carl, 146
McClelland, Robert, 34, 250, 314, 326
McCloy, John, 18, 329, 333, 334, 339
McHugh, Godfrey, 34, 309
McKeown, Robert, 190, 191, 418
McWillie, Lewis, 184, 187, 188
Mellen, Joan, 53, 114, 330
Methodist Hospital, 276
Metzler, James, 34, 309, 318
Mexico City, 3, 64, 67, 68, 71, 80, 90, 100, 101, 119, 124, 126, 130, 139, 143, 150, 156, 157, 158, 159, 160, 163, 202, 204, 205, 212, 213, 214, 222, 229, 231, 330, 331, 332, 341, 371, 372, 377, 381, 396, 402, 417, 419
Meyer, Cord, 394
MH/Chaos, 8, 54
Miami, 44, 51, 57, 66, 69, 72, 78, 82, 104, 105, 187, 212, 226, 231, 233, 333, 365, 372, 377, 386, 395
Michigan State University, 367
Midgett, William, 34, 308, 326
Milam, Wallace, 267, 272
Miller, Donald, 287
Miller, Dusty, 189
Miller, Lyle, 76
Milteer, Joseph, 226, 233
Minsk, 110, 228
Mitchell, Bernon, 96

MK/Ultra, 8, 54
Moffet, Sandra, 371
Montague, Dave, 251
Montgomery, Emmett, 153
Mooneyham, Lillian, 169, 170,
    180, 418
Moore, Elmer, 287
Moore, Fred, 148
Morales, David, 66
Morgan, Russell, 301, 368
Morgan's Gun Shop, 140, 141
Moritz, Alan, 368
Morley, Jefferson, 68, 78, 94,
    100, 101, 126, 396
Morrow, Anderson, 153
Moscow, 90, 96, 98, 147
Mowrer, Edgar, 395
Moyers, Bill, 29, 334
Moynihan, Daniel Patrick "Pat",
    80
Murphy, Thomas, 280
Murret, Dutz, 186, 187
Nagell, Richard Case, 103, 125,
    201, 202, 203, 204, 205, 212,
    216, 217, 221, 365
Nashville, 148, 199, 200, 235
NBC, 371, 401
Nelson, Doris, 34, 272, 309, 326
Neutron Activation Analysis, 267
New Orleans, 7, 8, 44, 46, 48, 54,
    56, 72, 76, 81, 82, 89, 94, 95,
    100, 102, 104, 105, 109, 110,
    113, 114, 116, 117, 118, 121,
    123, 124, 126, 127, 152, 153,
    154, 155, 163, 183, 186, 187,
    201, 202, 205, 210, 216, 219,
    222, 224, 228, 237, 241, 244,
    330, 332, 333, 363, 365, 367,
    370, 371, 372, 386, 399, 405

New York, 8, 13, 54, 57, 58, 93,
    103, 109, 117, 118, 222, 224,
    229, 243, 258, 259, 273, 279,
    345, 346, 366, 373, 394, 395,
    398, 399, 402
New York Times, 8, 54, 57, 93,
    103, 109, 258, 259, 273, 279,
    366, 373, 394, 395, 398, 399,
    402
New York University, 58
Newman, Bill, 295
Newman, Gail, 295
Newman, John, 94, 96, 97, 98,
    100, 101, 105, 106, 118, 125,
    296, 396
Newman, Sam, 107
Nichols, John, 365
Nitschke, Ivan "Bill", 107
North Carolina, 95, 123
Noteboom, Gerald, 290
Novel, Gordon, 365
O'Connor, Paul, 34, 255, 309
O'Donnell, Joe, 34, 284, 309, 326
O'Donnell, Kenny, 284
O'Leary, Jerry, 395
O'Neill, Francis, 32, 33, 34, 37,
    84, 85, 274, 285, 286, 309,
    326, 327, 342, 349, 417
O'Neill, Tip, 284
O'Connor, Paul, 316
Odio, Annie, 149
Odio, Sylvia, 64, 89, 118, 125,
    149, 150, 151, 201
Odum, Bardwell, 269, 270, 419
Olivier, Alfred, 373
Olney, Warren, 339
Olsen, Robert, 64
Olson, Robert, 373
Operation Mockingbird, 9, 55,
    331, 394, 395

Operation Paperclip, 373
Osiokowski, Carmen, 225
Oster, Joseph, 115
Oswald, 1, 2, 3, 4, 5, 6, 8, 11, 19,
　20, 24, 27, 28, 29, 30, 31, 38,
　39, 40, 42, 43, 44, 45, 46, 49,
　50, 52, 53, 56, 57, 59, 60, 62,
　63, 65, 66, 67, 68, 69, 71, 73,
　74, 75, 76, 77, 79, 80, 82, 85,
　87, 88, 89, 90, 91, 93, 94, 95,
　96, 97, 98, 99, 100, 101, 102,
　103, 104, 105, 106, 107, 108,
　110, 113, 114, 115, 116, 117,
　118, 119, 120, 121, 122, 123,
　124, 125, 126, 127, 128, 129,
　130, 131, 132, 133, 134, 135,
　136, 137, 138, 139, 140, 141,
　142, 143, 144, 145, 146, 147,
　148, 149, 150, 151, 152, 153,
　154, 155, 156, 157, 158, 159,
　160, 161, 162, 163, 164, 165,
　166, 167, 168, 169, 170, 171,
　172, 173, 174, 175, 176, 177,
　178, 179, 180, 181, 182, 183,
　184, 185, 186, 188, 190, 191,
　193, 194, 195, 197, 201, 202,
　203, 204, 205, 207, 208, 209,
　210, 211, 212, 213, 214, 216,
　217, 218, 219, 220, 222, 223,
　224, 225, 228, 229, 231, 232,
　235, 237, 238, 240, 242, 267,
　272, 273, 275, 285, 292, 300,
　327, 329, 330, 331, 332, 333,
　334, 335, 336, 337, 339, 340,
　341, 344, 355, 356, 357, 361,
　362, 363, 371, 372, 381, 382,
　388, 390, 391, 393, 396, 397,
　398, 399, 400, 402, 403, 404,
　406, 414, 415, 416, 417, 418,
　419, 420

Oswald, Lee Harvey, 8
Oswald, Marguerite, 152
Oswald, Marina, 2, 64, 109, 115,
　124, 129, 139, 140, 142, 151,
　152, 163, 205
Otepka, Otto, 94
Owen, Wayne, 50, 51
Paine, Ruth, 31, 115, 125, 133,
　139, 142, 151, 152, 341
Paisley, John, 367
Palamara, Vince, 153, 205, 294
Paley, William, 395
Paolella, Joe, 291
Parkland Hospital, 34, 35, 36, 80,
　81, 170, 171, 182, 192, 193,
　239, 240, 241, 242, 250, 258,
　269, 270, 272, 273, 286, 288,
　291, 304, 305, 306, 307, 308,
　309, 310, 323, 341, 350, 354,
　368, 417
Pate, Mack, 145, 146
Paterni, Paul, 334
Patrick, Lenny, 79, 189, 190, 418
Pearson, Drew, 87, 395
Pease, Lisa, 182, 245, 270, 330,
　366
Pecora, Nofio, 188
Pena, Orest, 125
Peña, Orestes, 115
Pennington, James, 129, 131,
　132
Pennsylvania, 34, 124
Permindex, 53
Perry, Malcolm, 34, 238, 239,
　240, 241, 242, 250, 254, 258,
　286, 287, 288, 289, 308, 343,
　371, 417
Peters, Paul, 34, 308
Petty, Charles, 350

Phillips, David Atlee, 7, 66, 67, 69, 70, 71, 121, 125, 126, 158, 213, 219, 220, 231, 341, 381, 397, 419
Pike, Terri, 387, 388
Pincus, Walter, 394
Pizzo, Frank, 141, 142
Poland, 223
Popov, Pyotr, 96
Potocki, Anita, 213, 231
Power, Harry, 215, 217
Powers, Dave, 285
Powers, David, 283
Powers, Gary, 79, 90, 285, 326, 420
Price, Jr, Malcolm H., 137
Price, Malcolm, 138
Probe Magazine, 50, 60, 70, 365, 366, 379
Proctor, Jr, Grover, 121
Purdy, Andy, 315, 317, 348
Quigley, John, 114
Quiroga, Carlos, 119, 120, 121
Rackley, Virgie, 173, 174
Raikin, Spas, 101, 102, 124
Randich, Erik, 267
Rankin, J. Lee, 40, 114, 176, 183, 272, 334, 336, 339, 340, 344
Reagan, Ronald, 60, 124
Red Bird Airfield, 129, 142, 418
Redlich, Norman, 272
Reed, Edward, 317
Reid, Helen Rogers, 395
Reid, R.A., 177
Reid, Whitelaw, 395
Renas, Carl, 355
Reston, James, 394
Revill, Jack, 168
Rhodes, Richard, 245
Riddle, Frank, 215, 217

Riebe, Floyd, 34, 309
Rike, Aubrey, 34, 309
Rivera, Geraldo, 21, 420
Roache, Wendell, 56, 115
Roberts, Delphine, 107
Robertson, Randy, 274
Robinson, Marvin, 130, 418
Robinson, Tom, 34, 84, 309, 315, 326, 349
Rocca, Ray, 334
Rockefeller Commission, 8, 54, 64, 247, 330, 372, 373, 374, 375, 383, 409
Rockefeller, Nelson, 8, 54, 64, 247, 373, 374, 383, 409
Rodriguez, Arnesto, 125
Rogovin, Mitchell, 376
Roman, Jane, 94, 100, 101, 418
Romania, 223
Rose, Earl, 242, 243, 246, 251
Rose, Jerry, 222
Roselli, Johnny, 57, 187, 235
Rosen, Alex, 38, 215, 337
Rossen, Johnny, 225, 237
Roswell, 160, 161, 163
Rowland, Arnold, 170, 172, 179, 180
Rowley, James, 160, 211, 216, 217, 259, 268, 270, 287
Ruby, Jack, 4, 8, 29, 39, 42, 45, 50, 51, 53, 63, 64, 79, 87, 91, 124, 161, 181, 182, 183, 184, 185, 186, 187, 188, 189, 190, 191, 192, 193, 194, 195, 196, 343, 357, 358, 359, 360, 361, 398, 414, 418, 419
Rudnicki, Jan Gail, 317
Rumsfeld, Donald, 376
Russell, Dick, 201

Russell, Richard, 18, 41, 201, 202, 204, 205, 333, 344, 367, 372, 373, 393, 417

Russia, 11, 65, 74, 86, 88, 89, 92, 94, 95, 97, 101, 109, 117, 123, 124, 127, 129, 141, 148, 154, 155, 156, 163, 209, 213, 222, 331, 417, 418, 419

Russo, Perry, 125, 371

Sagner, Alan, 103

Sahl, Mort, 401

Salyer, Ken, 34, 308

Samoluk, Thomas, 81, 198, 386, 412

San Antonio, 140, 215, 216, 217, 218

San Diego, 243

Sartre, Jean-Paul, 103

Sayyed, Khaleel Sultran, 230

Schiff, Dorothy, 395

Schlesinger, James, 375

Schweiker, Richard, 9, 55, 56, 59, 60, 61, 97, 115, 123, 124, 184, 361, 362, 417

Scobey, Alfredda, 39

Secret Service, 4, 7, 34, 46, 62, 78, 81, 90, 106, 121, 153, 154, 160, 198, 199, 200, 205, 206, 207, 210, 211, 213, 216, 217, 218, 226, 227, 229, 232, 233, 234, 236, 242, 245, 252, 257, 258, 259, 268, 269, 273, 285, 287, 291, 292, 294, 300, 301, 302, 306, 307, 309, 330,334, 337, 353, 354, 386, 410

Selassie, Haile, 205

Shaffer, Charles, 39

Shaw, Clay, 8, 46, 47, 48, 49, 52, 53, 54, 63, 72, 81, 94, 95, 108, 125, 154, 201, 204, 220, 241,

244, 262, 264, 285, 330, 345, 365, 366, 368, 370, 372, 399, 406, 419

Shelley, William, 174, 175, 179

Shenon, Philip, 396, 404

Sheppard, Barry, 104

Sheridan, Walter, 371

Sibert, James, 32, 33, 34, 37, 84, 250, 274, 286, 309, 314, 327, 341, 342, 349, 417

Simpich, Bill, 212

Single Bullet Theory, 7, 29, 32, 38, 41, 42, 66, 285, 308, 333, 341, 365

Slack, Garland, 137, 138, 139

Smith, David, 115

Smith, Sergio Arcacha, 106, 229, 371

Socialist Workers Party, 104, 204

Somersett, William, 226

Spain, 224

Spencer, Saundra, 34, 83, 155, 305, 309, 326, 341, 349

Spitz, Werner, 373

Sports Drome, 129, 136, 137, 138, 139, 140, 162

Spotlight, 10

Sprague, Richard, 38, 70, 73, 75, 330, 377, 379, 417

Springfield, IL, 198, 234, 235

State Department, 94, 98, 100, 101, 130, 155, 163, 222

Statue of Liberty, 230, 235

Steadman, Martin, 241, 288, 417

Stewart, David, 34, 309

Stokes, Louis, 380

Stone, Oliver, 5, 4, 23, 81, 82, 243, 244, 248, 274, 371, 376, 402, 404, 405, 406, 407, 420, 421

Stringer, John, 34, 85, 244, 247, 248, 249, 253, 309, 326, 341, 348, 350, 417

Stringfellow, L.D., 145

Stuckey, William, 105, 118

Sturdivan, Larry, 300, 383, 417

Sturgis, Frank, 8, 54, 372

Styles, Sandra, 165, 174, 175, 176, 177, 179, 341, 418

Sullivan, William, 331, 336, 337, 356

Sulzberger, Arthur Hays, 395

Swabeck, Marjorie, 221

Swinney, Louise, 122

Taber, Robert, 103, 237

Tague, James, 30, 257, 273, 368

Tampa, 118, 197, 211, 212, 213, 214, 215, 218, 228, 229, 233, 235

Tanenbaum, Robert, 60, 70, 72, 73, 330, 365, 372, 377, 378, 417

Taylor Jr., Charles, 291

Terre Haute, 215, 216

Texas Employment Commission, 129, 143, 144, 163

Texas School Book Depository, 29, 30, 73, 116, 129, 130, 131, 132, 133, 134, 143, 149, 162, 163, 164, 165, 166, 169, 171, 173, 180, 210, 240, 265, 273, 275, 282, 355, 418

Texas Theater, 94, 144, 145, 162

Thomas, Don, 260

Thompson, Bernard, 153

Thompson, Josiah, 246, 258, 259, 280, 293, 296, 346, 407, 417, 419

Thornley, Kerry, 124

Tip O'Neill, 379

Tippit, J.D., 7, 31, 39, 95, 136, 145, 146, 181, 192

Tobin, William, 267

Todd, Elmer Lee, 259, 268, 269, 270

Tolson, Clyde, 44, 159, 335

Tom Maupintour Associates, 223

Tomlinson, Darrell, 34, 258, 309

Trafficante, Santo, 39, 187, 188, 189, 190, 191, 235, 418

Traveler's Aid Society, 101

Treon, Alveeta, 121, 122, 123

Truman, Harry, 334

Trump, 1, 4, 5, 331, 386, 396, 411, 412, 413, 421, 422

Tunheim, John, 82, 363, 386, 387, 412, 421

Valenti, Jack, 402

Vallee, Thomas Arthur, 207, 208, 209, 210, 211, 212, 213, 232, 234

Van Hoesen, John, 34, 309

Vanderbilt University, 200

Vazakas, Vasilos, 98

Veciana, Antonio, 60, 61, 66, 67

Vicente, Thomas, 124, 231, 237

Vietnam, 2, 9, 405, 420

Village Voice, 59, 123, 265

Vinson, Robert, 160, 161, 162

Voronin, Piotr, 90

Vrtacnik, Ken, 252

Walker, Edwin, 39, 134, 217

Wallach, Paul, 56

Walter, William, 114

Walther, Carolyn, 169, 172, 180

Ward, Theron, 34, 309

Warren Commission, 1, 5, 6, 7, 8, 9, 15, 17, 19, 21, 22, 23, 24, 25, 27, 28, 29, 31, 32, 33, 34, 35, 37, 39, 40, 43, 44, 54, 55,

56, 57, 59, 63, 64, 66, 70, 71, 73, 75, 76, 78, 79, 81, 82, 83, 85, 86, 90, 91, 93, 97, 105, 106, 114, 115, 116, 119, 125, 126, 130, 136, 137, 138, 139, 140, 149, 150, 151, 152, 164, 165, 166, 167, 168, 169, 170, 174, 175, 176, 177, 179, 180, 181, 182, 183, 184, 185, 186, 189, 190, 192, 193, 194, 195, 197, 200, 205, 209, 210, 213, 215, 216, 217, 222, 229, 233, 234, 243, 244, 247, 256, 257, 258, 259, 263, 267, 270, 271, 273, 276, 277, 279, 280, 281, 284, 285, 287, 300, 301, 302, 305, 318, 329, 330, 331, 332, 333, 334, 335, 336, 338, 340, 342, 344, 348, 350, 352, 353, 357, 361, 362, 363, 364, 367, 372, 373, 378, 384, 390, 391, 392, 395, 398, 399, 401, 403, 404, 405, 409, 414, 415, 416, 417, 419, 420

Warren, Earl, 18, 73, 330, 332, 344, 419

Washington, 18, 39, 57, 58, 60, 71, 75, 78, 100, 118, 147, 153, 160, 162, 163, 172, 195, 198, 204, 205, 211, 216, 230, 235, 242, 245, 259, 267, 268, 334, 353, 354, 355, 366, 394, 395, 396, 402, 413, 419

Watergate, 2, 8, 10, 54, 376

Watson, Marvin, 87

Webster, Robert, 97

Wecht, Cyril, 243, 246, 247, 251, 264, 272, 286, 373, 383, 384

Weiss, Mark, 50, 51, 64, 65

Weitzman, Seymour, 279

Weldon, Douglas, 291

West, Louis Jolyon, 195

Whitaker Sr., George, 291

White, T.F., 145

White, William Allen, 395

Whitman, James Q, 12

Whitten, John, 333

Wilcott, James, 89

Williams, Bonnie Ray, 168, 170

Williams, Edward Bennett, 375

Williams, John, 379

Wilson, Eugene, 141

Winborn, Walter, 280, 281

Winchell, Walter, 395

Wise, Wes, 146

Wisner, Frank, 394, 395

Wolf, Betsy, 65, 97, 98, 99, 418

Wood, Homer, 137

Wood, Sterling, 137

Worthington, George, 149

Wright, Milton, 34, 309

Wright, O.P., 258

Wyeth, Jamie, 413

Yates, Ralph, 129, 132, 133, 134, 135, 136

Young Socialist Alliance, 104

Young, James, 38, 274, 342

Young, Walter, 252

Yugoslavia, 223

Zapruder, Abraham, 3, 7, 8, 21, 22, 54, 64, 65, 70, 79, 80, 257, 272, 275, 285, 286, 295, 300, 302, 327, 331, 351, 372, 378, 383, 384, 397, 398, 400, 403, 420

Zedlitz, William, 34, 308

Zimmerman, Joan, 252

Zion, Sidney, 399

Made in the USA
Las Vegas, NV
23 April 2024

89055827R00246